Henry Watterson and the New South

Topics in Kentucky History

James C. Klotter, Series Editor

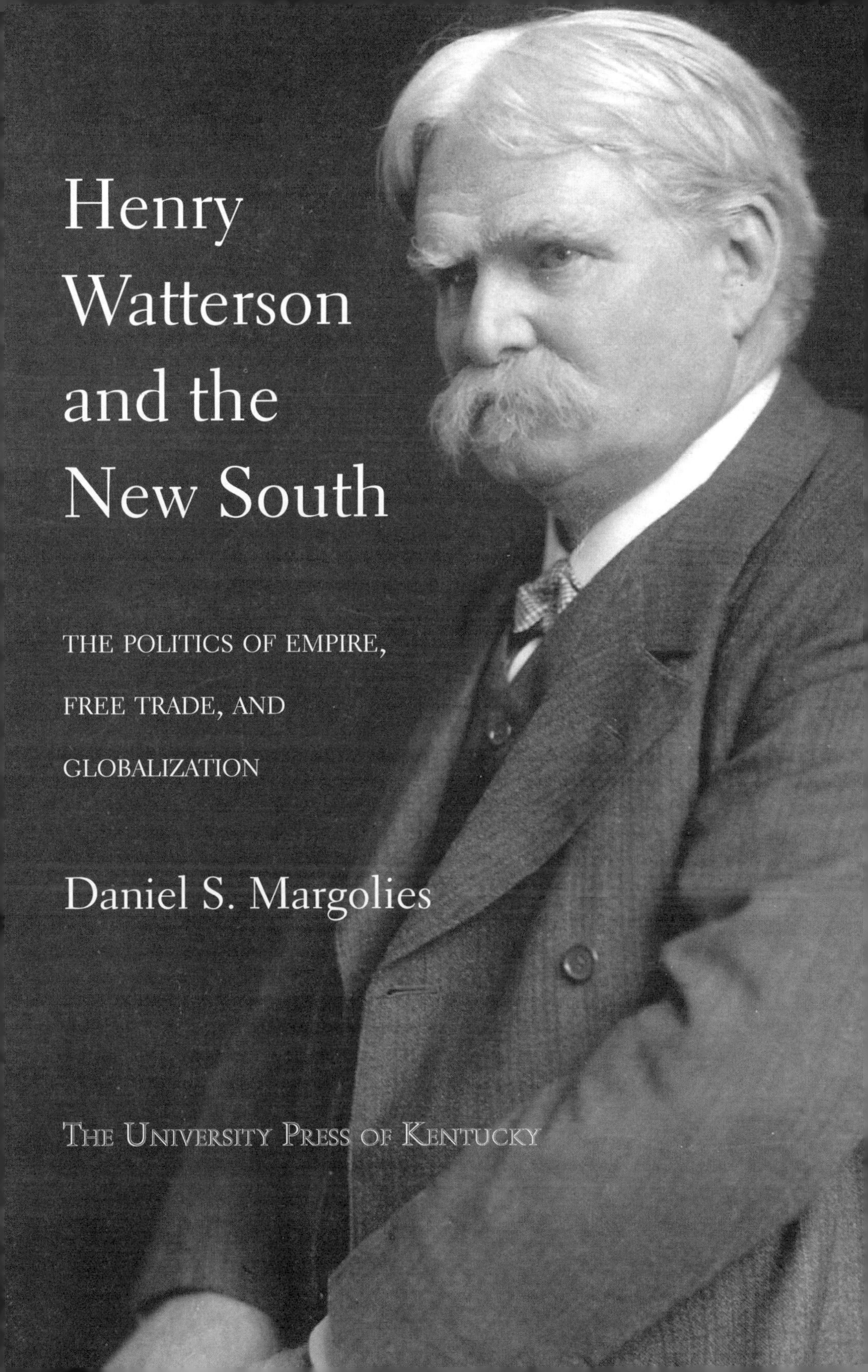

Henry Watterson and the New South

THE POLITICS OF EMPIRE, FREE TRADE, AND GLOBALIZATION

Daniel S. Margolies

THE UNIVERSITY PRESS OF KENTUCKY

Publication of this volume was made possible in part by a grant from the National Endowment for the Humanities.

Scholarly publisher for the Commonwealth,
serving Bellarmine University, Berea College, Centre College of Kentucky, Eastern Kentucky University, The Filson Historical Society, Georgetown College, Kentucky Historical Society, Kentucky State University, Morehead State University, Murray State University, Northern Kentucky University, Transylvania University, University of Kentucky, University of Louisville, and Western Kentucky University.

Editorial and Sales Offices: The University Press of Kentucky
663 South Limestone Street, Lexington, Kentucky 40508-4008
www.kentuckypress.com

10 09 08 07 06 5 4 3 2 1

Library of Congress Cataloging-in-Publication Data

Margolies, Daniel S., 1969-
Henry Watterson and the New South : the politics of empire, free trade, and globalization / Daniel S. Margolies.
p. cm. – (Topics in Kentucky history)
Includes bibliographical references and index.
ISBN-13: 978-0-8131-2417-9 (alk. paper)
ISBN-10: 0-8131-2417-4 (alk. paper)
1. Watterson, Henry, 1840-1921.6 2. Newspaper editors--United States--Biography. 3. Journalists--United States—Biography. I. Title.
PN4874.W3M37 2006
070.4'1092--dc22
[B] 2006019929

This book is printed on acid-free recycled paper meeting the requirements of the American National Standard for Permanence in Paper for Printed Library Materials.

Manufactured in the United States of America.

Member of the Association of
American University Presses

Contents

Illustrations

Series Foreword

Colorful, quotable, outrageous, unpredictable, iconoclastic, and inconsistent, Henry Watterson was also fascinating, influential, important, and respected. As the New South editor of the widely read *Louisville Courier-Journal*, "Marse Henry" became a national symbol of the southern colonel defending party ideals within the state, region, and nation.

No full and detailed explanation of Watterson's ideas and significance has appeared for a half century, and Daniel S. Margolies provides a fresh and revealing new interpretation of a key southern and American leader. He stresses Watterson's place in the emerging discussion of the nation's role in international and imperial affairs and restores the old editor to his key position in that crucial debate, a debate still important to us today. Watterson took his longtime support for free trade and a New Departure for the South to a world stage. Unusual for his region, the editor advocated free market expansion through globalization and territorial growth. Yet his political and world views on other issues required compromises with the idea of empire and the politics of party. Thus this man who had been the voice of southern moderation during Reconstruction, of angry Democrats in the disputed 1876 election, and of free traders in the endless tariff debates now became a spokesman for a diplomatic New Departure that he hoped would allow southern products to cover the world through both free trade and the new markets gained by American expansion. Increasingly frustrated with reactions to his views, Watterson finally retreated to a curmudgeonly discourse, though he won a Pulitzer Prize in the first year it was awarded.

Author Margolies provides unprecedented full coverage of Watterson's editorial philosophy and national importance, especially in regard to issues concerning the tariff, overseas empire, and the market economy. By studying the man, his journalism, and his diplomatic outlook in combination, Margolies does a particularly good job of stressing the changing nature of Watterson's views, his various metamorphoses, and his taking of his New South vision to an international arena. In that way and others, this book meets well the goals of this series.

Topics in Kentucky History is designed to publish works on the wide range of important subjects connected to the commonwealth, and ones with larger regional and national impact as well. Though the focus is historical, the interdisciplinary nature of the series encompasses other approaches to the study of the state. The goal is to publish both new authors and established ones, all using different methods to tell significant stories, whether studying virtually untouched subjects, looking at old questions in new ways, or offering fresh insights to familiar accounts. In the end, Topics in Kentucky History seeks to expand historical knowledge so that we know much more about our state, our nation, our world, and ourselves.

James C. Klotter
Series Editor

Preface

It is tempting to imagine that the role of the United States in the world was simpler and less challenging at the turn of the nineteenth century than it is today, but even a cursory study of history reveals that this is not the case. International affairs have such profound and dangerous immediacy today that it takes both imagination and commitment to recall that the transformations, opportunities, and challenges of empire date (at least) to many deliberate decisions made in the wake of the Spanish-American War. So often today do we hear it said in uncritical, approving tones that the United States is an empire that we must strain to hear the still quite relevant debate over the overseas empire at the time of its founding. In 1898, the question of empire was open in ways long since passed. What specific economic and political results, we must ask, did supporters of empire promise it would bring the country at that time and later?

The United States that decided to embrace empire after the War of 1898 was a modern nation easily eclipsed by its own superlatives. America was dynamic, productive, striving, eager, calculating, and industrious, but it was also prickly, racist, self-interested, tumultuous, violent, and expansionist. In studying it, we glimpse a fascinating young nation newly facing (and mastering, for a time) the challenges of globalization and the realities of imperial power. At the same time, we witness the passing of a nation with a relative simplicity and human scale that we might do well to remember today.

Perhaps nowhere were these changes brought by empire sensed more intensely than in the South, a distinctive region still struggling after the Civil War and Reconstruction to find social peace, to define its precise place in the nation, and to prosper. The South simultaneously faced both its past demons and future promise. This was challenging enough to accomplish within fin-de-siècle America, let alone within a developing global imperial system. Empire was sold as a balm for all national problems, but it must also be studied in regional terms. What did it offer to the South in particular?

Many answers were offered to southerners challenged by the confusion of this moment, the most coherent of which came from a group of politicians, editors, and activists called the New South ideologues. Supporters and promoters of southern development, prosperity, and autonomy within the Union, these New Southerners preached a program of economic salvation through social stability, investment, growth, and new market opportunities. None was more vocal or better known than Henry Watterson, editor of the *Louisville Courier-Journal*, a man commonly anointed in his time as "the greatest newspaper editor in America" (*Tampa Tribune*, June 17, 1906). Prominent and provocative, he provided an undistilled blast of New South ideology and southern nationalism alongside strident support for expansion and empire that distinguished him in the South and throughout the nation.

Watterson was as well known in his own day as he is virtually unknown today. In part, this is because of changing scholarly interests. Recent historians have deemphasized individuals in favor of social and cultural movements and are only now awakening to the importance of the vast middle stratum of politicians, journalists, editors, propagandists, and others who reflected and shaped the nation's political and economic interests at the turn of the nineteenth century. These editors, Watterson foremost among them, played the vital roles of interpreter and guide for the public at this moment when the United States transformed into its modern form and turned to empire and globalization.

In his editorials, speeches, and political action, Watterson shaped and explained complex foreign and domestic political economy for his readers throughout the South and the nation. He sought to reorganize the political economy to face the challenges of modernization and, consequently, spearheaded the movement for tariff liberalization and free trade for decades. Watterson believed in the promises of empire and the expansion of free trade in interconnected world markets for the South, and he fought for them.

This book is both a study of the trajectory that led Watterson to support empire as an appealing solution to the problems facing the South and the nation and an analysis of his ideas and their impact on the course of events. This book is also, more broadly, an exploration of the attractions of empire for Watterson and for a nation desperate for solutions to a wide range of social ills, economic disappointments, and (perhaps most important) unrealized ambitions. Foreign adventurism, war, empire, and globalization were viewed as the best means to achieve these varied ends.

Domestic problems were given foreign policy solutions. These solutions, in turn, came to define America's relationship to the world in the twentieth century, and they continue to form the core of its foreign affairs and political economy. As historians, we can study and understand their genesis; as citizens, we can continue to evaluate their legacies.

Studying Henry Watterson has been a labor of love and of years. It is a pleasure to research and write about a fascinating man with an enviable, if not unmatched, writing skill, a huge body of accessible materials, a sharp wit, and a continuing resonance. As with any project of this duration, I am deeply thankful for the assistance of a great many gracious people who have helped me to complete and improve it.

Joseph A. Fry has helped me in a great many ways too numerous to list here, even before I had the pleasure of meeting him in person. His book on John Tyler Morgan served as the model for this study, and my debt to his work on the South and American foreign relations is evident throughout. His many gracious and incisive criticisms of my analysis, structure, and presentation in several versions of this manuscript over a few years have improved it immensely. I am very thankful to him for his kind support. Tennant S. McWilliams provided excellent advice for strengthening my argument, and I am grateful to have had this assistance from the man whose own work on the New South I admire so thoroughly. It has been my great fortune to work with Joyce Harrison, editor in chief at the University Press of Kentucky, who has offered excellent suggestions and made publishing this book a real pleasure. I also appreciate the cheerful assistance of Ann Malcolm in getting the final manuscript together.

I have been fortunate to study under great historians who have inspired, challenged, and assisted me. It was a true honor and a pleasure to study under Thomas J. McCormick in Madison in the tradition of the Wisconsin school of diplomatic history. Tom is a fine person and great historian. He is also uniquely encouraging of independent thought and action. N. Gordon Levin Jr. of Amherst College first interested me in the study of American diplomatic history in his series of excellent classes. In my research and teaching, I strive to live up to both of their examples.

My colleagues at Virginia Wesleyan College have been very supportive, in particular Craig Wansink, who set a scholarly example and is a great friend; and the indomitable Ben Dobrin. Gary Noe invariably provided interesting conversations during many late nights in Blocker Hall, and John Aird provided irreplaceable assistance in digitizing the illustrations. I am thankful for the VWC summer faculty development funds and course release time that helped me to complete this project.

The fantastic collections and staffs at the Wisconsin State Historical Society Library and the University of Wisconsin Memorial Library made much of this research possible and pleasant. Also of tremendous help, support, and friendship were Tom Hefko, James L. Burghman, Jim Mathews, Bill Maltarich, Brett McNeil, Todd Cambio, F. Chuck Hornemann, Tony Gaughan, Ted Frantz, Eric Daniels, Honor Sachs, Van Mobley, Richard Schneider, and Dan Roth. Chip Landrum helped me to refine my argument over many arduous miles on the Appalachian Trail. I am grateful to Jim Holmberg and the Filson Historical Society in Louisville for allowing me to quote from their excellent manuscript collections.

I became interested in Watterson while visiting my large and loving extended family in Louisville, and I am grateful that my research there allowed me to spend additional time with my grandfather, Louis T. Roth, a man of charity, vision, and hard work. We all miss him. My greatest debt is owed to my parents, Lawrence and Sylvia Margolies. Their strong intellectual example, high expectations, and support over many years have been phenomenal. It is a pleasure to talk to both of them about my research and ideas. Both my father and my sister Allison gave excellent and insightful editorial criticism, while Alex and Julie Margolies and Rise Ochsner gave much love and support.

Lastly, I thank my lovely wife, Skye, who has been incredibly supportive and helpful during every step of this process, from brainstorming to editing. It is a blessing that we share the adventure of life together.

Introduction

A New Empire for the New South

Every Age has its interpreter. . . . This is the Age of the newspaper.
—Henry Watterson

Henry Watterson, or "Marse Henry," as millions affectionately knew him, was the legendary editor of the *Louisville Courier-Journal* and a central voice of New South iconoclasm from the Civil War through the Great War. Enormously influential in southern political and journalistic circles, Watterson enjoyed a broad national constituency that elevated him to the highest circles of American life. He was as contradictory and complex as the era in which he lived. He embraced change, development, and growth, yet he came to fear modernity and the transformations it brought. Watterson stood as the nation's premier advocate of free trade in a protectionist era. He proselytized for the cause of economic development and investment in the South and anticipated and supported the process of globalization before its inexorable logic became commonly accepted. A staunch Democratic kingmaker in a time when party labels mattered, he often gleefully infuriated the party faithful by supporting Republican foreign policies and conservative economic policies. Watterson was, variously, a Confederate, a unionist, an imperialist, an internationalist, and an isolationist, yet he always focused on modernization, free trade, and market expansion. Above all, he was a masterful polemicist on every issue imaginable. His ideas and actions were quoted, extolled, condemned, and ridiculed, but never ignored.

Watterson created the *Courier-Journal* and made it into a great and powerful newspaper with a lasting national reputation. Under his guidance, it became the authoritative paper of record for Kentucky, a major voice throughout the South, and one of the most respected papers in the country. The *Courier-Journal* was "the Koran of the Kentucky Democracy," wrote the *Lexington (KY) Leader*, "and Marse Henry Watterson [was] its prophet." The *New York Tribune* announced three decades after the launch of the *Courier-Journal* that "no name is better known in America—none carries more influence in the South—than that of Colonel Henry Watterson."[1]

Watterson shone on the editorial page. He coupled verve and political savvy with a characteristic outrage and a singular knack for forging memorable slogans and political battle cries. Sharp and provocative, his comments offered the best source for a quote on the controversies of the day. Even in a time before modern celebrity and instant reporting, everybody turned to see what Marse Henry had to say. He continually fascinated the national press, and his pronouncements about national and global events were reported as news.

An enormous array of papers across the country—ranging in size and significance from the *New York Tribune*, *San Francisco Examiner*, *Havana Post*, and *Chicago Inter-Ocean* to the *Morning Oregonian*, *Youngstown (OH) Vindicator*, and *Pueblo (CO) Chieftain*—reprinted and discussed his ideas as a matter of course. In 1908 journalist O. O. Stealey wrote, "Watterson is, and has been for thirty years, the most widely quoted newspaper writer of the country." Twelve years later, the *Houston Post*, with only slight hyperbole, announced, "There hasn't been a day in forty years when 'Marse Henry' could not wire a signed editorial to any representative newspaper in the country and have it appear on the front page." Even his relatively minor speeches were reprinted in newspapers across the country. The New York press in particular lavished attention on Watterson, further reinforcing his role as a national opinion leader. When he traveled there, which he did regularly, his activities and utterances were thoroughly documented, often on the front page. The *New York Herald* even ran a column called Wattersonia, which was simply a collection of particularly trenchant quotes from him on a variety of subjects.[2]

Watterson encouraged effusive language from all he encountered, whether it was praise or damnation. Perhaps writers felt that only excessive language could do his outsized character justice. By 1872, only four

Henry Watterson in the early 1870s, shortly after starting the *Louisville Courier-Journal*. Library of Congress, Prints and Photographs Division, LC-DIG-cwpbh-0

years after the launch of the *Courier-Journal*, great Kentucky knife-wielding abolitionist and newspaper editor Cassius Clay, who was not a fan of Watterson, described him as "virtually a dictator in my own state, and the most potent politician in all of the South." The *Tammany Times* called Watterson the "'Uncrowned King' of Kentucky," while the *Oakland (CA) Tribune* described him as "the Nestor of American journalism, . . . a prophet, sage, member of the modern magi, oracle, solon, Second Daniel and latter day luminary when matters of his own political party are under consideration." The *Fulton (KY) Fultonian* called him "not a dextrous mud slinger, braggart, or a cunning self seeker, but . . . perhaps the greatest personal force in American politics today." Tom Wallace, who succeeded Watterson as editor of the *Courier-Journal*, called him "the god who ruled things generally," a man who "possessed the circus instinct of Buffalo Bill, the personal glamour of Mark Twain and the dash of General [John Hunt] Morgan." Arthur Krock of the *New York Times*, the most famous of Watterson's Boys, as the *Courier-Journal* editorial staff was called, recalled Watterson as "an idol of every Kentucky family, including mine." When Watterson died, Krock compared him to Ulysses, King Arthur, and Titan and called him "the leading genius of the elder day." By 1898, Watterson was regularly described as a living legend, "an American institution," and the "dean of American editors." Even Oswald Garrison Villard, a liberal editor and bitter political opponent of Watterson, grudgingly called him "the darling of his Southern gods."[3]

Despite his lifelong prominence in the public eye and national politics, Watterson has essentially vanished from history. He is now remembered largely as a hyperbolic figure of legend. His ideas have been obscured. Colorful, comic images of Watterson have endured from his day to our own and have overshadowed more sophisticated understandings of his attempts to reshape southern politics and economy within a strong national union. The most lasting of these popular images, of Watterson as a half-mad ex-Confederate, first appeared in a *Harper's Weekly* cartoon in the midst of the 1877 Hayes-Tilden presidential election controversy. Thomas Nast drew the editor as "Henry Fire-Watter-son," every inch the crazed Rebel, exploding in revolutionary ferment as he calls for an army of ten thousand Kentuckians to come protest the disputed election and guarantee Tilden's victory. In contrast, calm, dapper, and bemused, *Cincinnati Commercial* editor (and prominent Republican) Murat Halstead douses Watterson with water; "FIRE AND WATER MAKE VAPOR," the caption

"FIRE AND WATER MAKE VAPOR. What a cooling off will be there, my countrymen!" The famous, scathing Thomas Nast cartoon of "Henry Fire-Watter-son," drawn during the Hayes-Tilden election dispute in 1877. This image of an unhinged and rebellious Watterson has proven to be the most enduring, despite its exaggeration. *Harper's Weekly*, February 3, 1877 wryly notes.[4] This unhinged, distorted image stuck with Watterson for the rest of his life, to his dismay, and continues to color the historical understanding of his politics.

Another lasting characterization, this time of the eccentric "Marse Henry," drew from the first radical image but moderated over time into the malleable public persona of an eccentric old southern gentleman. Throughout much of his life, Watterson was referred to either by the traditional southern honorific "Colonel" or by "Marse," an old regional variation on "master." Anointed with the name by the Louisville mayor in a poker game, Watterson was soon known as Marse Henry across the country. In 1919 the *Boston Transcript* called Watterson "a true Southerner of the old school" and noted that "people call him 'Marse Henry' no doubt after the old time plantation fashion."[5]

As editor, southerner, and Democrat, Watterson achieved national prominence as the voice of his section, but as Marse Henry, he stepped into the realm of celebrity. Marse Henry was a relentless bon vivant who took his entertainment and vacations as seriously as his politics. The national press regularly portrayed Marse Henry Watterson in cartoons as an old Rebel, playing cards, smoking tobacco, playing the banjo, brandishing pistols, betting on the horses, cutting shady backroom political deals, and generally continuing to raise hell. A standard feature of these images was, in Watterson's weary words, "the everlasting mint-julep joke." A cartoon from the *Washington Post* in 1907 presented this persistent stereotype, with a smoking Watterson playing cards with an enormous pile of chips. The caption read, "COL. WATTERSON'S SECRET OF PERPETUAL YOUTH."[6] Although privately professing to dislike this sort of portrayal, which was not so far from the truth, Watterson also found it to have a certain utility. He even titled his autobiography "*Marse Henry*" to capitalize on it. The public adored these images of an irrepressible character, and Marse Henry's classic southern bearing and rascality reserved a certain freedom for him in the political arena closed to other, less colorful public figures.

During his life and shortly thereafter, Watterson was the subject of a stream of laudatory personality sketches throughout the popular press, but scholarly attention to him has been limited. The best full-scale biography, by Joseph Frazier Wall in the mid-1950s, covers Watterson's historical significance and personal vitality but concentrates on the narrative of events up to 1876 and compresses all subsequent ones. Wall's biography arrived

"COL. WATTERSON'S SECRET OF PERPETUAL YOUTH." The national press loved to draw Watterson and emphasize his predilections. *Washington Post*, January 5, 1907

just prior to an explosion of scholarship on the New South and Reconstruction, and it quickly became the standard reference book on Watterson. No large study of him or his ideas has been written since. Repeating the hackneyed images of Henry Fire-Watter-son and following Wall's able but incomplete analysis, subsequent scholars have presented Watterson as merely one more representative of sectional harmony and development.

Even the most recent study of New South editors rests its understanding of Watterson upon Wall's dated biography.[7] Watterson is overdue for the full reappraisal found in this book.

Watterson belonged to a small group of New South editors, including Walter Hines Page, Henry Grady, Richard Hathaway Edmonds, Daniel Augustus Tompkins, Francis Warrington Dawson, and Edwin B. Craighead, who jointly created, honed, and spread a coherent and attractive ideology of post–Civil War development. Great southern newspapers like the *Courier-Journal*, *Atlanta Constitution*, *Raleigh News and Observer*, *Manufacturer's Record*, *Memphis Commercial-Appeal*, and *Charleston News and Courier* were usually under the control of a dominant personality, and all were springboards to varying levels of national influence for their editors. None rose to greater prominence throughout the country than Watterson, and few were around as long.

This group of New South ideologues supported economic modernization and industrialization, a strong union with sectional equality, and social tranquility free of radicalism from both the left and the right. They created a vital connection between the reading public and the policy elites, giving a national voice to southern concerns and disseminating their own idiosyncratic understandings of regional interests. During his life, Watterson was credited for his singular role in the reconciliation and development process, but retrospectively, he is often described as little more than a pedestrian New South thinker. He is frequently placed second in importance to *Atlanta Constitution* editor Henry Grady, who commands a small but unassailable position in history despite his early death. College history students today invariably read Grady's "New South" speech but, unfortunately, never engage Watterson's far more voluminous and significant output.[8]

Watterson represents the New South ideology as well as the unique journalistic moment between the era of the "personal journalists," who dominated much of the shape and color of American politics throughout the nineteenth century, especially between 1830 and 1890, and the rise of modern commercial journalism. He liked to quip that he straddled the eras when editors went from defending themselves in duels to defending themselves in libel suits. Watterson was often anointed the last of the personal journalists because of his writing style, unique ideology, political influence, and longevity. In fact, he was an important transitional figure during a time of massive upheaval.

"THE NATIONAL POLITICAL PHRENOLOGIST. 'The Democratic party has in front of it a great opportunity, if it but knows how to improve it. For the first time in thirty years it is the Republicans who are at sea.'—Henry Watterson, in a Washington letter." Watterson gauges the true nature of the national political scene and the opportunities for the Democratic Party, including the possibility of running for president himself. *New York Daily Tribune*, March 18, 1902

The great founders of personal journalism are now as much the figures of legend as of history: Horace Greeley and the elder James Gordon Bennett, George D. Prentice (who preceded Watterson at the *Louisville Journal*), Murat Halstead, Henry Grady, Charles A. Dana, E. L. Godkin, Whitelaw Reid, Samuel Bowles, William Cullen Bryant, and Henry J. Raymond. These great personal editors of the past, famously tough and opinionated, had an immense impact on national political discourse. The newspapers they created showcased their grand partisan rhetoric and embodied their ambitions and idiosyncratic personalities. Many became the nation's best papers. This ascendancy took decades of effort and hard partisan fighting to achieve. The personal factor, in fact, was often the papers' greatest strength and appeal.[9] Historians have written extensively and recently on all of the great personal journalists save Watterson. He deserves a prominent place on this list as one of the most important editors of his time, in the South and beyond.

Watterson approached the ongoing, bitter political disputes of his day by hammering editorially on key issues with the hope that sheer effort and repetition could transform ideas into actions and prescriptions into policy. Mark Wahlgren Summers notes the "distortion and politically engaged qualities of Southern journalism" and "the language [that] was truculent and apocalyptic." With the South as his major constituency, Watterson understood that strident language and support for southern nationalism could translate into a broad base of popular political power and influence. And he knew that it would sell newspapers. Although he was quite effective at getting his ideas heard, he obviously could not single-handedly manufacture public support. Like any politician, Watterson had to court the public for success and influence. Public persuasion required mastery of rhetoric. Like other partisan editors, he enlisted the strong traditions of southern oratory to shape and influence the public discourse.[10]

"In New York [the politician] becomes a Boss," Watterson announced in 1903. "In Kentucky and Texas, an orator."[11] Thus he discerned the special political role of editors in the South and aggressively set about to establish himself and his paper as the voice of his section. Louisville, the vital commercial and geographic link between North and South, provided the context, and the *Courier-Journal* provided the platform. With each new public controversy, Watterson vied to prove that he alone understood the true southern perspective on all political questions. He framed the practical benefits of his ideas on all political and economic matters for a descending list of preferred constituencies: Kentuckians, southerners, Democrats, and Americans.

Politicians and writers like Watterson understood two critical facts: that abstract and seemingly distant events and changes in world trade and international relations had great potential effects on regional and local affairs, and that it was essential to interpret these events in terms that were understandable and useful to the public at large, in particular to the all-important voter. These connections seem obvious today but were relatively novel to highlight in the nineteenth century. They had to be made explicit to be effective, and one of the best ways to clarify them was to emphasize their regional impact. This was especially true in the debates over foreign affairs in the 1890s. Although there was a strong consensus on domestic (and especially racial) affairs in the South following Reconstruction, there was much room for dispute over the proper relationship of the region and the United States with the rest of the world.

Southern editors emphasized regional interests in national debates more strongly than did journalists in other sections of the country. They often had two vocabularies, one for the southern readership and one that appealed to northern interests. The editors also had an intensified role to play in interpreting and explaining questions of power in regional terms. As Tennant S. McWilliams argues, southern society was especially drawn to editorial persuasion because of the massive disruptions in work, culture, and society wrought by Reconstruction and industrialization, and further because of nonresponsive governments. The relatively weak federal government did not yet have its "modern bureaucratic tentacles," he writes, and "in this limbo of public uncertainty, newspapers gained enormous power."[12]

Watterson sought to guide the southern discussion on foreign affairs. He believed that foreign policy should be the direct extension of his struggle to maintain Democratic dominance and achieve southern prosperity through global free trade. This emphasis on foreign policy has been lost on virtually all historians, who have viewed Watterson in terms of his domestic political actions. Yet one immediately notable aspect of *Courier-Journal* editorials was the extent of Watterson's discussion of international politics and trade. These topics often overshadowed coverage of local issues; Watterson tended to discuss even Kentucky state political battles in terms of their foreign and economic dimensions. He argued that global markets were the logical place where the South should seek results, and he labored extensively to make foreign policy relevant to the isolated people of the South.

This book focuses on Watterson's unique program for southern autonomy and prosperity within a stable and powerful American empire. He was motivated by a relatively simple goal: to solve the problems of the 1870s as well as those of the 1890s. Empire and free trade, he thought, promised to usher in the final resolution of persistent sectional inequality and economic instability. Watterson viewed an imperial foreign policy as a means of transcending the impediments to southern prosperity and achieving free trade that was elusive at home. He saw the opportunities of expansion and globalization as "God's promise redeemed" to the nation and to the South—final proof that the bonds of union forged in the Civil War were eternal. These opportunities offered answers to the sovereignty, development, and racial questions that had persisted in the South since Reconstruction, and to the national crisis of social disorder and overproduction that developed during the depression of the 1890s. Empire and free trade could neatly solve both the region's and nation's problems. Watterson equated southern advancement and modernization with American international dominance, especially in Asia. He therefore championed, as he put it in 1899, a "policy of national expansion, which, as far as it relates to the Pacific, is but another name for the development of the South."[13]

Watterson organized his development program around three linked tasks that he folded into a single expansionist policy: strengthening the bonds of national union, establishing a conservative and prosperous public order built upon free trade, and achieving southern political independence and economic supremacy within this system. He believed that only the Democratic Party could realize all three goals, although both it and the nation had to discard a few outworn ideologies as the price of admission to all the world's markets. "The trend of the modern World is set," Watterson intoned at the end of 1898, when he was fully in support of imperial expansionism. "We lag behind at our peril." Watterson struggled to convince the Democratic Party to heed his advice and to recognize that it had "always been the party of National progress and expansion."[14]

To mold the popular political discourse and rally the southern Democracy to his side, Watterson collapsed his basic interests into simple propagandistic slogans. He distilled his three major goals into an evocative holy trinity of southern freedom and national glory: "Home Rule, Free Trade, and Sound Money." He used this phrase repeatedly in editorials and speeches for more than five years to indicate "the distinguishing marks on the contents of the Democratic bottle." It opposed what he considered to be uniquely Republican policies: "centralization, protection, fiatism."[15] Watterson's holy trinity perfectly captured the seamless connections he made between domestic and foreign affairs. Free trade was its heart.

Home rule was Watterson's shorthand for southern local autonomy, with economic, social, and political independence protected from outside (northern and Republican) interference. It meant limited government, no unconstitutional "experimentation," and no radical efforts to reshape social or racial hierarchies. The home rule battle cry helped burnish Watterson's longstanding credentials as a conservative and a southern nationalist.

In calling for sound money, Watterson sought the maintenance of a stable currency system and reliable investment environment in the United States and an international system of currency convertibility based on gold. He believed both of these were essential for future prosperity. Sound money was an essential sinew of global trade. Watterson vigorously opposed free silver in particular, since it threatened the integrity of the economic system he sought to expand and liberalize.

Finally, Watterson considered free trade to be the cornerstone of the trinity and of his politics. He saw a free and expanding market as the unifying force of the future. A belief in the transformative power of free trade therefore formed the backbone of his expansionist position. It also became the backbone of the process now termed "globalization." Watterson, the nation's premier voice for free trade after the Civil War, deemed "a tariff for revenue only" the first step toward the establishment of a wholly open international trading system, in which American manufacturers could undersell and outproduce all competitors without impediment or restriction. Raw materials, goods, services, and capital would all flow freely in liberalized markets. The United States, and particularly the South, would in turn benefit enormously. Watterson believed home rule, free trade, and sound money in an expanding world empire meant prosperity, social stability, and political liberty.

Imperialism in the 1890s was an especially attractive issue in these terms because it required the Democracy and the South to jettison free silver and follow an expansionist free trade policy with national appeal. Empire included the embrace of globalization. Watterson cleverly grafted his perennial obsessions with the tariff, the party issue, and the sectional question onto his expansionist program. By the turn of the century, he pushed hard for an expansionist New Departure in foreign policy as a means of realizing all three aspects of his holy trinity of home rule, free trade, and sound money. Like the New South ideologues, who pushed their own New Departure from the past during Reconstruction, Watterson sensed a vital moment for change after 1898. He slowly discarded his fifty-year-old isolationist view of foreign relations and reoriented his entire political outlook around an aggressive internationalism that accommodated big government, imperialism, territorial aggrandizement, the open door, and globalization.

Watterson's New Departure in foreign affairs was an often contradictory amalgamation of war and humanitarianism, decentralized home rule and overseas imperialism, racial accommodation within a system of white supremacy, and, most of all, free trade in an ever-expanding, interconnected world market dominated by the United States. Watterson stressed as significant components of his New Departure policy both the reinvigoration of the South through free trade imperialism and the establishment of a free trade system *within* an insular colonial system. Other supporters of imperialism tended to support one or the other and only infrequently argued for both simultaneously. As long as free trade was accomplished in a new empire, Watterson ignored the problems of formal colonialism that were clear to others at the time. He was willing to utilize both approaches and to elide or, alternatively, to embrace any contradictions or costs so long as they were compatible with free trade.

Open markets dissolved all complications. An empire of free trade was, by definition, an empire of freedom. Conversely, Watterson interpreted the Republican mixture of colonialism and protectionism as an affront to both liberty and world order. He blamed protectionism for panic and depression, insufficient markets, social disorder, political radicalism, and paternalism. He equated free trade with peaceful national expansion, southern prosperity, political liberty, and even Christian purity. "We shall go on in religion preaching the Gospel of Christ, and Him crucified, and in politics, the doctrines of Honest Money, Home Rule and Free Trade," he wrote in a typical formulation.[16]

Watterson's transformation from an isolationist and antiexpansionist free trader into a joyously land-hungry, imperialist free trader was virtually unique among southern Democrats. Most of the region's politicians and editors either had always supported expansion or were adamantly opposed to the new policy. One exception was Joseph Bryan, Democratic editor of the *Richmond Times*, who moved toward imperialism as part of the reaction to domestic radicalism. Like Watterson, Bryan opposed foreign adventurism until he recognized its broader domestic political and economic advantages. Bryan was especially concerned about "the bulwarks of Southern traditionalism—the gold standard, white supremacy, and elite rule." The major difference between the two editors was that Bryan was a minor figure outside Virginia, while Watterson was considered a representative voice of the New South.[17] The connections between Watterson's ideas and those of other imperial propagandists are difficult to trace conclusively, but his formulations certainly powerfully influenced the terms of the debate in the South and in conservative Democratic Party circles.

Watterson shared an interest in market expansion with prominent southerners like John G. Carlisle, Hannis Taylor, Clark Howell, James C. Hemphill, and Lucius Q. C. Lamar. Yet Watterson's intellectual trajectory toward imperialism remained fascinatingly unique, fortified by the confidence and self-righteousness most often found among the newly converted. His program was in fact nearly identical to the "large policy" of the familiar cast of American imperialists, most of whom were Republicans, who sought markets, strategic bases, and a foreign policy solution to domestic economic problems and social instability.

In his support for expansion to solve these problems, Watterson demonstrated the extent of the expansionist consensus at the turn of the century. Yet his monomaniacal obsession with free trade distinguished him. It also anticipated some of the essentials of twentieth-century bipartisan foreign policy, with its central goal of achieving prosperity and stability through expanding global markets and the open door.

When historians refer to the United States' "becoming a world power" after 1898, they are partly describing the cascading impact of globalization on American politics, economy, and society and the corresponding attempt to harness this process. Global interconnectedness was driven by advances in communications and transportation, the spread of goods and information, a growing coherence in world trade, and burgeoning American economic supremacy.[18] Faced with unprecedented industrial capacity and productivity and a desire for new markets and outlets at the end of the nineteenth century, the United States sought to rapidly enter and direct world affairs. In responding to the complex globalization process with empire and an ideology of liberalized trade, the United States sought to configure international markets and power relations for maximum domestic benefit. Recognizing the potential opportunities in international affairs, Watterson sought a keen advantage for the South in this fluid situation. He aimed to clarify the significance of this imperial moment and, in particular, to convince the South of its value to the region.[19]

Watterson's singular program for southern Democratic dominance within a broader American empire of globalized free trade was matched in vehemence only by that of Senator John Tyler Morgan of Alabama, who "made foreign policy so fundamental to the South's economic and political prosperity and autonomy." The editor's mutability and fitful development toward expansionism are thrown into sharp relief when compared with the ever-focused Morgan. The critical difference between the two was undoubtedly between Morgan's uncompromising campaign for complete "Southern autonomy" from northern rule and Watterson's program for southern home rule, growth, and prosperity embedded firmly *within* a politically decentralized but spatially expanding federal union. Yet both men, paradoxically, supported a limited federal role in domestic matters, particularly in the South, coupled with an activist role abroad. As Joseph A. Fry argues, Morgan "considered strict construction [of the Constitution] necessary to protect the South's political and racial autonomy at home, [but] he judged sweeping federal authority and action abroad necessary to obtain the South's economic and political liberty."[20] Skating this line was not for the fainthearted.

Watterson's major contributions to the political debates at the turn of the century were his plans for Democratic reorganization along imperialist lines, his program for southern advance within a vibrant and expansive system of free trade, and his embrace of the logic of internationalism and globalization. These plans entailed streamlining the Democratic Party and its platform around his New Departure, improving the South's position in the nation, and transforming America's relationship with the rest of the world. Only then could the United States herald a new, integrated system of liberty, development, and prosperity. Watterson believed that the expansionist New Departure would realize his old visions for the South and the nation in a decidedly modern fashion and would extend the eternal truths of home rule, free trade, and sound money into a new system of international preeminence.

1

Toward the Star-Eyed Goddess

The Democratic party, except in the person of imbeciles hardly worth mentioning, is not on the fence. It is a free trade party or it is nothing.
—Henry Watterson, quoted in the *Kentucky Leader*, July 26, 1888

Henry Watterson's political outlook was shaped at the center of power from the time of his birth, in 1840, to a wealthy and politically prominent Tennessee family. Despite having only four years of schooling, he matured quickly during his childhood in Washington DC and imbibed the politics of the late Jacksonian era directly at the source. "I was born in a party camp and grew to manhood on a political battlefield," he wrote. "I have lived through stirring times and in the thick of events."[1] His grandfather, William S. Watterson, had served under Andrew Jackson during the War of 1812 and lived "within the inner circle of Jacksonian Democracy in Tennessee." William Watterson's ambitious son Harvey also became "an undoubting Democrat of the schools of Jefferson and Jackson." At a young age, with help from family connections, Harvey took James K. Polk's seat as the representative for the Ninth Congressional District of Tennessee and served as the youngest member of Congress for two terms. For a brief time, Harvey served as a special trade emissary to Buenos Aires, a position largely engineered by his father to keep him from drinking and carousing in Washington with his good friend Franklin Pierce. Harvey remained in politics in Washington or Tennessee for his entire life, later serving as Speaker of the state house of Tennessee.[2]

Harvey Watterson moved comfortably through tense antebellum

Washington politics, and he passed this political sangfroid on to his son. He also handed down a belief in southern economic development and a tradition of unabashedly partisan journalism that young Henry learned well. Harvey was involved in railroad and telegraph construction throughout the South and strongly supported modernization of the region. He served as a newspaper editor, first at the *Nashville Union* and later at the *Washington Union*. Both papers were stridently Democratic and supportive of the aggressively expansionist Young America wing of the party. When Pierce rose from this wing to the White House, the *Washington Union* became his favored paper.[3]

Like his father, Henry Watterson possessed impeccable political credentials and a remarkable set of connections that helped him rise to political and journalistic prominence at a young age. This pedigree also strengthened his image as a political sage. The legend of Marse Henry that developed at the end of the nineteenth century revolved around the singular trajectory of a man who seemed to have been born at center stage. Through his family connections, the young Henry met all of the great politicians of the 1840s and 1850s in Washington. This access set a pattern for his later years, when he knew personally (and often played cards with) most men of importance and maneuvered with ease in elite circles. As a child, Henry bounced on Andrew Jackson's knee at the Hermitage, had his curls stroked by Zachary Taylor, Millard Fillmore, Lewis Cass, and Franklin Pierce, and was even on the floor of the House when John Quincy Adams fell dead. Watterson later knew each successive occupant of the White House through the Wilson administration. In 1919 he remembered the troops returning from the Mexican War as "but yesterday," just as he could recall other soldiers marching off to the Civil War, the Spanish-American War, and the First World War.[4]

From the start, Watterson viewed politics through the filter of his inherited political traditions. He remained true to his Democratic political birthright throughout his life and consistently drew direct connections between the nation's current situation and the verities of the past. "The Jackson creed, as to the relation of the Federal and State governments, is the creed of the Democratic party to-day," he wrote in 1879. Nearly twenty years later, he used identical language.[5] Watterson collapsed history into a unified whole in which Democratic ideals ostensibly never changed, no matter how much the times themselves did. For decades, his editorials and speeches claimed to fight the same battle based upon the same truths that the Democratic Party had supported since the days of Jefferson. These battles, like the biblical struggle between good and evil, were eternal and replicated in each political generation. Over time, Watterson anointed himself as the rock on which party traditions stood. The *Courier-Journal* later reflected this position by claiming to have always supported whatever position Watterson chose.

Although his goals and language may have been born of antebellum politics, Watterson did not limit himself to the tools of his forebears. He did not fetishize established Democratic politics, and he was not a hidebound conservative. Absorbing totally the lessons of national union, expansionism, limited government, and free trade expounded by the Democrats of his father's generation, Watterson displayed enormous flexibility in the means of attaining these unchanging ends. Without admitting to contradictions or party irregularity, he often radically challenged the existing consensus in his party. For much of his life, he pushed innovation while demanding an unyielding conservatism based upon the ever-malleable legacies of Jefferson and Jackson. The contradictions in this approach (which certainly appeared) were smoothly subsumed in torrents of rhetoric.

Despite having lost one eye to an accident and much of his vision to scarlet fever, Watterson settled on a career in journalism. With his father's help, Watterson started the *McMinnville (TN) New Era* and edited it for two years, from 1856 to 1858. The young Watterson received national attention in Democratic circles when one of his strident editorials in support of James Buchanan was reprinted first in the *Nashville American*, then in the *Washington Union*, and finally made "the rounds of Democratic papers all over the country." Shortly thereafter, Watterson left Tennessee and spent a brief stint in New York covering the arts for a variety of papers, including *Harper's Weekly*, the *Times*, and the *Tribune*. At this time, he aspired to be "one of those damned literary fellows," but he never succeeded. In his autobiography, Watterson explained, "My destiny has been casual. A great man of letters quite thwarted, I became a newspaper reporter." Throughout his life, he loved music and the theater, and he always highlighted the arts in the *Courier-Journal*. Much of his autobiography is given over to reminiscence about various performers he knew and saw. In New York, Watterson became good friends with, among others, aspiring poet (and later secretary of state) John Hay. "Whether Henry Watterson would have been a bigger frog in the New York puddle, no man can say," Hay later recalled. "Certainly there is not today in the New York puddle a frog anything like so big as Mr. Watterson."[6]

Lacking artistic talent, Watterson returned to politics in Washington. He also returned to the vibrant epicenter of assertive antebellum expansionist agitation. At first, he acted as "a go-between and . . . a figurehead" at the Democratic *Daily States*. He gained this opportunity based on "the strength of being my father's son and [being] a very self-confident young gentleman." Soon he moved to political reporting, and he had his first scoop when he reported, in the summer of 1859, that Buchanan was going to choose Alexander Dimitry to head the Central American mission. The *Daily States* was started by John P. Heiss (who had also founded the *Washington Union* and who once worked for the *Louisville Courier*) and edited by Colonel A. Dudley Mann, who had been an arms dealer during the European revolutions of 1848, an assistant secretary of state under William Marcy, and later the Confederate commissioner to France. Watterson learned the rudiments of journalism from Heiss, but it was one of the paper's lead writers, Jane McManus Storm Cazneau, whom Watterson credited with teaching him to write. Although Robert E. May has argued that Watterson did not know Cazneau as well as he claimed, the fact that, late in life, Watterson so deliberately associated himself with her speaks volumes.[7]

If the broad outlines of Jacksonian Democratic politics ran in Watterson's veins because of his lineage, his association with Cazneau honed this legacy and gave it teeth. Certainly her stamp on his political outlook was enormous and long lasting. Cazneau led a remarkable and unique life, and in many ways she characterized the acquisitive energy of the 1840s and 1850s. She was a terrific propagandist and popular writer (writing as Cora Montgomery), a champion of territorial expansion, a government secret agent during the Mexican War, a presidential advisor, and a diplomat, and she may even have been Aaron Burr's mistress. Drawn to adventure and the opportunities of the frontier, Cazneau was a pioneer Texas settler, an international land and guano speculator, an owner of silver mines, and a supporter of filibusterers like William Walker, who took over Nicaragua with her support. According to Watterson, it was Cazneau who immortalized Walker as the "gray-eyed man of destiny" and gave General Winfield Scott the nickname "Old Fuss and Feathers," thereby pioneering the kind of instantly memorable phrasing that Watterson himself later practiced. Her most recent biographer makes a convincing case that it was in fact Jane Cazneau who coined the term "manifest destiny" in the *United States Magazine and Democratic Review*, rather than John L. O'Sullivan. Cazneau supported hemispheric union under U.S. control, American dominance of the Caribbean, and a Central American canal so "Mississippi Valley merchants could undersell Europeans in Asian markets."[8]

Watterson later pushed identical reasoning, much in the same fashion. He supported the ideas of a Central American canal and union, and he always remained interested in expanding southern and national trade in the Caribbean basin. He considered this region a "natural market" of the United States. Under Cazneau's guidance, Watterson adopted and supported commercial and territorial expansionism as the solution to national problems. When Watterson took over the *Louisville Journal* in 1868, Cazneau offered him weekly contributions from St. Thomas discussing the great opportunities awaiting Americans in the Caribbean. "The Western and Southern men are extending their arms in this direction," she wrote, and "you will soon hear of exciting events here." Soon after writing this, she disappeared. "A braver and more intellectual woman never lived," Watterson wrote, even though he was not given to appreciating the female intellect. He described her as "a born insurrecto and a terror with her pen" and noted, "She took great pains with me and mothered me in the absence of my own mother." Watterson thus claimed the mantle of one of the greatest supporters (and practitioners) of antebellum Democratic expansionism.[9]

In addition to apprenticing him to masters of partisan journalism and aggressive Democracy, Watterson's position at the *Daily States* gave him the opportunity to gain a name as a political reporter and to witness firsthand the disintegration of the national union. In a chance encounter that he later emphasized, Watterson met Abraham Lincoln immediately upon the new president's secret arrival in Washington in 1861. A few days later, the young reporter served as the press representative to pick up a copy of Lincoln's first inaugural address. Watterson stood at Lincoln's elbow during the inauguration and, he later claimed, would have held his hat if Stephen Douglas had not reached over and taken it first.[10]

At the time, Watterson had no sympathies for Lincoln or for the Republican Party. Yet these initial impressions later transformed into a belief in Lincoln's infallibility and good intentions that would permeate Watterson's thought and words for the rest of his life. Throughout the postwar period, he played a critical part in furthering the Lincoln mantle by delivering flowery, patriotic orations about the martyred president, arguing historical controversies about his decisions, and helping to establish a memorial at Lincoln's boyhood home in Kentucky. Watterson claimed Lincoln as a southerner and an exemplar of moderate politics. "Mr. Lincoln was not an enemy, but a friend to the South," he wrote. In line with this admiration, Watterson later paraphrased Jesus: "With respect to Abraham Lincoln, I, as a Southern Man and a Confederate solider, here render unto Caesar the things that are Caesar's, even as I would render unto God the things that are God's."[11]

As the Civil War approached, Henry Watterson was snugly ensconced in a sinecure in the Interior Department, courtesy of his father's old friend Secretary Jacob Thompson. As Watterson quipped in his autobiography, "When the troubles of 1860–61 rose I was literally doing a 'land-office business' with money galore and to spare." The collapse of the Union seems not to have disturbed him at the time. "I could not wholly believe with either extreme," he wrote in retrospect. When Lincoln took office, Secretary of War Simon Cameron offered Watterson a position as private secretary in the new administration, as well as the surprising rank of lieutenant colonel. Watterson turned it down out of fear of being something of "a confidential middle man" involved in corruption in the new administration, although there is some indication that he had previously agitated for the position. He decided instead to return quietly to Tennessee, to "go back to my books and my literary ambitions" and wait out the coming conflict between the states. He did not think it could last long.[12]

Although a strong unionist like his father, who was busily trying to keep Tennessee from seceding, Watterson ended up opposing the national union he repeatedly proclaimed to be immortal. He eschewed any sympathy for the radical fire-eaters who brought on the war but nevertheless was drawn to the southern cause for ideological and emotional reasons. Watterson did not immediately heed the call to arms but slowly drifted toward Confederate service. He found he could not simply wait out the war at his family homestead in Tennessee: "The boys were all gone to the front. The girls were—well, they were all crazy. My native country was about to be invaded, Propinquity. Sympathy. So, casting opinions to the winds in I went on feeling. And that is how I became a rebel, a case of 'first endure and then embrace,' because I soon got to be a pretty good rebel." One historian has pointed out that Watterson actually joined the Confederate cause after the southern victory at First Manassas, which indicates perhaps that he straddled the fence until he thought that the South might have a chance of victory. After the war, Watterson constructed an elaborate defense of secession based around the claim that "resistance to invasion" and fear of being treated as "a conquered province" were the major issues behind the war. He bolstered his defensive theory of southern rebellion by arguing that "the people of the South, like the people of the colonies, were used to self-government and self-defense."[13]

Watterson justified the Confederacy on the limited-government theory that underlay most of his postwar positions. He argued that the Constitution supported slavery and that secession was legally defensible, if morally confused. "Unfortunately, the organic law, as it originally stood, recognized an institution that was logically opposed to all for which the union professed to exist," he wrote in 1885. More than ten years later, he wrote virtually the same argument, declaring secession still "an open question." When he became extremely distressed by the growth of government under the progressives in the early twentieth century, Watterson even found the seeds of the Civil War in "the failure of the framers of the Constitution to fix the exact relation of the several states to the Federal Government." He argued that the Union was destroyed in 1861 because the federal government had not adhered to strict limits on its power.[14]

Although he recognized slavery as a constitutionally protected system, Watterson did not defend it. This claim helped strengthen his long-lasting postwar reputation as a moderate on race relations. In 1901 he told the *New York Tribune* that even "with a grey jacket on my back for four years, I was an outspoken, sentimental free soiler." Watterson rarely discussed the moral dimension of slavery, instead deferring to arguments that stressed its impractical, inefficient, and anachronistic character. He conceded that slavery "was the clumsiest and costliest labor system on earth." After the war, Watterson wrote that all but the zealots in the South had known that slavery was outmoded and doomed in any case. The Democratic Party defended slavery only because, he claimed, "it stood for the promise of the Constitution and the letter of the law." This was in keeping with his reasoning that, even in rebellion, the southern Democrats had stood for honest principles, personal liberty, and limited government.[15]

Watterson absolved himself of any personal guilt for slavery by often retelling the story of his brief personal experience as a slaveholder. Given a slave by his grandfather, the young Watterson maintained a friendship with the slave and eventually granted him freedom. Watterson recalled fighting the overseer when this slave was whipped, and hating the experience. "That was the only 'nigger' I ever owned, thank god!" Watterson wrote in 1894 in one of his most famous and widely given addresses. Clearly, his use of the word "nigger" set a tone for the story that deliberately reaffirmed his broader views on race even as he distanced himself from slavery. Later, he attested that this experience as a slaveholder had reinforced his convictions as a conservative insurgent, as it "set me a lesson in the true relation of human freedom to despotic power." From that point forward, Watterson refused to submit to arbitrary power, especially as he saw it manifest in tariff protectionism.[16]

Characteristically, Watterson filled a number of different roles as a Confederate soldier. To call his service fitful and unusual would be an understatement. He joined (and left) different units according to circumstance and whim. It all began, he liked to say, when he simply "leapt into an empty saddle" in Colonel Nathan Bedford Forrest's squadron as it rode away from Fort Donelson. "For the next six months, it was mainly guerilla service, very much to my liking," he recalled cryptically. Watterson also later rode with General Leonidas Polk, was chief of scouts for General Joe Johnston, and served as an aide to General John Bell Hood during the siege of Atlanta. Despite all of this action, Watterson's memoirs yield scant information about his military service.[17] His military record, aside from his sectional allegiance, does not seem to have interested him much. In looking back, he emphasized a few amusing stories of mistaken identity and misadventure (often involving hearty eating and drinking), but little else. Relatively uncommitted to the cause, Watterson was an ineffectual Rebel in uniform. He frequently left military service for journalism, in a variety of cities, and ultimately it was as a newspaperman that he became a major voice for the southern cause. He made his biggest contributions to the war effort with his pen.

After brief stints as assistant editor of the *Atlanta Southern Confederacy* and the *Nashville Banner*, and as a writer for the *Mobile Register* and the *Augusta Constitutionalist*, Watterson rose to prominence as the editor of his own paper, the *Chattanooga Rebel*. This paper, which showcased Watterson's acerbic personality and flamboyant style, soon became the most widely read Confederate paper in the western armies. Watterson moved the paper with the southern forces and gained a reputation for independent thought and vibrant writing that would follow him for the rest of his career. He also created a name for himself as a journalist throughout the states of the Confederacy that would serve him well in decades to come. Confederate soldiers enjoyed reading quips like "of course [General William S.] Rosecrans will cross the river as soon as the supplies of whisky come up. The 'desperate courage' of his Dutch and negro army is all kept in barrels" and typical Wattersonian calls for "universal exaltation. Such a thrill as [has] never yet run through Southern veins."[18]

Even while producing propaganda, Watterson did not hesitate to criticize the Confederate command and war effort. The independence and stridency that typified his later editorials were fully evident in his writings for the *Rebel*. "Criticism is the lamp of life. It is the light of the world—the city which sitteth on a hill—and cannot be hid," he wrote in a characteristic example. Most of all, the *Rebel* both reported and dissected the war news, and it was in this capacity that Watterson eventually sowed the seeds of his forced resignation. After a long string of bitter attacks on the competence of General Braxton Bragg (and after Watterson had the misfortune of accidentally insulting the general to his face at a party), the *Rebel* faced censorship and ruin unless Watterson stepped aside. He resigned. Failing to acquire an officer's commission and sensing the looming end of the war, Watterson quit the Confederacy and fled north, ending up penniless but proud at an uncle's farm near Cincinnati.[19]

Never having wholeheartedly supported secession and war as the answer to the southern question, Watterson abandoned what he viewed as a lost battle. He had a bigger vision of his role in southern life, and he now turned his sights to reconciliation and reunion, to the postwar settlement and the opportunity for "a new spiritual life, with manlier aims, broader ideas, and a larger perspective." Recognizing that the South's redemption and prosperity could now be attained effectively only within the national union, Watterson sought to establish himself as the arbiter of this new future. He left the Confederacy "an imprudent upstart . . . little better than a carpetbagger," he wrote. Yet "it never crossed my fancy that I could fail."[20]

It may seem surprising that Watterson the ex-Confederate decided to first practice his craft north of the Mason-Dixon Line in Cincinnati, but he unabashedly went where opportunities seemed available. In short order, and after an accidental drowning of the former editor, Watterson became editor in chief of the *Cincinnati Evening News*, a Republican paper. In this post he began writing the reconciliationist editorials that came to typify his approach to Reconstruction and that brought him national notice. He also seems to have been courting northern favor, and maybe even faintly flirting with Republicanism. Certainly, Watterson briefly relaxed his staunch, self-proclaimed eternal party ideals. Historian Lena C. Logan wrote, "No amount of explanation, however, can allay the suspicion that Watterson was over-supple and over-subtle in switching from the position of a pre-war Southern border Unionist, to a wartime Confederate soldier and propagandist, to a position as a Northern border unionist crying down vengeance on the Southern leaders."[21] There may never be a clear explanation of why Watterson tried his hand at a Republican paper in a Union city. Equally curious and noteworthy is that he succeeded.

Watterson's quick switch away from Confederate propaganda to reconciliationist crooning aroused the partisan press in Cincinnati. Great Republican editor Murat Halstead of the *Cincinnati Commercial* regularly reminded readers that Watterson was a Rebel and called Watterson's paper the "Chattanooga-Cincinnati-Rebel-Evening Times." Loving a good political brawl, Watterson did not slink away. He told his editorial assistants, "He is my personal meat. You boys shinny on your side and leave Murat to me." Watterson honed his editorial skills in this conflict. The two men later became close friends despite their political differences and ongoing skirmishing, and a friendly personal rivalry developed that mirrored the commercial rivalry between Louisville and the Queen City.[22]

Despite his flirting with sectional and party irregularity, Watterson longed to return to the South. He did so with the assistance of his father, who had political clout with Tennessee governor William G. Brownlow as a result of having remained a unionist during the war, and who further was in such favor with the postwar unionist order that President Johnson sent him on a tour of the South to report about conditions at the war's end. Henry was soon allowed to return to his native Tennessee without hindrance. There he began an intense and very successful revival of his wartime employer, the *Nashville Banner*. Watterson gave the southern orientation of the *Banner* a decidedly reconciliationist bent. "We want repose. We are weary of agitation," he wrote. Brownlow's *Knoxville Whig* archly diminished him as "little henry watterson," but the former propagandist proved his merit as an effective editor.[23]

It was at this time, on December 20, 1865, that Watterson married

Rebecca Ewing, whom he had met in Chattanooga during the war. Ewing, who came from a southern political family in Tennessee, had waited for Watterson to return after the war. Their marriage was long, prosperous, and happy. Watterson's often acerbic public personality was nowhere evident in letters to his wife, filled as they were with pet names and gentleness. He was similarly gentle with his children, whom he adored. The couple eventually raised five children and traveled very widely with them while maintaining an estate, Mansfield, outside Louisville. Henry and Rebecca remained married for fifty-six years. On the occasion of their golden anniversary, Watterson explained to the *Havana Post* that a long marriage was not difficult: "There is no secret about it. Mrs. Watterson always lets me alone, and I have let her alone."[24]

The success of the *Banner* under Watterson's guidance was so rapid and impressive that his friend and fellow ex-Confederate John Hatcher easily convinced Isham Henderson, owner of the *Louisville Journal*, to hire Watterson to revive that moribund paper. He therefore replaced legendary editor George D. Prentice, a Whig who had been widely credited with keeping Kentucky on the Union side of the war. By 1868, however, Prentice's influence, political power, and vaunted abilities had faded, and the *Journal* was suffering. Watterson eagerly set out to restore the paper's former glory and claim the Prentice mantle as the political conscience of Kentucky and the South.[25]

The Kentucky that Watterson moved to was, in many ways, a more reactionary environment than the defeated Confederate Tennessee in which he had been working. Despite its wartime loyalty to the Union, Kentucky "presented a more solidly Confederate-Democratic front" than any other southern state during Reconstruction. In part, this hardening of attitudes was a delayed response to Union wartime actions. It was also, significantly, an expression of economic self-interest. Louisville stressed its southern character and loyalties in order to reestablish its commercial credibility in the deeper South. Kentucky depended on being a commercial link and highway between the sections, and Louisville's prosperity in particular revolved around this carrying trade to the South. The state moved to slough off its wartime unionism with fierce struggles between "rival trade, commercial, social, agricultural and even personal groups." These tensions came to a head in a "power vacuum."[26] Watterson arrived to fill the vacuum in this border state with his idiosyncratic policies, preaching a gospel of southern independence, reformed Democracy, and prosperity for Kentucky within a strong Union.

Within this charged postwar atmosphere, Watterson pushed to create a prosperous and viable partisan newspaper. As he had done in Nashville, he immediately set out to improve the dying circulation of the *Journal*. In line with a similar pattern of newspaper consolidation all over the country, Watterson soon sought to combine his *Journal* with two other papers: Walter N. Haldeman's *Courier*, a strongly Democratic paper edited by former Confederate lieutenant general Simon Bolivar Buckner, and the less significant *Democrat*. Watterson saw economic and ideological advantages to this consolidation. He thought it was better to put the paper's energies toward fighting rival papers in other cities like Cincinnati and St. Louis than toward fruitless circulation battles at home among the city's three Democratic, English-language papers.[27]

After some negotiation and Buckner's stepping down, the new *Courier-Journal* appeared on November 8, 1868. Haldeman, a conservative businessman and committed Rebel who had fled Kentucky for the Confederacy in 1861 with his paper in tow, proved to be an ideal business partner for Watterson. According to Watterson, the two "were newspaper men to the manner born and bred . . . operating as one mind in the close and constant supervision not only of every department, but of every incident." In reality, the two men reinforced each other's conservative politics but, in the interest of efficiency, remained on opposite sides of the paper's administration. Watterson was sole master of the political content, while Haldeman concerned himself with the paper's market competitiveness. The two sides were complementary, as partisanship made for interesting reading and sold newspapers. The *Louisville Commercial* quipped on November 13, 1885, that "in State matters the Haldeman paper is Democratic for revenue only, no matter what it may be as Mr. Watterson's paper."[28]

Although the new paper was, in Watterson's phrase, "a double-headed monster," the public quickly accepted it. The partners' interesting combination of Democratic politics, unionism, and southern nationalism, as well as their setting in the vital Kentucky Democratic stronghold, soon created a paper with the widest circulation west of New York. Watterson rapidly made a national name for himself as an editor and as a spokesman for sectional reconciliation and economic development. The *Courier-Journal* grew tremendously between 1868 and 1875 and continued to prosper after that. Daily circulation rose to 30,000 by 1894. In 1870 the

Engraving of Henry Watterson in 1872, from a photograph by Matthew Brady. The accompanying article noted that he believed journalism was "yet in the infancy of its development as a science and its power as a political, social and moral engine." *Harper's Weekly*, July 6, 1872

Courier-Journal started a weekly edition, which raised its total circulation by another 144,000. Haldeman's involvement in establishing the Western Associated Press deepened news coverage and also afforded the paper an even wider circle of influence in national markets. The *Courier-Journal* was technologically advanced. It consistently purchased "the most modern press equipment outside of New York," including the Mergenthaler Linotype machine, the development of which it helped finance. The paper was also the first to print halftone photos in its daily edition.[29]

Alongside this growth and willingness to innovate, the *Courier-Journal* matured in its first twenty years from a fledgling southern paper with a strong regional bent to one self-consciously and deliberately absorbed in national and international issues. In the 1870s, the paper ran a prominent discussion of news from each southern state and a column called Keeping Tabs on Old Kaintuck. It often provided bemused or exaggerated coverage of events in areas such as eastern Kentucky. This coverage was soon overshadowed by discussions of international political economy. Like all papers at the time, the *Courier-Journal* covered every topic imaginable, from events around the world to literary controversies to obscure local issues, but it always centered on the American political economy. If an issue especially interested Watterson, as did free trade, it was not unusual for him to run multiple editorials on the topic in a single day. The *Courier-Journal* covered the tariff issue in particular almost every day, often several times a day, for over thirty years.

Watterson set out to shape this new paper into a reflection of his politics and a vehicle for his ambitions of being an important voice in his region and party. He deemed "the make-up of the newspaper . . . an autocracy. The product of one man, the offspring of a policy . . . fixed, sober, and alert." Watterson therefore directed most of his energy to the editorial page, which he considered to be the centerpiece of the paper and the product of individual vision. He insisted on overseeing all aspects of the *Courier-Journal*'s production throughout his reign as editor, but he was in actuality little interested in most of the mechanics of newspaper production. Partial to afternoons at the Chili Con Carne Club in Louisville and to long vacations and business trips to New York, Florida, Texas, and Europe, Watterson often sent in his editorials and left the daily business to his subordinates. The *New York Tribune* joked that "Marse Henry's office hours are more nearly 12 to 1 every other Wednesday."[30]

Nevertheless, Watterson's editorial production was monumental. His editorials were often immense tomes divided into chapters spanning six or more columns in the large-format paper. To help with this daily dissection of the news, Watterson employed more assistant editors than he did reporters, and he rapidly indoctrinated each in his way of thinking. Many of these assistants, who were known as Watterson's Boys, later became significant journalists in their own right, Arthur Krock foremost among them. "Each subordinate must be so drilled and fitted to his place as to become in a sense the replica of his chief," Watterson advised other aspiring editors. The national press considered all *Courier-Journal* editorials to be the opinion of Watterson, even the ones he may not have written. Although it was true that editorials written by Watterson's subordinates reflected his views, his writing was so distinctive that there was virtually no danger of someone actually confusing his editorials with one of his "boys'."[31]

With this degree of control, Watterson dedicated the newspaper to the promotion of his plans for the resurgence of the New South through free trade. He did not waver on this issue for the following fifty years. "Equivocation is fatal," he warned. Watterson ordained himself as the voice of those victimized by power, as "the watchful guardian of the people's interests and liberties." In particular, he assumed the responsibility of defending the South against all dangers, especially the abuses of the federal government and the Republican Party, and expanding opportunity for the South. The *Courier-Journal*, as the conscience of the Democratic Party and the voice of the South, was to be the vehicle of regional liberation. In order to gain control over popular political discourse and, thereby, to gain useful political influence, Watterson sought to educate the South about what he considered the reality of its political subordination and economic backwardness. "Emancipate the press from its thralldom to mammon by making it self-sustaining!" he commanded an Indiana audience in 1873. "Bind it with hooks of steel to the service of the people. Acknowledge no master except that of which you yourself are component parts . . . the mastership of public opinion."[32]

Given the ongoing upheavals of the period after the Civil War, this mastery of public opinion required providing a framework for political action and an interpretation of power in both regional and partisan terms. New South editors, significantly, provided this role through the turn of the century. Watterson understood that his role as an editor, as he later told his friend John Hay, was to "tell the truth and shame the devil."[33]

By this Watterson meant guarding southern interests while outlining his understanding of acceptable policy.

Watterson was one of the major propagandists of the New South idea during and after Reconstruction, and he concentrated on a positive message of rejuvenation rather than on recrimination. He called for the Democracy to differentiate itself clearly from the Republicans by jettisoning failed ideas and clearly staking territory as the party of prosperity and increased trade. The *Courier-Journal* regularly condemned the "despotism" and "tyranny" of Radical Reconstruction for conspiring to keep the South politically and economically subordinate and the Republican Party in power. The paper warned southerners never to vote for the "Republican Moloch" and constantly to fight "the materialization of their nefarious and treasonous plans." Watterson envisioned a triumphant New South, free of Republican rule, from which goods would flow to the markets of the world, and from which the Democratic Party would return to national power. C. Vann Woodward wrote, "The constant theme of New South editors and orators was cheap resources, business opportunities, railroad developments, and commercial enterprise." Henry Watterson exemplified these ideas.[34]

Watterson had one of the most powerful and persistent voices in this New South chorus. Arguing that southern development was the key to national prosperity, he sought capital investment from the North and Europe in railroads, foundries, and mills. He looked to the North for investment since he feared his message was not fully taking root in the "hidebound Bourbanistic" elements of the southern Democratic Party. Northerners had the money to invest and the votes to help the party. He sought the opening of "new routes of commerce and improve[ment] of old ones," and the overall modernization of the industrial and commercial systems in the region. "It is at length the aim of the Southron to out-Yankee the Yankees," he stated in one of his most memorable lines.[35]

Personally consumed by the need to develop the commercial sector, modernize agriculture, promote industry, and find new markets, Watterson never ceased to remind the South of its long-term interest in adopting his program. Once he articulated his theory of southern independence through commerce in the early 1870s, he felt he had created a solution to all future problems. He returned to the New South arguments for the rest of his life; they later formed the backbone of his plan for southern prosperity within an expanding global empire. In the following decades, Watterson argued that southern interests could be safeguarded only through tariff reform and free trade and, a bit later, through war, colonialism, and expansion into world markets. He never wavered in his emphasis on the southern aspect of national problems and foreign affairs.

In line with the Kentucky Democratic leadership, Watterson supported a New Departure program for the party that complemented his calls for a New South and anchored his other politics throughout his life. According to Hambleton Tapp and James C. Klotter, the term "New Departure" was coined by the Kentucky *Yeoman*, the main organ of the state party. Watterson accepted the need for change and consistently pushed his party to adopt new methods of achieving the New South's long-term goals. He told his readers that "there can be no peace as long as the carpetbagger reigns in Dixie," but his defiance was largely rhetorical. Despite his bravado, Watterson was willing to compromise in the interests of stability and the restoration of home rule. The New Departure ideal he embraced recognized the need for some unpleasant but necessary changes in the social structure of the South. He called for both North and South to end the entire Reconstruction system: the injustices in the carpetbag governments on the one hand and the recalcitrance and violence of unreconstructed attitudes on the other. Only by abandoning the failed policies of the past, he argued, could the South realize political independence and prosperity.[36]

"The hand of the South was in the Lion's mouth. The first essential was to get it out," Watterson explained. "The *Courier-Journal* proposed to stroke the mane, not twist the tail." He therefore urged the Democratic Party to absorb some of the changes of Reconstruction. Watterson became an early and important voice in the South calling for acceptance of the Reconstruction amendments as the treaty of peace. Eric Foner described this New Departure movement as a centrist, if cynical, effort to prove that the Democratic Party was not reactionary and to reassure the occupying North. Realizing that the passage of the amendments was "inevitable," Watterson accordingly advised the Democratic Party to be on the progressive side of history. Democrats needed to practice moderation and compromise if they wished to end Republican rule in the South and begin southern commercial development. The Democratic Party, he wrote, should be a "great, national, free-hearted, open-handed, order-seeking, and peace-loving organization."[37]

Watterson understood that conservative politics occasionally required innovative solutions. He valued stability, order, and progress, not retrenchment or reaction. Yet, like any good politician, he unhesitatingly coupled his calls for change with appeals to tradition. "The truth is there is no 'new departure,'" he wrote in explaining his fusion of conservatism and change. Instead, he argued, the reforming elements of the New South merely sought an innovative way to regain the old rights guaranteed by the Constitution. At other times, Watterson claimed that the New South fulfilled its core beliefs through compromise with the new order. In this sense, the New Departure was actually the fulfillment of Democratic traditions: "The South . . . seeks *principles*, not men or measures, as the foundation of its future fabric. It goes back to Jefferson—a thorough liberal and reformer—and takes its new departure from the founder of our Democracy." If another newspaper questioned his methods and compromises, Watterson denied its fitness for moral leadership. He sought to "lead and reform," he explained, "not to follow and fall in line behind the selfish and shortsighted timeservers."[38] Watterson preferred the middle road of compromise to the extremism of both fellow southerners and Radical Republicans. He followed this pattern for the rest of his life on all issues save the tariff, on which he was an extremist.

Watterson demonstrated his willingness to compromise on the issue of race. He claimed he did not consider race relations to be a uniquely southern problem and worked diligently to expedite their removal as a political question. He thought the major problem was, in fact, the Republicans' use of racial issues as political weapons with which to bludgeon the South. There were "Negrophobiacs" all over the country, he often wrote, describing the Republican North as even more cynical and racist than the South. Indeed, he argued, "Massachusetts and Mississippi are convertible terms." In one of his popular addresses from the Reconstruction era, Watterson assured his audience that the race question was a universal concern, not a southern curse: "The negro is an African in Congo or in Kentucky, in Jamaica or in Massachusetts." Rejecting the validity of race as a political issue because of its damage to the South, Watterson urged the Democratic Party to become the vehicle of moderation by preaching a "New Gospel of Peace." The South should "form new alliances, based on the altered conditions of our life. These alliances cannot be constructed upon by-gone issues and obsolete interest. . . . They must be liberal and provincial."[39]

Unlike other conservative Democratic politicians, Watterson judged the race issue to be far less important than questions of political economy.

Watterson's moderate position on race was based almost entirely upon political expediency. Because he believed that commerce was the most important aspect of national life, he was willing to accept limited revolution in the social realm as the price of development. With this reconciliationist rhetoric, Watterson portrayed himself as a racial moderate. "I have been something of a crank on the benevolent and sentimental side of the question," he wrote in 1890. Elsewhere, he noted, "I ask no privileges for myself and my children I am not willing to grant to the Negro and his children."[40]

According to historian George C. Wright, however, Watterson's New Departure positions on race were taken "not out of genuine concern for [freedmen] but out of fear that the federal government would intervene in Kentucky." Wright argues that "Watterson consistently opposed black involvement in politics." Watterson saw a "sentimental" motivation and expediency in allowing freedmen political freedoms, rather than a moral obligation, and he abandoned even this sentiment, when possible, years later. Watterson's relatively sympathetic Reconstruction-era attitude did indeed harden significantly in the 1890s. He came to judge African American suffrage a mistake, a "dangerous adventure," and a failure. He repudiated the wisdom of his Reconstruction-era positions and declared that political reality no longer allowed room for benevolence. Watterson recommended "dealing with him [the African-American] as a man and a brother, certainly, but as an inferior." He also rarely passed an opportunity to burnish his racist credentials, which were an effective and necessary political tool in the South. "In the South when a Nigger goes a niggering he generally does the thing at first hand, in an original niggerly way," he wrote in this vein. "A White Man is a White Man and a Nigger is a Nigger equally in Swampscot and Hell-for-Sartin, in New Orleans, New York, and Akron." Watterson also told "old darky" jokes to loosen up the crowd before his serious speeches and in letters to his friends.[41] Nevertheless, he accepted that political reality necessitated a change in the southern system, if not in southern attitudes.

Like other New South thinkers, Watterson hoped that, by emphasizing economic development, the South could move rapidly beyond the racial problems that plagued society and diverted attention from important issues. He advised the South to view its problems in economic terms. "The prosperity and happiness of the black people are indispensable to the prosperity and happiness of the white people," he wrote. The *Cou-*

rier-Journal thereafter became Kentucky's "most significant advocate" of the rights of freedmen to testify in court and to vote in the 1870s. It also led the fight against the Ku Klux Klan's lawlessness, social instability, and violence in Kentucky. During Reconstruction, Watterson often ridiculed those Bourbons whose politics consisted entirely of "Be-Damn-to-the-Nigger." Throughout his life, he strongly condemned lynching and "mobocrat" perpetrators as thugs who threatened both social order and, importantly, the willingness of outsiders to invest in the South. Thirty years after the war, Watterson still mocked those who stood only "for fight, sir, eternal fight, sir, and down with the nigger and the Yankee."[42] In the end, Watterson supported a modus vivendi on the race question in the interests of his broader program for southern independence and prosperity. This approach foreshadowed his rejection of racism as a barrier to economic development. Watterson was always more interested in the expansion of material benefits than in the persistence of what he considered to be reactionary and obstructive ideas.

As part of his New Departure program, Watterson moved to make the *Courier-Journal* "the recognized standard of the commercial interests of the Valley of the Mississippi." To accomplish this, he aggressively pushed the development of Kentucky's agricultural and industrial production, the establishment of Louisville as the dominant commercial city in the middle of the country, and the expansion of foreign trade for the South. Few places in the South were more in touch with the importance of foreign and domestic trade than Louisville, given its linkage of North and South and reliance on the outlet of the Mississippi. Watterson wanted the nation to consider Louisville "the natural gateway to the South" so that the city could dominate the carrying trade between North and South. As the South came to dominate the nation's economy, Louisville would become its first city. "A union of pork, tobacco and whisky will make us wealthy, healthy, and frisky," Watterson wrote with characteristic verve.[43]

The *Courier-Journal* was filled with Kentucky boosterism and calls for the expansion of its trade across the country and around the world. In the inelegant phrase of two great Kentucky historians, "Louisville commercially was Kentucky commercially." Watterson typically encouraged Kentucky and the South to develop their industries and cultivate broader markets for their products. He related all matters to their value to Kentucky's economy and waged a "relentless campaign" against rival city Cincinnati over domination of the trade routes to the South, particularly railroads such as the Louisville and Nashville.[44] This focus was very easily transferred to support for new foreign and imperial expansionism.

Watterson never forgot the potential transformative power of trade expansion for the South. Southern political independence relied upon economic freedom, he argued, and what was good for the South's premier city was good for all of Dixie. His fight for Louisville's commercial dominance in the South demonstrates his understanding of the city's and state's interests in terms of the expansion of national and international trade networks. Watterson, along with other New South editors, persistently pushed the idea that southern control of the international trade of the Mississippi River valley offered the opportunity for dominance of the nation's commercial life. *DeBow's Review*, for example, urged control of "this vast commerce, [because] it will bring us capital, votes in Congress, [and] diplomatic treaties. . . . We look, then, to the Mississippi as our mighty liberator and deliverer."[45]

While preaching reconciliation, Watterson remained at heart a southern nationalist. He built support for his vision of a resurgent South on a strong sectional appeal. He supported the Union, to be sure, but sought a return to a stable and limited system so that the South could dominate it economically. He warned the South that, in the end, it could not trust its freedom or prosperity to the North. For example, in wrangling with Cincinnati, he advised the South that "there is nothing Southern in or about Cincinnati" and stressed the city's inherent "malignity toward the Southern people." Watterson felt it was acceptable for friendly, honest competition to replace the unfair dictates of "sectional bigotry" and Radical Reconstruction. "To keep a leading place in the Union, or to keep a place of measurable influence, ought to be the aim of the Southern States," he wrote when describing the legacy of Reconstruction. He argued for this "not in the spirit of sectionalism, of course, but in the spirit of liberality to all portions of our Union." In other words, he thought all sections should be at least equal (if not the South more so). He feared Reconstruction threatened to make the South "another Poland" or "another Ireland." Within a mighty and newly unified nation, the South had a chance at salvation. "To sectionalism and partyism we owe our undoing," Watterson told southerners in 1877. "We shall owe our restoration to nationalism and nationalism alone."[46]

Watterson quickly gained a national reputation as a reasonable and fully reconstructed southerner, and he became famous for flogging what he called "the old sectional war-horse." Well into the 1890s, he attacked politicians for using the bloody shirt "to smite the living present with the jawbone of the defunct past." His speeches on reconciliation retained a remarkable uniformity and consistency over time, which is perhaps why historians have tended to view Watterson only in the context of Reconstruction. The culmination of his reconciliation effort was often considered to be his speech to the Grand Army of the Republic encampment in Louisville in September 1895, although Watterson continued to deliver orations on reconciliation until he gave up public speaking in 1914. He made it a personal crusade to end sectionalism. "Two things only remain," he wrote in 1895. "Ignorance and prejudice; ignorance and prejudice; ignorance and prejudice North and South. These finally removed, all will be well."[47]

But Watterson's support for the end of sectionalism was also based on a deeper understanding that conflict derived from fundamental inequalities in the national political economy. He told Republicans that "the Solid South has been from the beginning a simple protest against proscription." The South wished not to be hobbled, and it was Democrats who offered the only defense.[48] Watterson envisioned the riches awaiting a united nation if only the party were given a chance to shape policy and usher in his program.

Accordingly, Watterson viewed the "black flag of sectionalism" as a source of political oppression of the South and the Democracy. Under these ideological conditions, the region was unable to determine the limits of governmental power or to find the appropriate outlet for its commercial energies. New Southerners like Watterson saw that "sectional stress" was "grounded in economic competition" and sought to modernize the South to mitigate its effects. Watterson thought Reconstruction had to end for the South to attract needed investment and seek better markets at home and abroad. Prosperity and independent political power were symbiotic. Only the end of Reconstruction would bring "the pacification of the sections and the restoration of prosperity at the South."[49] Watterson's struggle to reorient the South to the politics of free trade was partly based upon a desire to limit sectionalism and dangerous governmental centralization through unrestricted and growing international commerce.

By the early 1870s, Watterson preached that the Democratic Party had to strengthen its national appeal if the South was going to obtain economic independence and accompanying home rule. The Horatio Seymour campaign in the presidential election of 1868 had failed precisely because it lacked national identity. At that time, Watterson was just beginning to consolidate his power as editor of the *Courier-Journal*. But by 1872, he was prepared to lead an expansion of the party's vision and to end the "rank old partyism of by-gone times." "We, in the South, need moral emancipation no less than political enfranchisement," he wrote in July 1872. "The South wants to be restored to its rightful place in the Union. . . . what we should strive for is moral enfranchisement. . . . [which] is identity with things national."[50]

In an attempt to make the New Departure a reality, Watterson therefore became one of the first prominent Democrats to support the breakaway Liberal Republican movement. He thought that the end of Reconstruction and the return of home rule for the South, as well as the end of corruption in national government, could be had only by alliance with northern interests. As Joseph Frazier Wall argued, "It was characteristic of Watterson to look to the Northeast for a candidate, for in that section could be found the capital for the industrial development of the South."[51] In his first major foray into national politics, Watterson joined important editors Murat Halstead of the *Cincinnati Commercial*, Horace White of the *Chicago Tribune*, and Samuel Bowles of the *Springfield (MO) Republican* (and later Whitelaw Reid) to form a group they labeled the Quadrilateral. This group intended to seize control of the Republican Party and create an overwhelming groundswell for Charles Francis Adams.

Like the others involved, Watterson thought that he had an unerring political sense and that the Quadrilateral was too powerful to fail. This was neither the first nor the last time he was wrong. The nomination instead went to fellow editor Horace Greeley, and Watterson subsequently endured the first of a long string of presidential elections in which he backed the losing candidate. He gamely and aggressively supported Greeley, but the campaign ended in the reelection of Ulysses S. Grant. After this defeat, and in Greeley's death soon after, Watterson found some hope in the loss by wishfully claiming that "Greeley's martyrdom shortened the distance across the bloody chasm; his coffin very nearly filled it."[52] The editor knew that sectionalism and the bloody shirt had killed the Democrats, just as they were preventing the South from attaining prosperity.

The loss of his chosen candidate in this election, and in the next two presidential contests, convinced Watterson that only emphasizing economic issues could bring a Democratic victory and a prosperous, independent South. With Grant's victory, the interests of the South were sublimated and the issue of free trade virtually ignored. Watterson did not yet have the power to shape Democratic issues and was only beginning to become consumed by the tariff. As historian Joseph P. Kenkel argues, in 1872 "the Democrats' innocuous tariff plank and their endorsement of Greeley attests to their lack of unity on the questions and to its insignificance."[53] Watterson would not allow this loss of focus again. By 1879, he had fully committed himself and his paper to the free trade cause, and he spearheaded the national move to the tariff as the single great political issue of the Gilded Age.

Watterson's first taste of political action at the national, rather than only the regional, level marked the beginning of his central involvement in all subsequent presidential campaigns through 1916. The election of 1872 had brought both Watterson and the *Courier-Journal* a great increase in national prominence and importance. Watterson began to be regularly quoted in the New York newspapers, and his own paper's circulation increased so much that, by 1875, it claimed it had "the largest and most widely diffused circulation throughout the West and South of any paper published." The *Courier-Journal* also stated that it was "taken and filled by more Boards of Trade, Chambers of Commerce, Hotels, Young Men's Christian Associations, and Public Libraries than any other paper outside of New York."[54] With this prominence, Watterson sought to nationalize southern concerns.

Four years later, Watterson supported Samuel Tilden, another knight-errant from the East. Watterson was the New York reformer's strongest southern supporter, and he played a significant role in the nomination, campaign, and subsequent bitter controversy over Electoral College votes. In August 1876 he became the congressional representative of Kentucky's Fifth District, filling the vacancy left by Edward Y. Parsons's death. Watterson had always insisted that he had no interest in political office and had, in fact, made this a point of pride. "I knew too much of the national capital to be allured by its evanescent and lightsome honors," he wrote. "Familiarity may not always breed contempt, but it is a veritable eye-opener." Tilden asked Watterson to accept the appointment so he could act as a friend in the House, and the editor agreed. Tilden offered nothing tangible in exchange for this support. He told Watterson, as well as *New York World* editor Manton Marble, that although they would have no official position in a new Democratic administration, they could expect "big influence." Walking out of the meeting with Tilden, Marble, who had badly wanted a position, said to Watterson, as Watterson later recalled, "Do you know—blank blank him—that he meant every word of it?" Watterson claimed that he would have been satisfied with the potential for vast influence.[55]

Aside from his speechmaking during the election dispute in 1876–77, which electrified the nation, Watterson did not accomplish much in office. In the end, Watterson was pleased with his sole experience in political office, although it did not increase his sympathy for politicians. He considered his tenure mostly a "kind of a seal upon the victory" of his long struggle for "personal and political recognition in Kentucky." He took James G. Blaine's seat on the House Ways and Means Committee and offered a number of minor bills for debate. Samuel Bowles of the *Springfield Republican* encouraged Watterson to "put away childish things and buckle down seriously to your great opportunity" in politics. After a tour of Kentucky, Bowles told Watterson, "I am miserly of such power as you possess and not willing to see any of it wasted." Nevertheless, Watterson returned to editing as soon as his appointed term expired. The national press continued to discuss his name for Kentucky governor or senator (he was nominated twice), but Watterson preferred the freedom of the editorial page.[56]

Yet, while in office, Watterson did have an important role in the events of 1876–77 that ended Reconstruction and gave the presidency to Rutherford B. Hayes. So much has been written about Watterson's role in the election and compromise that his role will be discussed here only briefly.[57] Watterson's experience during these events deepened his sense that the reins of government could be honestly held only by Democrats and that the specter of Radical Republicanism always threatened to return. He again demonstrated a willingness and ability to compromise out of political expediency, which he continued for most of his life. Despite his strident pronouncements, Watterson was always enough of a politician to recognize the value of a strategic retreat, and enough of a journalist to understand the necessity for proper spin on this withdrawal.

Watterson was the chairman of the national Democratic convention that chose Tilden, and he told the Democrats that the country needed "administrative relief from administrative ritualism; embraced in the simple creed of home rule, reduced taxes, and a living chance for the South as well as the North." Watterson managed to ram through a vigorous free trade plank that was the "strongest anti-protection plank of the entire period." After the election, Watterson served as a member of the commission that oversaw the electoral vote recount in Louisiana, and he remained, in his own words, "Mr. Tilden's personal representative in the lower House of the Forty-Fourth Congress."[58]

In this capacity, Watterson took a hard position on the disputed election that some thought flirted with renewed rebellion. The *Courier-Journal*, to which Watterson continued to send editorials in the form of long letters, anchored anti-Republican resistance in the South but was not overly belligerent. He wrote, "Civil war is not a red-tape affair. . . . Nor is it likely to happen ever until all the peaceful methods for the redress of grievances have been exhausted." These words came with an undercurrent of revolutionary ferment. Watterson described these "peaceful methods" in a speech on January 8 (a day Watterson called St. Jackson's Day in honor of the Battle of New Orleans) that drew a great deal of attention at the time and remained etched in the national memory for decades. He called for the assembly of one hundred thousand unarmed citizens in Washington to deliver a memorial in favor of justice. In addition, he called for "the presence of at least ten thousand unarmed Kentuckians in this city." Joseph Pulitzer, Watterson's friend, spoke next and called for one hundred thousand people, "fully armed and ready for business." This alarming cry was associated with Watterson, who was better known at the time, and reported around the country as a threat to lead a new southern army into Washington. This quote supposedly calling for ten thousand armed Kentuckians and the controversy surrounding it haunted Watterson for the rest of his life. It finalized his public image as a Rebel and bolstered his reputation for impetuosity.[59] Most biographical entries on Watterson continue to reprint the ten thousand unarmed Kentuckians statement as if it wholly represented his politics.

Watterson and his paper may have sounded radical, but he in fact quickly accepted the compromise that put Hayes in the White House and gave the South its "redemption." In private, Watterson continued to call the Republicans "the jobbers of corruption and assassins of liberty," but his public stance stressed sectional harmony and mild forgiveness. He accepted defeat for Tilden as long as it meant the end of sectional agitation and occupation and the beginning of home rule. He compared the unequal sectional relations to a loving "but never quite married couple," which confirmed that "submission and affection have not proved to be convertible terms." Watterson traditionally associated weak positions with effeminacy, while he linked independence with manhood. He thought the worst part of this situation was that "to-day it is the South which represents the woman in the quarrel." Were the North to finally release the South to home rule and obey constitutional limitations in the future, Watterson thought, the nightmare of Reconstruction could be left as a dim memory amidst the exponential growth of national prosperity.[60]

Once home rule was established following the Compromise of 1877, Watterson believed, a revision of the nation's economic policy would usher in stability and prosperity. The basis of this new order had to be a combination of home rule, free trade, and sound money. He considered free trade the linchpin in this holy trinity of national power. In tandem, these three policies promised the liberty, stability, and foreign markets necessary for the South to prosper within the Union. When "the relation of the South to the Government is still sufficiently equivocal to tempt partisans to rush in," he warned, the necessary commercial spirit would never triumph. On the other hand, when sectionalism was dead and political certainty and stability were reestablished, the South would have the opportunity to rebuild and expand its commercial horizons.[61] Watterson considered Democratic control of tariff reform the first major step, and his agitation for tariff reform intensified each year until the end of his career.

Watterson also renewed his appeals for more investment and greater attention to the expansion of foreign markets. Delivering a speech entitled "The New South" to the 1883 convention of the American Bankers Association, Watterson assured his audience that "commercially, financially, morally, we are one people." The end of Reconstruction had opened the possibility for the South to realize its potential, if the nation's business class was willing to drop the divisive ideological issues and invest its capital. "Capital is as unsectional as [it is] unsentimental," he told the group. "You have money to loan. We have a great country to develop." And Watterson assured these investors that he favored a conservative system supportive of business interests. "We want good money, honest money, hard money, money that will redeem itself," he said. He felt secure in ushering in a new era based upon unfettered commercial interests and, in turn, welcoming northern money into the New South. Things had changed with the passing of the war and Reconstruction. "Under the old system we paid our debts and walloped our niggers," Watterson told the gathered bankers. "Under the new we pay our niggers and wallop our debts."[62]

As he rose to national prominence, Henry Watterson declared the tariff to be "the question of the future," and this issue thereafter became the medium of all of his political expression. He became obsessed with the tariff and its relation to southern prosperity and liberty. Historians consider Watterson to have been "the leading free trader of the country" and "a fanatical advocate of tariff reform." Protectionist papers like the *Birmingham Age* skewered Watterson for relentlessly "grinding [his] tariff-for-revenue-only organ." In fact, Watterson tapped into a long-standing southern opposition to a tariff, and he argued that protection was the ultimate "live difference between Republicans and Democrats." He equated support for "the dogma of protection" with both anti-Americanism and secession and pushed for tariff reform at every national Democratic convention after 1876. "I wrote many of the platforms, and had a decisive voice in all of them," he recalled in his autobiography.[63] Each successive platform between 1880 and 1892 had a stronger tariff reform plank. All of them enshrined his famous shibboleth, "a Tariff for Revenue Only." By the 1880s, the *Courier-Journal* touted his true love for "the Star-Eyed Goddess of Reform" virtually every day on the editorial page. At times, as many as eight columns were dedicated to tariff exegesis.

The tariff was the perfect political issue for Watterson to champion. In it he found the totality of American political, economic, and social interests. He linked the "urgency of commerce" with political freedom and national cohesion. "What we suffer from is not too much but too little freedom, and that as long as trade is restricted our natural liberties are denied us," he wrote during the tariff debate of 1893. "To a free ballot, to a free church, to a free school, this generation must add free trade." This was a common linkage in free trade arguments, although Watterson tended to sound more apocalyptic than many free trade supporters. John G. Carlisle, a free trade–supporting U.S. representative from Kentucky and later Speaker of the House, wrote, "Politically we are free; commercially we are not." John H. Allen argued that "commercial freedom is more to be prized than political liberty. Without the former there can be but little else than mere pretense of the latter." Free trade was the basic

"'LET HIM RIP!'—Samson H. Watterson." The mighty Watterson rips the Democracy in half over the issues of free trade and protection. *Harper's Weekly*, April 5, 1884

precondition of globalization and the creation of international American economic supremacy. Liberalized world trade would enhance the American economy and create continual benefits at home. Watterson argued that extending free trade to Mexico, for example, would eventually create a union between the two countries. "Establish commercial union and the long step will be taken to political union, which will come about through natural agencies." Watterson argued that the only hope of his party and of the South to realize prosperity and independence was through tariff reform and the establishment of free trade.[64]

Watterson was hardly alone in emphasizing the tariff issue in the 1880s and 1890s, or in using free trade as a catchall cure. The tariff became, for a variety of reasons, the dominant national political issue between Reconstruction and the Spanish-American War. Both parties had an interest in using the issue as a shorthand to define their broader political positions; "it constituted a process of self-identification and self-explanation." In 1870 Henry Adams declared that for a southerner to support free trade was so expected that it "was like 'having worn a rebel uniform or having been out with the Ku-Klux Klan.'" Some important Democratic newspapers in the South, such as the *Atlanta Constitution*, the *Nashville American*, and the *New Orleans Times-Democrat*, favored protectionism, although the issue tended to tack to party lines.[65]

Watterson and other tariff agitators like Carlisle and William L. Wilson understood that the issue was ultimately as much about political power as it was about economic policy. The two parties agreed that "the political uses of the tariff were infinite," and they used it to subsume all other potentially destructive issues, such as sectionalism. "The remarkably malleable qualities of tariff rhetoric allowed them to claim that their tariff positions offered something for everybody," one historian wrote.[66] The Republicans used protectionism to further the North's industrial supremacy and the party's own political hegemony, to reward party supporters, and to limit the industrial advancement and political independence of the South. It was no accident that Watterson spent so much time perfecting his free trade arguments. He desired the same political benefits for the Democrats. He was constantly searching for the ideal construction that would provide both ideological clarity to the party faithful and popular appeal to the South at large. The tariff combined southern regional, economic, and partisan differences into one potent issue that could create Democratic electoral success.

Most important, Watterson understood that the tariff debate was over means rather than ends. It was a real and often vicious political dispute that, ironically, drew from a deep consensus on the desirability of expanding American opportunity, development, and competitiveness. Both Republicans and Democrats were deeply committed to a program of economic expansionism and international commercial supremacy, but they differed fundamentally on the role of the government in this program.

The parties battled over tariff revision as a way of girding the domestic system to a debate over the role of the government in international trade expansion. "The hyperactivity about the tariff was also anticlimactic in that both Republican and Democratic leaders agreed by 1890 that expansion of American exports was necessary and could be achieved by manipulating the tariff," argues Tom E. Terrill.[67] The tariff issue was a way of structuring the nation's response to globalization, not a challenge to it. This confluence of the two positions left free trade agitators like Watterson scrambling to explain how Democratic policies offered ever-greater and purer benefits, especially to neglected areas like the South. It was time for the South to begin to create its prosperous future through the magic of tariff reform and free trade in ever-expanding world markets.

Subsequently, Watterson described free trade as a tool of southern independence. The party that controlled the economic debate would, in turn, shape the trajectory of the government in domestic and foreign policy. Watterson thought that the South's struggle for home rule and prosperity could be won on the terrain of national economic policy. If the Democrats achieved supremacy in the tariff battle and limited the role of the "paternalistic" state, he argued, then the South could finally achieve home rule. The New South would reap the benefits of liberal trade expansion in the form of expanding foreign markets for regional products. Home rule together with free trade formed the answer to the southern problem. One could not exist without the other. In 1880, Watterson wrote these ideas into the Democratic Party national platform with phrasing right out of one of his editorials: "Home Rule; honest money . . . the strict maintenance of the public faith, state and national; and a tariff for revenue only."[68]

If Democratic tariff reform could rescue the South, then Republican protectionism sought to reenslave it. Watterson presented protectionism as the economic equivalent of Radical Republican rule of the South and as a giant conspiracy to impoverish the people. "The Republican programme is to ruin the southern people," he wrote in 1879. This program destroyed all opportunity for individual freedom and skewed the entire political-economic system for northern exploitation. "Protectionism is robbery and Republicanism is its prophet," he told the *Elizabeth (NJ) Evening Times*.[69] This sort of radical misrule endangered prosperity, provoked a dangerous reaction in the South, and unleashed instability in the form of labor agitation and inflationary movements like Greenbackism.

Watterson wished to draw the attention of all southerners away from the political inequalities and economic dissatisfaction of the domestic system by focusing on the wonderful cure-all of free trade in creating unfettered access to foreign markets.

In the wake of the "mongrel tariff" of 1883, Watterson began heavily stressing this precise linkage. This new tariff bill, the first general revision since the high tariffs were put in place during the Civil War, resulted from growing dissatisfaction with tariff rates and government surpluses. Despite initial calls for dropping tariff rates 20 percent, the final bill did not much alter the protectionist system or fully placate either party. The rates were insignificantly lowered, on average 1.47 percent. The "mongrel tariff" was, in the words of one historian, "a half-hearted attempt . . . to maintain a system of high protection, [while making] . . . some concession to a public demand for a more moderate tariff system." Watterson thought the tariff simply imposed unconstitutional taxation while shuttering opportunity in these desired foreign markets. For years, he had been arguing that "there is no protective organ in the country today [that] can show how protection is going to give American manufacturers foreign markets. It has not done it, and does not do it, and it will not do it." Since the northern mills were protected and well financed, he argued, the South was unable to end its dependent relationship under the Republican system of high tariffs. The southern mills were therefore kept in chains and isolated from their natural global markets. In 1883, Watterson declared, "The strength of southern competition is limited by the protective tariff. . . . Our laws do not permit the South to make the cotton cloth Mexico, South America, or China wants and would buy of us."[70]

In editorials throughout the early 1880s, Watterson regularly wedded southern prosperity with foreign trade expansion and stressed the need to limit state intervention in the economy. Only by linking investment, development, and free trade in a coherent system of limited government, he argued, would the region expand rapidly. "In this direction lies lasting prosperity, and nothing else than this should satisfy us, for nothing else is safe." By this, Watterson meant that there was no other policy that promised both prosperity and the continuance of social and racial stability, labor peace, and unencumbered home rule. A safe policy for the South had to include limitations on federal government interference as well as economic opportunity abroad. "It will not do to turn aside now and follow some will-o-the-wisp into the quagmire of protection," he wrote to emphasize these points. "The South can build cotton mills enough to furnish not America alone, but China and Brazil with all the cloth they need, but this she will never do under a protective tariff. The first step toward the accomplishment of this object is a tariff for revenue only."[71]

Watterson waged his tariff battles daily in the *Courier-Journal* and in his speeches throughout the 1880s, always stressing the advantages of free trade and market expansion for the South in particular. "The tariff," he wrote, "which is taxation, [is] the chief impediment to the substantial growth of the South, and of the whole country."[72] The virtues of free trade were so complete that Watterson could scarcely restrain himself on the editorial page. The year 1887, when the Democrats embraced free trade, marked one of the high points in his effort.

Alongside Speaker of the House John G. Carlisle and another southerner, Texan Roger Q. Mills of the Ways and Means Committee, Watterson had played an important role in convincing President Cleveland to support sweeping tariff revision in his December 6, 1887, annual address. Although the president "hung back from the extreme doctrines of [E. L.] Godkin and Watterson," the annual message still attacked protectionism. Cleveland declared that "our present tariff laws, the vicious, inequitable, and illogical source of unnecessary taxation, ought to be revised and amended." He tried to push past the static labels of "protection" and "free trade" and instead argued, "It is a *condition* which confronts us, not a theory . . . the question of free trade is absolutely irrelevant." Nevertheless, Cleveland's words unleashed a massive struggle for free trade. The message had an explosive and lasting public effect, and the tariff came to dominate the presidential campaign of 1888. As Watterson had sought for years, the fortunes of the Democratic Party were now tied to tariff revision.[73]

Throughout the campaign, Watterson clarified the positions he had developed over the previous decade. His clearest single statement on the "dogma of restriction [and] . . . gospel of mammon" appeared in *Harper's Monthly* one month after Cleveland's message. Soberly, without employing his usual verbal pyrotechnics, Watterson dissected the ills of protectionism as a limitation on development and market growth. He promised to avoid both "visionary theories" and the impossible, like "converting an Irishman into a Scotchman, an Ethiopian into an Anglo-Saxon, [or] extracting sunbeams from cucumbers." Rather, he provided clear analysis of a critical but solvable problem and displayed an appreciation, if not an

"Our Champion Infant on Real Protection. 'Nor will the people be misled by the appeal to prejudice contained in the absurd allegation that we serve the interests of Europe, while they will support the interests of America.'" Grover Cleveland depicted as the powerful defender of tariff reform. This image would not last long, as Watterson grew extremely dissatisfied with the president over his perceived failures. *Louisville Courier-Journal*, November 3, 1888 understanding, of hard economics. Amidst this discussion of wages and prices, Watterson still managed to convey bluntly that protection brought the worst possible results on all levels of economy, society, politics, and culture. "There is but one way, however, to tell the truth, and that is never complex," he explained. Although it might seem beneficial to some in the short term, protection actually produced "glutted markets, excessive competition, strikes, lock-outs, and the survival of the fittest." Ultimately, he wrote, a high tariff could lead only to "bloody revolution."[74] Conversely, free trade opened markets, calmed social strife, and brought peace, prosperity, and development.

Watterson's hard-line arguments on free trade and foreign markets were matched by those of other prominent Democrats in 1888, especially his close ally Carlisle. This group coordinated its efforts in order to control the party's overall stance. They sought to maintain focus on extreme tariff revision to usher in an era of free trade and expanded global market opportunities. In a very clear statement of the connections between tariff reform and the cultivation of such markets, Carlisle wrote, "We want not only the home market, but all the markets of the world for the varied products of this great country. We want to send our agricultural products, our cotton, and our breadstuffs and our provisions to the naked and hungry manufacturing people of Europe, and our manufactured products to the agricultural people of South America, Mexico, and Asia."[75]

These arguments created a great deal of momentum for the free traders and helped them force the Democrats toward the extremes of the tariff debate. After an all-night conference at the 1888 national convention, and over the rigorous challenges of Maryland senator Arthur P. Gorman, Watterson pushed through a strong platform statement in support of tariff revision. The platform reaffirmed Cleveland's positions as, in Watterson's words, "a declaration of principles to which Democrats may subscribe without looking around the corner . . . a statement of facts inconvertible." In reality, it transformed the movement for basic tariff revisionism into outright agitation for free trade. Historian George T. McJimsey calls the plank "another disaster" created by an overeager Watterson.[76]

Watterson saw the 1888 platform as a great personal victory. He thought it proved that he alone was responsible for "the authorship of the Democratic policy and idea of Tariff Reform." In a third-person screed he wrote for a profile in the *New York Sun* in 1888, Watterson declared himself to be the pioneer and consistent leader of tariff reform, to the exclusion of all others: "In view of these facts, how can any one say that Henry Watterson, with his Star-Eyed Goddess of Reform, did not beget the policy, and rock the cradle of Tariff Reform, claimed now by men who were unheard of when he was at work in the fields arrayed to meet all comers, whether Radical Republicans . . . or Conservative Democrats?"[77]

In making the cause of tariff reform personal as well as ideological, and in setting himself up as the ur-Democrat, Watterson created a situation in which he was doomed to clash violently with Cleveland. He had been supportive of the president in his first term, often played poker with him in the White House, and had even prevailed upon him for patronage for some Kentucky cronies. When Cleveland won in 1884, the Haldeman-Watterson-owned *Louisville Times* ran a life-size rooster on the front page celebrating the victory. In 1887–88, when sentiment for tariff reform was strong, Watterson supported Cleveland effusively. "One single digit among the clumsy fingers of Cleveland is worth all the brilliant, graceful and alert qualities of a dozen Blaines," the editor gushed in this spirit in 1887.[78] After the Democrats lost in the election of 1888, Watterson had soothing words for Cleveland and promises to the South that the cause of tariff reform would be reborn in four short years.

In 1890 Watterson embarked on a national speaking tour to promote the cause of tariff reform and to start the next presidential campaign early. He consistently wrote to Cleveland to encourage him to remain true to the free trade cause and to look forward to 1892. "I think the Republicans have 'bit off' more than they can 'chaw,'" Watterson wrote in April. "Assumedly, they will find their Tariff Jordan 'a mighty harsh road to travel.' It is inconceivable that a party so dishonest and reckless can again carry the country." Watterson told Cleveland, "For twenty-five years, under all circumstances and with every application, I have been preaching that sermon." The editor believed that support for free trade was growing all over the country, especially in the South, where it was "universalist."[79] As he would continue to do for the rest of his days, Watterson overestimated the public support for his free trade program.

One clear sign that the 1888 loss had endangered tariff reform was the passage of the McKinley tariff of 1890, the highest tariff in American history, with rates as high as 49.5 percent, including duties on raw materials like wool. Tariffs on raw materials and staples were especially galling to advocates of liberalized trade. Watterson repeatedly called this new tariff an abomination and blamed it for all the country's ills over the next five years. Yet he tentatively supported its last-minute reciprocity provisions, as long as they opened foreign markets. In retrospect, it is clear that the reciprocity provisions in the bill marked the beginning of partisan convergence on the tariff issue around the benefits of globalization that Watterson embraced. From this point on, alongside protectionism came a concerted push to use bilateral reciprocity agreements to liberalize trade and expand global market access, particularly in Latin America.[80] Tariff reform had become a tool of globalization.

Watterson welcomed the idea that lower tariffs could be used to open foreign markets, although he saw reciprocity as only a first, very limited step. When Secretary of State James G. Blaine pushed hard for reciprocity, Watterson declared Blaine "the new apostle of Free Trade." In September 1890, just as the tariff was coming to a vote in the Senate, Watterson told the *New York Tribune*, "I agree with him [Blaine] that the home market is no longer sufficient; that we must find sales for our surplus production; that the system of foreign exchanges, which I have always advocated and he now advocates is becoming indispensable." Despite this praise of Blaine, Watterson still believed that Cleveland could successfully carry the free trade battle forward. "I consider your nomination indispensable," Watterson wrote to him in late 1890.[81]

Watterson's concern over the McKinley bill heightened when it was discussed at the same time as Henry Cabot Lodge's "force bill," which called for federal supervision of congressional elections. Like other southern Democrats, Watterson feared this legislation would disrupt the white-dominated social structure of the South and expand the reach of Republican power.[82] He envisioned a combination of high taxation and expansion of federal arbitrary power, and he propagated fear that the tariff represented the vanguard of a new Republican effort to destroy home rule in the South in addition to strangling development. The moment perfectly fit Watterson's long-standing perspective. He easily equated the dangers of protectionism with Republican intervention in the southern system of white supremacy. He praised "the Southern white man, who has been unable, conscientiously, to accept the gospel of Force and the doctrine of Protection from lips laden with malediction." The South could not trust the Republicans to produce an honest tariff policy any more than it could trust them to respect home rule. "In truth as I see it, the extremists of 1890 have exchanged places with the extremists of 1860," Watterson wrote.[83] Not until the campaign of 1892 did he became convinced that the promised land of free trade was at hand or that the South would finally find relief from Republican attacks on its independence and prosperity.

The early 1890s marked a high point in Watterson's political power. His role as a spokesman for the New South, his ongoing campaign for free trade, and his skill as a writer and politician all combined to make him an influential and nationally known figure. He delivered the opening address, "Our Expanding Republic," at the world's fair in Chicago in October 1892, an event often touted by historians as a defining moment in fin-de-siècle America. This speech, a fine example of Watterson at his most florid and patriotic, announced the death of sectionalism: "There is no geography in American manhood," he told the crowd. "There are no sections to American fraternity." Watterson, a good speaker despite his high-pitched voice, was eagerly sought to speak before diverse groups and political organizations around the country. He toured the country in package tours with well-known speakers like John Brown Gordon and John J. Ingalls in which he covered topics as disparate as Lincoln, John Paul Jones, "Money and Morals," and, in his best-known address, "the Compromises of Life." These popular talks were often covered in great detail on the front pages of local newspapers, with photographs or engravings of the editor. They were also reprinted in magazines and books. A political organization called the Watterson Club was founded to agitate for free trade, and a Hotel Henry Watterson soon opened in Louisville to capitalize on the editor's fame. The editor became so famous that Henry Watterson brand cigars were sold, as was Henry Watterson Whiskey.[84]

In addition to his centrality in the Democratic Party's discussion of tariff reform, Watterson was touted as a potential candidate for either the presidency or the vice presidency in 1892. The *New York Herald* repeatedly called for him to run, especially because he was so well known and liked throughout the country: "The nomination of Mr. Watterson for President would, we believe, be more generally acceptable to his party all over the country than that of almost any other man who can be named." Many other politicians were put forward, of course, including Carlisle, Gorman, and William Vilas. Watterson himself aggressively pushed for his ally Carlisle. The editor had abruptly abandoned Cleveland as a potential candidate because he thought the ex-president could not possibly win and because he preferred a southerner. "But, to me, it seems that if we go" to Cleveland as a candidate, Watterson told the Kentucky state Democratic convention in Louisville, "we shall walk through a slaughter-house into

Henry Watterson Whiskey bottle, marketed to capitalize on Watterson's fame.

an open grave."[85] This statement, which quickly made the rounds of the national newspapers, became one of Watterson's most famous expressions despite the fact that it ultimately did not change the party's nomination or even make a lot of sense.

In 1892 Watterson once again parlayed his prominence and power within the party into control of the platform's tariff plank at the national convention. He determined the public image of the Democratic Party's economic policy and, of course, strongly reemphasized free trade by hardening the statement of 1876. One historian archly called Watterson's plank "the tariff plank of John C. Calhoun—not of Jefferson, Jackson, and Cleveland." Another described the plank as the "boldest and most radical pronouncement against the tariff ever put forth by a responsible political party." Watterson smoothly declared that it evoked "the wisdom and the benediction of the spirit of that sage and saint of Democrats, Samuel J. Tilden."[86]

The Watterson-penned plank not only attacked protection in general terms as unconstitutional, but it also described the McKinley tariff as "the culminating atrocity of class legislation." At the convention, Watterson received twenty-six votes for vice president, but his real triumph was in once again realigning the Democracy clearly with radical tariff revision. Cleveland, appalled, wrote to Secretary of the Navy William C. Whitney, a mild tariff revisionist, that as soon as "this fellow Watterson" was "given his place in the furtherest back seat the safer we shall be."[87]

As the campaign unfolded, Watterson pressured Cleveland to stay true to the hard-line free trade policy. Those who disagreed with him and the policy of free trade, Watterson wrote to Cleveland during the summer, "are not, as to the Tariff, Democrats at all." Watterson beseeched the candidate to return to his 1887 annual message as a guide. "I know it by heart," the editor purred. "Take it as your guiding star . . . emphasize it, amplify it, but do not subtract a thought." Cleveland disregarded Watterson's advice, as might be expected after the editor's slaughterhouse comment, and made the mistake of showing insufficient deference to him. "One thing they [Watterson's letters] demonstrate beyond any doubt, to-wit; that you have not—I think I may say—the slightest conception of my disposition," Cleveland bitingly told Watterson. The president accused Watterson of "platform smashing" and denied that the editor ever had any influence on tariff policy. After a final letter to Cleveland refuting these insults, Watterson officially ended his "personal relations" with the presi-

HON. HENRY WATTERSON.

The Bluegrass Editor Is In the Lead, But Cleveland's Friends Are Arrayed Against Him.

LEADERS

TALK TO THE TIMES

Situation Full of Lively Interest and Enthusiasm.

Zack Phelps Slated For Kentucky's National Committeeman.

BOOMING

MARSE HENRI.

Has an Undoubted Lead, According to Present Calculations,

But Cleveland's Friends Are Opposing Him With Vilas.

Booming for Marse Henri. Clipping touting Watterson's presidential possibilities. *Louisville Times*, circa 1892 dent. Cleveland was reportedly pleased not to have to grapple with the editor any longer. The two never spoke again, even when they attended the same Democratic functions.[88]

During the campaign and into 1893, Watterson allowed neither his personal dislike for Cleveland nor the disavowal of his influence to interfere with his desire to achieve tariff reform. Watterson told Whitney that, since Cleveland "has his uses, and very great uses, but he also has limitations," he could be supported "solely on the grounds of expediency." Watterson considered the Democratic platform's tariff promises to be "promissory notes" that had to be paid to the voters. With Cleveland's victory, Watterson felt he had "a great constituency behind" him that could force immediate action on the tariff. He was to be disappointed.[89]

As soon as Cleveland won, the *Courier-Journal* increased its already stupendous discussion of the tariff until it crowded out almost every other issue. By January 1893, the editorial page daily discussed the benefits of free trade and market expansion. "Under a tariff for revenue only we would do justice to all concerned . . . and then American manufacturers would command not only our home market, but all markets," it promised. After the inauguration, the *Courier-Journal* declared "Triumph" and pronounced it "the Day for Friends of Reform to Rejoice." Watterson hoped that the president would "take his place in the Valhalla cloisters of Democratic saintship along with Jefferson, Jackson, and Tilden." Through the rest of the year, the *Courier-Journal* talked about little but the tariff and the fact that the party was "specifically pledged to open new markets."[90]

It is hard to believe how much Watterson found to write about the tariff over the next year. "The face of the country is turned toward free trade," he wrote in April. "The Democratic party received its marching orders last November. Forward!" Watterson discussed the tariff in terms of foreign markets, busy southern ports, southern independence and home rule, sound money, the Civil War "pension robbery," Canadian annexation, organized labor, the "bonny liquor of the Bluegrass and the Pennyrile," Wall Street, sectionalism, jingoism, high wages, low prices, trusts, the world's fair, and almost every other conceivable topic. He characterized "a Tariff system half protection and half revenue . . . as incompatible with American institutions as a labor system half slave and half free" and declared the issue "an irrepressible conflict." When he did not have a suitable topic, Watterson rallied the faithful with editorials that increasingly read like sermons: "It is for Mr. Cleveland to exclaim in trumpet-tones:

'to your tents, O Israel!' It is for Mr. Cleveland to call the Lord's anointed about him and to set out upon the march which is to smite the Philistines hip and thigh. We are not here to conserve Republican policies, but to destroy them. . . . The revolutions are not evolved out of rose-water." The religious tone helped reinforce Watterson's other attacks on the Republicans, and the excessive language helped keep readers interested. When running one or more tariff editorials every day, Watterson understood that his writing had to be at least as entertaining as it was enlightening if anyone was going to read it. He had to keep interest in the tariff perfectly honed. "He who dallies is a dastard," he warned Cleveland. "He who doubts is damned."[91] This was a pattern he continued throughout the decade: returning to exhortations to strengthen his points and alternating outrageous editorials with sober policy analyses. Soon Watterson printed his editorials in double columns that consumed the page, and his language inflated to fill this space.

It was not until December 12, 1893, that Representative William L. Wilson's tariff reform bill was introduced in the House. Watterson's constant barrage on tariff reform produced a great deal of discussion in the national press just as the congressional debate began. Although the bill passed the House quickly, with a large list of duty-free items (including wool, coal, iron ore, and sugar), the Senate arrested its progress, gutted virtually all of its reform elements, and added 634 amendments. The final version, dubbed the Wilson-Gorman bill, offered only mild reductions, put a very limited list of raw materials on the free list, and effectively ended reciprocity on sugar. Overall tariff rates were not much lower than they had been in the "mongrel tariff" of 1883. Indeed, the new bill was not a truly significant change from the 1890 McKinley tariff. Watterson called the failure to completely overhaul the tariff "a miserable betrayal." Instead of the redemption he had anticipated for years with such verve and consistency, he got failure. Watterson's disgust hit new highs. He described the bill as "a mongrel piebald of patches and pusillanimity, a grotesque hodgepodge of pretense and pettifogging, a nondescript abortion of incompetency, selfishness, cowardice and treachery." He would not even call the new tariff the Wilson-Gorman bill but, cleverly, the "Bill McKinley, Jr."[92]

When Cleveland, "exhibit[ing] his usual ineptitude," allowed the unsigned bill to become law in July, Watterson brought his personal hatred into public and, for the next several years, wrote vehement anti-Cleveland screeds. Until his death, Watterson was sure to remind his readers angrily that Cleveland had helped kill tariff reform and weaken the party. "It was all Cleveland's fault" was Watterson's defiant claim. The *Cincinnati Tribune* sarcastically asked in a headline, "OH, WATTERSON, How Could You Say Such Awful Things?" Since his personal fortune and influence were directly tied to the free trade issue, Watterson personalized the conflict. A journalist who knew him wrote that "the break with Cleveland not only made political history but also revealed a prima donna quality in Watterson's make-up."[93] More important than the personal issue was Watterson's desire to reestablish his dominance in the Democratic Party, to squash growing Populist radicalism in the South, and to rescue the cause of free trade from the morass into which it had fallen in the wake of the Wilson-Gorman revision. His desire to implement free trade increased as the depression of 1893 intensified and seemed to threaten the whole American system.

By 1895 Watterson had joined a growing national movement to solve the problem of economic stagnation through the coordinated pursuit of international markets. He knew this focused emphasis on foreign markets required a more assertive and proactive international stance. Accordingly, Watterson supported Secretary of State Richard Olney's bluster in the Venezuela boundary dispute with England, in which the United States claimed the Monroe Doctrine prevented Great Britain from fulfilling its territorial claims on the boundaries of British Guiana. Olney famously rebuffed the British by announcing that the United States was "practically sovereign on this continent, and its fiat is law upon the subjects to which it confines its interposition." This kind of posturing—which bolstered America's developing claim to hegemony in the Western Hemisphere and led to a short-term boost in Anglophobia at home—thrilled Watterson. Using his universally applicable analogy, Watterson declared "the conflict between Monarchy and Democracy is an irrepressible conflict." He warned the British, "We are a vast imperial Republic, and we mean to be respected and felt among the nations. We mean absolutely to control, to dominate in [Latin] American affairs. . . . Our words shall be law."[94]

Yet Watterson still struggled with the implications of adopting an aggressive international posture if it meant European-style imperialism. He feared the expansion of the federal government, the expense of a big navy, the danger of a standing army, and the threat of perpetual war with other imperial powers. Watterson believed that free trade could supply all the

OH, WATTERSON

How Could You Say Such Awful Things?

"IT WAS ALL CLEVELAND'S FAULT."

The Democratic Party Is on the Verge of Destruction.

NIGHT WITH THE STAR-EYED GODDESS.

Henry Watterson in His Home, His Office and His Club—Views on Great Public Questions, From Free Trade to Seven Up.

From a Staff Correspondent of THE TRIBUNE.

LOUISVILLE, KY., Nov. 11.—I came down here to interview Henry Watterson.

Surely in these days of degenerate and despairing Democracy there is no character

"OH, WATTERSON, How Could You Say Such Awful Things?" Watterson blasted Cleveland for the failure of true tariff reform and for weakening the Democratic Party. *Cincinnati Enquirer*, November 12, 1894

benefits of imperialism without the costs of war and threats to liberties. American goods and products could flow unimpeded into the nation's "natural markets" in Latin America and Asia. "The markets of the world are open to us if we have the sagacity to take possession of them," he promised. He decided that the expansion of unencumbered foreign trade was the necessary next battle of independence and particularly sought its gains for the South. Over the next five years, Watterson increasingly saw the benefits of expanding the area of free trade around the world through imperialism. In 1895, however, he was happy to support "Home Rule, Free Trade, and the flag of the Union wherever it can find a ship at sea to carry it at its masthead."[95]

2

Sound Money, Home Rule, and Free Trade

> The top-loftical, high-falutin, free-silverites. . . . We consider the whole riff-raff of them a lot of crazy children astride a spavined, broken-winded, wooden jackass.
>
> —Henry Watterson, February 27, 1897

During the free silver contest of 1896, Henry Watterson addressed the most vexing of the political questions at the end of the century: how to reconcile development and growth with stability and order. The depression of the 1890s complicated these questions just as it sparked disorder, political radicalism, and violence across the country. Southerners and northerners alike wondered how to maintain a vibrant and expanding economic system without disrupting the established social order. As part of this decisive movement, Watterson argued that there was only one way to save the Democratic Party and the South from being swallowed by either the shortsighted radicalism of the Populist left or the paternalistic protectionism of the Republican right. He envisioned a symbiotic system of limits on intrusive government and unrestricted access to the international commercial system. What would link it together? His ever-expanding area of free trade, of course. Free trade, "as a rule," stabilized the whole system at home and abroad and liberated all who engaged in it. Watterson thought the solution lay in repairing and expanding trade in global markets rather than retarding it by tariffs, by currency manipulation, or by governmental experimentation.[1]

Despite his longstanding emphasis on trade issues, Watterson saw free silver as the paramount danger in 1896. He and other southern conservatives were so terrified by the uncertainty and radicalism unleashed by hard times that they formed an unlikely alliance with the Republican Party. All southern goldbug editors were torn between their ideals and their "fealty to the Democracy." Some chose ideology and interest over partisanship. A few, most notably Watterson and Joseph Bryan of the *Richmond Times*, later continued to defy party regularity with a trajectory toward expansionism similar to that of Republican editors and politicians.[2]

In the interests of defeating silverism and maintaining the New South economic development program, Watterson helped rend his party, almost destroyed the *Courier-Journal*, and aided his sworn enemy from the tariff battles, William McKinley. To not defend the righteous path of development and prosperity from the immediate threat of Populist radicalism, he feared, would warp the American future even more than four additional years of protectionism. Only after helping to ensure a Republican triumph over free silver in 1896, which all but negated his political gains of the previous quarter century, did Watterson return to Democratic regularity to rescue his vision of home rule and free trade. As it turned out, his desire to achieve these ends and increase American access to foreign markets brought him back again to the Republican fold.

Watterson left the United States for Europe with his family early in the winter of 1896, intending to retire. He sought peace and time in his beloved Switzerland to write his long-postponed biography of Abraham Lincoln. Had his career ended at this point, Watterson would have been remembered much as he often appears in the general historical literature: as a colorful Reconstruction-era figure who helped guide Dixie to an acceptable threshold of modern success, agitated excessively for tariff reform in the heady days of the Gilded Age, and then gracefully faded away to allow younger New Southerners a chance to obtain southern (and national) glory. As he explained, the original intent of his exit "was my desire never again to trouble myself, or anybody else, about politics; and to leave to younger hands the responsibility and details of my own particular business. . . . I thought I had earned my right of discharge."[3] Conscious of his place in history, and a frustrated litterateur from the early days, Watterson seemed eager to settle into the gentleman scholar's life in Europe, educate his children abroad, and write his final memorial to Lincoln.

Henry Watterson en route to attempted retirement in Geneva, Switzerland, in 1896, as he appeared on the front page of the Paris edition. *New York Herald*, November 8, 1896

What more satisfactory way to cap a career as a southern conciliator and politician than to write a biography of the hero Lincoln and leave the daily political skirmishes behind?

There are questions about how long Watterson intended to be gone, but it is clear that he meant to concentrate on his private life and limit his exposure to the daily grind at the Old Lady on the Corner, as he called his paper. He likely intended to return to Kentucky, as he had recently bought his estate, Mansfield, and his name was still carried on the *Courier-Journal*'s masthead. However, there is no evidence that he planned to return before the Lincoln book was finished. Watterson's name was a major selling point for the paper, and Haldeman may have left it on for this reason. Watterson was confident enough of the nation's direction to bow out of the fray in a critical election year. It is mysterious, however, that this partisan warrior of the old school left the country just as the radicalism brought on by the depression was gaining national influence in the presidential contest. Since he had reached his greatest power in earlier electoral screeds, his willingness to leave the country indefinitely was a notable, if curious, sacrifice. In American politics, gone was forgotten. "A single year often carries with it the force of a cycle of time," he noted shortly before leaving.[4]

Watterson knew that his longstanding political goals were either finished or impossible to complete in the near future. The union and home rule issues of the 1870s seemed satisfactorily settled for the moment. Advertising revenue and circulation of the *Courier-Journal* had boomed despite the depression that started in 1893. Daily and Sunday figures had risen by 10,000, and the weekly edition's circulation had increased by twice that, to 145,000. Hard times nationwide may even have been fading; the economy looked to be in something of a minor upswing from the dark days of 1894. Neither the political violence that continued in Kentucky (with forty-eight murders in the forty-eight days between July 1 and August 17) nor the labor violence that flared around the country, sadly, was unusual. "The year 1895, it seems, is to be a bright one after all, though few have begun so gloomily," Watterson wrote in the spring.[5]

Most of all, Watterson's bitter disappointment about the tariff reform battles of 1892–94 indicated that it was time to bow out. He later drew parallels between his discouraged position and Lincoln's losing interest in politics before becoming rearoused by the repeal of the Missouri Compromise. Watterson claimed the same prerogative after the travesty of the Wilson-Gorman tariff. "I confess," he wrote later, "that, with the failure of the victory of 1892 to record itself in the results it promised, and with selfish greed and embittered faction rising like a noisome tide, or vapor, all about me, I felt very much as Mr. Lincoln says he felt." The failure of free trade was a dark stain on the glorious cause of union; the conflict with protectionism was irreconcilable. So Watterson left for Geneva.[6]

Yet he did not actually disappear. Watterson's defiant persistence in national politics for another two and a half decades after his attempted retirement derived from his intransigence on the basic direction of American economic policy and market expansionism. Whether or not the Democracy and the nation felt a need to be rescued, Watterson appointed himself savior. In so doing, he reentered the vital national political debate just as the nation contemplated empire in the aftermath of the Spanish-American War. The quiet life of an expatriate biographer simply could not compare to that of a selfless patriot who rescued the country from iniquity, inflation, and protectionism. "It is necessary about once every generation to cast out the fiat devils," he wrote.[7] And it was always the right time to fight for free trade.

Watterson thought that maintaining a sound currency in conjunction with free trade would increase American access to world markets as well as revive the Democratic Party. As they had since the tariff battles of the 1880s, Watterson and his editorial staff stressed this point repeatedly, often several times a day. There was little subtlety to Marse Henry. And why should there have been? As he saw things, "Truth is always simple and easy of comprehension." He linked "National Prosperity" founded on conservative economic principles with international competitiveness and "National Honor" abroad. The gold standard was the basic medium of exchange, and a necessity if international commerce was to develop further. It was, according to one historian, "the accepted, orthodox doctrine" to use the gold standard to grease the wheels of global commerce. Conversely, free silver, Watterson argued, would "collapse American credit abroad and destroy business confidence at home."[8] Adherence to the gold standard helped keep the United States competitive in the most lucrative markets and predominant in both commercial and financial circles. Free trade coupled with the gold standard was the clear solution with the strongest partisan and doctrinal appeal and the greatest economic promise.

Watterson also argued that the stability of gold was of great importance to a South hungry, if not starved, for capital investment and outlets for its agricultural goods. Since the Civil War, the *Courier-Journal* had founded its southern development program on creating modern, reliable, and stable systems for investment within the South and trade in foreign markets. Inflation would only hurt its supposed beneficiaries, the "fellows who hew the wood and draw the water, and otherwise keep the official pot boiling."[9]

What Watterson saw clearly was that there was no economic magic to silver, despite its seductive appeal. Agitation for it only distracted attention from the central issue of tariff reform. Historian Joseph Frazier Wall justly noted that, "being a doctrinaire himself in blaming all economic ills on the protective tariff, [Watterson] had only contempt for other men who clung tenaciously to another doctrine, cheap money." The simple ideas of the Populists, Watterson believed, would only create further complications and undo the entire home rule project. "In their disordered brains, all things are topsy-turvey," he wrote in 1895; "they have eyes but they see not." If the Populists could fix everything by manipulating ratios, he asked, why not adopt a 1,600-to-1 ratio? It would be "just as effective and [would] result in oceans more of good silver money."[10] In Watterson's eyes, manipulating the money supply was an ill-conceived plan that could only cloud the real solution to depression: expanding the area of free trade and developing new markets abroad. Furthermore, he thought increased federal manipulation of the currency meant either granting undue power to a centralized authority or empowering the lunatic fringe.

The most important aspect of Watterson's understanding was that nothing—not price or wage manipulation through inflationary measures, silver coinage, or government control—would stop the cycle of depression without tariff reform. "Bryanism represents the outcry, the excess, the exaggeration of the depression that the country has suffered from," Watterson told the *New York Times* in 1896. "That depression," he argued, "is due to the protective idea." He saw tariff reform and expansion of free trade as the keys to improving the system and the worker's lot, as they always had been. Currency manipulation was "perversion of Democratic truth, [the] sacrifice of the substance of economic reform for its shadow." Its evil twin, protectionism, was simply a means of using one set of paternalistic falsehoods to protect a batch of economic falsehoods.[11]

In Watterson's trade-oriented view, the radical agrarians failed to understand that the nation's price problems were almost entirely caused by agricultural overproduction and insufficient markets. "The general trend of prices has been downward because production has been enormously cheapened in many departments, and because there has been overproduction," went a typical Watterson argument. Hardest hit were the central commodities: corn, beef, wheat, and cotton. The *Courier-Journal* tantalizingly pointed to Guatemala as a "Land of Opportunities" that offered "great chances for American enterprise" and recommended "we should better turn our attention to China."[12] The key, then, was to seek out new markets and to free those markets toiling in tariff slavery, not to follow half-baked currency schemes.

Watterson, like many other New Southerners, increasingly reflected the growing obsessions of the business community. By denying the significance of the currency in the national economic crisis, Walter LaFeber argues, "the Cleveland administration and other goldbugs [had] to claim that overproduction, not the lack of money, was the prime cause of the depression." Thus this group, in conjunction with similarly minded Republicans and businessmen, sought to increase markets to alleviate what they perceived as a production glut.[13] Watterson became one of the loudest of these voices, insisting that market expansion be the essential focus of any solution to the nation's ills. The *Courier-Journal* first concentrated on the agricultural interests that dominated the broader southern outlook and trade systems and then, after the Spanish-American War, put even greater emphasis on manufacturing.

In adopting these positions, Watterson aligned himself with other prominent sound money Democrats in the South. Many of these same ideological allies also broke with the party over Bryan, although few later became expansionists. Alongside Watterson, James C. Hemphill, the anti-Populist editor of the *Charleston News and Courier*, argued for this brand of fiscal conservatism from the perspective of a resurgent, independent South interested in expanding its trade. Hemphill wrote that free silver betrayed everything sought and built by the New South. Certainly, financial relief for farmers and others was desirable, but it was only to be had through tariff reform. Inflation would not adequately meet southern needs. The people of the South, declared Hemphill somewhat wishfully, "do not want free silver. They would prefer free trade, that they might sell their products in the dearest and buy their supplies in the cheapest markets of the world." This was identical to Watterson's program for southern and national advance via globalization.[14]

Hemphill and Watterson rejected the idea that the American farmer needed protection in world markets. To breathless reports that Asian farmers had the competitive edge because of their compensation in silver, the *Courier-Journal* responded that it was true that "American farmers have been obliged to sell their products in the markets of the world in competition with poorly paid labor." But, it argued, wages were not the issue, xenophobia was not an effective argument, and silver was not the answer. These issues were used to obscure the importance of opening new markets. "Wherever the system of trade restriction falsely called protection prevails, the practice of abusing and calumniating foreigners prevails," Watterson wrote. Paternalistic constraints on the home market dulled America's competitive edge. American goods, farmers, and workers would dominate international markets "if they had not been taxed to pay bounties, direct or indirect, to other industries." Agriculturists, particularly those of the South, were paying tribute to the manufacturers and corrupt cane and beet sugar interests. This, not gold, raised all costs and inhibited their ability to sell abroad.[15]

The New South boosters demonstrated their interests in numerous southern expositions, heavily stressing expanding markets and exports as the keys to both national and regional prosperity. Watterson envisioned a bright future when he visited the important Atlanta Cotton States and International Exposition of 1895. "Old things are passing away," he declared in an editorial he sent back to the *Courier-Journal*. "The New South has come to stay." Finally, it seemed, the South had adopted his New Departure message from the 1870s. He had visions of the South industrializing and then spreading its goods around the world once free trade was established. "The iron scepter of Pennsylvania, needing no other tariff protection than that supplied by God and nature in the soil and climate of the South, is being transferred to the uplands of Kentucky, Tennessee, Alabama, and Georgia," he told his readers. Whereas the North had used the illiberal crutch of protection to industrialize, the natural advantages of Dixie would flourish in an unencumbered system of free trade.[16]

Although Watterson enjoyed the support of some other southern editors, he knew that he had to build a strong national consensus for free trade and market expansion if the Democratic Party was to survive. Bipartisanship looked slightly promising. There had been limited harmony between conservative Democrats and Republicans over the gold issue stretching back at least to the mid-1880s, and even back to Greenback days. But the threat of increased centralization, and the profound differences over the tariff and the treasury surplus it produced, hampered cooperation and kept the party divisions ripe. Democrats like Watterson favored tariff reform to respond to radical pressures and end the surplus, but they seemed to be losing ground in the mainstream party. The party unity that existed before the depression and the Wilson-Gorman battles had faltered during hard times. Critical voting populations in the northern cities were becoming as disenchanted as southern farmers. As historian Paul Glad puts it, by this point in 1895, "The Democratic party was widely regarded as the party of depression and economic nonsense, and it would be a long time before those scarlet stains could be wiped off the Democratic escutcheon."[17]

In 1895, Watterson devoted extensive editorial attention to the silverite threat to the Democrats. The only suitable way to fight the "fanatical folly" of free silver, he wrote dramatically, was "hand to hand." In Kentucky, this battle was critical. The silver issue was a "fruitful source of Democratic dissension." In significant respects, Watterson's involvement in the struggle for a sound currency was identical to his earlier efforts regarding the expansion of southern markets, greater credit and investment, and social stability after the Civil War. Watterson felt that he was facing the same groups of opponents: "There are two kinds of Popocrats. One is the plain, old-fashioned, dyed-in-the-wool greenbacker and red-nosed cherub; your cross-roads yawper by day and toll-gate raider by night, who prides himself upon going the whole hog in his politics and be damned to the nigger! The other is the silly-billy, half-educated, would be political economist."[18] Here Watterson effectively linked Populism to the disruptive and terrifying campaign for "free roads" in Kentucky, which exploded in the 1890s after seething for years. These so-called night riders, rich with the reborn spirit of the post–Civil War guerrillas and Ku Klux Klan, robbed and destroyed tollgates throughout Kentucky. Through terrorism, they limited the power of county governments and defied the state, rendered turnpike stock worthless, and effectively suppressed commerce in many areas. This group was seen, in short, as a strong threat to the commercial order and to the rule of law, bringing "perennial lawlessness, violence, and crime that ran through a generation."[19]

In typical fashion, Watterson united the disparate elements of national, regional, and local politics into an easily understood (and easily maligned) single entity. Populists threatened to produce even greater forces of anarchism than the raiders disrupting midstate life and would finally kill all economic advances. Similarly, Watterson presented protectionism as a pseudoscience foisted upon the people by ignorant, self-appointed experts and every bit as dangerous as the night riders. Struggle against both had to begin at home, as the gains of Watterson's New Departure Democracy faced erosion or destruction.[20]

Again, the *Courier-Journal* and its state allies refused to allow the radicals in Kentucky to "try to lead the country away from the great and ab-

"FREE SILVER! FREE SILVER! FREE SILVER!" Advertisement for the *Owensboro Daily Messenger* taunting the gold Democrats. *Louisville Courier-Journal*, May 25, 1895

sorbing issue of tariff reform." To the disdain of both state Republicans and Populists, Kentucky Democrats often wrapped state issues in the broader national issues that consumed Watterson and others. The state party platform for 1895, for instance, reaffirmed the Watterson-crafted tariff policies of the 1892 presidential platform and praised Carlisle and Cleveland by name. It stood strongly for gold and sound money, but the candidates, vacillating under popular silverite pressure, obscured the issue.[21]

By the mid-1890s, Populism had grown aggressively, and Watterson's grip on the state party organization was weakening. A survey of the positions of the state's newspaper editors in 1895 revealed that about a third of Kentucky's Democratic press had declared for free silver, particularly in the rural areas in the southern and western portions of the state. The state's premier silver journal, Urey Woodson's *Owensboro Daily Messenger*, was so emboldened that it even ran ads in the *Courier-Journal* attacking the gold Democrats and their newspapers and directing readers to its own pages. The ads' headlines screamed "FREE SILVER! FREE SILVER! FREE SILVER!"[22] In Louisville, the four major papers were for gold, although two of them, the *Courier-Journal* and the *Times*, were under the same Haldeman ownership.

In the state elections of 1887 and 1891, Democrats demonstrated their weakness. The 1893 depression radicalized politics further and gave greater importance to the most divisive national issues. Free silver elevated Watterson's enemies, like Senator J. C. S. Blackburn, to greater prominence and power in the state party and put the editor's state allies on the defensive. Gold Kentuckians such as Senator William Lindsay, Secretary of the Treasury John G. Carlisle, ex-governor and former *Louisville Courier* editor Simon Bolivar Buckner, Congressman James McCreary, *Courier-Journal* publisher W. B. Haldeman, and Watterson saw how the money issue could wreck the state party organization (and particularly their position in it), and they fought aggressively.[23] These same men subsequently hardened their positions when the national Democratic Party followed this route with equally disastrous consequences. The problem was that the silver issue involved not simply who controlled the economy but who was going to control the party as well.

The 1895 Kentucky governor's contest clearly demonstrated the growing weakness of the state party organization and the vulnerabilities of Watterson's New Departure program itself. This campaign laid the groundwork for the party disunion that, in 1896, put the dark and bloody ground in the Republican camp for the first time ever in a presidential election. It marked the end of the post–Civil War era, when, as one observer put it, the "Democracy has always won out in Kentucky where it had the assistance of Marse Henry and has always lost out when opposed by him." Silver politics greatly complicated and weakened the state Democratic Party structure. At a meeting in Owensboro, the party voted to support silver despite its earlier declared positions. Gubernatorial candidate P. Wat Hardin announced he was a free silverite. "Despite the protests of the conservative and thinking elements of his party," thundered the *Courier-Journal*, Hardin thereafter "hazarded his nomination upon the prevalence of the fiat craze." The election now turned "upon the effectiveness with which the ignorant and thoughtless can be threshed into a blind frenzy for a fifty-cent dollar."[24]

The Kentucky political mood shifted beyond Watterson's sway. "Turn, sinners, turn!" he warned, but to no avail. Watterson failed to see which political position was, in reality, headed for banishment. He had declared that those who continued to propagate free silver "will lie shipwrecked along the shores of the Dead Sea which awaits to engulf political wrongdoing and partisan disloyalty," but the first victim was the Democratic Party itself. Talk of a third party—the New Idea Democrats—went nowhere, although the pattern of bolting the party over silver was established. As a result of the turmoil, a Republican, William O. Bradley, was elected governor of the commonwealth for the first time. Soon thereafter, amidst "turbulence, ruffianism, madness, [and] anarchy," the General Assembly sent the state's first Republican senator, William J. Deboe, to Washington and helped give the Republicans control of Congress. At the governor's inauguration, the *Courier-Journal* reported that, with the transfer of parties, "the inspiring strings of Dixie blended with the patriotic strains of the

'Star Spangled Banner,' while above all rose the dear old air of 'My Old Kentucky Home.'"[25]

But the shape of the crisis was clear to Watterson. "Public opinion was never farther at sea in Kentucky than it is at this moment," he wrote toward the end of 1895. The official history of the Kentucky Democratic Party called this period a "political drama or burlesque . . . a mere curtain raiser in Kentucky and the nation, compared with the bigger show of the summer and fall that followed." The election of 1895 destroyed "the old dynasty" and created a meaningful two-party system in Kentucky.[26]

Because of disasters like the governor's race, gold Democrats tried to rally support throughout the region. In May 1895, as part of this effort, John G. Carlisle toured the South, speaking at the Sound Money Convention in Nashville before going to Kentucky. For Watterson and many others, Carlisle was a favorite son of the southern Democracy, both "the intellectual head of the sound money party" and a reliable, staunch free trader. His tour "was plainly an effort to hold the South in line" for the upcoming national duel, as this was to be the decisive region. Carlisle was quite effective on the stump. Champ Clark of Missouri, temporarily voted out of Congress, reported that Carlisle's speech on April 16, 1896, was "the best single Gold Standard speech ever delivered since the world began." To press the sound money position in the region, Cleveland also used the other southerners in his cabinet: Secretary of the Interior Hoke Smith of Georgia, Secretary of the Navy Hilary A. Herbert of Alabama, and Postmaster General William L. Wilson of West Virginia. Despite all the prominent figures and high-powered rhetoric, "their efforts proved unpopular and the public response was generally unsatisfactory."[27]

The *Courier-Journal* trumpeted Carlisle's visit to Kentucky in the face of this popular opposition. It lavishly covered his two-and-a-half-hour-long "cool, surgeon-like dissection of the free silver craze" in his hometown of Covington. In this speech, Carlisle called upon the "great conservative force" of the Kentucky Democrats to fight "radicalism and paternalism in all their forms . . . agrarianism, communism, populism and fiatism." Free silver, he announced, would "destroy credit and undoubtedly produce the most serious financial disturbance this country has ever witnessed." In line with these imperatives, the *Courier-Journal*'s editorial pages were consumed with attacks on silver and support for Carlisle. The headlines announced, "Kentucky Talks of Nothing Else." Carlisle's trip was cut short because of the death of Secretary of State Walter Q. Gresham, and he never delivered a planned Louisville address.[28]

Watterson called for the creation of sound money clubs to "educate the ignorant and to prevent the party machinery from being seized by the demagogues." He denounced silverites William A. Peffer, William M. Stewart, and Ben Tillman as fools, knaves, and anarchists with "revolutionary" and "dangerous" programs. Watterson declared that "the people" would not be swayed by their "pure demagogy" and that "the people of the United States will never Mexicanize their currency." The "Mexicanization" idea became one of Watterson's favored images, and he applied it to whatever situation seemed to threaten the purity of U.S. traditions, be it currency manipulation or a possible third-term presidency. Watterson persistently contrasted the chaotic politics of Latin America and Asia with the purity and stability of their North American counterparts. Regarding silver, he wrote, "The tail may wag the dog in Persia and India and China and Mexico and Peru, but it has never done it in these United States and it never will." Other papers responded to goldbug shrieks about Mexico by drawing attention to the perceived failures of gold standard countries such as Spain and Turkey. Both sides attempted to smear the opponent by associating it with spectacular examples of failure.[29]

Although Watterson often left the racial dimensions of his comparisons implicit, they were deliberate. He picked up echoes of other southern racist ideas of the meaning of "Mexicanization" to tar the Populists. For instance, at the same time Watterson used the term as a shorthand for the evils of free silver, Josephus Daniels of the *Raleigh News and Observer* was using it to refer to the threat of the North's pushing miscegenation to "Mexicanize the South." It was critical for Watterson to trump the race card. Although conservative elements in the South found Bryanism disgraceful, "few Southern Democrats were willing to destroy party unity and invite the breakdown of white supremacy by joining a third party movement."[30] Watterson sought to save the party from itself using the language it knew best.

Overall, Watterson trumpeted a stubborn, unyielding conservatism despite shifts in the party and the likelihood of alienating his audience throughout Kentucky as well as farther south. Positions such as these were especially damaging for the weekly edition of the *Courier-Journal*, which was distributed in heavily Populist and rural southwestern Kentucky, as well as Tennessee, Mississippi, and Alabama. Nevertheless, Watterson reclaimed the state as a conservative bulwark in editorials titled "There Stands Old Kentucky" and "Here Stands Old Kentucky." He attacked those who went "deflecting from the straight, open highway of Democratic Truth into the bushes of mere speculation and experiment, temporizing for some imaginary advantage that never comes to pass." His editorials provided no mercy for the arguments of the Populists and their supporters, dismissing "the universality of [their] hallucination." Watterson gained special note for sticking William Jennings Bryan with the moniker "Boy Orator of the Platte" and for clever turns of phrase like "It is a paradox of nature that a man all mouth can be at the same time all cheek."[31]

Shortly before leaving for Europe, Watterson summarized his view of acceptable courses of future action. In an editorial that reads like a valedictory farewell, Watterson called for a newly flexible conservatism to meet the challenges of the coming and future elections. The Democrats lacked leaders, he wrote, and were "without a policy and without a head." Of course, Cleveland was to blame. He had failed miserably on the tariff issue, squandered his mandate, tried obstructionist "Protectionist gibberish," and, most of all, left the party dangling without an effective issue. "He has been a woeful scourge to Democracy," Watterson wrote. But the age and incompetence of the party leadership had taken a toll as well, and "their public usefulness is expended." Watterson believed that Democratic Party frustration would continue until 1900. An effective issue had not yet appeared, and a new tariff revision was far off. The Democracy was left warding off radicalism and attempting to survive. Watterson typically started election campaigns by fishing for "The Issue" upon which to unify the party and win, but for once he could only recommend circling the wagons. "The battle of the future is not yet fairly on."[32]

The key was to not lose sight of the ultimate party and national goals. The Democracy should be "comprehending the vastness of the interests embarked under the Government of the United States." If the Democrats began to attack corporations, railways, banks, or organized capital merely to be popular, Watterson warned, they would dissolve into diffidence, without hope of return. The party should accept change—even embrace it—to steer between radical rule and chaos. The party "must seek to make itself the organ of the great middle and conservative element; made up of the better classes who labor and produce," whether these folks worked in field, mine, bank, or shop. Tariff revision would have to wait for these coming times of greater stability; "every intelligent man knows the evils arriving from frequent tampering and constant uncertainty." Better to accept the flawed tariff and "the flag universally adored" than to give aid at this moment to the forces of disorder.[33]

Finally, Watterson dropped his bombshell. This great party warrior was willing to acquiesce to a party bolt to arrest radicalism and end further party disunion and economic depression. "If the Republicans do right, support them. Antagonize nothing because it does not emanate from ourselves." He could not bring himself to become what the Bryanites were calling a "Hanna-crat" and urge the party faithful to vote for McKinley. Rather, Democrats should vote *against* Bryan. Watterson claimed, wishfully, that the heart of the Democratic Party would retain its effectiveness and public confidence. As he put it several months later, it was not a waste to vote against a platform that was not truly Democratic: "In the end . . . all who are Democrats . . . must come back to the old beliefs, and start afresh from where we left off in 1892."[34]

This discouraging farewell was Watterson's last major editorial on domestic politics before his departure for Europe. His views continued to be solicited by William Randolph Hearst for the *New York Journal* and by various other papers, like the New York and Paris editions of the *Tribune*, the *Times*, the *Herald*, and the *London Chronicle*. Watterson did not retire to obscurity, and he in fact increased his published attacks on Bryan as the summer political season began. Ensconced in Europe, Watterson placed ever-greater stress upon his own strict rationality and neutrality. He wrote from abroad "out of the sincerest obligation to truth as I am able alone to see it; being wholly and forever withdrawn from political activity and nowise personally concerned about the issue of public events."[35] The distance allowed Watterson to perpetuate his position as the Democratic sage and to act as the self-appointed conscience of the party. He presumed to speak as an impartial, true Democrat from Europe, rather than as just another goldbug editor attempting to stem the tide of southern radicalism at the source.

Back in America, the tide had turned, and William Jennings Bryan received the Democratic nomination. The ignominy of "the so-called Democratic convention" in Chicago, as John M. Palmer referred to it, ensured that the heavens had indeed fallen and that "fiatism" and anarchism were riding among the ruins of civilized economic policy. *Courier-Journal* publisher Walter N. Haldeman was first among gold Democrats to take his paper defiantly out of the party despite "being cursed and abused roundly by the free silverites in Kentucky." He privately assured Watterson that he was "losing no sleep in the matter, and my digestive apparatus is unimpaired." The *Courier-Journal* stood fast in opposition and called for a true Democracy to rise to the Bryan challenge. Haldeman, a conservative businessman and a founding member of the Western Associated Press, was certainly aware that the Democratic papers across the country that had endorsed Bryan and free silver faced massive advertising losses from the business community. Yet he showed no hesitation in choosing between party regularity and the economic positions the paper had supported since the Civil War. Many other major metropolitan southern papers bolted the party, including those of Nashville, New Orleans, Montgomery, Galveston, Mobile, Richmond, Charleston, and Baltimore. Many of these papers suffered the same fate of advertising and circulation losses as did the *Courier-Journal* after the election.[36]

William Jennings Bryan, for his part, was unperturbed that wealthy, urban newspaper owners and editors like Haldeman and Watterson opposed his crusade, particularly in a state that seemed beyond their control. He believed that the Populists held the cards in Kentucky, and a swing through "impressed [him] with the belief that the electoral vote of the State was safe beyond a peradventure." A warm welcome from the likes of Senator Blackburn, Governor Hardin, and editor Urey Woodson certainly supported this viewpoint. Bravely entering the nest of snakes in Louisville, Bryan attacked the newspaper opposition directly. "An editor only votes once," he noted, "and I have known some editors who have had so little influence that they could not even control the one vote which the law gave them." Rather than have the papers, conservative all, on his side, Bryan preferred the people.[37]

Unwilling to give Bryan the rope to hang the Democracy, Watterson sent a cable to Louisville with perhaps his most famous lines: "Another ticket our only hope. No compromise with dishonor. Stand firm." This telegram was reprinted in many gold-supporting Democratic papers the nation over, and it became a rallying cry for the gold elements of the party. Watterson was now firmly committed to a party split that essentially guaranteed that the Republicans would triumph. Writing from Geneva to Cleveland's former secretary of the navy William C. Whitney, Watterson warned that the Bryanites would swallow and destroy the Democracy if action were not taken immediately. "If we are to have a future, we must lay the foundations now." He told the *New York Tribune* that he feared the "beginning of the end of republican institutions."[38]

Watterson occasionally sent similar views home to Louisville, where they covered multiple columns of the editorial page and then radiated to the Democratic Old Guard throughout the country. In the middle of the summer, Watterson phrased the question as one of both social stability and economic freedom. The former Rebel announced clearly that "liberty is nothing unaccompanied by order." To step away from a conservative order of solidly sober capitalism was "the first step in the down hill journey of agrarianism toward anarchy and despotism." He compared the U.S. government to the management of a bank or railroad and implied that it should be run on the same simple, antiradical economic calculus. Watterson cried for the country to be unfooled by the "overproduction of heroes" and easy answers of the free silverites. In typical fashion, he presented this battle as an unprecedented attack on every major aspect of the American system. It was uniquely destructive of national institutions, ideals, and destiny. Certainly, some of this grandiose rhetoric was exactly that—partisan bluster designed to destroy Bryan's drawing power. But Watterson, echoing Carlisle three months earlier, pressed the need to create a third way between "the two monsters of Radical Paternalism and Radical Anarchism." He wanted to shout damnation from the middle, where he was happiest and where, he was convinced, the most successful policies thrived.[39]

Watterson argued that the radicalism of the Bryan platform created the need to forward a third slate of candidates to split the vote and allow the Republicans to win. The party had to be purged to save it. An electoral loss would actually help: "The fewer votes Mr. Bryan gets the easier will be the reorganization of the Democratic party." Only then could the Democracy renew its program along acceptable lines. Playing the role of a mugwump in reverse, Watterson agreed with Haldeman: "A positive victory for McKinley would settle the free silver craze for years to come." Watterson understood the twin dangers of creating a third party and reaching accommodation with his declared foes. A new party might inoculate the Old Guard from the Populist contagion, but it would ensure that the party of Reconstruction would again reach the White House. Watterson therefore forwarded his advice with the emotion of a man "behold[ing] the work of a lifetime dissipated upon the passions of the hour." But he was willing to make that sacrifice; the question had become one of national interest rather than immediate party gain. As Watterson described it after the election, "All of the evils foreshadowed by the Republican platform the country has tried and survived . . . but the menace of the Chicago platform is immediate and radical . . . and therefore the house being actually on fire, our first duty is to put the fire out, not be too particular what agencies are employed toward this paramount object."[40] Yet he carefully skirted outright support for the Republicans until shortly before the election.

Watterson claimed he saw little difference between the two parties. Both were peddling forms of government paternalism, although McKinley's brand was at least a known quantity that promised stability. Watterson characterized the election as really "between radical paternalism masquerading as a Democrat and radical paternalism open and undisguised, pressing the pretensions of radical Republicanism. The triumph of either is bad enough." The only saving point was that McKinley would not "tamper with the money and credit of the nation," whereas the Populists promised to wreak havoc. Watterson wrote that, in Populist movements in Colorado and South Carolina, the United States had "broken doses" of Bryanism, and, "having tested these homeopathic experiments, we may well draw back aghast before the thought of applying it, allopathically, to the General Government."[41] Given the choice of paternalisms, the one likely to expand economic opportunity won. Watterson, the strict constructionist, would make similar decisions when choosing between expansion and market gain on the one hand and anti-imperialism and lost opportunities on the other. Democratic truth was organic and eternal unless it was faced with material danger, in which case expediency and economic development won out.

Although he preached bolting the party, Watterson did not wish to end his retirement to lead this futile battle. For the time being, he left saving the Republic to his subordinates. Publisher Haldeman and his son William, the general manager of the *Courier-Journal*, kept Watterson abreast of the struggle. The gold Democrats had met in Chicago in July and August to discuss their options and potential candidates. William Haldeman was named to the executive committee and given the job of organizing southern delegates to the upcoming Indianapolis convention. "It was by no means an easy task," he wrote to Watterson in Geneva, "for the free silver heresy had thoroughly permeated the South."[42]

The Kentucky gold Democrats met in Louisville at the end of August.

Watterson was discussed as a possible presidential candidate along with other native sons Buckner and Carlisle. Some advocated that Watterson play the part of sacrificial candidate. With Bryan's inevitable defeat, Watterson would be poised to control the party. Haldeman asked Watterson if he would "accept the nomination from the Indianapolis Convention" despite that it would require him to interrupt "the work in which you are engaged to take up a forlorn hope."[43]

If he was not the candidate of the people, Watterson was at least a polarizing force for national opinion leaders in the party and the press. On August 22, Haldeman related that he "threw cold water on the proposition," but he nevertheless proceeded to describe the plan for Watterson's final step on the national stage. According to Haldeman, *Chicago Chronicle* editor Horatio W. Seymour and Illinois gold Democrat leader John H. Hopkins wished Watterson would "sacrifice" his retirement and return for a large rally at Madison Square Garden. Then, with a speaking tour of strategic areas, Watterson would be a formidable candidate. Both men put great emphasis upon Watterson's ability to rally and guide influential opinion in the United States. Seymour believed, reported Haldeman, that the two hundred Democratic papers that were then vacillating would come out "enthusiastically" for Watterson. Haldeman and the others anticipated that the election returns would guarantee Watterson's control of the party and "certain" nomination in 1900. Haldeman thought the editor could "obtain from two to three million votes in this country."[44] This movement for Watterson's candidacy provides evidence that he had a high standing among conservative Democrats of both the North and South despite his bitter anti-Cleveland activities for the previous two years.

Watterson had declined to run for or hold office since his experience in the House in 1876–77. At this point, he was not interested in running when there were other qualified men from which to choose, notably his old comrades Carlisle and Buckner. In the middle of July, he was already denying any intention to run. Watterson gently demurred in an interview with the *New York Herald*: he would run, he said, only if all other possibilities were exhausted. He was firmer a few days later, when he declared, "I have not now, and never have had, the faintest political ambition." In fact, he was quoted on the front page of the European (Paris) edition of the *New York Herald* as saying lightheartedly, "If anything would make me bolt the forthcoming Indianapolis convention, it would be my own nomination." Watterson supported a return to "the best traditions of the great

Democratic leaders before its machinery was engulfed by Populism," but he shunned office seeking. "You will bear me witness," he told the same paper a week later, "that I regarded the possibility of my own nomination with a kind of terror."[45]

Watterson was not interested in the rigors of the campaign or in the potential limits on his freedom. His lifelong antipathy to public service, aside from the year in Congress, had deep stirrings. This entire period of 1896, including the chance to run for the highest office in the land, was not mentioned in his autobiography (neither, however, was Bryan, despite their three decades of interaction). In several places in this memoir, however, Watterson denied an interest in holding office because, "to me as to my father, office has seemed a badge of servitude." Although he admitted that, upon starting journalism, "I did this . . . with a big 'J,' nursing for a while some faint ambitions of statesmanship—even office," the impulse did not last. Instead, he "discard[ed] everything that might obstruct my entire freedom, for I came into the world an insurgent, or, as I have sometimes described myself in the Kentucky vernacular, 'a free nigger and not a slave nigger.'" Certainly, his deliberate words were meant to relate the strongest disgust for the slavery of public office. The officeholder was a slave to a constituency and to a party bureaucracy, rather than the master of public discourse. Politicians were beholden to their constituency, whereas editors, Watterson thought, created and managed national ideological debates. He saw himself as the guardian of truth and a freeborn man, not a foot solider or a slave. In using this language, he also emphasized his role as instigator and played up his image as Marse Henry. A common southern racist trope—"the Kentucky vernacular"—was that the free African American generation born after the Civil War was insolent and uncontrollable compared to those who had been reared under slavery. In a few brief lines in the beginning of his autobiography, Watterson belittled the idea of holding office as unfit for a man of his caliber, emphasized his southernness, and declared himself free from all constraints.[46]

In this context, Watterson wrote to his son Ewing after the nominations were made, "I took no stock in the Presidential business and am rejoicing and relieved that the nomination went elsewhere."[47] He was not simply being coy about wanting office, and his disposition was not particularly suited for it. Possibly he still had visions of a gentleman's life in Geneva. His fondness for European tours, regular vacations in Naples,

Florida (a town founded by Walter Haldeman), and for dining, drinking, and playing cards at thc Manhattan Club seemed incompatible with a strenuous fight for the presidency, let alone a term in office. Watterson, under the direct guidance only of his good friend Haldeman, was free to speak his mind on any subject in his paper. The life of a critic was preferable to the strictures of public office. Drawing self-conscious parallels to Lincoln, Watterson intended to return to politics and save the country, but he would do so by returning to the platform of the *Courier-Journal*. At the helm of his paper, Watterson was free to be an insurgent.

When the goldbugs gathered in Indianapolis to nominate a slate for their newly formed National Democratic Party, Watterson was still considered "a very attractive candidate" with "lots of friends here, men who consider him entitled to any honor." One major sticking point, besides that Kentucky's delegation was already sworn for Buckner, was that Cleveland, unsurprisingly, opposed his enemy Watterson's receiving the honor. This was described as a rumor in the news report, however, and Cleveland remained officially silent on the specific candidates. Other potential candidates included E. C. Bragg and William F. Vilas of Wisconsin, Senator George Gray of Delaware, Carlisle, Daniel W. Lawlor of Minnesota, William D. Bynum of Indiana, and Secretary J. Sterling Morton of Nebraska.[48]

William B. Haldeman and the *Courier-Journal* were major organizational forces for the convention's success, and they trumpeted its start with a huge, front-page banner headline of Carlisle's remark, "Agrarianism, communism, Populism, fiatism have no place in the Democratic creed, and can not be incorporated into it." Other conservative papers, northern and southern, directly supported the National Democratic bolt, including the *Chicago Chronicle*, *St. Paul Globe*, *Brooklyn Eagle*, *Detroit Free Press*, *Richmond Times*, and *New Orleans Picayune*. Some of the Republican press welcomed the ticket but did not support it: "A splendid ticket. Don't vote for it." Bryanite papers were vicious in their dismissal of this "sham Democracy."[49]

The convention produced a platform upon which Watterson could have easily and happily run. Of course, it condemned the free silverites. In line with the program long supported by Watterson, the platform prominently stressed the tariff as the only legitimate focus for Democratic attention. It "denounce[d] protection and its ally, free coinage of silver, as schemes for the personal profit of a few"; reaffirmed "the historic Democratic doctrine of tariff for revenue only"; and pressed for free ships as well as free goods. The National Democrats decried that "the stars and stripes [are] an almost unknown emblem in foreign ports" and called for coordinated action to reduce impediments to the expansion of American commerce in global markets.[50]

The candidates were two quite grizzled generals from either side of the Civil War: for president, Senator John M. Palmer of Illinois (born in Kentucky), and for vice president, former Kentucky governor Buckner. Watterson was so consumed by the ostensible threat to civilization that he passed up what seems like a ripe chance to bask in the light of such a fulfilling display of postwar national union, as he did at almost every other opportunity. He believed that the candidates were representative of the good fight for the American system and all that it encompassed. "They stand for honor of the nation among the nations of the earth, and for the moral being of commercial society." To Watterson, Democratic ideals of freedom and commercialism were complementary, if not identical. With this ticket, salvation would be reached, the Democracy salvaged, and McKinley made president. The *New York Times* observed at the time that "the certainty that neither [Palmer nor Buckner] can be elected does not in the slightest degree restrain the enthusiasm in the cause."[51]

Two years later, Watterson granted that the gold Democrats were "neither fish, flesh, fowl nor good red herring." The cause had been a good one, he thought, but the National Democratic campaign could not fix the problems plaguing the rank-and-file Democracy. As it turned out, neither could Watterson's unusual and quixotic Democratic expansionism four years later. Certainly, the success of the third-party movement in influencing the Democratic Party was limited. Watterson wrote six months after the election that "the mainspring of the Indianapolis movement" was that it created "an indispensable diversion and made a bridge over which at least a million of Democrats might pass to McKinley." In reality, the gold Democrats "talked with exaggerated optimism" but garnered only a "minute portion of the vote."[52]

Watterson's formula for national advance never became mainstream thought among southern Democrats. It was finally subsumed by a sophisticated new political order that itself steered his sanctified middle course. International and domestic interests became more clearly fused, as Watterson anticipated and sought. His political struggles for the next twenty years were, in many significant respects, a response to this new system inaugurated by the McKinley surge. The development of what Walter Dean Burnham has called the "System of 1896" heralded a new politics more "appropriate to 'capitalist democracy'" and to empire.[53]

The end of reliable electoral returns in critical states constituted a prominent part of the new political system. That Kentucky's electoral votes went to McKinley is one of the most-cited results of this campaign. The *Courier-Journal* played no small part in this action, although it cost the paper dearly. The election polarized the state, and more people voted than in any other election in the commonwealth's history. Bryan showed strength in the old Jacksonian areas in western Kentucky that Watterson had traditionally presumed to lead as the voice of the true Democrats. The mountain, urban, and conservative "old agrarian" elements voted for McKinley. These latter groups were traditionally supportive of Watterson's tariff positions and heeded his call for a known paternalism over a foreign anarchism. The Democratic dominance of the state ended, and Kentucky became "a doubtful state."[54]

The *Courier-Journal* barely stayed afloat. Breaking the bad news to Watterson, William Haldeman wrote, "The free silver people throughout the state and the South and West are malignant and vituperative, and I fear it will be some time after the campaign before they get over their soreness with us. We have lost a great number of our old subscribers whose comments in leaving us have been bitter in the extreme."[55] There was no way to tell when new subscribers would arrive. The *Courier-Journal* had lost many loyal Democratic readers, and no Republican readers replaced them. After all, the paper had not endorsed the Republicans in the election. The *Courier-Journal* limped along on the edge of collapse. The weekly edition, with its circulation in the rural and deep southern areas that were heavily supportive of Bryan and therefore bitter, was suspended. It had earlier reached the level of almost 145,000 subscribers spread out through every state and territory, as well as Canada. The vast bulk of out-of-state subscribers were in the old Confederacy, especially Texas (21,454), Tennessee (12,076), Mississippi (9,490), and Arkansas (7,252). Daily readership in Kentucky dropped from a high of 34,722 to only about 17,000 during the weekdays, and from 37,000 to 29,500 on Sundays. Other city papers, especially the independent *Commercial* and some of the other papers in the state, picked up the slack. There were, after all, 298 papers in the state from which to choose. Advertising revenues at the *Courier-Journal* dropped $100,000 in the wake of the 1896 disaster, largely as a result of these circulation failures. The *Louisville Times*, an evening, urban paper that was also part of the Haldeman stable of papers, was not so hard-hit. Because its sound money stance was not injurious in Louisville, the *Times* helped the *Courier-Journal* survive even as most statewide readers went elsewhere for their news and politics.[56]

Thus the Democracy's electoral losses were mirrored by a similar popular disavowal of the *Courier-Journal*. Although Watterson had the luxury of a permanent soapbox on which to criticize government policy and offer guidance from on high, he also faced the potential pitfalls faced by all politicians. He was, in many respects, not quite as independent of immediate material interest as he liked to portray. The *Courier-Journal* needed readers, especially loyal party readers, to continue its financial success. Both Watterson and Haldeman knew they could not forever alienate the people. In 1896 they tried to lead the public entirely on their own principles, without compromise and without further ensuring that they were being followed by loyal consumers and voters. The paper paid the price for this misjudgment.

Paducah lawyer and U.S. representative John K. Hendrick remembered Watterson, absent but still identified as the voice of the *Courier-Journal*, being "abused and slandered on every stump, by all the cross-road politicians who could muster a half dozen men to speak to." Feeling the crushing economic effects before the election was even over, Haldeman wrote to Watterson, "We will be glad to have you back to steer the ship out of troubled waters." An irascible and defiant Marse Henry had built the paper, and he could presumably restore it. Writing to a friend about that rebuilding experience, Watterson later recounted, "I have done as hard and continuous work the last ten years as I ever did in my life. Indeed, it cost me as infinite labor to save the property from destruction between 1896 and 1900 as it did cost to create it thirty years before."[57]

Watterson's crafty public image, as perpetuated in the nation's press and the Democratic Party's elite circles, was not nearly as damaged as the immediate financial health of the *Courier-Journal*. Watterson's national stature was not due entirely to the circulation of his paper, which was very wide but quite small when compared with the giants of New York and Chicago. Rather, the editor was looked to by much of the nation, and especially by the northern and eastern press, as a representative voice of the conservative and Democratic New South. Despite the heated politics of the moment, his storied role as spokesman was not finished. In many ways, his "No Compromise" position, so widely touted, could even strengthen the lasting popular persona of the old "Henry Fire-Watter-son" of the 1870s.

In line with this logic, Watterson had already decided to come home. Despite his hesitance to run on the National Democratic ticket and his insistence that he had forever left party politics behind, the need to save his paper, the party, and the nation was too great. His decision to fight again came when the Democrats imploded at Chicago. In a nice turn of phrase, Watterson wrote that he "miscalculated the amount of Populistic alloy which had gotten mixed up in the pure gold of Democracy." Having been rudely thrust back into politics with this talk of his candidacy—"a certain relation to political warfare which has never had any personal attractions to me"—he could no longer stand by and watch the party of conservative government and liberty go down in flames. He sailed for home, "ready to take all the blows it may please Heaven to send, please God they shall be returned with interest."[58]

Watterson returned to New York on November 29, 1896, humbled but unwilling to retreat from his long-term goals. After quickly dispensing with pleasantries in an interview with the *New York Times* on the day after his return, he immediately launched into the program he would propagandize for the next five years. As might have been expected, Watterson attacked the tariff and stressed the need to expand market opportunities. He instructed the Republicans to follow the example of the great Blaine and totally revamp the tariff and lower or remove all restrictions. The United States was, simply, poised to dominate the world if the adequate measures were taken. And, as always, Watterson saw the fires of anarchy on the horizon if his self-described straight middle path were abandoned: "The American manufacturer no longer needs protection. He manufactures everything, down to collar buttons, better than the manufacturers of any other country. We could soon control the markets of the world. It would be the salvation of the Republican party if it would abandon the tariff as their share in a National and generous policy. . . . The policy of protection shall be abandoned by the Republican party or overthrown by a mob." As usual, Watterson offered a choice only between establishing free trade and facing socioeconomic ruin. He thought it unlikely, however, that McKinley and the party of state thievery would find it possible to join the National Democrats in their program for national honor and power through free trade. After all, the Republicans were peddling a brand of paternalism that differed only slightly from Bryan's. "The differences [between the two parties] are too doctrinal and radical," he said. Watterson did not expect a union of the sound money forces to last, and he no longer thought it expedient to pretend they shared any other interests. As he put it several years later, the Republicans represented "organized rascality" and the Democrats "organized folly." Given this "choice between the fools and the knaves," Watterson chose the fools.[59]

The *New York Times* interview covered issues of national interest and not conditions in Kentucky, about which Watterson reserved comment. He had set the tone for the coming turmoil in 1897. With his party seriously divided on all levels, his paper's survival in question for the first time since its founding, and the confluence of tariff, market, and expansion issues weighing on his mind, Watterson girded himself to remake the Democracy according to the rough precepts he had long heralded. The free silver threat had passed. "The free coinage of silver at the ratio of 16 to 1 is as dead as the institution of African slavery," he declared.[60] What remained to be determined was how McKinleyism could be brought to heel.

3

Democracy Unterrified and Undefiled

> In Kentucky we have a great deal of politics. All of us are born statesmen.
>
> —Henry Watterson, September 8, 1897

When he returned to Kentucky at the end of 1896, Watterson had a variety of political goals focused on a single vision of attaining southern prosperity and independence through free trade. His short-term goals complemented this broader project. These goals included healing and reforming the national and state Democratic Party organizations after the silverite fiasco and reaffirming tariff reform as the party's primary focus. Watterson also had to return the *Courier-Journal* to prosperity and lead the fight against the protectionist Dingley revision of the tariff. Most of all, he sought utter transformation of the Democracy's outlook and goals in order to create, as Jefferson had done in 1800, "a great, enlightened, conservative National party . . . having a single voice in each of the sections and all of the States." The goal was free trade, nothing less. It was time, he wrote, to "stop following a set of bankrupt leaders in a wild-goose chase and come back to the principles of Democracy, unterrified and undefiled."[1]

Between 1897 and 1900, Watterson's struggle for the soul of the Democracy and the salvation of the South first occurred at the state and national levels but ultimately turned on international affairs and global trade. Only after consolidating his position in the party could he turn his attention to the nation's new imperial policy. Before a new program of national renewal through globalization could be launched, Watterson thought, it was necessary to purge and purify the party "along tenable lines." Amidst all of the social and political ferment of 1897–98, he produced a new program for reform and reunification of the Democratic Party based upon reaffirmation of the free trade ideal and support for territorial expansion. If capital and labor, and organization and anarchy, could be unified at home through free trade, he thought, then surely the American empire should be organized along similar lines for the benefit of all involved. This was the ultimate goal of his party reform fight of 1897–98.

In many ways, Watterson sought to destroy the party as much as save it, although he would never have admitted as much. From this period until his death, he adopted a defiant independence within the Democratic Party that challenged its traditions as much as strengthened them. Watterson had his goals and his work laid before him, and during this time he produced some of his most memorable editorials. But his language alone could not shape reality. The path to financial health and party approbation proved to be a harder road to travel than it had been at any time since 1868, when he started the paper. Watterson faced the sharp consequences of his 1896 party bolt for three years, as the Republican victory in the national election only intensified the divisions in the Democratic Party. Political passions in the nation in 1897 were not easily cooled, and party betrayal in the South, more specifically, was no small matter. In Kentucky, it was often the source of bloodshed, riots, and feuds.

As he had throughout his political life, Watterson preached his political cause from the high middle ground, selling himself and his ideas as the third way between a revolving cast of dangerous Populist radicals on one side and the reactionary, paternalistic Republicans on the other. Watterson claimed that only a rejuvenated Democracy coupled with flexibly conservative politics could save the nation and allow the political attention to turn elsewhere: "With firmness and intelligence; with malice toward none; assailing no man, but defending ourselves; reasoning with ignorance; pleading against prejudice; as Kentuckians, as Democrats, as Americans, let us go forth shoulder to shoulder in support of good government founded on the public credit and order. The worst that can happen to us is political annihilation, and better to die a thousand deaths, both natural and political, than yield to a fanaticism, whose only end, if it is not checked, must be civil war, the overthrow of liberty, and the degradation and ruin of the people." Watterson repeatedly emphasized this need for

Democrats to hold the line against both social disorder and excessive government control. He deliberately echoed Lincoln's second inaugural address to stress the dangers of radicalism of the right and left and the need to hold a reasoned middle course. Three months earlier, Watterson had expressed the same sentiment, using almost the same words and invoking the spirit of the Great Compromiser, Henry Clay. The only true solution, he wrote, was a "sound and safe policy," based on the broad ground of compromise. "All else," he warned, "is straight-out Republicanism on the one hand and straight-out Populism on the other hand."[2] Watterson believed he was, in the tradition of Clay and Lincoln, bringing salvation and tolerance to a Manichean world.

Historians have largely ignored the period between the election of 1896 and the start of the Spanish-American War. In political terms, the realignments of 1896 were of such long-term importance that the immediate fallout of this political shift is sometimes overlooked. Likewise, the early McKinley administration is usually discussed only in terms of the Cuban revolt and the encroaching war with Spain. The internal Democratic Party maneuverings of 1897 seem to pale in comparison. Kentucky historians also often slight this period, concentrating instead on the riveting political crisis caused by the assassination of Democratic gubernatorial candidate William Goebel in front of the Frankfort statehouse on January 30, 1900. Because of the drama and importance of that election and aftermath, historians have not given much independent emphasis to the earlier, 1897–98 period. A more detailed discussion is warranted. It was in this period that Watterson reshaped his role in the Democratic Party and sought to finally dominate southern attitudes toward free trade. The collapse of the *Courier-Journal* after the 1896 campaign freed him to attack all of his enemies even more strongly than before. His politics were angrier and less compromising. He relished this new freedom; it was "a period where it is every man for himself, the devil get the hindmost!"[3]

Rebuilding the national party along new lines was a long-term project that Watterson momentarily deemphasized in 1897 because of the immediate crisis in the state party. Kentucky politics had, for the moment, greater excitement and violence, as well as more immediate repercussions. Watterson sought to consolidate his position within the state party to serve as a base for strengthening conservative southern control on the national level. The national battle for free trade could be waged successfully only from the local level, where the tariff issue resonated with working people. “If the Sound-Money Democrats hold the balance of power nowhere,” he warned, “they can nowhere form a nucleus for the rehabilitation of the old Democracy.” Watterson wanted to reaffirm Kentucky as a conservative bulwark around which the nation could rally, as he claimed it had been throughout the nation’s history. The commonwealth, this breeding ground of statesmen that had given the world Henry Clay, Abraham Lincoln, and Jefferson Davis, alone could “lead the vanguards of liberty through the trackless forest” of radical politics. Watterson pushed a recalcitrant and unwieldy Kentucky into the forefront of his free trade battles, although this forced him to interpret gymnastically the legacy of Clay’s archprotectionism and Davis’s less than conservative actions. Kentucky was not going to “resign her great place among the States of the Union to play second fiddle to the Rotten Boroughs and the mining camps of the faraway West.”[4]

Watterson soon relearned the hard lesson that, in politics, it was necessary to build as well as to destroy. His command of the state party machinery, and of state politics generally, was unsettled and insecure. As both politician and businessman, he had to cultivate supporters. While Watterson directed much of his energy toward national issues, the Watterson Club of Louisville, created in his honor, led an effort to retake municipal governments from Republicans. Watterson’s political standing was closely tied to the health of the *Courier-Journal*, so he made special efforts to restore his former political power on the state level by reclaiming the role of party sage and guardian of truth. He set out to rebuild his paper over the ruin of his party opponents and journalist rivals.

The *Courier-Journal*’s actual survival was in grave danger. No paper could survive in the tense atmosphere of Kentucky in the late 1890s without a combination of loyal, party-based readership and unabashed political vehemence. Watterson was well fortified for this sort of battle and expected to draw blood from his rivals rather than retreat. He attacked the “six-by-nine disfigurements which imagine themselves to be newspapers” as “donkeys, one and all.” The *Courier-Journal* presented itself as part of the future rather than “a thing of the past,” because it alone understood the dangers of splitting the party and the crisis of the moment. But the fallout of 1896 did not make the paper look like a harbinger of the future. Falling circulation and advertising were almost the least of Watterson’s problems. His incendiary editorials provoked his opponents to hold public burnings of the paper and to lodge bomb threats against its offices. The *Courier-Journal* did not yield. "We shall end where we began," a determined Watterson wrote. "The *Courier-Journal* as a property is beyond the reach of attack. The *Courier-Journal* as a newspaper has always held its own."[5]

Watterson and Haldeman's stance on sound money in 1896 had, in a sense, restored the *Courier-Journal* to the sort of vibrant and violent existence that editor George Denison Prentice had made famous in the days before the Civil War. This political turmoil, and the attendant shifts in political alliances, reflected traditional, if sometimes tragic, Kentucky politics. The situation in the state had been divided and tense since the 1895 governor's race. The peaceful transition of political power and the maintenance of the public order itself faced serious challenges for the next several years.

Despite the commercial and physical dangers of the moment, and in keeping with the tradition of the gunslinging Prentice, Watterson displayed no timidity in his editorials. He invoked, if a bit jocularly, the code duello: because of his poor eyesight, Watterson offered to face all challengers at a handkerchief's distance. He also taunted and attacked the silver Democrats and their Populist allies without pause, subtlety, or variance, exactly as he had in 1895–96. This defiance and exaggeration should not be surprising, given the long-standing surplus of self-righteousness, bluster, and independence Watterson had displayed since his days at the *Chattanooga Rebel*. He was fond of drawing parallels with past party crises, like those of the 1860s and 1870s, to sharpen the political differences within the party and to energize the readership. Watterson saw continuities in the *Courier-Journal*'s positions on all controversial topics since Reconstruction. In each instance, including the Reconstruction amendments battle, the New Departure, support for Tilden, and, of course, tariff reform, he believed that the paper stood for truth in the face of revanchist foes. He maintained the same certitude through the 1900 election and the imperialism fight. "Truth ever remains the same," he wrote.[6]

The *Courier-Journal* had long stuck to a plain format that differed significantly from the popular, sensationalistic "yellow" journals of the larger cities. By the 1890s, the *Courier-Journal*'s old-fashioned approach had compounded its circulation difficulties. Watterson himself thought that yellow journalism threatened journalistic integrity and that, because of it, "people were beginning to believe nothing they read in the newspapers." This sort of sensationalism was ushering in a world where people expected the worst of their papers and received the same. For his part, Watterson believed that "telling the truth" was enough, and he did not temper the editorial style or tone of the paper. He continued to fight party battles as he always had, which was a form of entertainment in itself. Watterson liked to claim that the *Courier-Journal* spoke with the voice of reason and truth, whereas other dailies were merely the "thick-and-thin twaddle of the fast-and-loose, self-constituted oracle." To meet the competitive challenge of this twaddle, however, the *Courier-Journal* was forced to make some cosmetic changes. It altered typeface and headlines, lowered advertising rates, increased its number of pages, expanded its Sunday features, and augmented its use of illustrations, "colored supplements," and cartoons. The paper also expanded its incentives for multiple subscriptions, including free accordions, guitars, mandolins, and banjos; sets of *The Leatherstocking Tales*; loads of coal; sewing machines; pocket watches; sheet music collections; and other items of interest to the Kentucky populace.[7] These changes had greater effect on the "counting room" (the business office) than on the editorial room, and Watterson liked to contrast the two. The paper's problems were compartmentalized, and its partisan mission via Haldeman and Watterson was still stressed, even as the Old Lady on the Corner was given an overdue makeover.

The paper's surface changes did not affect Watterson's routines, and he continued to write his editorials on national Democratic politics as if his political power in Kentucky had remained intact. The *Courier-Journal* was "not the least disturbed about its material fortunes either in the present or the future." Many of Watterson's earlier critics and political enemies had "gone to their account," and he planned to outlast the current batch. With a few exceptions, he did not regularly contribute to the expanded Sunday paper, and the editorials on that day tended toward the literary rather than the political. On the other six days, when Watterson exercised direct control of the paper, the focus was mostly on Democratic politics and the tariff, as it had been for years. Increasingly, the paper addressed events in "furrin parts," as it jokingly called them.[8]

The national and European press continued to solicit Watterson's opinions, even if his voice was not popular within the state at the moment. For example, the *New York Herald*, on December 8, 1896, carried a front-page report about Watterson's interview in the German *Anzeiger*, in which he had criticized Cleveland. This ongoing prominence derived almost entirely from Watterson's singular ability to electrify and entertain the public and to shape the nature of political debate in the South and around the country. Despite the concessions to short-term fiscal viability, he was determined to fight his way back to the top on his own terms. Within two years, he would succeed, and could claim that the paper's "measure of material prosperity was never so great as it is now." In 1899 the paper would carry two slogans astride the title on the masthead: "More than QUADRUPLE THE CIRCULATION of any morning paper in Kentucky" and "Largest morning circulation in the South."[9] This was a situation quite removed from the dark days of 1897.

Stressing a new "independence" as he sought to seize the reins of the party, Watterson continued to claim that he alone spoke for the true Democracy and the one true path. This position allowed him to attack from within the comfortable confines of party regularity while gaining freedom to emphasize his impartiality and offer a new Democratic direction. He preached salvation: "As a Democrat, we appeal to Democrats to come out from the body of death which envelopes them in the camp of Bryanism and to march with us upon the broad open highway of Democracy." The true Democracy had to remain true to "the faith of the fathers," and the radicals must not be granted relief if the party hoped to return to national power. Watterson continued to refuse any compromise with the silverites, even if it meant more Republicans being elected in the short term. He rejected "'Harmony' with a very big 'H' for the sake of Office with a very big 'O.'" He liked this phrase. Four months later, he claimed, "'Harmony' with a very big H for the sake of Office with a very big O, is just what has wrecked us. It is vile and most abominable, and is preached only by scamps having jobs up their sleeves, or donkeys, who possess neither a sense of reasonable intelligence, nor any convictions of their own." Watterson thought that supporting the mainstream party, currently under silverite control, out of some ossified sense of loyalty was out of the question. After all, was it not important to remain independent, truthful, and vigilant when one's silverite and Populist opponents were "mean and mousing, malignant, splenetic and envious, [the types] who, to gain a little cheap glory, or to carry some crazy project, would burn a baby at the stake"?[10]

One of the biggest retrospective misunderstandings of Watterson's politics in these years is the assumption that, after a brief flurry of independence from party strictures, he was chastised by the public and by his readers and came crawling back to true regularity. According to this view, the experiences of almost losing his paper and of vicious political disavowal by the voters convinced him to fall in line.[11] Although it is true that Watterson, wholly at odds with the Democracy, tried valiantly to return to the mainstream party fold, his attempt was not a sign of newfound humility or an acceptance of defeat. Rather, he was seeking to strengthen his regional political position as a basis for selling expansionism throughout the South. Throughout 1897 he remained within what he considered to be the only rightful party, the gold wing of the Democracy, regardless of Bryan's claim that it was a Republican front. He intended to stay within his own party as a troublemaker and a reformer. After 1896, Watterson wrote many times that the *Courier-Journal* had "abdicated all question of leadership and signified its purpose to fall in line at the rear of the column . . . prepared for everything, responsible for nothing."[12] But he did not become a mere soldier in the ranks, blindly following orders passed down by party leaders. Rather, the *Courier-Journal* was part of the rank and file that intended to exercise the right of all common soldiers to complain vociferously without having to be responsible for others or be the first to lead a suicidal charge.

It is difficult to overstate how aggressive, repetitive, and merciless Watterson's attacks on his party enemies were in his effort to regain ideological sway. He trotted out the familiar arguments for sound money and the "public order" and coupled them with the equally familiar references to "Truth for its own sake, for God's sake, and for the people's sake." As always, many of his attacks rested more on emotion than on rational discourse. He poked at the "16-to-1, go-as-you-please, stick-in-the-mud Free Silver short horse" from the impregnable "bed-rock of thorough conviction, entrenched by the forces of all human experience." Among many other epithets, he called Populists bigots and "glow-worms," dismissed them as "loose-jointed, joggle-brained fellows from somewhere out in the wild and wooly west," and described them, bizarrely, as "some combination of sea serpent, mastodon, and airship." He used the image of Populism as "a short horse" quite often, likely because of its resonance with the horse-breeding Kentucky culture and because Watterson believed Populists were "very short of a jackass." At other times, he accused them of having "sworn the horse to be sixteen feet high and they stick to it," and he referred to different factions of Democrats as "a gray horse of another color." He characterized Bryan as a "dodger and a coward" and, better yet, an "oratorical stormy petrel."[13]

Watterson restated the Democratic truth in "passing events and as to political economics" so aggressively and so repetitively that state papers begged for a change of tune. The Democratic *Stanford Interior-Journal* cried, "Give us something fresh or give us a rest, Marse Henry, please!" But Watterson was convinced that support for the free coinage of silver had to be extirpated. Bryan still drew power from the persistence of the silver issue. Watterson feared that, if the idea itself were not finally and utterly demolished, Bryan would rise again in another four years, with equally disastrous results.[14]

Long after the 1896 election, the *Courier-Journal* continued to condemn Populists for scaring off investment in the South. It praised Hilary Herbert of Alabama, Cleveland's secretary of the navy, for recognizing the need for a new conservative business regime in the region, the development of corporations to organize this wealth, and more equitable distribution of federal monies throughout the South. The first step in this development program was, of course, ending the threat of Populist "fiatism" and financial instability. Only honest money could be "efficacious" and used for "universal acceptance and interchangeable value."[15]

Watterson called Kentuckians to arms and appealed to them on myriad levels, all centered around a notion of the "Kentucky Idea." If the state Democrats were going to blaze the trail back to honest politics for the national party, they had to draw on both tradition and innovation. Watterson believed that, as a border state, Kentucky was uniquely qualified to gather the best elements of national politics. Supporting free silver in 1897 made as little sense as continuing to support secession had in 1865. His omnipresent analogies to the war period again were used to push the party forward on an acceptable middle path. Only then could it regain its rightful position as the nation's political leader.[16] Not unimportant in these calculations was the realization that Watterson would not long be considered the voice of the South if his political positions had no relevance to those held by the bulk of his party.

Watterson's "Kentucky Idea" also included an appeal to masculinity, which he consistently equated with his political positions. "Where is Kentucky's Manhood?" he asked. The decision to overthrow the Populists depended on "an intelligent and manly acceptance of facts." In a clever turn of phrase, Watterson called for sound money backed by the only silver standard the state needed—"sterling manliness." These appeals had a dual purpose. On one hand, Watterson was encouraging Democratic Kentuckians to think of themselves and their party as the essence of masculine truth. On the other, he was throwing out a challenge to the public to rise and prove its "manliness" by following his advice, much as he would do later in support of expansionism. To do otherwise, he implied, would be to succumb to weakness and femininity.[17]

On January 8, "St. Jackson's Day," 1897, Watterson and his gold Democrat allies gathered in Chicago to reaffirm their program and reassure themselves that all hope was not lost. This group included old stalwarts like Franklin MacVeagh, Simon Bolivar Buckner, John P. Irish, and Assistant Secretary of the Treasury Charles S. Hamlin. According to the *Courier-Journal*, all of the speakers spoke in honor of "DEMOCRACY OF THE JACKSON KIND" and congratulated the gathered for offering an "unsullied" platform in the last election. Each speaker pressed the party to regain its former glory by maintaining these conservative first principles. Cleveland's rather vague letter on this idea received mild applause. The newspaper reported that "the enthusiasm was even greater" for Buckner's speech on Kentucky and that Watterson was greeted with "several minutes" of "ringing cheers."[18]

Watterson, speaking on his favorite topic, the "Future of Democracy," declared that a mighty Democratic spirit ran directly from Jefferson, Jackson, and Tilden to the gathered forces, who stood alone for the public credit and the public order. Speaking with his usual grandiosity, Watterson declared, "Let us consecrate this noble theater as a temple of Democracy, of Democracy unterrified and undefiled, the only kind of Democracy which Jefferson taught and Jackson practiced." He defended all concerned for bolting the party in 1896 and said that he would always follow the forces of public credit and order, even if doing so required abandoning the party again. "As far as I am concerned, and no man's Democracy can go back of mine," he told his allies, "whenever good morals against bad morals, good money against bad money, Government against the mob, are the issues, I shall go with the party which stands true to the public credit and order, no matter where it takes me."[19]

Watterson was willing to tolerate an interlude of Republicanism because he believed the nation would survive it and rise to a better future in four years. The public had not given the Republicans a mandate, Watterson said, but had merely suppressed dangerous radicalism. It had been wiser to accept the known dangers of Republicans than to risk the unknown consequences of Populist rule. The duty of the Democrats was to create a system that ensured public credit and order "for all time." It was time, in short, to end the brief alignment with McKinley and begin to fight. Watterson self-servingly announced that he had "surrendered none of [his] original, individual ideas" and was ready to lead this fight.[20]

To introduce this new program, Watterson declared that the battles of the future were to be fought only over economic conditions, the search for markets, and class identity. The ideologies of the previous century were no longer relevant, he told the crowd, as industrialization and the new corporate order in America necessitated a new focus and new tactics. "In 1800 we were a few millions of people and we loved liberty," he said in his standard construction. "In 1897 we are eighty millions of people, and we love money." The dollar was now king in all politics. Society was newly divided between capital and labor, and the Democrats had to be the unifying, synthesizing force between them. If the party did not reconfigure itself for this struggle, the conservative forces would not achieve their rightful primacy.[21]

Watterson blazed a new path, founded on free trade. He predicted that the election of 1900 would again be fought between "organized capital," in the form of Republicans, and the "organized anarchy" of the Bryanites. The future of Democracy was then "the unification of liberty and order" through the "reconciliation of capital and labor." Watterson claimed that capital and labor "ought to be convertible terms."[22] Like many of his most strident pronouncements, this idea (although again deliberately echoing Lincoln) was never given any more precise explanation. On what terms could the two possibly be reconciled without disrupting the very social order Watterson wished to preserve? There is no denying that such ideas had appeal in a public speech, as they sounded important and innovative while promising the final resolution of socioeconomic conflict. This pronouncement actually meant nothing, and it was never explained in later writings. It did, however, bring Watterson back to his one true love; the keys to achieving this wonderful convergence were, as might have been expected, tariff reform and free trade.

This neat fusion of an almost seriocomic allegiance to the memory (but not the substance) of a pantheon of political saints with a divergent new program that sought free trade at all costs became Watterson's trademark. He saw an opportunity not only for a union of sectional and party interest but for a seamless extension of his shibboleths. First, free trade had to triumph at home. This required an unforgiving purge of the radicals in the Democratic camp and a radical pruning of Republicanism. "The only possible ground" on which to wage these battles, Watterson told the Chicago audience, was "at once high enough and broad enough to draw from each of the two extremes." As usual, his idea of a newly centered Democracy rejected the two extremes that were equally "joined to their fleshpots" of illegitimacy. Radicalism had to be squashed, and the "fixed tenet" of protectionism had to be destroyed. Wresting the power of tradition from McKinley, Watterson accused him of utterly misunderstanding Henry Clay's "temporary expedient" and of subsequently retarding the entire future. He announced that protectionism was "at war with the genius of American institutions, an assault upon the intelligence and capabilities of American manhood," and "an abject [*sic*] lesson to every agrarian, anarchist and populist in the land" in how to destroy American liberties and opportunities.[23]

Skewing history to his own purposes, Watterson compared Republican intransigence on protectionism to the slaveholding "patricians of the modern South" who refused to concede their "imagined rights in the territories" and therefore caused civil war. He called for a return of the revolutionary battle against tyranny and the midcentury battle against sectionalism. Since he also likened silverite Democrats to this same group of reactionary slaveholders, it is clear that the radicalisms of the right and left were merged in his mind. Following a similar logic, he compared Republicans to the "nobles of the ancient regime in France," who failed to compromise with modernization and liberalism and so ignited revolution. This idea fit nicely with Watterson's regular characterization of the Populists as Jacobins. At other times, he reversed the image and put the *Courier-Journal* in the role of revolutionary vanguard and declared that, under the National Democrats, "the Bastille of Kentucky ignorance and intolerance will topple to the ground."[24]

All of these confused but grand historical analogies were meant to prove a lineage in extremist thought leading to protectionism. Watterson thought the divine right of kings, slavery, and "taxation for private purpose" were all equally "prescriptive" measures that would be obviated when the great liberal middle came to power. Paraphrasing Lincoln again, and equating the tariff with slavery, Watterson declared, "If taxing the whole people to pay tribute to a part be not wrong, then nothing is wrong." The war for the security of the country from revolution was on, and it was going to be fought on the issue of free trade. The Dingley tariff represented but the first battle. Treason in the form of nullification had been squashed with "a withering blow," as had "treason in the form of anarchy." Watterson girded the party for the new round of patriotic battle, to be directed in the service of "the pursuit of prosperity and happiness" and against the treason of protectionism.[25]

But first, the unvanquished silverites still needed thrashing, as they posed a greater immediate danger than did Republican protectionism. Consequently, Watterson staked his political power, and the *Courier-Journal*'s revival, on the unlikely race for clerk of the Kentucky Court of Appeals, which was the only statewide office contested in 1897. The election became especially important because the Republicans in the Kentucky assembly had just rejected the gold Democrats' choice and made William J. Deboe the U.S. senator. Watterson campaigned intensely in support of minor candidate James R. Hindman in a desperate attempt to restore the conservative Democratic presence in the state and meet all silverite challenges.

The *Courier-Journal* entered the race with its usual mix of grandiosity, repetition, and partisan instinct. It called dramatically for a fight to the death if necessary: "The National Democrats must stand together like a stone wall. Theirs is a battle for conviction. . . . Wherever the Free Silver candidate shows himself we must oppose him with a Sound-money candidate. Man for man, vote for vote, foot to foot, must we stand and fight this great battle for the right, with the weapons of reason and truth, with the flag of our country, and our whole country, over our heads; resolved, if need be, to die rather than see a single star in that bright galaxy of stars dimmed by the fever-breeding mists, the foul vapors, of repudiation and anarchy." Historians Hambleton Tapp and James C. Klotter describe the campaign as "the most exciting feature of the year to the sensation-loving people." It "became extremely acrimonious and violent [as] hatred and vindictiveness magnified the contest out of all proportions to its actual importance."[26] Hindman was the former lieutenant governor and had been the chair of the Kentucky National Democratic convention in Louisville in 1896. The regular Kentucky Democracy, still in silverite control, ran Samuel J. Shackelford; the Populists, Republicans, and Prohibitionists also ran candidates.

In a triumph of symbolic politics, the gold Democrats met in Louisville in July in a convention on a scale wildly out of proportion to the significance of the office. This campaign was not about Hindman for the clerkship; it was about winning all future campaigns and rescuing the party. The theme was unity, and politicians from all over the state were trotted out to indicate this singleness of purpose. "FOR THE RIGHT," declared the headline, "Battle-Line of National Democracy Is Now Formed." The gathering, according to the news report, "represent[ed] the brains and the honor and the manhood of all the Kentucky communities"; it was billed as the greatest such event since the Civil War. It included a collection of all those who had "fought the good fight for the party in its dark days." Former secretary of the treasury John G. Carlisle, attending his first state party convention in ten years, was chairman of the proceedings. Simon Bolivar Buckner headed the platform committee, which also included Watterson, Senator William Lindsay, editor and politician W. C. P. Breckinridge, and other state notables. This was "the National Democracy, the sound-money Democracy, the old-fashioned Democracy, the true Democracy. And as long as such a gathering of such men is possible in this State there is assurance that in Kentucky at least, there shall be no compromise with dishonor."[27]

All of the men in attendance agreed that the purpose of the convention was to defeat silverism and boost free trade, notwithstanding that none of these issues had anything whatsoever to do with the duties and responsibilities of the clerk of the Kentucky Court of Appeals. The *Courier-Journal* printed the platform on the front page, under an oversized engraving of Jefferson surrounded by a wreath of (old) hickory leaves. The party reaffirmed the sound money Louisville and Indianapolis platforms of 1896. It pledged, in Wattersonian language, "the complete reorganization and perpetuation of the Democratic party, not only for the campaign, but for all time." To carry the Democracy forward into this eternity, the platform touted a tariff for revenue only, global free trade, and a universally convertible currency based upon the gold standard. "With suitable revenue and navigation laws," promised the National Democrats, the United States would regain "supremacy of the seas," inaugurate civil service reform, and maintain public order and prosperity. Once again signaling the need for the Democrats to move forward, away from the failed and dangerous systems of the past, Watterson declared, "As a political issue the free and independent coinage of silver at the ratio of 16 to 1, or any other ratio, is as dead an institution as the institution of African slavery."[28]

John G. Carlisle, free trader. Library of Congress, Prints and Photographs Division, LC-DIG-cwpbh-04036

Speeches by Carlisle, Watterson, and Lindsay were long and heavy with rhetorical flourish, in the style of the day. Carlisle, in his workmanlike way, used class warfare to condemn the old enemy of paternalistic government. He called free silver "a Chinese monetary system to expel gold from the country" that served the interests only of mine owners and the nonproductive elements of society. It was complemented, he said, by a system of protection that formed "a Chinese wall to exclude competition and give a fictitious value to the products of the favored classes." [29] The hackneyed image of the "Chinese wall," the Great Wall of China, permeating rhetoric and writing on the tariff throughout the nineteenth century, was meant to evoke the mismanagement, stagnation, and hopelessness that accompanied schemes of cultural and economic isolation.

Carlisle linked sound money, national development, and international trade and investment. A sound and stable currency was needed to galvanize the domestic commercial system and trigger broader global opportunity. He thought both inflation and protection were designed to isolate the United States from "civilized" markets just as these outlets were needed the most. "Many of our industries are depressed for want of a market for their products . . . many of our most profitable commercial enterprises are languishing for the want of a profitable trade." Money had to be free of suspicion, instability, and taxation so investment and the search for markets could go forward without impediment. The conservative forces had to dedicate themselves to the "repudiation of fiatism, protectionism, socialism and every other undemocratic and un-American theory or project."[30] Carlisle had used virtually the same phrase in Covington two years previously.

Watterson's speech was a bit more philosophical, and it drew deeply on his past role in the Democratic Party. He cast himself as the new great compromiser and grouped his actions of the previous three decades into a seamless example of struggle against the forces of reaction from both ends of the spectrum. To be a true conservative was to adhere to an eternal set of beliefs while also continually moving the party and nation forward. Watterson was always honing and improving the New Departure, seeking not retrenchment but development, growth, and expansion. He thought Bryan's radicalism had disrupted the high ground upon which the Democracy had supposedly always stood, because Bryan had proposed "more than a New Departure, . . . it was to all intents and purposes a revolution." The editor meant to rally the conservative elements among the people and, in his standard formulation, "interpose between the warring extremes of agrarianism and rapacity the strong arm of a Democracy, unterrified and undefiled." Thus Watterson struggled valiantly to preserve free institutions and maintain a middle course, "to stay the hand of imperialism at the North; to restrain the turbulent elements at the South."[31]

Here Watterson made an interesting comparison. Because a middle course of compromise had prevented Radical Reconstruction from forever rending the nation, "the South [was] rescued from historic companionship with Poland and Ireland," while "the North [was] spared the disgrace of Russia and England." The direct relationship he saw between conquest and subordination in imperialistic relations would later stand at the center of his critique of Republican expansionism after the Spanish-American War. Watterson used the same analogies of blighted, illiberal control of conquered provinces to attack both colonialists of the Right and anti-imperialists of the left. As a partisan of the middle, Watterson constantly shifted his equilibrium; the perfect balance was always to be found by incorporating the best elements of each new program or policy as it developed. Watterson's speech to the convention was of a single piece with virtually all of his writings and speeches between the election of 1896 and the Spanish-American War.[32]

The only idea Watterson expressed in this speech that he had not already honed repeatedly in his editorial columns of the past several months followed up on Carlisle's description of the "Chinese wall" of protection. In classic Wattersonian fashion, he linked the idea of the destructive silver–high tariff system with every other foreign, and therefore pathologically backward, system he could fit into a single sentence. This feat was accomplished in a section devoted to the situation of the Kentucky farmer. "Mexicanizing our currency and building a Chinese wall around our commerce," warned Watterson, would reduce the state's farmers "to a condition little better than that of the peon of Latin America or the poor Sicilian peasant, who never saw a golden coin in all their days, but who eke out precarious lives on shinplasters and copper." He skillfully, if oddly, cast even the most local concerns in terms of both an international and a nativist context. Watterson tried to persuade farmers to think globally and assign all their troubles to the protective tariff, as well as to connect the program of the silverites with foreign systems of domination and control. Convinced of his unique ability to find the true answer to all problems, Watterson, a politician's son who lived on a gentleman's spread east of Louisville and who was not given to oversympathizing with rural Kentucky life, claimed "to be something of a farmer myself" and blamed all agricultural problems on the general system of tariffs and "excessive tribute."[33]

Energized by a new electoral battle, the *Courier-Journal* editorial page relentlessly discussed the party issue almost daily between July and the election in November. Watterson's writings were drone-like in their repetition. The titles of the editorials only hint at the tone: "In Battle Array," "Stand by your Guns, Democrats," "Now, or Never!" "Before, After, and Always," "All There is To It," "Party Duty and Pirate Law," "The Coming Verdict," and so on. One phrase he used as the title of several editorials was "Vae Victis!" which he liked so much that he continued to use it as a title during the First World War. An important editorial of September 22, 1897, titled "True Democracy," laid out two major issues. It described the split situation in Kentucky and in the state Democratic Party and forwarded the basic Wattersonian critique. It also viciously attacked Grover Cleveland for failing to preserve the Democracy. Specifically, the editorial blamed Cleveland for the Chicago platform of 1896. If Cleveland had not been so coy about his "quasi-candidacy," argued Watterson, then John G. Carlisle would have been free to divert the Kentucky delegation away from silver, and Massachusetts governor Russell could have rallied the eastern sound money interest. Because Cleveland neither led nor followed, the cause of sound money was destroyed before the Chicago convention, as well as left leaderless, and the gates were opened to the "visionary Paternalistic Populists."[34]

In his struggles to restore his own vision of the Democratic Party, Watterson felt it necessary also to remove the Cleveland stain from the party's pristine garments. Watterson had, of course, turned against Cleveland when he hopelessly bungled tariff revision in 1893–94. The editor described any praise of Cleveland as "the union of genteel hypocrisy with profound dissimulation." He called the ex-president "a man wholly ignorant not merely of theoretical and doctrinal questions of any kind, but equally so of the public life and the public men of the time, and very nearly so of all Democratic traditions."[35]

Watterson's strongest criticism was, as would be expected, reserved for Cleveland's utter failure to unify the Democrats on the tariff issue. And it was in this failure that Watterson made the connections between the "the trouble" in 1897 and the solution offered by reaffirming the party's support for free trade. He believed that, since tariff reform had "literally died in his [Cleveland's] arms," the only hope for future revenue reform was for the issue to be "born again."[36] This rebirth could come only when the Democratic Party was fully united and the proponents of fiat money purged. "The Remedy" that Watterson proposed in September 1897 was twofold. First, the Kentucky Democracy had to crush "the various 'isms'" and unify around the conservative principles of public order, in the form of home rule, and sound money. The party then had to move forward on the third essential element of the holy trinity—free trade.

Watterson thereafter turned the bulk of his attention to the national party, to the situation of the South generally, and to foreign policy. The Hindman campaign did not help create the unity that Watterson thought was the precondition for restored party unity on free trade. As he had said wishfully time and again, the National Democrats appealed to the people. He felt sure the people were listening. The *Courier-Journal* even printed

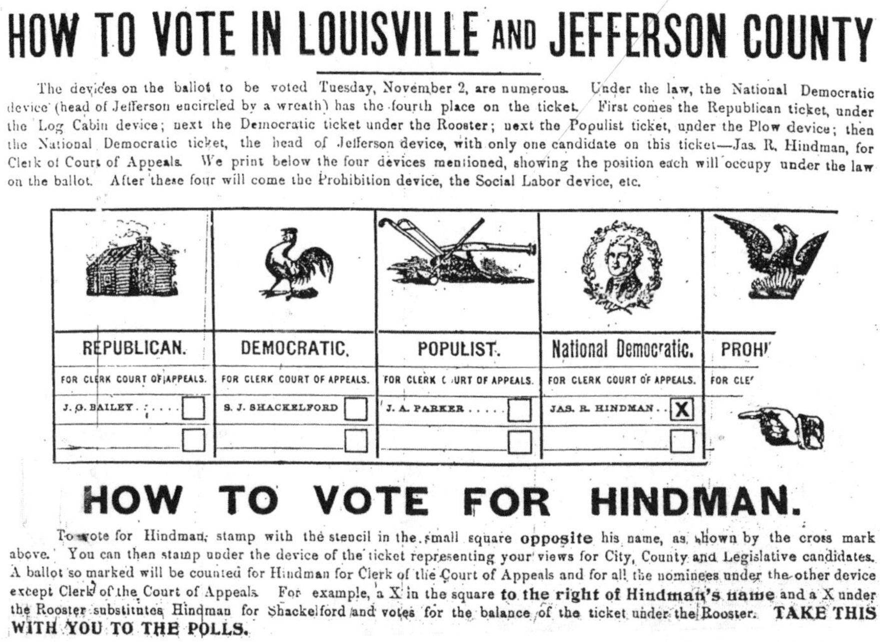

HOW TO VOTE IN LOUISVILLE AND JEFFERSON COUNTY

The devices on the ballot to be voted Tuesday, November 2, are numerous. Under the law, the National Democratic device (head of Jefferson encircled by a wreath) has the fourth place on the ticket. First comes the Republican ticket, under the Log Cabin device; next the Democratic ticket under the Rooster; next the Populist ticket, under the Plow device; then the National Democratic ticket, the head of Jefferson device, with only one candidate on this ticket—Jas. R. Hindman, for Clerk of Court of Appeals. We print below the four devices mentioned, showing the position each will occupy under the law on the ballot. After these four will come the Prohibition device, the Social Labor device, etc.

REPUBLICAN.	DEMOCRATIC.	POPULIST.	National Democratic.	PROH'
FOR CLERK COURT OF APPEALS.	FOR CLERK COURT OF APPEALS.	FOR CLERK C URT OF APPEALS.	FOR CLERK COURT OF APPEALS.	FOR CLE'
J. G. BAILEY . . . . . ☐	S. J. SHACKELFORD ☐	J. A. PARKER . . . . . ☐	JAS. R. HINDMAN . . ☒	
☐	☐	☐	☐	

HOW TO VOTE FOR HINDMAN.

To vote for Hindman, stamp with the stencil in the small square **opposite** his name, as shown by the cross mark above. You can then stamp under the device of the ticket representing your views for City, County and Legislative candidates. A ballot so marked will be counted for Hindman for Clerk of the Court of Appeals and for all the nominees under the other device except Clerk of the Court of Appeals. For example, a X in the square **to the right of Hindman's name** and a X under the Rooster substitutes Hindman for Shackelford and votes for the balance of the ticket under the Rooster. **TAKE THIS WITH YOU TO THE POLLS.**

"HOW TO VOTE IN LOUISVILLE AND JEFFERSON COUNTY." Sample ballot to explain to voters how to vote for Hindman and the National Democrats during the tumultuous 1897 campaign season. The *Courier-Journal* ran a variation of this ballot several times, to no avail. *Louisville Courier-Journal*, November 1897

a sample ballot to clarify the differences between the Democrats and the National Democrats, to be clipped and taken to the polls. Yet, again, the people rejected Watterson's positions. Hindman lost by an enormous margin, and the silver Democrat Shackelford was elected. Shackelford had 187,482 votes to the Republican James G. Bailey's 169,687, while Hindman polled a weak 9,562, just 2,000 more than the Populist candidate, Joseph A. Parker.[37]

By the time of what one historian called the "horripilating gubernatorial campaign of 1899," Watterson had larger fish to fry. His coverage of the race between (among others) Democrat William Goebel and Republican William S. Taylor for the Kentucky governorship never became as breathless as his attacks on the Populists, although news coverage of it was intense. The *Courier-Journal* often lavished critical attention on tumult and violence in state politics, particularly in the contentious eastern mountains. This time was no different. This election and its bloody result were as exciting as politics got at the time and almost caused civil war within the state. Goebel was the author of a controversial state election law expressly designed to prevent Republicans from "stealing" electoral victories, as they supposedly had done in 1896, and Watterson believed that the law virtually guaranteed Goebel a victory. As it turned out, it did not. The campaign for governor turned in large part on Goebel's attacks on Watterson's old ally, the Louisville and Nashville Railroad. The L&N supported Republican candidate William S. Taylor and started a paper, the *Louisville Dispatch*, to woo Democratic voters and confront the *Courier-Journal*. Goebel lost the election, and the attempt to seat him by manipulation of his own election law also failed. He was shot on the Frankfort statehouse steps and sworn in as governor before dying from his wounds. The incredible turmoil in Kentucky thereafter was heavily reported in the *Courier-Journal*.[38]

Biographer Joseph Frazier Wall gives greater attention to the Goebel campaign than to Watterson's attempt to reconfigure the state and national Democratic Party. Wall believes that Watterson's support for Goebel was evidence that, at last, "Watterson and the *Courier-Journal* rejoined the Democratic party." Wall's best example of Watterson's change is that "the wreath-framed picture of Thomas Jefferson, emblem of the Gold Democrats which the paper with dogged determinism had carried for two years at the top of its masthead, disappeared, and once again the cocky little rooster of orthodox Democracy adorned its editorial page." Contrary to Wall's view, however, Watterson sought to reshape the party along radical new lines and did not desire reentry into the ranks as a party hack. The *Courier-Journal* refused to "be saddled with the desire of the purpose to resume its abandoned leadership in Democratic councils. . . . It enjoys its freedom too much to surrender it."[39] Instead, Watterson would remain faithful to his own politics and to the traditions of Jefferson, Jackson, and Tilden, and he would wait for the party to follow his advice and drop the silver issue. He refused to be sidetracked by this campaign aside from its relevance to broader issues affecting the National Democracy. Although the Goebel campaign turned on many critical issues of governance in the state, it did not have clear national implications. In short, it was not relevant to Watterson's broader project of remaking the Democratic Party. He used Goebel to emphasize the crisis caused by the political tyranny of the Republicans and the dangers of the silverites.

Watterson therefore placed himself above the partisan warfare in the state. By early 1900, his primary editorial interest had turned to consolidating America's international gains rather than to the Goebel issue. Although he framed many local issues within an international context, Watterson concentrated his writings on what he considered to be the larger picture. In the case of expansionism, his ideas for southern advancement were far outside the Democratic mainstream. Nevertheless, he believed he could convince the party to adopt his program once he made the free trade issue unavoidable. The *Courier-Journal*'s "bread and meat and respectability are wholly independent of party majorities and minorities." Watterson would not fall back into line. The parties were "in a liquid, fluid state," and the fight would be carried as far as was necessary to reestablish true Democracy. The *Courier-Journal* would go on at its self-designated post and would not abandon the cause until the party "clear[s] the breakers and sweep[s] out into the mid-ocean of 1900, as trim and taut as in 1800, bearing Jefferson's flag with Jackson's emblems at the fore, having a chip off the same old blocks of granite and hickory on her quarter-deck!"[40]

Watterson failed to reform the state Democratic Party, and his attempt on the national level in 1897 was also futile. His central hope in national politics was to limit the extent of William McKinley's plan to reinstate "ample protection and encouragement to the industries," as the president vowed in his first inaugural address. McKinley came into office bound and determined to raise tariff rates and immediately called a special session for this task. The resulting Dingley revision of the tariff during the first half of 1897 achieved the central Republican Party objective of raising rates and putting in a mild reciprocity component. The Dingley tariff restored the McKinley tariff wool duties that the Wilson-Gorman bill had eliminated and increased duties on fruit, hides, sugar, and other items. Tariffs on steel and iron were dropped.[41] It was the most important portion of McKinley's economic program before the Cuban revolution changed the political equation.

Democratic tariff reformers were not surprised. Realistically, as Watterson had written during and after the election, such a revision was the Faustian bargain for Bryan's defeat. Gold Democrats had accepted "protectionism, to save the country from the anarchy and repudiation that immediately threatened it." The president's discussion of "further experiment and additional discretionary power" for reciprocity provisions in a new tariff bill indicated to Watterson that Republican paternalism might be softened.[42] Just as a hint of Populist disorder could bring chaos, he believed, so too could a sliver of reciprocity perhaps bring free trade.

The reciprocity idea marked a significant shift in American foreign trade policy toward incremental globalization. McKinley's new emphasis on the "New God" of a more flexible and powerful system of reciprocal trade relations dominated U.S. policy for at least the next four decades. By integrating and opening markets via liberalizing trade agreements, the move to reciprocity formed the heart of globalization.[43] The idea of using lowered rates as an economic carrot signaled a compromise with the idea that freer trade could drive an ever-expanding marketplace. The relatively fitful moves toward a new politics of concession and compromise in the Dingley bill emboldened free traders like Watterson, who favored any concessions leading inexorably to their own system of economic fundamentalism.

The tensions between these reciprocity and free trade approaches made the events of 1898–1901 especially interesting. This was the period in which the constraints and opportunities of different forms of globalization were recognized and tested. The McKinley administration experimented with various political and economic configurations in constructing a system of world market expansion during these years: outright colonies in a scattered island empire, closed trading systems, managed free trade, and structured reciprocity, to name a few. Watterson supported the long-term goals but sought uniform application of the free trade and home rule ideas as the definitive answer to all economic, political, and social interests: "The Free Trade prescription goes to the root of the disease. It grounds itself in the law of supply and demand. Starting out with the premise that we are the greatest people on earth, with more abundant and accessible natural resources, and that we are also the most skilled workmen in the world, Free Trade would enlarge our markets by a system of international exchange and barter, which it believes would recover to us, but which Protection has driven off, and give us an equal showing in all the neutral markets."[44]

Watterson considered free trade to be the policy of a strong nation. Since the United States was on the verge of global economic supremacy, he argued, should it not be willing to adopt the essential basis of liberal economics? He slyly warned his readers that American acquiescence to protectionism compared unfavorably with the repeal of the British Corn Laws fifty years earlier. When the British realized their economic potential in world markets, he wrote, they liberated the home market. In making this comparison, Watterson aligned the protectionist Republicans with the reactionary, aristocratic Tories, just as he compared them to the "property interests in France in 1788, [and] the slave-holding interests in the South in 1860." The inherent strengths of American manufacturing would eventually require sloughing off the unneeded protectionist system. American businesses, competitive, growing, and with "superior resources," would eventually recognize the tariff as, "in reality, an obstruction." Following the great examples of the past, they "will fling it aside, precisely as the manufacturers of England did fifty years ago." Watterson beseeched, "Come, where is our Republican Sir Robert Peel?"[45]

Watterson knew that the Republican Party would never accept his "allopathic treatment" of free trade, but he sensed the GOP "coming out as a full fledged Free Trader on the homeopathic plan." The two approaches to trade policy sought the same end: the dominance of American goods in world markets. Together, they formed a bipartisan consensus on a system of market expansionism to solve the problem of overproduction. Globalization offered a clear solution to both domestic instability and the limitations of the home market through a policy of "exporting the social question," to use historian Thomas McCormick's elegant phrase. Watterson saw that the key differences between the parties were to be found strictly in a dispute over means. Drawing on the points of conflict and agreement between these "allopathic" and "homeopathic" programs, Watterson created a unique *new* New Departure for the maintenance of southern social order, political dominance, and economic development within an expansionist U.S. foreign policy. He understood that economic supremacy and free trade were necessary and complementary in a capitalist world system.[46]

First, however, Watterson struggled with the Dingley tariff. His decision to oppose McKinley so sharply after an election in which he implicitly endorsed him was relatively unremarkable, given their massive differences on the crucial tariff issue. But it also had a personal element. Accustomed to a close proximity to those in power, regardless of party affiliation, Watterson believed that his valiant sacrifice at personal and professional cost in the campaign of 1896 entitled him to a certain amount of influence in the incoming administration. Watterson reported that he was gratified to aid McKinley and "shall be glad if I can help to make his way smooth after he reaches the White House." Although the editor did not have a direct personal relationship with McKinley, his parents had been regular dining companions and "close friends" of Mr. and Mrs. McKinley during the late 1880s. Indeed, Watterson told A. K. McClure of the *Philadelphia Times* that Mrs. Ida McKinley was "like a daughter to my dear old father." Watterson believed that he deserved at least some private acknowledgment and, perhaps, a minor voice in the creation of the cabinet. For example, he wished to influence the president-elect's choice of secretary of state, but he could not figure out how to inform McKinley. The editor believed that, if he did it directly, "it would be a kind of impertinence."[47]

The real affront came when McKinley did not reappoint Watterson's friend Benjamin Ridgely as the American consul in Geneva. Watterson pursued this end through the offices of Herman Kohlsaat, a staunch Republican and owner of the formerly Democratic *Times-Herald*, who had been instrumental in organizing editorial support for McKinley. Kohlsaat was the only man Watterson knew "with any reach whatsoever [among incoming Republicans] at Washington." Despite a series of appeals, McKinley did not reappoint Ridgely. Watterson was embittered. He wrote John Hay, an old friend from the 1870s and later McKinley's third secretary of state, that it was this "personal inconsideration of which I feel myself to have been made the unmerited object [that] has disturbed me more than any other consideration." His contribution to McKinley's victory was made at "great cost to himself," a disappointed and petulant Watterson wrote Hay, and he had hoped, at least, to be the president's "private friend." All he had sought was an "inexpensive" favor and the opportunity for "some service to the Administration." Writing to moderate Republican senator William B. Allison, Watterson was less charitable and quite a bit more direct. McKinley should have felt "some sense of obligation to those Democrats without whose interposition he could not have been elected," complained the editor. All Watterson wanted was "a slight mark of recognition." This failure of political decency offended Watterson's honor as well as his sense of justice. He wrote Allison, "There has been no time in these thirty years when any person occupying the White House would have treated me with the inconsideration, not to say incivility, observed by Mr. McKinley in this business. . . . What kind of man is this you have elected to the Presidency? . . . Am I a slave, or am I a vassal, am I simply a worthless shotgun, which, having ceased to be suitable may be thrown aside with impunity and indignity?"[48]

Watterson clearly expected reward for his troubles in 1896. He was not a man to let personal affronts die quickly. He was used to having politicians, even a president from another party, show him at least the minimum level of respect he felt was his due and, perhaps, his birthright. It is hard to know how Watterson's approach to the McKinley administration might have differed if Ridgely had been reappointed. Certainly, Watterson stressed issues of policy and did not bolt the Democratic Party to gain patronage privileges among Republicans. Yet his claim to be unconcerned with political isolation and irrelevance as long as truth triumphed was belied by the clear sense of entitlement in his letters. In any case, no matter how many political appointments could have been given away, Watterson's differences with McKinley over the tariff guaranteed a certain amount of dispute and histrionics.

Watterson's return to the tariff question was as inevitable as seasonal change. The tariff issue had been subsumed by silver in the election of 1896, despite its centrality to McKinley's whole program for development. The Chicago platform of 1896 had put off consideration of the tariff question until the money issue was solved, and the National Democratic platform had necessarily emphasized the fight against silver alongside its call for a tariff for revenue only. Watterson was determined that the silverites would get no mileage out of the issue now that the election was over. He wrote, "Every now and then we hear some Free-Silver organ pipe a very weak and, in most cases, a very discordant note about Tariff Reform, as if Tariff Reform had not been sent to the rear by the Chicago Convention." Nor would Watterson allow Bryan to participate in the tariff debate. Bryan, foreshadowing his actions over the Treaty of Paris two years later, had "urged the speedy passage of the Dingley tariff bill in the hope that McKinley would fall into a hole." The *Courier-Journal* refused to consider Bryan's position on the tariff, claiming that it was also "too busy to speculate about what Bryan would do if he were President or about what would happen to Niagara Falls if the moon fell into Mammoth Cave." With the victory in the stable currency battle, Watterson decided attention should return to the tariff on his terms alone. "You might serve notice on Dingley and his crowd, that the gold-standard Democrats also expect to vote against protection at every opportunity," wrote Watterson in the closing days of the Cleveland administration.[49]

The story of the congressional debates and passage of the Dingley tariff has been told many times and does not bear repeating here. The Republican platform of 1896 called the Wilson-Gorman tariff "a National calamity" and declared, "Protection and Reciprocity are twin measures of American policy and go hand in hand." The party stressed the need to reestablish a system of "the most ample protection." In his inaugural address, McKinley reiterated these goals, although he emphasized "the re-enactment and extension of the reciprocity principle" to expand and create "new and advantageous markets for our surplus agricultural and manufactured goods." His call for a special session of Congress to pass this new tariff, in the words of one historian, "staked the success of his administration on the prompt passage of protective legislation." The Dingley tariff is always noted largely for its high duties, which were increased slightly from those of the McKinley tariff of 1890, the heyday of protectionism. But McKinley himself "clearly wanted a modest revision without a riot of protection," and the critical parts of the new tariff law dealt with recapitulating the reciprocity provisions of the 1890 law.[50]

The president and his congressional allies in the debates over reciprocity structures in the new law had motivations other than the traditional, now almost anachronistic, system of protectionism. Trade policy was now subordinated to the central concern of the administration: the search for foreign markets in which to dump America's excess goods. Margaret Leech nicely described reciprocity as "the resolution of the intellectual predicament, the reconciliation of the protective principle with the practical necessities of a superabundant production."[51]

Though he agreed with this end, Watterson was a free trade fundamentalist. He argued that any protection stifled trade. Before McKinley entered office, Watterson did his best to poison the political waters and grab the moral high ground by insisting that it was the Democrats who had always supported reciprocity based upon "the true principles of tariff construction." These "true" tenets maximized both trade and revenue without creating "bounties" for rapacious private interests.[52] Democratic reciprocity was also designed, the *Courier-Journal* argued, to allow American trade and shipping to expand without any unnecessary, counterproductive protection.

The disagreement over subsidizing American shipping was a good example of Watterson's essential conflict with McKinley over the means rather than ends of expansionism. Watterson understood the necessity of expanding the American fleet to encourage commerce, but he believed that direct government action to protect American-built ships would be more destructive than useful. In his inaugural address, McKinley had sought exactly this sort of governmental "bounty." He had called for "the restoration of our American merchant marine, once the pride of all the seas in all the great ocean highways of commerce." In response, Watterson dismissed the protection of American fleets as "a primitive and vicious policy." Limiting commerce in the true fashion, the paper's argument held, would "work a revolution in our foreign commerce" by denying American farmers access to international markets through trade and carrying restrictions inevitably imposed by foreign competitors. Foreign ships would arrive at American shores laden with foreign goods, the paper warned, and leave empty.[53]

The *Courier-Journal* welcomed debate over the Dingley bill with a chorus of huzzahs. Watterson, in an editorial titled "TRUE FRIENDS OF TARIFF REFORM," noted that the Republican Party presented "horns and hoofs, the same old money devil it always was and is, and not a whit less cunning, arrogant and greedy than in days of yore." Although protection would likely bring short-term prosperity, Watterson predicted, the pendulum would swing back over the coming long years, and the Democracy would again be in a position to establish its control of trade policy. As he had in 1892 and would again in 1900, Watterson argued that only the free trade issue could bring Democrats to their rightful position of national political power. "If the Democrats cannot unite on the Tariff, then upon what can they unite?" he asked. "Certainly not upon free silver." As usual leaving the technical discussions of the tariff's flaws to his large editorial staff, Watterson concentrated on the political implications of the bill, sometimes in multiple editorials a day. He cast all local politics and the Kentucky senate race in terms of the "atrocities of the Dingley bill."[54]

By the time the Dingley bill was signed on July 24, 1897, Watterson had accepted that "any tariff is better than perpetual uncertainty." He knew that business simply wanted a stable, clear system in which to carry out its natural and inevitable expansion. The new tariff, he wrote, would "no doubt . . . stimulate manufacturing enterprise, [and] call into activity much capital which has been hiding." It would not, however, solve the long-term problems of overproduction, high prices, and limited markets. Whatever temporary boost to the economy followed would not indicate that the Dingley bill was anything but a "mongrel" with "no right to claim any Free Trade paternity whatever." Free traders, Watterson was confident, would flock to the Democracy, and he was willing to wait for business leaders to abandon Republican paternalism and find their true home. In an interview with the *Florida Times-Union* on November 20, 1897, Watterson declared that Republicans "began with the Dingley Tariff to build an impassable wall between themselves and their recent allies."[55]

As he had said so often before, Watterson believed more strongly than ever that the Democratic Party would finally unify around international economic supremacy and free trade. The creation of a system of free trade (first symbolized by the Star-Eyed Goddess of the tariff for revenue only) was to be the capstone stage of national and regional development. Using political language that resonated deeply with both North and South, Watterson declared, "If we are to have a reunion, a reconstruction and a restoration of the Democratic party . . . the terms must be so specific that no man can escape them."[56] The South and the Democracy would rebuild and rise again on the clear principles of home rule, sound money, and free trade. Watterson soon decided that expansionism was the means of achieving these goals. Following this logic, his holy trinity became deeply intertwined with the vital debates over imperialism, and not a little transformed.

4

The Idiosyncrasy of the Market

> It is beneath our dignity and antagonistic to our interests to swagger up and down the earth, chips on our shoulders, our coat-tails trailing on the ground, blood in our eye, bluster on our tongue, slapping the back of one dirty hand in the face of all decency, and plunging the claws of the other greedy one into the possessions of the weak.
>
> —Henry Watterson, January 19, 1898

Before 1898, Henry Watterson believed strongly in isolation from political entanglement with foreign powers, although he embraced international commerce. His conversion to an expansionist program was unorthodox for a southern Democrat but a logical development in his lifelong struggle to establish southern home rule and to expand the global area of free trade. This shift in his thinking displayed his ability to dramatically alter his outlook as political conditions changed. Watterson abandoned his isolationist views only when he realized the advantages expansionism and globalization offered to the South, to the Democratic Party, and to the nation.

Watterson's isolationism drew from a deep sense of American exceptionalism, a distrust of foreign entanglement, a distain for European imperialism, and a strong belief in the transformative power of free trade. Like many at the time, he thought that the United States had honed a unique and prosperous society liberated from the iniquities of the Old World. "The American people are free from the conventionality of European ideas and traditions," he wrote in a typical formulation of this view, "free from the enervating sense of the past with its defeats and vast responsibilities."[1] Watterson did not dwell on the ideology of exceptionalism, as he was apt to do on tariff reform, but he did mention it regularly. He keenly tried to hamstring overexcited jingoes, self-styled patriots, and self-interested filibusters who sought to breach the isolation that kept America both safe and different. In line with the general Democratic standard of the time, Watterson thought the United States had to avoid all foreign entanglements except trade relations, aggressively maintain the Monroe Doctrine, and defend a clearly articulated American idea of liberty within the Western Hemisphere.

Watterson wished commerce to be free and favored foreign policies that were unencumbered and cheap. In his public orations, he presented this position as a patriotic ideal, but he also connected it to more concrete discussions of America's industrial supremacy and democratic mission. American economic strength underlay national security and afforded it a unique place in the world system. Watterson argued that the singularities of American politics had "revolutionized" the systems of thought and politics that typified the Old World. Because of this liberation, he told national audiences in his popular addresses, the United States was "destined ultimately to absorb all the resources of the earth and air, and all the arts and powers of man in his state of final and complete development."[2]

Despite the military weakness of the United States relative to the European great powers, Watterson believed that America held an unassailable position in secure isolation. "The United States are a first class power," the *Courier-Journal* declared, because of geography and a dominating economic position. The paper proffered the argument that, if agitated, the nation would destroy all attackers. "The empire that battles with this great republic will be no empire when the strife is over," it cheerfully chimed. Echoing Jefferson, Watterson warned that no power would challenge the United States because "a conflict with us would be a conflict with republican institutions and a conflict with the granary and storehouse of the world."[3] He thought maintenance of this economic supremacy, coupled with a resistance to experimentation and centralization, was the best guarantor of national liberty and survival.

As a first step in the process of realizing this vision of economic supremacy, Watterson wanted to finalize America's control of its "natural markets" on solely American terms. He saw that the geographic separation that created the special American character also created a division in the world's markets. These natural markets were those in the Western

Hemisphere, which Watterson thought the United States should rightfully dominate. Americans have "never yet consulted Europe about the management of our own affairs in [this] half of the world," he wrote. Watterson did not consider this idea of America's dominance in its own hemisphere to be outsized. "This is not a spread-eagle gasconade," he advised, but a product of "the American spirit, backed by American resources."[4]

Accordingly, Watterson harnessed his understanding of the American traditions of commercial expansionism and diplomatic isolation to the politics of development at the regional level. As the *Courier-Journal* had pushed for the Democratic South to follow a New Departure from its anachronistic social structure and political-economic system during Reconstruction, so now did it call for an entirely new New Departure in national foreign policy to liberate the South from its subordinate position. Both departures were designed as flexible responses to changing times, offering a clear path to southern development and autonomy. Watterson deliberately reused the label "New Departure"; the domestic and foreign policies he proposed were linked in his mind.

Watterson formulated his New Departure in foreign affairs in response to the coming era in which the market, and the relationship between capital and labor in this market, would become the dominant, defining element in American political and social life. He envisioned a new empire based upon the expansion of the international area of free trade to supersede Jefferson's famous "empire of liberty" with its enlarged area of freedom. "The idiosyncrasy of the century we are leaving behind us was Liberty," Watterson wrote and said often between 1898 and 1900. "The Idiosyncrasy of the century we are about to enter will be Markets."[5] Watterson adored this phrase, and he used it for years to explain his entire approach to the political battles over trade and expansion. Economic development and competition for global markets were going to define politics and diplomacy in the future, he thought, just as sectional and slave questions consumed the Revolutionary, Jacksonian, and Civil War–Reconstruction eras.

Now that questions of liberty and order had been settled by war, Watterson thought, future domestic and foreign politics would focus purely on economic issues. As Jefferson understood how to reconcile liberty and order and created the theory of states' rights, Watterson declared, so must "the Democratic party, led by a new Jefferson . . . [provide] the reconciliation between Capital and Labor." Without saying so explicitly, Watterson presented himself as this new Jefferson, just as he had drawn parallels between himself and Lincoln during the election of 1896. He had returned to save the Democratic Party from Populist chaos, Watterson told his readers, and now he planned to reconfigure the party for the political economy of the future. Both actions required moderation and caution, but also vision. He warned the Democracy and the country to "steer between the two extremes of commercialism and anarchism" so as not to be torn asunder.[6]

Since he believed that the market governed modern life and social order, Watterson applied these same economic imperatives to national policy as well. "This age is a commercial and mercenary one," he wrote early in 1897. "The best minds are not devoted to the fine arts or to statesmanship, but to the accumulation of money in vast business enterprises." In his view, "Modern civilization [is] largely due to the development of commerce and especially of international commerce." Protectionism and the creation of closed international trading systems threatened not just the United States but civilization itself. Watterson viewed unencumbered global commerce as "an agency for peace" and argued that limited markets and paternalistic protectionism threatened social order. The growing pains of industrialization that had so violently shaken the system—in the Great Strike of 1877, at Homestead, at Pullman, and in hundreds of other, smaller places around the nation and in Kentucky—threatened to destroy American institutions if not ameliorated. Watterson believed that both rapacious capital and seething labor were to blame, whereas "the market" and conservative compromise offered peace and a hope of redemption.[7] The market had brought these socioeconomic changes, and the market could provide solutions.

After 1897, Watterson returned incessantly to the need for expanded international markets to bolster American economic supremacy. In July 1897, the *Courier-Journal* declared that "no man can look over the items [in the U.S. Bureau of Statistics report on national commerce] without becoming convinced that the United States are destined to control the manufacturing markets of the world, as they now control the markets for agricultural products." The prospect of this impending greatness was tempered with an understanding that, in both of these markets, there was as much "under-consumption as overproduction." Tobacco, a product particularly important to Kentuckians, faced these two dangers. Watterson echoed the broader business chorus about industrial and agricultural overproduction, especially the positions of the National Association of Manufacturers and other proponents of wide expansion into foreign markets. At one point, the *Courier-Journal* observed that the manufacturers association's president's speech "reads like an extract from an editorial in the *Courier-Journal*."[8]

Yet Watterson differed from the manufacturers on one critical point: he grafted the assertive push for "the commanding share" of the international market onto his long-standing emphasis on tariff reform. He believed the best response to a structural economic crisis was not the expansion of government involvement and activism but its contraction. Perhaps, he mused, the National Association of Manufacturers would eventually push for free trade, as the manufacturing interests had done in England. Since he thought free trade solved the problem of overproduction, Watterson did not advocate grabbing colonies or similar accoutrements, like coaling stations. High tariffs were the only thing limiting national opportunity, including access to both the "natural" markets of Canada and Latin America and the "neutral" markets of Asia. Watterson remained convinced that establishing a free trade system in the nation's natural markets could solve any and all problems without the social or economic costs of imperialism and government expansion.

This combined search for stability, liberty, and markets finally required a level of governmental action that Watterson had never imagined but belatedly decided to support. He had long been a champion of small government, arguing plainly that "the country is too much governed" and calling for "the Constitution, strictly constructed, above all." He never budged from his insistence that "the principle of home rule" had to be practiced "equal[ly] in counties, cities and towns, and in the states of the union, exempt for the tampering of those who have no immediate responsibility, or concern." Watterson initially thought the federal government had virtually no role to play in the new, market-oriented world, aside from setting up the opportunities for increased trade by lowering tariff rates and helping to maintain social stability and national security. His party alone could guarantee these limitations. The Democratic Party, he announced, had "always grouped itself about the organic law of the land, a written constitution, explicit in its terms. . . . The Democratic party made the idea of strict construction the essential principle of its being."[9]

Yet Watterson profoundly challenged the very Democratic traditions he claimed to defend by neatly straddling an internationally oriented market capitalism guided by the modern state and a self-consciously decentralized, Jeffersonian republic. It was possible, Watterson thought, to expand into foreign markets without destroying American institutions or establishing "Caesaristic" forms of government. He argued free trade would produce prosperity and economic liberation both at home and abroad without danger to the Constitution. Watterson championed limited government in almost perfectly inverse proportion to its actual growth. In so doing, he ignored the trends that defined the expansion of governance in the post–Civil War era. His support for an increase in state power was based on an outmoded, mid-nineteenth-century idea of the state's administrative power.

Although he forwarded a rather modern program of market expansionism in 1898, Watterson opposed the accompanying explosion of governance and bureaucracy. He did not understand or anticipate the deeper structural changes that were beginning to define and shape the federal government, and he did not anticipate that even a system of free trade imperialism would ultimately rely upon at least moderately increased levels of governmental activism. For example, he could not tolerate the creation of a commerce department at the federal level, "because commerce is private business." In his view, the nation could have rapid economic expansion even as the size and scope of its government contracted. According to this logic, the constitution was not being changed but recentered and reaffirmed by the expansion of free trade.[10]

Watterson became vague when arguing these points, no doubt because he knew this position was unsustainable. His stance on imperial policy was rife with contradictions, but he did not abandon these guiding ideological principles until the potential benefits to the South became clear. He disputed only the nature, not the idea, of empire. Until the Spanish-American War, Watterson remained convinced that peaceful expansion into foreign markets, conservative social order, and southern development could be successfully reconciled with isolation. However, his rigid limits on the role of government and the isolation from foreign entanglements became quite malleable over time, when he wanted to accelerate the blessings of free trade.

Watterson linked isolationism, market expansionism, and exceptionalism with strong partisanship. He believed that the parties differed fundamentally in their approaches to world affairs. Only the Democratic Party provided the blend of ideas and honesty needed to realize the inherent promises of this system, and Watterson condemned those who supported aggressive foreign involvement as "hot-heads" and "chuckle-heads" interested in "a policy of acquisitiveness and general all-around entanglement abroad."[11] He laid such a policy at the feet of his political enemies, the Republicans.

In significant respects, and especially in the continual disputes over trade policy, Watterson thought, partisan differences were heightened when they reached the border. If the formulation of foreign policy was simply an extension of domestic political battles, Watterson did not want the democratic light of the world to be represented by Republican paternalism. Just as Democratic foreign policy had always enshrined the truest American principles, Republicans would only project their failed values abroad. Watterson argued that the Democracy was the only party that understood the true meaning of national glory and a "vigorous foreign policy," because of its expansionist past. He was initially unwilling to grant any sort of dispensation from this iron law to the incoming McKinley administration, and he dismissed Secretary of State John Sherman's announcement of such vigor as "a great deal of talk."[12]

Watterson accused the Republicans of being insufficiently expansionist and weak-willed because he thought it made good political sense. He argued that the Republicans were merely the successors of the party that had supported Britain in the War of 1812 and also, shamefully, had opposed the Louisiana Purchase and the Mexican War. "Both our great acquisitions of territory were made under Democrats," he mocked the Republicans. Even Alaska had been bought when a Democratic president was in office. Watterson stressed that the Republicans had "never . . . fought a foreign war or acquired a foot of territory," to remind his readers that the party had proven itself only in defeating and exploiting the South, not a common enemy.[13]

Just as he claimed that no one could impugn his personal Democratic credentials, Watterson argued that his party had a monopoly on national glory and land-grabbing. He treated the two as if glory were entirely dependent on expansionism. In so doing, he collapsed decades of history, foreign policy, and party changes into a single, uninterrupted flow of events and intents. Although he stood fast on isolationism as the true, traditional American diplomatic posture, Watterson also found it expedient to lay claim to the more aggressive policies of the past. Tracing his political lineage to Jefferson and Jackson, he constructed continuities to validate his own contemporary position. He fortified himself to defend his new imperialist positions as the culmination of all previous actions taken by legitimate Democratic administrations and unabashedly called the continental United States an empire long before it became politically useful to do so in support of his imperialist program of 1899.

How Watterson reconciled this aggressive viewpoint with his attack on jingoes of both parties and his standard appeal for isolationism may well be a good example of managing cognitive dissonance. In the end, he attacked members of both parties who did not agree with his own personal understanding of any particular issue. Therein lay an important aspect of his recurrent willingness to endanger party allegiance during the Spanish-American War. As he had in the silver issue, Watterson claimed to articulate the true national interests, as opposed to the groping partisanship of all those who disagreed. He presented himself as the voice of the great, reasoned middle, that mysterious agglomeration of the "moral element" and "the American people."[14] He did not consider it the slightest bit unusual that this position could change quite suddenly or be internally inconsistent.

The nature of Watterson's isolationism at this time was clearly evident in his positions on the ongoing diplomatic crisis triggered by the crumbling of the Ottoman Empire (known as the Eastern Question), which he addressed regularly between 1895 and 1897.[15] It is notable that he felt it necessary and appropriate to respond to crises of European imperial diplomacy at the same time he was facing the momentous domestic political challenges discussed in the previous two chapters. To the average Kentuckian, and even to members of the Louisville merchant class, problems in the Ottoman Empire were undoubtedly irrelevant. They do not appear in any history of Kentucky. (Nor, for that matter, does Kentucky political opinion figure in the standard histories of the Eastern Question.) However, Watterson did not think international imperial controversies were insignificant or irrelevant to the lives of his readers, and the *Courier-Journal* regularly covered all manner of issues pertaining to these affairs on the news and editorial pages. The paper discussed a broad array of world imperial politics in detail, especially German, British, and French political economy. Global issues mattered to Watterson, and he considered it essential to unveil their relevance to his readers. Articulating the meaning of international affairs was his goal. That Watterson was interested in the broader political impact of these issues was evident most of all in the fact that he consistently wrote about them in his editorials.

Certainly, Watterson saw imperial news as an effective way to sell newspapers, given the public's fascination with the inherent drama and spectacle of great power conflict. Yet the *Courier-Journal* was not a sensationalistic yellow journal, and it was not given to reporting on events solely for their salability to the public. In keeping with Watterson's basic materialist orientation, the paper tended to interpret international crises like the Eastern Question primarily in terms of power and economics, not ideology. It dismissed other approaches, based on less palpable interests, as irrational crusades or worse. Watterson covered the Turkish issue in terms of its inherent interest and importance to the stability of the international system. As the situation had little potential for a direct impact on the United States or the South, he made no attempt to invent one. Indeed, he insisted that America should not be dragged into this potentially entangling situation because involvement in international problems would compound the dangers of domestic radicalism.

Although he supported assertive action on the part of the great powers to act as "a receiver" for the Ottoman Empire, Watterson wanted the United States to have no part in any action. From this point until the end of his life, he thought that any open-ended commitment to policing the world could end only in a disastrous morass that would corrode domestic liberty and prosperity. He deemed it the responsibility of American policymakers to follow international developments but not to participate in them. Sarcastically, he wrote, "Let those who clamor for an aggressive American policy turn their eyes to the East. Wisdom comes from the East. . . . The whole entanglement is indeed like a nightmare, and its names are Foreign Policy and Manifest Destiny. . . . The Turkey of Thanksgiving is to remind good Americans that their happy fortune absolves themselves from all need of troubling themselves about the Eastern Question . . . and the policy of acquisitiveness and general all-round entanglement abroad."[16] Even as Watterson punned about turkey as a reminder of the isolationist ideal to avoid foreign squabbles, he understood that the country was tightly linked with, and affected by, a world system of trade and diplomacy.

Watterson saw clearly that international technological, economic, and political changes were transforming the character of American interests, and he made certain to understand and interpret them. This insight was at the basis of the slowly developing consensus on internationalism. Once the link between domestic and international affairs was clearer and the opening of foreign markets was viewed as essential, the logic of market expansionism abroad via globalization arose swiftly in both parties. This connection between domestic and foreign interests only grew more intricate as the century closed. It was a small step for public figures like Watterson to proceed from evaluating discrete foreign events because of their relevance to urging involvement in these events because of this same relevance.

Watterson also refused to allow the United States to get dragged into China before 1898, despite the growing threat that European powers might establish markets there closed to American involvement. Watterson had long been an ardent supporter of gaining access to the China market, and he never wavered from this goal. He understood that opening trade in foreign markets was the key means of expanding business activity at home. He encouraged American farmers to grow ginseng, an important crop in the southern mountains, and tantalized his readers with the classic argument for Chinese trade: "The demand for it is practically unlimited, as all the 400,000,000 Chinamen use ginseng if they can get it." He urged the Pacific Northwest to switch from wheat to rice cultivation so it could grab Japanese and Chinese markets. Watterson called for treaty rights to be upheld but rejected any collusion with the European powers to enforce these rights because he did not want the United States to get snared by the imperial powers. "It is clear that we want nothing of China except a chance to trade there and the protection of our citizens who may go thither to trade," the *Courier-Journal* claimed in a typical editorial. Nor did America have any business intervening in China or acquiring colonial possession there. Watterson declared, "Our country has not heretofore been noted for rapacity or territorial aggression, at least outside of North America."[17]

Watterson's opposition to an active, imperialist foreign policy in Asia on the eve of the Spanish-American War came from a desire to avoid foreign entanglement and the complications that accompanied an imperial foreign policy and colonial experimentation. He saw no possible benefit from active U.S. intervention in China, and he feared that anything greater than improving trade relations through an expanded American commercial presence would involve entangling alliances with countries with which "we have no interests in common." The United States had no procedures or "place in our system of government" for dealing with "dependency of this sort," declared Watterson. Any territory in China would be "a source of embarrassment, trouble, and expense with no countervailing advantage."[18] This was a classic anticolonialist formulation that appealed to Watterson's fundamental concentration on the commercial bottom line. Adventurism abroad simply did not pay, but trade would.

Furthermore, Watterson saw an unpleasant racial dimension: China was "inhabited by Mongolians" unsuited to the American system. The racial antipathy of nonwhites was a basic component of later anti-imperialist positions in the United States, especially in the South.[19] The curious aspect of Watterson's support for these ideas of racial exclusiveness was how quickly and remorselessly he abandoned them while he, like the flag, followed the American freighter to the markets of the world. He used racial arguments when they supported his positions and when emotional appeals were most useful. When he sensed new opportunities for commercial gain, he dropped the discussions of race because of their irrelevance to the central issues of economics.

Watterson also refused to allow private citizens, especially missionaries, to drag the United States into power struggles or complications in that "land of benightment." The U.S. government had typically increased its involvement in international affairs by responding to the problems of missionaries. Watterson was not given to sentimentality, and the *Courier-Journal* warned individuals of the perils of proselytizing abroad. He strongly argued that the American government should not take any responsibility for missionaries caught in foreign turmoil, despite the fact that this was an issue that had a great deal of resonance with the public. The federal government should never act to protect those missionaries who were foolish enough to become embroiled in troubles overseas. No misplaced sense of duty or responsibility divorced from verifiable material interest should lead the United States to defend missionaries, no matter how endangered.[20]

When British missionaries in China were killed in the summer of 1895, Watterson took a clear position that the United States should not "supply a gunboat or a file of soldiers to protect every American citizen in his peregrinations about the world." The role of the government, he reminded his readers, was merely to establish the broadest possible guidelines for trade, not to intervene actively in specific international squabbles. If the State Department intervened for American citizens abroad, it would "keep us perpetually embroiled with foreign nations and perpetually in the wrong." Watterson also reminded Americans that, since their own treatment of minorities was often harsh, there was no reason to go abroad to protest like mistreatment. How could America be outraged at the deaths of a few missionaries at the hands of the Chinese, the *Courier-Journal* asked archly, when "we remember the wholesale massacre of Chinese in Wyoming"?[21]

Finally, Watterson believed missionaries were entirely irrelevant to U.S. foreign interests and, therefore, unworthy of much sympathy or support. In fact, he thought that missionaries were simply confusing the important economic issues involved. In an excellent example of his rejection of nebulous appeals to civilization, God, and destiny in favor of a strict materialism, Watterson wrote that, in China, "the missionary has followed the merchant. If only the interests of Christianity had been at stake, China would have been left undisturbed in her isolation. Commerce unlocked the reluctant ports of China to European and American trade. The missionary was only an incident."[22]

Although he had rejected activist participation in European power struggles in China, Watterson was willing to engage the powers in structures that promised what he considered to be beneficial returns. For example, he sought bipartisan support for the Olney-Pauncefote arbitration treaty signed in the final months of the Cleveland administration. The treaty, which had developed in the aftermath of the Venezuelan boundary dispute, put all disputes between Great Britain and the United States into arbitration, within certain procedural limits. Edward Crapol calls opposition to the treaty "one of the last outright displays of anti-British nationalism" in America. Yet Watterson aligned himself with various social and corporate associations and local governments all over the country that supported it, as well as with intellectual figures like John Fiske. Watterson endorsed Fiske's views and summarized them on the editorial page.[23]

Brushing aside the fact that he had inveighed so aggressively against Britain in 1895 during the Venezuela boundary dispute, Watterson welcomed the treaty, in typically overblown fashion, as "the longest stride that has ever been taken toward universal peace" and as "a great monument of human and Christian diplomacy." This great defender of conservatism welcomed the "novelty" of the treaty and considered it an example of the best politics for the future. Notable, too, was that Watterson tended to support Cleveland in all his foreign policies despite their irreconcilable differences over domestic policy. Watterson was not concerned that the treaty established a new international system of adjudication that could be construed as entangling, because he thought it was a different, better type. Recalling his earlier defenses of the Monroe Doctrine, Watterson declared the party issue dead on this point. That policy was indeed "of Democratic origin," he wrote, "but the Republicans with practical unanimity have now ranged themselves" in its favor. Since the treaty did not threaten the Monroe Doctrine, there were no grounds to oppose it. When necessary, Watterson presented his chosen policies as pinnacles of bipartisan achievement. Following this inclusive logic, he declared flatly that all who opposed the treaty were "enemies of their country." He dismissed the charge that the treaty was entangling as "equally insipid and foolish," an appeal to "ignorance and prejudice."[24] These descriptions were reminiscent of Watterson's treatment of the Populists, in part because the silver interests also opposed the treaty.

Watterson reserved his most vicious attacks for silver Democratic senator John Tyler Morgan, the "Ambassador from Alabama," who led the opposition to the treaty. Morgan was long one of the South's preeminent expansionists and a central supporter of the South's dominating the "natural" markets in Latin America, though he did not share Watterson's emphasis on free trade. In early 1897, Watterson gave Morgan both barrels on the editorial page. The editor called Morgan's position against the treaty "pure rot" and personally attacked him for having an intemperate lack of self-control, for putting his "pet aversion" in front of the nation's interest, and for having "foamed and raged as deliriously as to make considerate people fear for his sanity."[25] Watterson's invective, as was often the case in the 1890s, had little direct effect on political opinion. Morgan prevailed in the end, and the treaty failed in the Senate by three votes.

The differences between Morgan and Watterson were reflected in the consistency of their attitudes toward Great Britain's role in the world and its effect on the South. While Watterson was in the process of converting to imperialism, his editorials wavered significantly between twisting the lion's tail, musing in racialist fashion on the glory and superiority of the Anglo-Saxon race, and promoting commercial self-interests. For example, in an editorial celebrating Queen Victoria's jubilee, the *Courier-Journal* praised "the good and virtuous queen" and the English race at the same time that it noted "the poverty and persecution of Ireland, . . . the butchery of helpless Africans and the debauchery of the South Seas." Morgan was consistently anti-British on economic and strategic grounds. Watterson commended the British for understanding that "commerce wants peace" but wrote, "We are accustomed to associate the foreign policy of Great Britain with all that is truculent, aggressive, domineering, acquisitive." He acknowledged that Britain was "our traditional foe" but also "our best customer." Watterson allowed that the Monroe Doctrine, an important structure that kept the hemispheric system both healthy and secure for the United States, also depended upon the British for its existence. Given the relative advantages of the Anglo-American relationship, Watterson accepted this tacit strategic alliance, whereas economic nationalists like Morgan called for an "American Doctrine."[26]

Although he would recommend its dissolution in a few short years, Watterson believed throughout 1897 that the Monroe Doctrine was the single best guarantee of free trade in Latin America. It was a symbol of American exceptionalism in the region and around the world and proof that territorial annexation was not necessary to secure all foreign markets. The United States, wrote Watterson in 1897, was "the Great Power of the New World" that stood as a shield between Latin America "and the despotisms of Europe." He stressed that stability and order, including class and racial hierarchies, needed to be maintained for the benefits of commerce. The Latin American countries understood, Watterson continued in a paternalistic vein, "that all America is a brotherhood, and that the older brother holds the sword and spear for the protection of the junior members of the great Pan-American fraternity." He saw the relationship between North and South America as one of subordination. Watterson recognized some "jealousy" on the part of the Latin American countries because of U.S. power but believed that they understood that American hegemony in the hemisphere was "the most effectual guaranty of their independence and security against the encroachment of European powers."[27]

Watterson had no doubt that the United States rightfully should have control of the markets of the hemisphere and should enjoy a monopoly of power in the region, but he never clearly explained how American power would be utilized. Given his other statements about the limits of adventurism abroad, it was easier in this case to be vague. The Monroe Doctrine as a policy and a lodestar was one of the few historical concepts that Watterson discussed without arbitrarily cutting it to fit his own positions. He understood, and wrote regularly, that the policy was a joint

Anglo-American one, run at the convenience of both countries but long dependent on British power. Unlike his expansionist contemporaries—and unlike Morgan, who pressed for an American doctrine—Watterson began to consider the Monroe Doctrine as having fulfilled and maybe outlived its historical purpose by the turn of the century, and he called for its abolition rather than its expansion.[28]

Again differing from Morgan and other southern nationalists, Watterson was not troubled by either foreign investment in the South or by a supposed colonial relationship with Britain that was stifling independent development in the region. Fear of this subordination was intensely and widely held. Watterson desired only political and strategic isolation and never attacked the expansion of capital or investment. He sought instead to increase these contacts, because he understood that British capital kept the world economic system alive and flowing without creating a threat to the integrity of American isolationism or to southern home rule. Increased international trade and investment in the South would only strengthen these tenets.[29]

The *Courier-Journal* elided the hot political issue of extensive British investment (or "colonization") in the South, largely because it viewed investment as a boon and not a threat. The paper pushed aggressively for *more* investment, foreign and northern. In the same vein, it supported tax incentives in the South to trigger greater industrial development. Editorials such as "The South Wants More Factories" encouraged foreign investment and called for expanded international connections. Watterson linked the increase in capital availability with expansion into new markets and southern prosperity. These editorials calling for investment ran regularly, reflecting the wider appeal of commercial arguments in the political discourse of the time. The South needed to encourage capital development and project its power and riches abroad. It also needed to jettison its persistently obsolete ideas.[30]

It was in this spirit that Watterson called for his New Departure in American foreign economic policy, in the form of a new program to finalize his incomplete Reconstruction-era plans for southern development. Since the social, political, and racial issues of the Reconstruction period finally seemed to be resolved, Watterson refused to accept any obstacles to the implementation of the economic vision he had expounded for thirty years. The new New Departure moved away from the lies of protectionism and big government and the dangers of foreign entanglement, toward an engagement with the world on the broad economic terms of globalization. It was time, wrote Watterson, to recognize "the insufficiency of the home market" and to embrace the need for a new global system of trade. In so doing, he rejected the protection of domestic industry but not its promotion abroad. It was time for the United States to modernize its international outlook and for the Democratic Party to rid itself of its "ordinary vision" in favor of an entirely new orientation toward the global economic system. The foreign and domestic goals of this vision could not be separated because there was no difference between them. Watterson believed that the Democratic Party could regain national dominance only with an entirely new outlook based upon the expansion of free trade.[31]

Watterson characterized protectionism as equivalent to the lies of the slaveholders (that cotton could not be grown profitably without slaves), just as he had previously compared free silverites to slaveholders. The "whole trend of modern thought—the movement of the civilized world" was against all of these ideas. He argued that slavery, free silver, and protectionism were lies successively sold to the southern public to prevent modernization and development. The first had brought war, destruction, and economic backwardness; the second had unleashed radicalism; the third obscured the realities of the market, challenged the social order, and maintained illegitimate Republican rule. Protectionism and governmental paternalism limited the advancement of the nation as a whole and sabotaged the advances coming to the South from international trade. Now that the "sectional and sentimental questions—the race question and the local autonomy question" were settled satisfactorily in the wake of the defeated "force bill," Watterson could not allow "the solidarity of the South" to "break up before the new questions—the economic questions—which were bound to follow."[32]

Watterson's New Departure at the turn of the century reflected his New Departure of the Reconstruction years in its emphasis on constructing an enlightened commercial policy free from the restricting, reactionary ideologies that limited southern growth. In both instances, Watterson emphasized the transformative power of free trade in economic development and the centrality of commercial considerations in political choices. As he believed the Democratic South had honestly redeemed itself after the "hari-kari of 1860," he thought it was time again to realize its potential in the international realm after the hari-kari of 1896. Folding sectional, economic, social, and partisan interests into a single vision of expanding global markets, Watterson told his southern readers that the new New Departure would counter these destructive lies. He thought his policy could produce prosperity, utterly eliminate racial strife, provide for a stable and orderly Union, and rationalize the national political system in the Democrats' favor.[33]

The new New Departure centered on widespread theories of overproduction, a desire to trade industrial goods for raw materials from abroad, and support for a proactive economic policy that did not require excessive governmental centralization. It drew deeply from a belief in an integrated capitalist world system based upon the free flow of goods. Watterson intuitively understood the hierarchical character of this flow. The main industrial powers were to sell finished goods to the lesser states of the Western Hemisphere in exchange for raw materials. So long as currencies remained stable, Watterson indulged his interest in the producer and the transfer of goods. "International commerce is essentially the interchange of products," the *Courier-Journal* intoned. Befitting a spokesman for industrial, commercial, and agricultural Kentucky, Watterson emphasized the centrality of production for world markets. Trading one set of goods for another quantity of goods "extends our [own] foreign markets," he wrote, and that was "an exceedingly desirable thing to do."[34] The actual transfer of gold or silver was, in some ways, irrelevant; the flow and expansion of trade was primary. After all, the money that did exchange hands was usually paid for by British loans.

This attitude was tempered by a realistic understanding that, under a free trade system, the United States was forced to woo its foreign customers. It could not coerce them. In this sense, Watterson reaffirmed that he fundamentally understood all political relations as delicate economic couplings and interactions. He was sensitive to the interplay of trade relations, the fickle role of the consumer, and the need for innovation and competitiveness. He never broached the idea of forcing trade onto weaker countries. Rather, it was exactly the weaknesses of these countries that made them the "natural" markets for the United States. Watterson felt that Latin American trade had to be earned despite its natural attraction to the American orbit. The United States thereby would avoid the artificial force that typified Republican foreign economic policies, even reciprocity. "We must make it [trade] to their interests . . . [and] consult their convenience," he advised. It would not do to try to forcibly expand markets. Competition was fierce, he warned his U.S. readers, and "trade is reciprocal." America had to offer "inducements" in the form of low tariffs and hire "commercial agents" who spoke the languages of the countries. Proactive government policy was acceptable along these lines, provided it acted to lower barriers and ease trade. As Watterson's criticisms of the Dingley tariff revealed, he did not believe that it was necessary to create punitive tariffs with weak reciprocity features when simply lifting the barriers could have an immediately beneficial effect.[35]

This view of international trade also held that the market alone determined where institutional structures would develop. "Trade does not follow the flag, but the flag follows trade," the *Courier-Journal* argued. Likewise, credit institutions would develop "where they are needed, perishing where they are not." The *Courier-Journal* did not support the independent creation of an "International American Bank," as had been suggested in Congress during the first Cleveland administration. Watterson did not believe it prudent or effective to attempt to pick the areas where a government could create market growth, but he was eager to capitalize on such growth whenever it appeared.[36]

Under his new New Departure program, as he had since he arrived in town in 1868, Watterson intended the Falls City to be the fulcrum of a great economic revival of the South even as it surpassed its commercial rivals St. Louis and Cincinnati. The difference this time was that economic development would be directed outward. Watterson urged Louisville to seize the opportunities offered by globalization in new, important markets like Mexico. "There is a big and growing demand for a large number of articles which are produced in Louisville factories," he wrote. "The Mexicans are our neighbors . . . [and] they would be glad in the opportunity to buy in our more advantageous market."[37]

In the March 1897 Prosperity Edition of the *Courier-Journal*, Watterson highlighted Louisville and Kentucky's dominance in world tobacco markets (over exporter nations such as Turkey and Hungary) and featured an illustration of an angel dumping a cornucopia of coins over the city. In Watterson's description, Louisville was a city of superlatives. The facts that it had the world's largest burley tobacco leaf and bourbon whiskey markets were widely used to advertise the city, as was the fact that it "makes more plows, jeans, cement, and oak tanned sole leather than any city in the world." Louisville had the largest handle factory in the world, the biggest pipe iron foundry in the United States, and the cheapest coal and potato markets in the South. Watterson understood that true prosperity depended on both "the full granary and the busy factory," and he put Kentucky in the "race for commercial, agricultural and manufacturing supremacy." Louisville could be "a second Chicago," given its important rail links to southern ports and its prominence on the Ohio River. As he had in the 1870s, Watterson counted and worried over Cincinnati's greater number of workshops and factories. Watching the cotton mill campaign that was transforming the Deep South, Watterson called for Louisville to develop its own cotton mills and markets. Covetously, he advised his readers that the Indian Head Mills of Cordova, Alabama, had sold its production for the next five years to China. Clearly, he argued, it was time to develop a comparable mill industry in the Ohio River valley. Kentucky had the climate, the transportation facilities, the coal supplies, and the will to dominate in these markets. "What is true of the South" in terms of economic advantages "is also true of Kentucky and Louisville," Watterson announced. He called for investment in and dedication to expanding this crucial business within the commonwealth.[38]

These plans to make Louisville the Chicago of the South never came to fruition, and the rather fanciful idea of making the city a cotton hub failed. Watterson remained concerned, however, that the agricultural and manufacturing overproduction that were becoming such important public issues threatened to derail the new prosperity of the South and the country as a whole. Since economic health was the key to social order, Watterson took the same approach he had followed during the Populist revolt: he sought reasoned change. His essentially conservative outlook on the processes of development and change was equally applied to domestic and foreign policies. Although he was not totally averse to change, Watterson required assurance that new conditions would not unnecessarily complicate or destroy the existing system: "In public affairs, as in amatory affairs, it is well to be off with the old love before we are on with the new; that is, all government being more or less experimental, we should not undervalue stability, not be quick to quarrel with things existent, nor seek to change the established order, until we are sure of the shelter above us and the footing beneath."[39] He believed that the laws of the free market, untainted by the experimentation of the left or the paternalism of the right, would govern American relations with the rest of the world just as they would define relations in the domestic sphere. This was the safest guarantor of stability and liberty. In early 1898, Watterson saw no reason to move beyond market expansionism and diplomatic isolationism. It was in this context that he dealt with the smoldering Cuban revolution and the outbreak of hostilities with Spain. When he became sure of the "footing beneath" and saw the possibility of quickly installing his New Departure through territorial expansionism, Watterson hastened to trade his old love for the comely lass of colonialism.

5

The *New* New Departure

> The *Courier-Journal* is a jingo; but it is a jingo having an ample and a soaring soul. When it goes a-catting, it goes a-catting! If we want Mexico, let us take it. If we want Canada, we'll do the same thing. . . . Let us establish the Christian religion in India, China, Persia, and plant the stars and stripes over the seraglio of Abdul the Damned on the Bosphorous. Or, if it is islands we want, there is the owld emerald isle itself . . . let us annex Ireland! But Hawaii—them cannibals—them lepers—them cholera-stricken, God-forsaken, hell-bound Kanakas! Lord, it causes one's blood to thicken, and one's digits to freeze and fall off, the bare thought of it!
>
> —Henry Watterson, December 23, 1897

If one reads Henry Watterson's editorials on single subjects over a long enough period, excluding the relentless tariff writings, one observes the small contradictions in each eventually blossom into sweeping shifts in his political positions. On the critical issue of recognition of Cuban belligerency, this certainly was the case. In fact, the totality of Watterson's change of position on Cuba was matched only by the reversal of his opposition to Hawaiian annexation. Both changes reflected his mutable responses to new political conditions, but more important, both revealed his evolving approach to America's position in the world.

As he sensed an unfolding opportunity to fulfill his new New Departure for the South by achieving regional development and autonomy through globalization, Watterson did not hesitate to abandon his guiding isolationist, anti-imperialist principles. Although the *Courier-Journal* did not join in the sensationalism that characterized many of the country's newspapers, Watterson did become a vocal and important member of the chorus urging American action, expansionism, and internationalism. This transition was slow but ineluctable. By May 1897, Watterson was advocating recognition of Cuban belligerency, marking his first step toward ardent support for territorial expansionism and foreign entanglement of the highest order after the Spanish-American War. He used a variety of appeals—racial, strategic, ideological, and economic—to support his arguments as he shifted toward expansionism in the wake of the war, but he ultimately stressed the policy that he thought offered the best and most immediate benefits to southern independence and prosperity.

The Cuban revolution against Spain had been brewing long before it broke in 1895, with American interests in the island going back further still. The *Courier-Journal* covered the issue often in 1895, and its editorials were uniformly reserved and supportive of American neutrality. This position contrasted markedly to the one held during the earlier Cuban revolt of 1879, which was only minimally covered as news and not at all on the editorial page. In February 1895, when the insurrection began, Watterson was in the unusual position of defending President Grover Cleveland's policy of neutrality toward the revolution. Some Democrats roundly attacked Cleveland, but Watterson praised the president for following "the old Democratic policy of 'peace with honor' and the avoidance of all needless complications with foreign nations, whether strong or weak." Unlike some expansionist southerners in a long line stretching back to Thomas Jefferson, Watterson did not think that Cuba was the key to southern prosperity, and so he had never been much interested in grabbing it outright.[1] His only sustained discussion of Cuba in the prerevolution period, predictably, dealt with the inequalities of the sugar bounties under each successive tariff.

Watterson, expectedly, stressed economic self-interest and filtered his position through his understanding of free trade. There was to be no action without it. Eight months before the revolution began, Watterson rejected the idea of supporting the Cubans in their struggle because he saw no clear economic benefit for the United States. Critical racial and language differences would mean "assimilation [into the United States] would necessarily be slow and difficult." Watterson took special pleasure in noting that "the men who wish to buy or steal Cuba" were the same ones who pursued protection for big sugar in Louisiana. They did not understand that "annexation would be equivalent to a commercial treaty establishing free trade between the United States and the countries annexed." Watterson believed that territorial expansion required a subsequent expansion of jurisdictional authority. He could envision only two options in the Cuban situation: either neutral noninvolvement or annexation as a state, with the requisite extension of the area of free trade. "If Cuba comes to us," he wrote, "she might come first as a territory, but ultimately she would become a state." Statehood, in turn, would give Cubans social and economic parity with Americans even though they were notably "incapable of self-government."[2]

Watterson did not consider the Cuban revolt to be a harbinger of greater things to come, mostly because he was not impressed with the rebels themselves and feared revolutionary instability on the island. The *Courier-Journal* admitted a tepid "natural sympathy we have with any people struggling to throw off a foreign yoke" but did not suggest that this struggle superseded the legitimacy of the established Spanish order. "A revolution is like a forest fire," Watterson explained. "Every day that fire is allowed to smolder increases the danger." He considered Spain's exploitative and extractive colonialism to be "an anomaly in our enlightened age," and he professed to understand why the Cubans desired freedom. It was, however, "as much as we can be expected to do [to] maintain a strict neutrality in the matter." Rather than intervene, the United States should remain a shining example of a "great republic" toward which Cuba could strive. This attitude reflected well the long tradition of American isolationism.[3]

To maintain this distance and aloofness, the *Courier-Journal* refrained from hysterical reporting. Equivocation was typical among papers like the *Boston Journal* (which was considered to be only mildly sensationalistic) and the *Chicago Inter-Ocean*, a Republican sheet, whereas the excitable *New York Sun* boldly declared "Cuba must be free!" from the start. Watterson condemned such journals for acting "with the indiscriminate recklessness of partisans," and he remained a sharp critic of yellow journalism and the commercialization of news reporting, which he deemed irresponsible and dangerous. He distinguished between sensational reportage and editorial argument, no matter how outrageous. The former was a relative innovation that was founded upon strictly commercial calculations; the latter had long-standing American traditions of "personal journalism" behind it. Watterson felt he had a responsibility to provide the public with reasoned interpretations of America's evolving interests. Since he wrote for a national audience, Watterson presented himself as the voice of reason and Americanism, the thinking man's alternative to the hysteria of the Hearst empire. His paper lagged considerably behind other papers in joining the bandwagon for war and even in calling for recognition of Cuban belligerency. Unlike many New York papers, the *Courier-Journal* did not even report the Spanish firing on the American merchant ship *Allianca* in March 1895, let alone become frenzied.[4]

Instead, the paper approached the Cuban issue gingerly. A strong antijingoism permeated the *Courier-Journal*'s coverage of the revolution and its supporters throughout 1895. It considered reports from the island "conflicting" and those from Cuban propagandists in the United States, such as the "cigarmakers in Tampa," untrustworthy. Overall, Watterson thought it was "hard to discuss intelligently the situation in the island." He never wavered in his attacks on what he called "the blatherskite press," and he continued to bemoan the loss of decorum in journalism until the end of his life. That did not keep William Randolph Hearst from asking Watterson if he would, "as [a] personal favor, . . . wire the [*New York*] *Journal* a stirring signed editorial for free Cuba?" Watterson did not respond. He did not yet support a free Cuba, and he disdained Hearst's sensationalism. "There is scarcely any matter of news in recent years which has not been similarly distorted, perverted and fabricated by this utterly unscrupulous crew of systematic, habitual and mercenary liars," he wrote in disgust in 1898. Although Watterson obviously relished editorial histrionics and hyperbole, his journalistic code of ethics did not allow for the same on the news page.[5]

As the months passed in 1895, Watterson's thinking evolved incrementally: he sharpened his attack on "the throttling fingers of Spain" and supported a change of rule in Cuba based largely on the incompetent administration of the island. Cuba was the size of Kentucky but with a million fewer people, wrote Watterson, and "the public debt" was "about $300 for every man, woman and child, white, black or yellow, the unhappy island possesses." This "black record" of mismanagement was a sign that "barbarity" had descended upon "one of the oldest Christian nations on the globe." He called Spain a "decayed and viperish land" that had failed as a colonial power. By the end of July, Watterson carefully supported a change of rule in the colony, although he feared "the people of Cuba may not be capable of self-government." At this point in his thinking, American "strict neutrality" meant that it would not support either side as the legitimate power. Watterson also did not think it was necessary for the United States to silence supporters of the rebels. This marked quite a transition from his position in the spring.[6]

Still, Watterson hesitated because he did not consider the Cuban revolutionaries a legitimate alternative government. They were merely a group of "insurgents," not yet an independent political entity like the Confederacy had been. Watterson balked at the rejection of established rule, however corrupt it might be. The United States could recognize only legitimate governments with established lines of control, he argued, and "it would be a queer proceeding to recognize a number of unknown insurgents without a head as constituting a belligerent power." This question of whether to recognize belligerency was hotly disputed at the time in the popular press and in law journals. It formed the basis for the overall American approach to the revolution and had particular resonance in a South only a generation removed from its own revolution.[7]

Watterson rejected the clear historical parallels. The Cubans were unlike the American revolutionaries because they lacked the appropriate civil, racial, and intellectual structures to make a smooth transition to self-government. The United States had had "a nearly homogenous population bred in the school of Anglo-Saxons and colonial liberty." It is unclear what exactly Watterson meant by "colonial liberty." Presumably, he believed that a history of at least some local self-government (or "home rule") had prepared American colonists for independence. This same tradition likewise had been the source of Confederate legitimacy. Watterson explained that the racial problem had been avoided in America because the various ethnic groups "had been assimilated in a great measure, except for the negroes, who had no political power." Cuba, on the other hand, had no individual of Washington's caliber, no tradition of home rule, and no hope of establishing "a stable government" unless the United States followed an intervention with annexation. Watterson awaited evidence of a decent Cuban government to recognize.[8]

Standing on international law as a guide, Watterson discussed his fear that recognizing the revolution as anything more than an "insurrection" would set "a precedent that might be troublesome in the future." The United States might have to side with subsequent national liberation movements, which was the equivalent of declaring war on the governing imperial power. Watterson also doubted that the Cubans were really worthy of something as important as official recognition. Although the

United States had indeed recognized other Latin American states, "their experience as republics has not been particularly exhilarating," he wrote. Despite sympathizing with the Cubans, he thought involvement would create an unnecessary entanglement; moreover, he did not believe that the public supported a radical break with the traditional patterns of foreign affairs. In response to Republicans who were busy attacking Cleveland for not recognizing the Cubans' belligerency, Watterson relished a quote from "that somewhat well-known American and Republican, General and President U.S. Grant." Grant had advised decades earlier that "to justify a recognition of [foreign] belligerency there must be, above all, a de facto political organization of the insurgents, sufficient to constitute it . . . a State."[9]

Watterson's own experience in Kentucky demonstrated to him both the potential dangers of an unchecked rebellion and the folly of choosing sides. The insurgency on state toll roads had grown into a small-scale war that was deeply affecting Kentucky. In a sardonic editorial titled "They are Belligerents," Watterson drew many parallels between the Kentucky raiders and the Cuban rebels. If Congress recognized the Cubans, he argued, it really should recognize the Kentuckians. The groups had had similar successes in disrupting life and commerce and terrorizing the populace. Both also had "made war on the tobacco industry." Given the "state of war" that existed in Kentucky, Watterson sarcastically argued, "the arguments brought forward in the Senate to prove the belligerency of the Cubans tend strongly to prove that of the turnpike raiders."[10] Although the Cubans fought for liberty and the toll raiders were criminals, Watterson did not believe either group was worthy of recognition. He easily linked local concerns with broader issues of national and foreign policy to emphasize his points in both.

As the public, and especially the congressional, mood shifted toward recognition of Cuban belligerency by the end of 1895, the *Courier-Journal* admitted that this shift was probably indeed supported by "a large majority of the American people." But, it warned, if recognition went through, United States policy should still be constrained, since there were no logical or material grounds for annexation. In admitting the depth of public support for the Cubans, Watterson revealed his flexibility on the Cuban situation. He demonstrated a willingness to follow, rather than attempt to dictate, public opinion.[11] In less than nine months, he had moved from being uninterested in anything other than the restoration of Spanish order on the island to quietly accepting that the situation on the island was worth conservative and careful reevaluation. Watterson was not wholly opposed to the United States' flexing its new international strength, but he was opposed to forceful action without a clear understanding of future consequences. He reveled in the idea that the United States could, if it chose, decide what sorts of regimes were appropriate in its "natural" orbit in the Caribbean. When he temporarily retired and left the country at the end of the year, he seemed to be leaning toward some acceptance of the Cuban revolutionary effort.

During the election year of 1896, Watterson's few contributions to the *Courier-Journal* ignored the Cuban issue. He was consumed with the internal, supposedly revolutionary, threat posed by the Populists. When he returned to the issue in early 1897, his position had hardened. He even raised offhandedly the possibility of conflict with Spain, yet until the war began, his writings and speeches spoke to his position in the Democracy and in battling the Dingley tariff's negative features. Despite that the Cuban issue appeared regularly in the paper, Watterson's editorial position on recognition did not shift appreciably between 1895 and May 1897. He continued to stress the economic aspects of foreign policy and the need to avoid the potential pitfalls of adventurism. He emphasized stability and conservatism at home and abroad, and he did not yet identify an activist policy with a winning political strategy.

The problems of investors in Cuba fell on deaf ears in Louisville. Watterson thought traders and investors, like missionaries, should not expect the U.S. government to break with tradition in service to their private interests. He remained concerned that individuals masquerading as American citizens were trying to pull the United States into the conflict and that the exaggerations about Spain's holding American prisoners would create a push for intervention similar to the one that had occurred with the missionaries in China. "The Government of this country is not an insurer," Watterson wrote. It was not responsible for stopping filibustering from its shores, or for anything beyond "good faith and reasonable diligence in enforcing its neutrality laws." Nevertheless, the United States could not tolerate the slightest intrusion on its neutral prerogatives, such as the searching of ships flying the U.S. flag. Watterson took these neutral rights seriously, especially as they affected trade. Such an intrusion, he warned, "would speedily lead to complications that would be unpleasant for the Dons."[12]

Despite these inclinations toward action, Watterson remained ambivalent about American intervention in the conflict, primarily because he feared damage to domestic political institutions and liberties. He did not find it difficult to oppose Republican congressmen on the recognition issue, since he thought the GOP habitually offended the true American spirit. And this was, of course, the party that had opposed recognition of the Confederates. But the increasing Democratic defection to the pro-recognition camp made the problem more visceral. Watterson expressed concern that pro-Cuban senators (and silverites), like John Tyler Morgan, Roger Q. Mills of Texas, and David Turpie of Indiana, were ignoring the Constitution and Democratic traditions by pushing so aggressively for recognition. Watterson called these senators extremists, which was the label he foisted on most who disagreed with his approach. He attacked the senators' jingoistic aggressiveness and compared the idea of congressional rule of Cuba to the "illegitimate" imperialist rule that Congress enforced during Reconstruction.[13]

This image of neo-Reconstruction tendencies in American imperialism soon became a standard part of Watterson's editorial attacks on all those who disagreed with him. For the moment, he thought Populism and paternalism clearly had made these men mad with power and self-righteousness, and they were seeking to make Cuba "the slave of a Congressional oligarchy." Watterson supported McKinley's cautious moves toward an interventionist posture. The *Courier-Journal* argued that the power to recognize belligerency lay only in the executive branch and that Congress had to remain within its constitutional limits by not forcing the nation to move unreasonably.[14]

By late spring, the *Courier-Journal* had hardened its tone and shifted its position. It presented the Cubans' revolution as a "struggle to shake off the European yoke and secure for themselves the right of free government as established in America." Drawing a parallel to American-style political freedom and referring to the concept of their political "rights," Watterson sidled away from the idea that the Cubans were incapable of self-government. The impetus for this shift seems to have been Senator Morgan's success on May 20, 1897, in getting the Senate to recognize Cuban belligerency. Morgan's biographer describes this action as a critical new Democratic alignment with the McKinley administration.[15] Perhaps the harsh Republican political and press attacks on Morgan convinced Watterson that this was a suitable issue on which to press his broader political agenda.

Sensing partisan advantage in this question of recognition, in short order Watterson reversed himself and came to aggressively support Cuban freedom. On May 28, in an editorial titled "Recognize Cuba," Watterson fused all of his usual political agendas into one strident call for action that thoroughly contradicted his earlier statements on Cuba. Throughout, he remained true to the one variation on his holy trinity: home rule, free trade, and the Monroe Doctrine. "The people of Cuba are struggling for the rights which belong to all men," he wrote, and their revolution was identical to the American Revolution. Watterson also now likened the Cuban revolt to the Confederate struggle for advancement and equality within a paternalistic Republican America. "They are struggling for home rule, for individual sovereignty, for freedom from foreign tax eaters," he announced. Ignoring his earlier pronouncements on the need to adhere to international law, Watterson announced that the United States could act as it chose within its sphere of influence. He also discounted his earlier test of verifiable self-interest. The United States should "be manly enough to express our sympathy in the right way, without stopping to count the possible cost to ourselves in dollars or blood, or without parleying and pettifogging over finely split hairs of international law." As usual, Watterson made grand pronouncements without concern for the details. Details did not matter. It seemed clear that the Republicans, lacking a clear and proactive policy, were vulnerable in light of popular support for the Cubans.[16]

This new approach to the Cuban problem also included some of the now-standard Wattersonian rhetorical techniques. Not the least of these were hyperbolic attacks on the Spanish and their culture, each editorial draped in patriotism and sometimes crude jingoism. These editorials contained the sort of language that characterized yellow journals and reflected the demagoguery that Watterson occasionally reverted to for political effect, as he had in the free silver campaign. He skewered the "many-titled" and "high toned aristocrats" who could not handle insults from Americans but could "shoot non-combatants and prisoners, outrage women, murder children, and leave hundreds of their own people to starve." He announced, "Spanish character has not changed a particle in 400 years." He warned Spain that it was "straining at a gnat and swallowing a herd of camels" and could no longer control events. Watterson agreed with interventionist Hannis Taylor of Alabama, U.S. minister to Spain, that Spain had demonstrated "utter incapacity" in its rule and should leave.[17]

Watterson could contemplate recognition of the Cubans only alongside a strong announcement of neutrality. Although he supported recognition of the island's independence, he remained unwilling to accept either intervention or annexation. He believed that this position reflected the mood of the country, whose citizens were "not interested in the acquisition of Cuba . . . [and] in fact are opposed to that." As with Hawaii, Watterson saw no unassailable benefit to noncontinental expansion. He did not revive his earlier idea that recognition of the rebels was akin to a declaration of war. Unlike a stereotypical yellow press editor, Watterson counseled calm and thoughtful diplomacy to peacefully resolve the dispute in the Cubans' favor. His conservative approach to social order also did not easily accommodate the quick and radical change required for a more interventionist policy. Since McKinley had "promised prosperity," wrote Watterson, it was unlikely that his administration could "contemplate any vigorous action." He feared Spain alone could start a problem by "an outrage upon our merchant vessels," so it was time for "some display of statesmanship" to head off a crisis.[18]

Significantly, Watterson's prescription for an independent Cuba also reflected his program for the maintenance of world order and national growth through the establishment of global free trade. As had been the case in the United States, Watterson claimed, liberal economic interdependence and stability were the best assurance of political liberty and social order in Cuba. It was in America's interest to expand the area of free trade by encouraging the Cuban rebels to end Spanish paternalism and control. This change of regimes would benefit the United States directly without requiring more than rhetorical support. By the end of 1897, Watterson believed that it might be possible for the United States to become diplomatically powerful and economically supreme without negative effects. Liberal rhetoric and the free market were the magic combination, a formula that would later come to typify the American approach to globalization and world order.

Therefore, the most important aspect of a new order in the island was self-control of its "foreign trade, and hence the control of tariffs, [which are] vital to Cuban interests." Control of the tariffs meant control of the whole system of power and prosperity. Whatever power controlled the tariff and access to the market held the key to national development. This view mirrored Watterson's long-standing approach to southern development, and it formed the immovable support for his imperialist program between 1898 and 1902. It also, incidentally, reflected the logic that lay behind American Cuba policy under McKinley and later American approaches to international political economy.[19]

Again and again over the next several years, Watterson returned to the tariff issue—whether American, Cuban, Puerto Rican, or Philippine—as the sole repository of honest politics and future prosperity. He sought to apply free trade in Cuba to liberate its inhabitants and to expand the general area of liberal capitalism, just as he had for years in the South. Free trade was his solution to all problems, foreign and domestic. It provided all the benefits of empire while smoothly avoiding its costs. Watterson was certainly in agreement with the globalizers under McKinley on this point.

Though Cuba could gain its independence through tariff policy, Watterson also understood the reality of its subordinate economic relationship with the United States. If Spain granted "autonomy for Cuba," then the establishment of free trade in the Caribbean would allow the United States to "nearly monopolize the import trade of Cuba."[20] Given the natural accretion of these economic benefits, Watterson did not think it was necessary to spend money to speed them along or, especially, to wage an expensive war to achieve them. If the United States was foolish enough to get involved in a war with Spain, he wrote, "one industry which . . . [it] would undoubtedly stimulate greatly would be the pension industry. It is awesome to speculate upon the magnitude of our pension expenditure if we should have another war." Watterson had long equated the huge expense of military pensions with the keeping of a standing army because he thought both corroded domestic liberties and economic health. This view mirrored a general southern resentment of the significant Grand Army of the Republic pensions as a major budget drain and a perfect example of Republican Party shenanigans.[21]

Although he desired and supported the benefits of market expansionism, Watterson was unwilling to accept a similar expansion of government or military responsibilities before the Spanish-American War broke out. Peaceful economic expansion was preferable. When war came, his entire outlook changed to meet the new reality. Conquest suddenly seemed to answer all of the country's problems, and Watterson was willing to exploit it. He agreed to support armies as well as colonies, to entangle the flag in international politics, and to pursue Dixie's future overseas through empire.

As with the Cuban question, Watterson radically changed his position on the annexation of Hawaii once the Spanish-American War began. Throughout 1897 and into the next year, he pressed antiexpansionism almost daily in the *Courier-Journal*. Watterson fused his arguments against free silver with his argument against expansionism, referring to these policies as jointly "a delusion and a snare." He argued against the annexation of Hawaii, a "monstrous scheme of spoliation," because it would violate America's democratic traditions, entangle the nation in foreign squabbles, muddle the races, and necessitate huge military expenditures.[22] Watterson typically appealed to economic self-interest, which he thought would not be served by any annexation scheme. Finally, a great many of the *Courier-Journal*'s antiannexation editorials appealed to southern and national racism. On each of these issues, just as he had done in the Cuban situation, Watterson reversed himself without hesitation or self-consciousness when he adopted a policy of imperialism.

Each successive editorial on Hawaii in 1897 reiterated Watterson's basic views, which had not changed since the last annexation craze of 1893–94. President Benjamin Harrison had forwarded an annexation treaty in his final moments in office in 1893, and Watterson always considered the treaty an illegitimate Republican conspiracy. In the early months of the Cleveland administration, Watterson heavily stressed tariff revision as a party matter and discussed the Hawaiian issue in similarly partisan terms. He played an aggressive role in the strong southern fight against annexation. He described the Republicans' plan as analogous to their attempt to rob the people through protectionism and argued that "it differed from other raids on the Treasury only in its methods." In line with his longstanding isolationism, Watterson opposed the annexation attempt in the early 1890s on economic, ideological, and racial grounds. He argued that the Constitution did not "make provision for a colonial establishment" and called the policy a dangerous British import. Watterson, like the majority of southern editors, declared, "We are not a nation of jingoes." In keeping with his hardening domestic stance on race after 1890, Watterson warned his readers that annexation meant taking in a people "more mongrel in character than any known to our domestic fabric . . . when we confess ourselves unequal to a serious race problem here at home . . . [adding] new and unknown risks to present dangers."[23] The annexation attempt failed.

The Hawaiian issue returned to public attention when McKinley submitted an annexation treaty to the Senate on June 16, 1897. As "resistance was immediately forthcoming" in Congress and attention was focused on tariff revision, the annexationists sent the treaty to the safety of John Tyler Morgan's Foreign Relations Committee to await a friendly reception in the winter session. Morgan went on a celebratory tour of the islands to "supplement his expansionist brief." Congressional debate finally recommenced in January 1898. During the six-month interlude, Watterson wrote regularly and vehemently against the idea of annexation. He considered Morgan's position to be a betrayal of the Democratic Party and of the South and argued that McKinley was pushing the United States down a new and dangerous path, in violation of both tradition and his inaugural address, in which he had reaffirmed a policy of "keeping ourselves free from entanglement" and had declared, "We want no wars of conquest; we must avoid the temptation of territorial aggression." Watterson warned that the annexation treaty was "the beginning of a new policy, a policy of territorial aggression against which President McKinley remonstrated." Imperialism brought an ever-greater series of problems with ever-diminishing returns. "This [first] accession of territory will be peaceful," Watterson warned, "but the next one contemplated will bring a war."[24]

Watterson's opposition to the annexation of the islands derived from the same isolationism that dominated his view on American relations with the rest of the world. That is, he opposed overseas expansion because of its moral, strategic, and, particularly, economic dangers. As he put it succinctly, annexation "will violate our national policy since our national existence, will reject with contempt the teachings and warnings of the founders and conservators of our institutions, and open the way for untold burdens and entanglements in the future." Annexation would "bankrupt the United States and keep them in continual complication and war with the rest of the world." This was, of course, the standard argument for nonentanglement, and the *Courier-Journal* used it consistently. The editorial page often ran this quip: "Speaking of Hawaiian annexation, it is pertinent to remark that if Uncle Sam would attend to his own business he would have more business to attend to." Given the ongoing social and economic turmoil after 1893, Watterson deemed it unnecessary to involve the nation in politics abroad. "We certainly have domestic troubles enough of our own without reaching out to the four corners of the earth for others," he wrote.[25] Only later did Watterson decide that these social crises could be solved or obscured by foreign involvement.

Concentrating on domestic issues and confining foreign policy to the Western Hemisphere meant that the United States could avoid being pulled into foreign conflicts. Annexation, however, was a potentially slippery slope: "Having annexed Hawaii in order to protect Alaska, of course we shall have to annex Australia in order to protect Hawaii, and annex the moon in order to protect Australia. Our national bird was not called a spread eagle for nothing," he wrote. Watterson attacked Hawaii as a strategic "weak point" upon which the nation could be broken. It was too distant to be of strategic value, and "no battleship, coaling on the Hawaiian Islands, could reach the United States in condition to fight." The islands were not the "key" to the Pacific, as annexationists claimed. "No country that is nearly a week away by the fastest steamer can be [a] valuable key to anything, as far as we are concerned," he wrote. Other papers joined the *Courier-Journal* in making this argument. Watterson approvingly quoted the "yellow" *New York World*, which claimed that Hawaii "would be a key—a new key to unlock the vault of the Treasury and pour out a fresh flood of the people's money."[26]

Watterson's fundamental idea, common to isolationists, was to "not render our country vulnerable when it is practically invulnerable." He meant this both in a strategic and an economic sense. He therefore denigrated American naval strength—contradicting other nationalistic editorials praising it—and emphasized the burden of the very expensive, "immense navy" needed to defend the islands. "As we have not enough ships to defend our own coasts, the reasoning is that we ought to acquire territory to defend in the middle of the Pacific," he wrote. "What sort of strategy is that?" Watterson, doing his best to sound folksy, called Alfred Thayer Mahan "one of those 'dam'd literary fellers'" and recast the supposed geopolitical threats from England and Japan as "scarecrows . . . set up by men who wished to use the government for the advancement of their private interests."[27]

Watterson strongly opposed using foreign policy to protect and promote private, largely northern interests. The enemy was familiar. As it was manifestly not in the nation's interest to take Hawaii, he thought, private conspirators must be involved. This "tireless" conspiracy of private interests was interested in illegitimate government investment in undersea cables, in expanding subsidies for the merchant marine, and in "making common cause with the other Robber Barons who have just accomplished the infamy of passing the Dingley-Jones Tariff Bill." Wrapping himself in the Stars and Bars and appealing to continued southern opposition to annexation, Watterson announced, "It is only white carpetbaggers and thrifty sons of missionaries who are pushing annexation for the 'swag' that is in it." He argued that the government should be establishing and maintaining only the most general structures for trade and security and could not bow to parasites from the Northeast. In this way, he portrayed antiannexation as a southern movement as well as one broadly based on national traditions. "Hawaiian annexation is in no way a popular movement," he warned his readers, "but simply a scheme of a few self-interested conspirators."[28]

Watterson evoked his political idol Jefferson to support all of these antiexpansion arguments. He did this self-consciously, noting that expansionists of both parties and sections used Jefferson as the ultimate source of political cover: "Whenever an American feels it necessary to bolster up some political theory, whatever that theory may be, he inflates his chest, rolls his tongue and invokes the name of Thomas Jefferson. No principle, heresy or ism born in the party calling itself Democratic, and few born in the party calling itself Republican, are, if we believe their advocates, without the warrant and sanction of Thomas Jefferson. It is said that all things in religion can be proved by the Bible; so it seems that all things in politics and economics can be proved by Jefferson." Indeed, Watterson would soon write about Jefferson and the legacy of Democratic expansionism so often and at such length that other papers, even as far away as the *Salt Lake Tribune*, begged him to stop. In this case, however, Watterson quoted Jefferson's idea that it was acceptable to absorb Cuba because the island was defensible, but that "nothing should ever be accepted which would require a navy to defend it."[29] Since Hawaii was so distant, Watterson would not let the annexationists use a Jeffersonian blessing for their plan. He reserved such affirmations exclusively for the Democracy.

But Watterson did not pretend that all of the Democracy was following Jefferson's sage advice, and he spared no ridicule for these interlopers. He blasted proannexationists like the "old gentleman" John Tyler Morgan for their stupidity and venality. Morgan, the leading Democratic voice for annexation and the chairman of the Foreign Relations Committee, was singled out for his "absurd" positions. In early 1898, Watterson even attacked the senator for misrepresenting Cleveland's position on Hawaii, after Morgan rather famously and inaccurately claimed that the president had supported annexation in 1893. Cleveland publicly denied this claim, and Watterson uncharacteristically leapt to his defense and attacked Morgan for "not understand[ing] himself" or anything else.[30]

Since Morgan typically presented extreme versions of the standard arguments for annexation—especially the idea that the islands were "indispensable"—Watterson used these pronouncements to attack the whole movement. In a typical editorial titled "We Must Annex the World," Watterson followed Morgan's logic to the establishment of a world empire where "there would be no resting-place for the sole of the jingo's foot" under "the Congress of the United States of Humanity, dominated by Senator Morgan and Mr. Dole, of Hawaii." Watterson also mocked Morgan's central idea that Hawaii would protect his pet project of a Nicaraguan canal by pointing out that, from Hawaii, "it would require guns of about the same range to 'control' the Nicaraguan and Martian canals." Or, he wrote the next day, perhaps the United States should be concerned "that guns mounted on the west coast of Ireland may be made to point directly at Boston harbor, or the city of New York."[31] Watterson attacked the senator for two reasons: he wished to maintain antiannexation as the dominant southern policy, and he feared Morgan's Democratic imperialism might overly encourage McKinley.

Watterson especially did not want Morgan and others to encourage the Republicans to implement their program at home, let alone begin an overseas empire that would project Republican paternalism abroad. "The Administration had better prove its ability to properly govern the United States as they are before going over 2,000 miles out into the Pacific for new territory to govern," the editor grumbled. With McKinley in Washington, Watterson understood that the Republicans would return aggressively to their interest in holding the islands, but he did not think that the country supported such adventurism. The 1896 Republican platform stated that "the Hawaiian islands should be controlled by the United States"[32] but did not specify the exact nature of control. Watterson was vigilant for signs of an expansionist turn and unwilling to compromise. He even stopped supporting reciprocity with the islands, rejecting it as ham-fisted "aid" to the self-interested planter class in Hawaii, and began targeting the administration as a friend to this group.

Paradoxically, Watterson favored the idea of erecting a revenue tariff on Hawaiian sugar. He thought that annexation would bring "absolute free trade with the islands" but that, in the absence of that action, there was "absolutely no good reason for sacrificing revenue in favor of Hawaiian sugar producers." Watterson had never considered reciprocity with Hawaii to be "real reciprocity" or anything more than "a scheme for giving some millions of our revenue to sugar-growers in Hawaii." The United States could have been taxing Hawaiian sugar since 1873, he wrote. The arbitrary enforcement of reciprocity created inequities. If Hawaiian sugar was free, then all sugar should be free.[33]

Watterson thus argued all sides of the debate. He opposed the annexation of Hawaii because there were no new, direct economic benefits to be had. He argued that the United States already derived all the benefits of trade with Hawaii without foreign entanglement, but he also attacked the system of reciprocity that brought this trade because it diminished American revenues from sugar. And, finally, Watterson famously opposed tariffs on principle but wanted to erect one against the self-interested sugar planters of Hawaii. On some days, these three conflicting positions were presented on the editorial page at the same time.[34]

Most of Watterson's racial language also was linked with economic issues. He supplemented the image of self-interested planters exploiting the American public with the bogey of "Mongolian cheap labor." These were two easy targets, considering McKinley's support for protectionism and Morgan's pretense that foreign peoples would be welcomed into the United States. Watterson linked all members of Hawaii as equal threats to the purity of the country, as he had in 1893–94. He singled out the "cholera-stricken, God-forsaken, hell-bound Kanakas," the "Mongolians," and, with great relish, the lepers. Watterson rarely just played a race card; he drew on racial and class hierarchies to form common groups. Thus he warned of "Asiatic labor" and of the Chinese "riff-raff population" that would come to the United States to be in "unrestrained competition with American labor." Why, asked Watterson, if McKinley wanted to protect American workers against "the pauper labor of Europe," did he want to annex Hawaii, with "its thousands of coolies and Kanakas"?[35]

Morgan, the unreconstructed southerner, had adopted a line of racial accommodation while supporting Hawaiian annexation that seemed highly suspect to Watterson and other southerners. According to the senator, Hawaii should enter the Union as an equal state. Watterson could not understand how the different racial groups could possibly fit into a state of Hawaii. Surely, he thought, bringing greater racial complications upon the United States was a mistake. "Are the Kanakas, the Chinese, the Japanese and the Portuguese to be full-fledged citizens, or virtual slaves?"

"UNCLE SAM—HEAVENS, MR. M'KINLEY, HAVEN'T WE HAD ENOUGH OF THAT SORT OF THING?" *New York World* cartoon emphasizing the racist case against Hawaiian annexation, with McKinley proposing to force a savage onto Uncle Sam. Reprinted in *Louisville Courier-Journal*, November 13, 1897

he asked. If these groups were to become citizens of a state, Watterson understood that their rights would have to be limited. "A great state it will make," snorted Watterson, "with its baker's dozen of Americans and its hundred thousand of Kanakas, Chinese, Japanese, and Portuguese." Better to leave the island to its own racial chaos. This view was representative of the standard southern antiexpansionism based upon racism. Nor could Hawaii become a dumping ground for black Americans, as some suggested. The *Courier-Journal* rejected that idea as foolish, since "they are here to stay unless deported against their will, which is impracticable." Even if they were deported, it would only make Hawaii "another Hayti perhaps." In this way, during 1897, the *Courier-Journal* mirrored the racial attitudes of the American press at the time. Watterson did not differentiate himself in this respect from other southern Democrats.[36]

Watterson's fullest statement against Hawaiian annexation and the inclusion of different racial groups came at the end of the year, a time he favored for writing sweeping, ebullient editorials on important topics, perhaps because he considered his audience more attentive at this time. Certainly, his editorial "A Matter-of Fact-View" contained some of his strongest and most exaggerated language on the Hawaiian issue. This editorial was a response to a *St. Paul (MN) Pioneer Press* editorial about the assimilation of foreign peoples in earlier cases of expansion, especially Florida and Louisiana. The *Pioneer Press* saw no problems containing and controlling "Indians, Spaniards, Frenchmen and Greasers" in these earlier actions and therefore wondered why Hawaii would be a problem. Watterson, who would soon make an identical argument in favor of expansionism, at this point distinguished between indigenous Americans and other barbarians. "Indian blood was clean blood," he wrote; "it was red blood. It was rich red blood. The Indian was a savage. But he was not a mongrel. He was not a maneater. There is no naming him with the loathsome natives of the Cannibal Islands, the blood in whose veins is ashen grey, tainted through countless generations of nondescripts, the offscourings of Asian filth."[37] This sort of racism did not create a very convincing argument, but that was not the intent. "A Matter-of Fact-View" was written to appease the racism of his readership and to gird antiannexationists for the looming treaty battle in the Senate. Such writing showed how Watterson could get caught up in his own rhetoric and allow it to become overblown. In the same editorial, he slipped in attacks on the ideas that the United States needed coaling stations and that there were any economic benefits to annexation. Rather than writing yet another straightforward political or economic treatise, Watterson played to the gallery and used the crudest sort of racist rhetoric. In conjunction with his jingoistic nationalism, this sort of language inoculated him from any charges that he was insufficiently southern. Just as no one could "get ahead of him as a Democrat," no one could impugn Watterson's credibility on white supremacy. When he later converted to expansionism, Watterson again usurped this position as, in his phrasing, a simon-pure patriot beyond reproach and disagreement.

The final paragraph of this editorial, though in a jesting tone, signaled how serious Watterson was about preventing annexation. "It will take a yoke of whales and a spike-team of sea lions either to get that treaty through the Senate, or to pass a joint resolution," he wrote. "And even then, we should construct a bridge of comets and asteroids between San Francisco and Honolulu to obstruct navigation and fumigate the atmosphere." He did not believe the treaty should pass, and he refused to consider the annexationists to be anything other than a tiny, anti-Democratic cadre. Antiannexationist messages like Watterson's definitely spread through the public, the sugar industry, and the Senate, and the treaty failed to produce the necessary two-thirds majority. Watterson interpreted this failure as a victory for the Democracy as well as for the nation's traditions. Increasingly, before the Spanish-American War changed the equation, he unfavorably compared the "feeble," corrupt, and conspiratorial annexation policy of the Republicans with the continentalist vision that had guided the Democrats in the annexation of Texas. He stressed the doctrine of "consent of the governed" and asked, "Is this a time to add a number of islands 2,100 miles away, inhabited by a hostile population that can only be kept down by force?"[38] In a matter of months, Henry Watterson would galvanize his readership throughout the South, and his party, by suddenly, aggressively, and unreservedly answering yes.

The Spanish-American War had far deeper roots in the imperatives of American political economy than it did in the quick succession of faux and real crises in the first four months of 1898 that finally produced hostilities.[39] Watterson, long opposed to adventurism and entanglement to protect these same political and economic interests, finally recognized in early 1898 that only war could supply the South and the Union with the means of realizing the nation's promise and dominance. Only imperialism served the twin goals of America's expansionist tradition and newer economic objectives.

Watterson came to see war and its spoils as the quickest route to national greatness and the solution to the disharmony, unrest, and instability that had marked the previous five years. The old Confederate and even older unionist realized that war as a process and an end was not something to be feared but, rather, embraced. The editor discovered that his basic economic goals and partisan political imperatives all easily converged in a globalized imperial system. War promised to solve all the nation's ills. A moral war would "exploit the United States of America as a power among the Nations of the earth . . . reinvigorate the national spirit . . . [and] divert the spirit of domestic discontent." Furthermore, he wrote, "it will animate the rising generation of the South, demoralized and debauched by the Republican attempt at Reconstruction by force of arms, with a new impulse and a new hope. [And] it will give the West something better than inflated money to think about."[40] Despite all of this wonder, Watterson's conversion to this view occurred gradually.

Across the country, the yellow press noticeably increased its hostility toward Spain when the news broke about Spanish Minister Enrique de Lome's letter insulting McKinley's fortitude in early February 1898. The New York *Journal* typified the outraged response: it published the letter on February 9 under the great headline "Worst Insult to the United States in Its History." As usual, Watterson did not allow the *Courier-Journal* to become hysterical. The story was reported on the front page of the paper on February 10, but, in typical disdain for the yellow press, Watterson did not comment on the letter until after de Lome's resignation. On February 11, Watterson wrote a subdued piece explicitly designed to deflate the cries for war from the "extremists" and to defuse the journalist-driven crisis atmosphere. He began, bluntly, "There is no occasion for excitement over the de Lome affair." After describing the circumstances and content of the letter, Watterson advised that it was, ultimately, of no significance and should not affect national policy. He similarly discounted the influence of "sensational newspaper correspondents" and other "featherheads" upon those in power and concluded that "the de Lome incident would seem to be closed."[41]

Having long prided himself for defining journalistic ethics, Watterson took special pleasure in attacking the "cockroach lofts of the New York poster sheets" early in 1898. In previous years, he had criticized Hearst and Pulitzer for muddying the craft and moral authority of journalism. As the situation in Cuba intensified, Watterson continued to group sensationalistic reporting alongside political jingoism, describing both as the refuge of knaves. To Watterson, both threatened the integrity of the public discourse and the national good. "The yellow journals substitute mendacity for enterprise," he explained. Despite the small cosmetic changes made to the *Courier-Journal* since 1897, Watterson had rather resolutely kept his paper from becoming sensationalistic. He presented his strong opposition to the venal yellow press as a sign of honor and sagacity. As might be expected, he considered himself to be the avatar of true journalism as much as of true politics. He shared this outlook with other southern and midwestern papers. According to historian George W. Auxier, these papers had "a decided provincial antipathy to the 'yellow sheets' of the East." Other historians have also contrasted midwestern reporting and attitudes with the archetypal sensationalism of the New York press.[42]

Despite Auxier's grouping of Watterson's approach with those of Democratic and Republican papers north of the Ohio River, the editor considered himself and his paper to be southern, not midwestern. Consequently, he did not have the commercial incentives to radically alter the paper's appearance and style in line with the yellow press. Watterson's stock-in-trade remained editorial power and the interpretation of events in a manner useful to his readers. Yellow journals used sensationalism to sell newspapers, whereas Watterson used his own persona and his ability to frame the issues in interesting and politically persuasive ways. Readers turned to Marse Henry to clarify the issues. His volcanic language eliminated much of the need for sensationalistic flash. Throughout the period of the Spanish-American War, the *Courier-Journal*'s main distribution, audience, and competition were in the former Confederacy. This orientation allowed the paper to ignore the sensationalist tactics of the East Coast in favor of a style of argument and declaration more suited to particular regional concerns.

The major Democratic papers throughout the South replicated Watterson's reliance upon rhetorical substance rather than sensationalistic flash, largely because of the political imperatives of southern political culture, which rewarded and demanded such a role for its opinion leaders. Southerners looking for insight into the complex issues of the day turned to the major newspapers for guidance more directly than did readers in other areas of the country. Joseph Bryan of the *Richmond Times* became a sharp critic of yellow journalism when he began to push an expansionist position quite close to that of Watterson. Other New South editors, like Edwin B. Craighead of the *Mobile Register* and Daniel Tompkins of the *Charlotte Observer*, also grounded their arguments in the particular imperatives of the southern system. All of these men reflected the region as much as they affected it. They made careful editorial decisions based on perhaps equal measures of broad ideological and economic calculations, but their final interest was in choosing the direction of the Democratic Party and maintaining a focus on southern development.

The major New South editors could not simply create "public opinion" on war and expansion in the South, as some have argued. Rather, they sought to dominate the style and substance of public discourse on these issues. Like his fellow editors, Watterson was less concerned with winning readers and increasing advertising in the short term than he was with gaining political adherents and allies in the long term. He tried to force change by commandeering the very structure of political discussion. Once in control of the public discourse, he thought, he could effectively shape the Democratic Party's positions and produce his final political program. Although he failed to convince the party on almost every issue save the tariff, Watterson did find success in shaping and dominating the broader debates.[43]

The *Courier-Journal* was not entirely an exception to the war hysteria that riddled the nation's press. Like its contemporaries all over the country, Watterson's paper increased its coverage of the Cuban situation as tensions on the island and anticipation at home grew. If it never became breathless, the *Courier-Journal* definitely exploited the growing tensions between the United States and Spain to the fullest extent possible. The explosion of the battleship *Maine* in Havana harbor on February 15, 1898, was a watershed event that finalized the growing journalistic frenzy and the nation's slide into war.[44] The incident also inaugurated the move of the *Courier-Journal* toward what should be described as a war footing.

When the "Horror at Havana" was first reported, the paper treated it not as an act of war but as a "calamity." Both the headline type and the illustrations were very large for several days, spanning seven columns and dominating the front page. The front page covered the inquiry into the explosion for the entire month. The paper ran no editorial comment for two days after the explosion, and when it finally appeared, the discussion was subdued. Editorials over several days stressed the mysterious nature of the explosion, the likelihood that it was an accident or unsolvable, and the belief that the common sense of the American people would keep peaceful interests in the fore. The *Courier-Journal* was willing to wait for the investigation by a federal tribunal before passing judgment or leaping to paranoid conclusions. After all, when the *Maine* was launched in 1895, the *Courier-Journal* had written about its "defects" and declared it a "second class" ship. Once again now, Watterson linked the excesses of the hysterical press and the opportunistic jingoes. The "whole yellow pack is in full yell," he wrote in a nice phrasing, but he believed that the people would resist. Despite that "the American people" were "a high-spirited and fearless people," Watterson was confident that they were "not going to get their facts from the yellow brigade of the press or the yellow brigade of the politicians."[45]

Watterson at first had nothing but praise for the caution and nonpartisanship of the McKinley administration. Shortly after the explosion, he counseled the public to ignore the feeling of uncertainty, the stock market fluctuations, and the other indications of "ticklish times" and, instead, to expect peace. Although there was no evidence of Spanish involvement in the *Maine* incident, several editorials warned that if indeed "Spanish treachery" were involved, then the United States would "strike back first and discuss terms of peace afterward." Entire issues of the paper were devoted to maps of Cuba, the positions of U.S. and Spanish ships, and the preparations for war.[46]

By the second week in March, Watterson experienced a sudden conversion to the complementary programs of military preparedness and "Cuba Libre!" This transformation jettisoned years of (somewhat varying) support for foreign nonentanglement, reversed a similarly long-standing commitment to smaller government, and defied the positions of the party Watterson had spent all of the difficult year of 1897 trying to court as well as rebuild. When he glimpsed the potential gains of a war against Spain for his new New Departure, Watterson decided that party issues should take a back seat during a war. Rather than make a divisive political issue out of involvement, he decided to exploit the emerging opportunities. As a first step in this new direction, he joined the movement to rebuild the American military. Again, the news coverage in the *Courier-Journal* signaled the change before the requisite editorials were released. On March

10, the entire front page was dedicated to preparedness, the *Maine*, and defense spending. The editorial page, however, only briefly mentioned the need to be ready for war.[47]

Even though he would soon argue that the Democracy could not be caught failing to support preparedness and militance, Watterson could not resist injecting some partisanship into the preparedness debate by attacking one of his perennial targets: the "pension raiders." He had long considered the Civil War pension issue to be an odious drain on the nation's treasury, second in its destructiveness only to the protective tariff. Both were symbols of Republican corruption and the continued subordination of the South. This was more than mere rhetoric. The pensions were indeed a significant drain on the federal budget, and historian Richard Franklin Bensel has argued persuasively that the complementary system of protective tariffs and military pensions was in fact the basis for northern economic and Republican political domination in the late nineteenth century. The American military was weak in 1898, Watterson wrote, because the Republican "politicians have squandered our money on the survivors of past wars instead of making ready for future wars." Had that money been put to better use, the United States would have a first-class rather than a fourth-class navy. Watterson had, of course, only shortly before, argued that it was precisely the nation's weak naval power that kept it out of unnecessary trouble abroad, but that position disappeared given the juicy opportunity to attack the pensions.[48] It is striking how, in times of war and political expediency, logic can reverse course.

Although opposed to self-interested spending, Watterson was not averse to spending money on arms or to joining forces with the Republican Party on the Cuban issue. The same day he ridiculed the Republican pension raiders, Watterson called for rebuilding the American merchant marine with government funds. This was the position for which he had castigated McKinley the previous year. Outside the context of war, Watterson viewed such aid as tribute to the private sector. Shortly thereafter, the *Courier-Journal* called for the development of a top-notch navy with all American-made ships, attacked the Spanish as bankrupt and failing, and praised McKinley's nonpartisanship in the preparedness campaign. The newly aggressive Watterson called for the country to "rise to a broader plane of patriotism" instead of "partisanism."[49]

In a long, historical editorial on these themes, titled "Politics and

War," Watterson sought to prevent the "intrusion of politics into a question that is not partisan." He cautioned his party not to make either of the classic mistakes of all minority parties in times of war: to criticize the persecution of the war for political gain or, conversely, to support the losing side of the war. As war seemed inevitable, he sought to ensure that the Democracy would not be tainted by an unpatriotic and unprofitable antiwar position. He offered examples of the Federalist Party's opposition to the War of 1812 leading to its demise; the Whig opposition to the Mexican War, which he believed finally killed it; and, of course, the Democrats' stance during the Civil War. That disastrous party position had handed the Republicans the federal government through the Cleveland era. Watterson appealed to the Democracy and to the South to avoid making this mistake again. And he did so in a declared spirit of national unity rather than from partisanship or selfishness.[50]

In so doing, he temporarily abandoned the party spirit that had always animated his foreign policy critiques and tariff agitation. Instead of seeking immediate political gain, as might have been expected given his natural Democratic instincts and well-established practice, Watterson rejected utilizing the current situation for political purposes. "The question of peace or war should not be made a party question," he declared. "It is beneath the dignity of the subject to discuss it on party grounds."[51] Much of the shift resulted from his quick realization that the war was going to be both popular and successful. Watterson wanted a share of the glory and the spoils for the South and for himself.

This idea that war should not be sullied with politics was very unusual for Watterson, but understandable in terms of the hierarchy of his beliefs. His dominant focus had always been the political dimension of all matters of public interest. He searched for the single great issue of the time to exploit effectively. This was particularly true for issues of both commercial significance and political expediency. After the successive party disasters of 1896–97, Watterson was not going to let the many potential gains of a war with Spain escape the Democracy.

Watterson's increasingly pro-war editorials in March and April 1898 clearly demonstrated a belief that war was an excellent vehicle for a Democratic Party resurgence. It is a bit glib, but not wholly inaccurate, to describe him as caught up in war fever. Watterson did not dwell at first on the economic or political consequences of the war, or on its potential gains, but wrote of war strictly in terms of its more attractive symbolic meanings. He showed a remarkable willingness to suspend, but not abandon, discussion of his deeply held political positions and regional goals. For the time being, he created a new set of slogans befitting a newly vibrant Union on the way to war, reveling in the "extremely dramatic tone to the opening of a struggle."[52]

In itself, Watterson's separation of war and politics for the purposes of national unity and rhetorical power was a profoundly political act. He understood that he could not allow Republicans to claim the war as their own, and he could not let a neocopperhead element rise again to bedevil the healing Democratic Party. The nation had not experienced a war in a generation, he wrote (ignoring the Indian wars), and initially it would be electrified by the experience. Once the initial war bloom faded, however, it would take a focused effort to offset the development of a "popular clamor" for results. To channel the civic energies properly, Watterson called for the recognition of "fixed principles" of political leadership. He stressed that only a few foolish politicians might disagree with militance; "in the present crisis the American people have forgotten party considerations and are united."[53] For the previous few years, Watterson had tended to write his editorials toward specific groups: gold Democrats, manly Kentuckians, conservative-minded southerners. In this period, he more often addressed the nebulous "American people," presuming, by this phrasing, the ability to speak for them all instead of only for the Democrats. He may have believed that the people actually were united, and that was why he wanted the Democracy to capitalize on this moment. As he usually did, Watterson warned politicians to follow the will of the people as he interpreted it. He further demanded unanimity in public opinion on preparing for war.

Watterson also separated the issue of Cuban independence from politics. If war were to begin and become a bipartisan issue, then Watterson wanted to ensure that the Republicans could not claim to be the sole saviors of Cuba. His editorials now treated the revolution as a matter of universal interest and support. Neither "the American people" nor "civilization" could "ignore this horrible condition of affairs" any longer, he lectured. In the editorial in which he made this statement and reversed his earlier writings, he repeated as a mantra the phrase he had a short time earlier sidestepped: "Cuba Must be Free." Almost a week later, he wrote "The Time Has Come." In this editorial, which traced American Cuba policy back to Cleveland, Watterson argued that independence for

Cuba and the end of Spanish misrule had been the essential Democratic policy from the start. "We expect to stop this some time; we should stop it now," announced Watterson. "To delay action further would be a crime against humanity." Watterson thus easily conflated and simplified the issues of Cuban independence, war, and national unity to remove any possible negative political repercussions for the Democrats. In this expedient frame of mind, he argued that "the question of humanity is not a party question; the question of the liberation of Cuba is not a party question; [and] the question of Americanism is not a party question. When we go to war it will be as the nation of the United States, not as any particular political party."[54]

Warming to the idea of a war at the end of March, Watterson wholly accepted that a war with Spain would double as a war of national liberation for Cuba. Watterson disregarded the need to wait for the impending release of the court of inquiry report about the *Maine* explosion, arguing that even the devastation of the ship paled in comparison to Spain's responsibility for "the destruction of Cuba." It was time to act, although the United States still needed a specific casus belli. For support, Watterson referred to "the general sentiment of the American people," the "manhood of America," and the "united and determined people." True to his word, to avoid the party issues, Watterson claimed that the reason for his shift in opinion was Republican senator Redfield Proctor of Vermont's powerful and understated speech on the situation in Cuba. Now that the nation knew the truth of Cuban suffering from a man of honor, not merely the lies and exaggerations of jingoes, it was time to act.[55]

Amid his numerous flip-flops, Watterson refused to compromise on the assertion that this universal fight for Cuban independence had to be exactly that—a war of liberation from all control. "Humanity demands that Cuba shall be free of Spain," he declared, "and Americanism demands that the United States shall be free of Cuba." The independence of Cuba, which Watterson had long sidestepped as a matter of national policy, had now become that special mix of universal and national interest. Watterson remained, from this point forward, steadfastly opposed to anything but close (and free) trade relations with Cuba until such time that Cuba petitioned for entry to the United States. In this sense, his prowar and anticolonial rhetoric actually had some substance. Although he could not claim to have supported action before the clamor for war gained strength nationwide (another example of Watterson following and not creating popular political opinion), he never wavered from the position that Cuba deserved independence from any sort of colonial rule, Spanish, American, or otherwise.[56]

The fullest statement of Watterson's reformulated approach to "the Situation and the Obligation" appeared on March 28, in a multicolumn format that had previously been reserved for major editorials on topics such as Populism and Democratic Party reorganization. The language was free-form, hyperbolic, and quite florid, as his larger pronouncements tended to be. It covered all the major aspects of his worldview, especially his idea that the United States was destined for greatness and world power. Watterson was still convinced that these ends were compatible with political isolationism. He pronounced that "a state of war exists between the United States and Spain" and proceeded to attack Spanish rule, character, history, and morality back to the time of Phillip II, a period he characterized as that "horrible, ghastly phantasmagoria of human woe!" After a long treatise on the horrors endured in Cuba, Watterson announced that "if the *Courier-Journal* were President of the United States it would not be halting for a policy." That policy was part humanitarian crusade and part free trade imperialism.[57]

Watterson envisioned a war fought solely on Cuba's behalf and the establishment of its independence under American protection and assistance. Protection and tutelage of an independent Cuba could potentially solve all of the problems facing the United States in the short term and would guarantee painless incorporation of a failed Cuban republic at some point in the future. "Upon the material side we have nothing to fear from war," he wrote optimistically. The United States could act proactively now and continuously reap the benefits. Watterson claimed that this war of plenty was also one of the deepest morality. Having described the brutal experience of Cuba under the Spanish and disputed the opinions of antiwar naysayers, Watterson reversed his own, earlier comments about the fitness of Cuba for self-government. "Admitting that the insurgents do not seem to be exactly the best materials out of which to make republicans," Watterson nevertheless supported experimenting with Cuban independence until it proved a clear failure. In fact, he considered temporary but real independence not only a vote of confidence in Cuba but a positive step for the United States.[58]

To support this position, Watterson borrowed much of the imagery of the traditional imperialists. Drawing deeply from paternalistic constructions of American power, he envisioned the United States nurturing Cuba as it would a child:

> To set up in the Queen of the Antilles, a little sister Republic—to see this little sister—to guide with gentle hand her early footsteps—to pin her bib and tucker round her neck—to keep the dogs away—and when she is able to go alone, to say "God Bless you, little sister," is to set an inspiration in the cold heart of this commercialized, materialized generation of Americans, which will elevate and strengthen the national character and, mayhap, be a means of extricating us from bossism and ring rule, from more office-seeking and money-getting, the bane of the present, the danger of the future.[59]

How exactly Cuban independence would produce reform of the boss system and end materialism at home he left tantalizingly vague. These arguments were, however, classic Watterson. When he considered his argument infallible, he saw no reason to limit the discussions of its advantages to anything less than unprecedented excellence. He shortly would begin to claim, fantastically but seriously, that war and expansion would usher in a classless and racially harmonious society.

Significantly, Watterson largely abandoned the Cuban race issue he had discussed in previous editorials in favor of a more benign paternalism. No longer needing arguments of racial exclusiveness, he quickly dropped them. Instead, as he had in the case of the freed slaves during Reconstruction, Watterson viewed the issue of race in pragmatic terms. He refused to allow racial questions to interfere with what he saw as the more important political-economic issues. Thus he became willing to welcome the "plenty of highly educated and patriotic Cubans" as American citizens when they decided to join the United States. Watterson envisioned Cuba's being rapidly "Americanized," as Texas had been, and slowly coming firmly into the American orbit. "Perhaps," he winked, "they might take [American consul general to Cuba] Fitz Lee for their first President."[60]

Having aligned himself in favor of a war with Spain for Cuban independence, Watterson turned his attention to McKinley and the need for immediate action. Until McKinley sent the war message to Congress on April 11, Watterson experimented with a variety of techniques, ranging from cajoling to threatening, to encourage war. He both praised McKinley and warned him to follow the sentiment of Congress, mirroring the efforts of politicians of both parties. "There is no necessity for a long [war] message," Watterson advised the president. "It can be put in two words—'sick 'em.'"[61]

At times, the last one on the wagon becomes the loudest. On two consecutive days, Watterson even renounced and apologized for his earlier reluctance to recognize Cuban belligerency. He called it "a grave mistake . . . of restraining our better nature in a smug observation of so-called international punctilio." Therefore, he resolved, "let the blow be as swift as our decision has been tardy." As the war parties eagerly awaited McKinley's message in early April, the *Courier-Journal*'s news reporting became almost entirely absorbed with the war. The paper ran front-page cartoons showing an American eagle attacking Spanish vultures, dwelled on the differences between the war-making capabilities of the "Anglo-Saxon" and "Latin" races, and devoted whole sections to rumors of war. The editorial pages were similarly consumed by the war. By Sunday, April 10, Watterson's war mania hit high gear, and he wholly rejected all compromise and negotiations with Spain. America's patience had been pushed to its limits, and still Spain did not "understand the Anglo-Saxon blood." Therefore, in clichéd but direct tones, he called for "the universal language that is spoken from the cannon's mouth."[62]

McKinley's war message of April 11 disappointed both Watterson and aggressive members of Congress. At some length, the president recounted conditions on the island, the disruption of American commerce, the path of negotiations with Spain, and the independence issue. Like Watterson, McKinley looked to both Andrew Jackson and the annexation of Texas as the appropriate "safe precedent" against expansion. Unlike the editor, McKinley thought it was not "wise or prudent for this Government to recognize at the present time the independence of the so-called Cuban Republic" in the absence of an appropriate government. The president did not even call for an immediate declaration of war but, rather, "measures to secure a full and final termination of hostilities."[63] McKinley did not present a war with Spain in the apocalyptic, transformative, and moralistic fashion of Watterson, and thus he came under attack.

Watterson, in conjunction with other Democratic papers, criticized McKinley for his indecision, for his unwillingness to accept Cuban independence, and for his request for "a power which should not be placed, and was not intended to by the founders of our Government to be placed, in the hands of one man." For several days following McKinley's war message, the *Courier-Journal* dissected the speech's flaws. Even in his war fever, Watterson refused to acquiesce in the expansion of executive power and firmly argued that Congress "should surrender it[s war powers] to no one." He called for Congress to take "the Cuban question into its own hands."[64]

Despite his rhetoric of reconciliation in the face of war, Watterson had no interest in abandoning partisan attack. The day McKinley delivered his message to Congress, Watterson ran a huge editorial, spanning several columns, titled "Some of the Whys and the Wherefores," that focused on war as a political issue. In it he skewered various voices of calm and pacifism, including George Foster Peabody, E. L. Godkin of the *New York Evening Post*, Carl Schurz, and all other "professional Mugwumps." This vicious partisan attack came from the man who had repeatedly sworn that the war was not a party question. Indeed, the day before, the *Courier-Journal* had run a cartoon in which Uncle Sam sat in a cannon cart pulled by a donkey and an elephant. "We'll turn them loose Monday," the top stated, referring to McKinley's impending message. On the bottom was written the moral "When These Horses Do Work Together They're the Best Team on Earth." In the end of his April 11 editorial, Watterson predicted confidently that the Democrats could use the war to reunify after the bolt of 1896, to reaffirm the "real national interest," and, finally, to "sweep the country."[65]

In the meantime, Watterson chastised antiwar reformers. He attacked mugwumps of the pacifist stripe for "pretend[ing] the world would be utterly too-too" and not understanding the need for vigorous action against Spain. The war, he demanded, would be first about freeing Cuba, second about forcing Spain to pay for "her treachery and inhumanity," and finally about teaching the world "that the United States of America is a nation, with the biggest kind of capital N." Antiwar attitudes, on the other hand, were craven and feminine and would "emasculate the human species."[66]

In following this line of thought, Watterson wrote such a blue streak against the mugwumps that it is worth quoting at length. This selection unifies his masterful writing style, his sometimes errant irrationality, and his fusion of all political, social, and economic questions into a single line of argument centered on the dangers of national emasculation.

> The writer of these lines, being the only offspring of the seventh daughter of the seventh son, knows all things, he is omniscient;

> all that was and ever will be has been revealed to him; indeed, having committed no sin, and done no wrong, having, in point of fact, gone on from grace to grace until he has arrived at a state of perfection, he don't mind telling the believing reader exactly what will happen when the world of real men and women has been unsexed, when the existing race of men and women has changed places, when luxury and vice have expelled toil and trouble, and Mr. Bellamy's co-operative society of amalgamated idiots has made life so easy that one has only to touch a button to draw a cork, or even a straight flush—as a body might say—and in short and fine, when every woman wears seven league boots and every man is his own baby-jumper! Know then that, just beyond the North Pole . . . is a thin, perpendicular sheet of ice. This sheet of ice is precisely like the drop curtain of a theater, but behind it are things more curious and terrible than were ever known in any theater. . . . On the outer side—that is on our side of this sheet or wall of ice—are great festoons of snow. . . . But on the other side, after the struggling tourist has passed a gulf of boiling ether, there is a world much bigger than the world we inhabit. This world has no seasons. It is perpetual summer there. The average height of the men is fifty feet; though of course there are people of undersize, from forty to forty-five feet, with the occasional hunchbacks and dwarfs of thirty. They are impervious to shot and shell; and their daily diet is dynamite. They are waiting to devour us and our little mimic world. About the time the modern reformers have succeeded in emasculating the human species, some fool with a pickax will break through the thin partition of ice which separates us from the real blood-and-iron world of the Amasagoosians, and they will swoop down upon us, a thousand million strong, and swallow us, the he women and she men, boots, babies and all, just as an elephant might swallow a mosquito![67]

In this part of the editorial, Watterson dissects and lampoons the "lucubrations of the paper warriors" by becoming a paper warrior of the highest order. Much of this was pure nonsense and pure style, demonstrating the final return of Watterson's self-confidence after the troubles of 1897. The tone of righteousness and attack, allied with an utter ridiculousness, would come to characterize many of Watterson's editorials over the next several years. Watterson often digressed from topical matters to the dangers of emasculation, equating all positions that opposed his own with femininity and weakness. From a serious pretext—in this case the complementary needs to go to war to free Cuba, to fulfill American destiny, and to silence critics—Watterson embarked upon a self-consciously ridiculous diatribe that ultimately fused his anxieties about gender roles, utopianism, and social disorder into a single, joyous attack on mugwumpery and pacifism.

Much of this type of writing was entertainment designed to bolster the image of a sassy and slightly loony Marse Henry. It also demonstrated a willingness to resort to pure style when reason failed and when repetition of a single point might have outlived its editorial utility. This was precisely the kind of bombast that was reprinted in the national press, rather than another pedestrian appeal for Cuba Libre. Watterson knew how to make news as well as interpret it. His standard practice was now to print his editorials spanning several columns, as if his ideas and the prospect of war with Spain were too exciting and significant to be contained in the traditional layouts. It was not unusual for his editorials to fill six columns a day. On this huge canvas, Watterson continued to print many more mainstream arguments as well, centering on criticism of McKinley.

Watterson further attacked insufficient war fever on both moralistic and political grounds. "Surely never had a nation greater provocation to go to war," he wrote in full battle cry. Spain was barbaric, exterminationist, arrogant, indecent, and graceless. The United States was "a perpetual peril to monarchy," and Watterson believed it was time to eliminate any calculations of foreign opinion in American policy. In fact, he broached the idea of fighting a crusade against monarchism in the New World, which directly contravened his earlier intonations against ideologically driven crusades abroad. "The slime of this old serpent of Europe has been too long over the fairest island of the New World [and] God is tired of kings," he wrote. A few days later, he pronounced the crusade against monarchism in the New World the moral equivalent of the American Revolution and the battle against slavery. Given the sacred nature of this struggle, Watterson attacked the "featherheaded maniacs who are bellowing for war only for war's sake," as well as those who supported "war for revenue only."[68]

The war was sure to have political repercussions, and antiwar elements in the Democratic Party faced political destruction. Assuring his readers that "the *Courier-Journal* is a friend, not the enemy of the Administration," Watterson averred that bad advice and bad policy could not be tolerated. Believing, and perhaps hoping, that McKinley's "colorless" message made him and the Republican Party vulnerable, Watterson declared that Cuba had to be free by November 1, or the people would destroy the party and "every public man who supports its timorous, heartless and time-serving policy." He was especially confident that those who had so bedeviled the gold Democrats in 1896, the Populist South and West, "will not leave a grease spot of the recreant who plays into the hands of Spain." Again, Watterson easily slipped into his comfortable role as partisan agitator. Partisanship, it seemed, was acceptable to Watterson only if it threatened harm to the Republican Party. Otherwise, the times demanded nonpartisan patriotism.[69]

Watterson supported the Senate war resolution because of the Teller Amendment, which denied "any disposition of intention to exercise sovereignty, jurisdiction, or control over said island except for pacification," and the Turpie-Foraker Amendment, which signaled recognition of the Cubans as "the true and lawful government of that island." He welcomed the strong declaration of Cuban independence and the establishment of "a free government on the island based upon the consent of the governed." Though he expected a strong movement toward annexation, Watterson thought it "would only mean more trouble," and he was quick also to establish that the federal government would never accept responsibility for the Cuban bonds. In the end, more than half of the votes for Cuban independence were cast by southerners.[70]

Alongside this aggressive support for an independent Cuba, the *Courier-Journal* (like most of the country) remained entirely silent about other Spanish possessions, save for one brief discussion of Puerto Rico. In this case, the paper declared, "Although small, it is a very desirable island." Since there was no revolt going on there, Watterson felt justified in casting a covetous eye. He discussed the island's commercial, strategic, and agricultural benefits in purely self-interested terms. In early April, the *Courier-Journal* announced that, after the war, Spain should not retain title to any island in the hemisphere, and Puerto Rico should be given the chance to request entry into the United States as part of "the general settlement." It is important to note that Watterson advocated a voluntary union rather than a forcible land grab.[71]

Despite these early expansionist stirrings, Watterson believed that the United States was going to war for honorable reasons. Even in his war fever, he did not accept any action that lacked propriety as he defined it. Watterson saw only purity in the American cause. Simultaneously, he called for the war for Cuban independence in violation of his long-held national principles and in defense of newfound traditions he had only begun to recognize as legitimate. When, on April 20, McKinley signed the joint congressional resolution and war looked to be inevitable, Watterson eagerly discounted any possibility of a peaceful settlement that might interrupt the unfolding of a war as passion play.

To bolster his case, Watterson attacked those who were, self-interestedly, mere "patriots for revenue only," as well as those "featherheaded maniacs" who wanted war merely for the sake of war. He wrote editorials that downplayed the congressional disputes over Cuban independence and self-government and announced that "bickering and caviling are swept away, factions and divisions are closed up. We are Americans all, for America against the World." He pedaled low-grade jingoism in an editorial titled "Right or Wrong, Our Country." In the boldest possible terms, Watterson presented the upcoming war as one massive struggle between "liberty and despotism," between "the twentieth century and the twelfth." He also, expectedly, equated the American cause with masculinity by describing the war as one between "manhood and kingcraft," a battle waged "by men against monkeys." In this final confrontation, he argued, the United States would usher in an era in which the autocracies of the Old World were banished from the Western Hemisphere forever and the power of the United States was respected and feared worldwide.[72]

Watterson's belief in the morality and honor of the war was more deeply held than one might initially suppose. He did place an importance on notions of national honor and moral right that went beyond his immediate interest in rallying public support and reflected his southern character. He had, after all, fought for the Confederacy despite a deeply ingrained unionism and antipathy to slavery. He had served out of a sense of obligation to his native South. In 1898 Watterson saw the opportunity for an honorable war to be fought by the whole country, which he hoped would erase the divisions created at Fort Sumter. He therefore continued to stress the idea that the war was a just war utterly bereft of self-interest, although he certainly recognized its potential benefits. Only later did he stress these more concrete motivations.

When bidding farewell to the Kentucky troops during a speech in Lexington on May 27, 1898, Watterson spoke primarily in terms of the

"YOU WANT ALL THE WAR NEWS." Top half of a full-page ad promising the best, "fresh and hot" Spanish-American War coverage in the region. The "CUBA MUST BE FREE" cannon at the top glorifies the slogan Watterson once belittled. *Louisville Courier-Journal*, May 8,

war's morality and the soldier's honorable duty. To be sure, he delivered a typical military farewell, even declaring it "sweet to die for one's country." He also announced, in Rooseveltian fashion, that "there is something even worse than war," meaning the pursuit of luxury, sloth, and "a few degrading dollars" instead of national glory. Echoing his language of the previous weeks, Watterson again connected insufficient nationalism and pacifism with social chaos and femininity. He told the departing soldiers, "Through the systematic violation of natural laws and amid artificial class distinctions and hideous contrasts of life, to emasculate the Anglo-Saxon species in America [was] . . . even worse than war." On the other hand, a war for Cuban independence would create much "less talk of the mass and the class from now on" and would provide stability and order for the nation. He argued that "the strengthening of national feeling and the obliteration of class distinctions that will follow will be more to us by far than the war will cost."[73]

The bulk of this speech, however, sailed beyond platitudes and imperialist rhetoric to concentrate on the morality and magnificence of fighting Spain as a united nation. Watterson anointed the war as the "first time since the Crusades [that] war has been levied for no cause of a purely material kind." He told the soldiers not to march under the cry "Remember the *Maine*," because it was "too revengeful." Rather, he advised them to dedicate themselves to the glory of liberating Cuba and to the greater glory of fighting to prove that the national union was solid. In a pointed phrase, Watterson announced that war "emancipated both sections of the Union from the mistaken impression that we were, or ever could be, anything else than one people."[74]

In his editorials, Watterson emphasized that the war fulfilled the promises of union forged during the Civil War, and he equated the war against slavery with the new one against Spain. In this sense, he found some inevitability, and a great deal of desirability, in the reunited nation's fighting a foreign war. He ridiculed peace supporters in the United States (inexplicably described as "those who diet on rice and peer through blue goggles") as overly legalistic and fearful. "If they had prevailed [in 1860]," he announced, "America to-day would be a slave-holding nation."[75]

Watterson's interest in proving the South's patriotism through war, his eagerness for redemption through battle, and his interest in leaving the "ignoble ruts" of the Populist years behind were all widely shared by southerners. It was one of the most notable legacies of the war for the South. The *Raleigh News and Observer* announced happily that "the war will kill sectionalism as nothing else could do. With Southern men bearing arms for old glory, no bloody shirt waver can hereafter obtain an audience." Gaines M. Foster argues that support for the Spanish-American War granted old Confederates both legitimacy and a new pride in the "Confederate celebration" that was ongoing in southern culture and brought about a "deeper sectional reconciliation."[76]

The reconciliation issue resonated deeply with Watterson's southern audience, and he never hesitated to trot out his purplest orations. At a celebration of Ulysses S. Grant's birthday at the Waldorf-Astoria Hotel in New York at the start of the war, on April 27, 1898, Watterson responded to the toast "the Reunited Sections" by declaring, "We are the most homogenous people on the face of the globe." He told the audience, "The true American neither consults geography nor counts the cost" of going to war with Spain. In later years, Watterson often described this reconciliation as the grandest of the many legacies of the war. He declared that only a "patriot and hero like William McKinley" could have laid the bloody shirt to rest by placing Joseph Wheeler and Fitzhugh Lee in charge of the war effort. War was "a scourge, [but] also a purifier," he wrote at war's end. "It has wiped out sectional lines and made us a united people as never before since the ratification of the Constitution."[77]

Watterson presented the triumph of national union as a teleology in which the reconciliation of the Union and the attainment of world imperial power jointly solved the problems of crass commercialism, Populist radicalism, and femininity that were the root causes of national stagnation. Watterson believed that the war finally unleashed southern regeneration and national advancement and provided a catalyst for lasting political cohesion. He described this belief in the preface to his *History of the Spanish-American War*:

> It annihilated sectional lines and solidified the nation. It proclaimed us a nation among the nations of the earth; no longer a huddle of petty sovereignties held together by a rope of sand. It dissipated at once and forever the notion that we are a race of mercenary shopkeepers, worshipping rather the brand upon the dollar than the eagle on the shield. . . . It rescued us from the turbulent discussion of many misleading questions of domestic economy, uplifting and enlarging all our national perspectives. Above all, it elevated, broadened, and vitalized the manhood of the rising generation of Americans.[78]

Watterson emphasized these blessings of war as part of his long pursuit of national reconciliation and the end of sectionalism. It also formed part of his common appeal to southern nationalism. Marshall E. Schott argues that self-interest took precedence over the desire for "national reconciliation and sectional redemption . . . in shaping the South's view of events in Cuba." Indeed, Watterson placed great emphasis on the idea that the war offered the South a new opportunity to concentrate fully on economic development instead of being sidetracked by old sectional or racial issues. As historian Patrick J. Heardon persuasively argues, however, "Neither the sectional conflict nor the [South's] effort to shape foreign policy ended with the Spanish-American War."[79] In Watterson's mind, the final settlement of the union and class issues at home allowed the South to focus anew on the benefits of activist foreign affairs.

Accordingly, Watterson accepted, supported, and used the old Confederate celebrations that permeated southern politics and culture to bolster support for his new national program of territorial and market expansion. "We are all Americans . . . but 'Dixie' is our war song, and ours alone," he wrote at the war's onset. Watterson and other opinion leaders in the New South considered unionism and expansionism to be equally desirable outcomes of the war. Both were likewise central to southern development. One year after the war, at a famous dedication of Union soldiers' graves in Louisville on May 30, 1899, Watterson clearly connected these ideas. He discussed southern advance in a system of war and expansion under the newly unified nation. Finally, he told the crowd, "the Confederacy, swallowed by the Union, lives again in American manhood and brotherhood." Sectionalism and racial problems were over. Although he was dedicating Civil War graves, Watterson looked toward the future meaning of the Spanish-American War. He saw the triumph in that war, coming after the great conflagration of 1865, as "God's promise redeemed." The imperialist period inaugurated by the war was the final fulfillment of the nation's promise: "The heroes of the new North and the new South . . . have side by side re-emblazoned the National character in the waters about Corregidor Island."[80] National union and economic development in the post–Civil War era were merely the first, preparatory steps toward imperial glory and great power.

6

War Has Its Compensations

> Expansion and Imperialism, we are their friends.
>
> —Henry Watterson, March 27, 1900

As soon as it became clear that the Spanish-American War was going to change domestic politics as well as the international stance of the United States, Henry Watterson searched for "The Issue" that the Democrats had to seize to win the White House in 1900. As the war brought forward "new issues and new men," Watterson called for disregarding all of the old issues in order to dominate these new ones. He sought a single overarching and unifying matter to serve as both the anchor for his party and a suitable foreign policy for the nation during the new century. After some vacillation, he concluded that territorial expansion and the extension of the area of international free trade through American leadership were the winning issues in both of these senses. His move toward support for expansion was slow to develop but, like all of his other positions over the years, all-consuming and unrelenting when it arrived. A single dose of free trade expansionism would eliminate the twin dangers of Populist-inspired experimentation and Republican protectionism. It would also provide an opportunity for the Democratic Party to heal itself after the debacle of 1896. Imperialism and globalization would lead the way toward a successful New Departure for the South.

After decades of partisan agitation for free trade, a conservative social order, and an independent and prosperous South, Watterson came to believe that only an imperial foreign policy was the answer to all of his goals. Although excited and even breathless at times, he was not merely intoxicated by the war. He sought a real solution to the intractable problems of overproduction, stagnant markets, Populist agitation, political subordination, and high tariffs that bedeviled the South. Accordingly, he directed his political and editorial efforts from the spring of 1898 through the end of 1900 toward convincing southerners of the need to adopt a new and aggressive posture in the world. Watterson told his readers that only through American expansionism could the South finally realize the economic development and dominance that had eluded it since Reconstruction. "War is an engine of waste," he advised, but "it has its compensations."[1] Here, at last, he thought he had found the firm ground on which the Democracy and the South could be reborn. In his mind, expansionism meant a victory for free trade that was otherwise unattainable.

As soon as he realized what was at stake, Watterson abandoned his long-standing misgivings about adventurism abroad and began to propagandize for imperialism with all of his power. In the middle of the Spanish-American War, he convinced himself that imperial expansion might also provide the political success that had consistently eluded him since the tariff battles of the 1880s. He thought that the anti-imperialists—like the Populists in 1896 and the secessionists before them—doomed the party to another divisive and disastrous defeat in the coming presidential campaign and threatened the free trade cause. Watterson was eager to identify the "altered conditions" brought by the war in order to determine how to dominate them as a politician and thereby reap their benefits for the South. The terms of the debate over foreign economic policy were themselves rapidly transformed by the war. The possibilities of globalization quickly became apparent, and there was renewed jockeying by the parties to shape the American response. Paul Wolman argues that "the defeat of the Democrat-Populist ticket in 1896 and the U.S. victories in the Spanish-American War would . . . nurture new theorizing on expansion and development that promised to supersede the old conflicts of 'home-market' protection versus 'tariff for revenue only.'"[2] Watterson remained fixated on wresting control of this conflict and finally seeing a victorious Democratic Party lead the country to free trade after 1900. His other interests were subsumed in this quest as much as served by it.

At the start of the Spanish-American War, Watterson concentrated on the war news and the public anticipation for action rather than on the broader issues of a possible postwar settlement. The *Courier-Journal* received its reports from the *New York Herald*'s Special War Service—which it called "by far the best war service in the world"—and advised its readers to file each issue so, at the end of the war, they would have "a complete history of the war." Freedom would triumph in this war as it had in the Civil War, Watterson the old Rebel wrote, and Europe should be wary of challenging America's "new proclamation of liberty." Although he remained opposed to expansion, Watterson invoked manifest destiny and described the "mission of America" as freeing Cuba and spreading "the gospel of equity in government—the lesson of individualism that Christ taught." He did not yet consider expansion inevitable.[3]

Watterson welcomed this particular war but advised caution. The situation was novel, the issues unknown. "We have never engaged in a war for humanity before," he wrote in the middle of the conflict, and "we have no precedents to guide us." In this spirit, and as he had for a decade, Watterson advised expansionists to lower their covetous eyes and forget about annexing Hawaii under the cover of war. In an editorial titled "Questions That Can Wait," Watterson directly addressed his old nemesis Senator John Tyler Morgan and the broader "conspiracy" to annex Hawaii. With pragmatic reasoning, he explained why the Hawaii question should "be left severely alone." At present, he argued, the United States was not responsible for defending neutral Hawaii but could still use it for a coaling station. He saw no reason to change that system: "We have all the advantages that we could get in time of war . . . and none of [the] disadvantages." Watterson refused to entertain any subsidiary issues that might interfere with war with Spain.[4]

Admiral Dewey's destruction of the Spanish fleet in Manila Bay on May 1, 1898, changed Watterson's understanding of which issues could wait for discussion after the war. Indeed, it slowly changed his entire perspective of America's war goals and of the best means of achieving his New Departure in the South. At first, Watterson was thrilled with the results. With typical hyperbole, he described Dewey's victory in world historical terms only a month after the battle. "The event was in some respects unparalleled in the history of mankind," he wrote, "and while it is too early to forecast its ultimate effects, it is at least possible that it will have the largest influence on the destiny of the human race." At the time of the battle, the *Courier-Journal* was starved for exciting war news and used its biggest headline ever to announce the victory. Within two days, it was calling for Spain to quit and sue for peace. In contrast, the *Raleigh News and Observer*, another important southern paper, gave Dewey's victory a rather subdued treatment.[5]

On May 3, the *Courier-Journal* also ran a large map of the "scene of hostilities in both oceans" that provides an idea of how these unfolding international events were interpreted for its readership. The United States was drawn in the middle of the map, with no line shown at the Canadian border. This portrayed an image of incredible size and dominance, as the United States filled the center of the map to the uppermost edge. Cuba was drawn almost the size of the United States, thus appearing important and worthy of the greatest attention. Europe and Asia, on either side of the page, appeared to be almost equidistant from the United States, although the Philippines were almost twice as far away as Spain (6,520 versus 3,120 miles). Thus, two days after Dewey sailed into Manila Bay, the *Courier-Journal* presented a graphic view of the United States linking and dominating the other hemispheres and collapsed vast distances to seem both inviting (in the case of Asia) and dangerous (in the case of Spain).[6]

Even amidst this triumphalism, Watterson's long-standing isolationism did not erode in the "flush of our first victory." Concerned about the new questions and possible complications raised by acquisition of the islands, he hoped "to dispose of them" as soon as possible. Counseling calm, the *Courier-Journal* immediately questioned the darker implications of Dewey's victory. It advised the American people to listen to anti-imperialist former president Benjamin Harrison and not seek to replace a European colonizing power in Asia. Assuming that the Filipinos were now allies of the United States, Watterson argued that it was appropriate neither to trade the islands away nor simply to annex them. Although he wondered if they were capable of self-government, he believed the Filipinos themselves should have a voice in their future, and he praised Filipino independence leader Emilio Aguinaldo throughout the summer. Watterson also returned to the same racial arguments he had used against Hawaiian annexation. "Even if they desired to become part of the great American republic," he thought it would be impossible to accept them. "They are of the Malay race mostly, though some are known as Negritos, and there is an intermixture of Spaniards." Although some of those with European blood might leave, the remainder of the population could not possibly be assimilated. "It is scarcely necessary to say that we do not want them as citizens," Watterson wrote.[7]

Most of all, in the early stages of the war, Watterson posed practical objections to creating an island empire because of its incompatibility with American sovereignty. He contended that the United States did not "wish to be responsible" for the Filipinos and had "no facilities under our system for governing a dependency." He had used the same constitutional argument against the movement for Hawaiian annexation. Although he saw a wartime strategic expedient in holding on to the islands, Watterson perceived no advantages in permanently possessing the islands. He thought such a move could actually do damage to the American system. Although willing to wage a war for Cuban independence, which was a step away from his earlier positions and perhaps from American tradition, Watterson could not accept the "featherheadedness" behind a new push for colonies in Asia. The *Courier-Journal* pointedly reminded its readers that the war was not being fought "for a few half-breeds" and that the nation had made a solemn and "formal disavowal of selfish motives."[8]

A week after the battle in Manila Bay, Watterson reaffirmed "our national policy against territorial aggression and foreign entanglements." Thereafter, he ran a series of editorials condemning the idea of acquiring the Philippines, contradicting his prewar declaration that he intended to concentrate strictly either on the war, and avoid the postwar settlement, or on partisan issues. In this latest round of anti-imperialist editorials, Watterson presented variations of the arguments he used to fight Hawaiian annexation, centering on appeals to tradition, as well as strategic, racial, and even climatic arguments that the tropics were unsuitable for white habitation. At this early date, he rejected the "dreams of empire" and invocation of manifest destiny. That latter idea was anachronistic, he said, dating from "the good old days of pristine Democratic purity, when it was everyman's right to larrup his own nigger and the Democratic battle cry was '54–40 or fight.'" It was not "theories" that shaped national destiny in the modern world, he wrote somewhat vaguely, but rather "events." Given that the war was going on, the United States had no way of knowing what strange problems might arise, and it was better off waiting for "events yet to come." Watterson bolstered his argument against annexation with his favorite historical examples. "The inexorable logic of events" drove the Louisiana Purchase, he wrote, and the Mexican War resulted from "events and not greed." In a short time, he used both of these analogies to support a policy of expansion, which may indeed have been a matter of his waiting for events to unfold.[9]

By the end of May, the *Courier-Journal* was convinced that Spain should not be allowed to retain the archipelago, even if the United States did not end up desiring it. "The flag of cruelty and oppression must be swept from the Asiatic as well as American waters," Watterson declared in the crusading spirit he had adopted to describe the war. Logically, he could not see how the United States could wage an anticolonial war and simultaneously grab colonies for itself. But change was afoot. The war had blown uncertainty into the Pacific and into national politics.[10]

Other newspapers and politicians across the country began to debate the same question at this early stage of the war, with the same combination of jubilation and ambivalence. The *Raleigh News and Observer* announced two days after Dewey's victory, "The country does not want Manila. . . . This is no war for territorial aggression." But it did concede that it might be necessary to take coaling stations there "to protect our commerce in the Pacific Ocean." The *Philadelphia Record*, citing America's vastly increasing commercial interests, agreed that some portions of the islands should be retained. The independent *Boston Herald* thought the United States should follow its Monroe Doctrine–based traditions and protect an independent and free Philippines instead of controlling it, whereas the Republican *Chicago Inter-Ocean* argued that the islands fell "outside of our sphere of influence." Other papers thought it was best to wait until the war was over before making any final, momentous decisions.[11]

Even archexpansionist Senator John Tyler Morgan's view of the Philippine issue was ambivalent and "evolutionary." In many ways, his attitudes early in the war were similar to those of Watterson. Morgan wrote in June 1898 that Cuba had to be left independent until it made its own choice to join the United States. The country could not "colonize by force," he argued, because that was "repugnant to our national creed." While denying that America was fighting a war of conquest against Spain, Morgan advised that it was necessary to accept the changes being produced by the war and to extend good governments and the blessings of American trade to the former Spanish colonies.[12]

Watterson's approach also evolved with events, although it might be more accurate to describe his position as reversing. Editorials on the expansion issue, especially regarding the Philippines, appeared daily. Although papers all over the country discussed the issue, few achieved the sheer volume of editorials that appeared in the *Courier-Journal*. Virtually every issue featured one of Watterson's trademark long editorials on the topic. This output was reminiscent of the earlier explosion of writings on Populism. Watterson's strong, prewar antiannexationist stance lasted through the month of May 1898 but then rapidly dissipated. In June he began to support territorial expansion and to sing the praises of an aggressive, imperialist approach to foreign affairs. By the end of the war in August, Watterson had settled into the roles and arguments that would carry him through the election of 1900. He claimed that the changing circumstances forced him to change; he was now an expansionist. He then supported this shift by echoing the positions of newspapers from all over the country that also called for retaining the Philippines.

Watterson told his readers that he was in the vanguard of contemporary opinion, and he was. Papers agreeing with the *Courier-Journal* included the *Baltimore News, Boston Advertiser, Chicago Inter-Ocean, New Orleans Times Democrat, Cleveland Leader, Kansas City Star, New Haven Register, Hartford Times, Atlanta Commercial, Washington Post, Savannah News, Topeka Capital, New York Times, New York Herald,* and *New York Sun.* Watterson was interested not in the party labels of these papers—many of which he had violently disagreed with in the past on a variety of issues—but in their congruence with his new ideas. He easily shaped his political allies to fit the new conditions.[13]

Nevertheless, Watterson moved fitfully toward a "national policy undreamed of by the fathers of the Republic." He insisted that the United States could abide by its traditions and avoid entanglements, although his editorials began to sound less convinced. He was beginning to anticipate how manifest destiny in the Philippines would assert itself. Returning to his increasingly frequent concerns over the decline of American society through encroaching femininity, Watterson thought that perhaps, with expansion, "the Anglo-Saxon species in America" could have "its downward course toward emasculation arrested." Just as he had argued that war would halt emasculation, now he concluded that imperialism would serve that function.[14]

Watterson's realization that the imperial gains created by the war offered the economic opportunity he had long sought for the South provided the principal motive for this change. In early June, he discussed "the Coming of Flush Times," making it clear that major changes should be welcomed. "Those who do not move forward may blame themselves," he cautioned. He thought the war dictated control of the island colonies as well as "a larger standing army and a large, efficient navy." This important and expensive change would ripple through the economy, creating employment opportunities and prosperity in the form of job and market expansion. It also promised to end economic discontent and the resulting politics. "The farmers of Kentucky and of the South now have their greatest opportunity," Watterson wrote. He encouraged them to profit from it and correct the imbalances created first by civil war and then by depression. Since 1865, the South had been excluded as the rest of the country industrialized and boomed. Now, as this productivity was replicated on the world stage, things would be different.[15]

Most important, expansion meant the final death of protectionism. "Adding largely to our domain brings with it the necessity of solving several interesting problems," Watterson predicted. It simply was not possible to seek international commercial dominance and, at the same time, protect the home market. Expansion into foreign markets required the leavening agent of free trade. The establishment of an American overseas empire was akin to projecting the American domestic system abroad, he argued, and international trade would have to work just as interstate trade did. This was the essential logic that later underlay the interconnected markets heralded by globalization.[16]

In his editorials, Watterson increasingly warmed to the subject of international free trade and open markets, and he slipped back into the comfortable rhetoric of tariff reform. After noting the irony of observing Republican protectionists suddenly emphasizing world markets, Watterson argued that the results of territorial expansion into the Philippines, Puerto Rico, and Cuba were very clear: "It means the breaking down in a great measure of the protective system. A nation with large possessions in various and distant parts of the earth, with a powerful navy and a great merchant marine reaching out for foreign markets wherever they are to be had will have little use for a Chinese wall around it." Watterson understood that, as the nation's involvement in the world grew in the aftermath of the war, the logic of "the diversification of products" required an inclusive system of trade. He saw an opportunity to prove what he had been arguing for years: protectionism was an anachronistic policy. Successful trade expansionism required liberal trading regimes in the form of free trade. American manufacturing was no longer "infant," Watterson declared, but overproductive. "We are obliged to run on half time, or find new markets."[17]

Watterson considered free trade the obvious, easy solution for finding new markets, and it formed the backbone of his support for expansion in 1898. By the middle of the summer, having found his footing, he no longer exhibited any hesitancy in his editorials. Daily he hammered on the need for the United States to expand into foreign territories and markets and spread the area of free trade. The nation had to recognize changing realities, he wrote in a barrage of editorials, and avoid "self-immolating obstruction." Watterson's arguments also covered the familiar gamut of imperialist rhetoric. He mentioned Christian and democratic "obligations," the imperatives of social Darwinism, Anglo-Saxon racial destiny, and the diplomatic need to stay ahead of quickly moving events. Most of all, he argued that the United States had to recognize that it was now a Pacific power of the highest rank and accept the responsibilities and benefits of its new status. He called for the "permanent occupation of the Philippines" and "the abandonment of our position of national isolation." His description of the benefits of this New Departure centered on the country's need to fulfill its commercial promise "in the great trade developing in the Pacific."[18]

The potential of the Asian trade, which Watterson had mentioned earlier but had not emphasized, suddenly became the focal point of subsequent editorials. He pronounced this trade the final solution to the nation's self-evident need for foreign markets. Its potential offered "a vastness that can hardly now be comprehended." He especially concentrated on enticing his beloved South with the image of these limitless markets. He promised fellow Democrats that support for expansion would have positive economic and political results. "In particular have the Southern states everything to gain and little if anything to lose," he wrote in a common phrasing.[19]

Watterson very quickly realized that, when writing for the South, the case for expansion had to be made on the basis of tradition and precedent, just as his earlier, antiexpansion position had been. He accordingly invoked the power of American national memory by directly relating this case of expansion with earlier expansion into the West. In this way, Watterson again employed arguments that were current and even dominant in other contemporary imperialist writings. He exploited the resonant myths of the frontier, of New World exceptionalism, and even of manifest destiny, which he had until recently discounted. These ideas, developing in Watterson's editorials and speeches throughout the decade, colored all of his future writings on the imperial issue. Even when he concentrated on the economic advantages of imperialism, Watterson was careful to evoke these powerful emotional touchstones. In a typical fusion, he wrote, "We must plant the flag of liberty in the far Eastern wilderness and we must let no petty accusations of selfishness deter us from providing new trade outlets that our farmers, merchants and manufacturers demand for their goods."[20]

Watterson compared the Philippines' importance to American trade with Asia to the significance of controlling the mouth of the Mississippi River as a factor in national development. This image resonated with the audiences of the entire Mississippi valley, both North and South. It also connected Watterson's case of expansion with earlier efforts designed to increase American control of critical economic outlets. In the same sense, Watterson began regularly to invoke Jefferson and Jackson (and, to a lesser extent, his father's old friend James K. Polk) as the guiding lights of any future national policy. Despite that he had earlier used these presidents to support conservatism and attack dangerous "experimentation," Watterson was soon decrying "obsolete conditions [and] old theories." In the case of expansion, he believed that the traditions were both continued and reaffirmed. He declared, "We shall not depart from the ideals of the Fathers of the Constitutions; we shall be realizing them though to a fuller and greater extent than they recked of."[21]

At the early stages of the war, Watterson was not yet sure how the imperialism issue could be fruitfully exploited by the Democratic Party. But he knew a losing horse when he saw one, and anti-imperialism fit the description. In a June editorial titled "'Imperialism' As An Issue," Watterson noted that national party lines were not yet clearly drawn and rejected the idea that "imperialism" was an issue. That term did not appropriately characterize the opportunities at hand. Although William Jennings Bryan may have already come out against something called imperialism, Watterson did not see any political value to such a stance. "At present it seems hardly possible to make a party issue out of 'imperialism,'" he mused. Watterson demanded new issues so that his party could be reborn, and he alone reserved the right to shape them. He certainly was not going to follow Bryan's lead, and he likewise refused to recognize the state party platforms of Arkansas and Indiana, which called for anti-imperialism as well as free silver. These declarations were vague and useless, the *Courier-Journal* intoned. Furthermore, since "they do not propose to drop the old issues," like silver, they were unacceptable. On the other hand, when the *Buffalo (NY) Express* forwarded the idea that all great powers should be involved in the decision on the Philippines, which would have sapped the issue of its domestic political resonance, Watterson snapped, "When an American, in America, sees such stuff . . . in a professedly American paper, he may be pardoned for the comment: 'Hell!'"[22]

In moving toward expansionism, then, Watterson kept a clear eye on the potential ways the issue would affect his party. As more Democrats entered the growing anti-imperialist movement, Watterson's political instincts took over. He sensed that only strong support for national expansion could win elections. Indeed, the events of 1898 inaugurated an era in which assertive overseas action was a key to political success. Within this partisanship (which, of course, contradicted his earlier declarations that the war was not, and could not be, a party issue), Watterson maintained a marked sense of friendliness toward the McKinley administration and the overall Republican war effort.

Watterson again placed himself in the unorthodox position of defending Republican policies to save the Democratic Party from itself. The developing anti-imperialist movement made for some unusual and, to his mind, unwelcome alliances. The *Washington Post* ran a cartoon with Bryan and Grover Cleveland sharing a single, narrow "anti-imperialism cot," with the caption "A PRODUCT OF THE WAR. It looks like a narrow bed, but they seem contented."[23] Once again at odds with the mainstream party, Watterson trod back to the self-appointed leadership of a third way between extremes. Perhaps he was most comfortable in the no-man's-land between the parties. He certainly thrived on conflict. Watterson essentially remained in this position for the next two decades: attacking his enemies and cajoling his perceived allies, shaping the public discourse but never fully finding victory.

Watterson believed that the new issues raised by the war gave him the means to finally rebuild the Democratic Party in his image by purging those who did not understand the New Departure of expansionism. He proclaimed the coming dispute over expansion "an excellent opportunity to perform the Caesarian operation not upon the country at large, but upon the number of his professional brethren who have edged their way imprudently near the march of the inevitable." This was an especially interesting turn of phrase and a good example of Watterson's classically mixed metaphors. He implied that the backward elements who opposed expansionism could be excised from the body politic through a caesarian section, even as he characterized imperialism itself as "Caesaristic."[24]

"A PRODUCT OF THE WAR. It looks like a narrow bed, but they seem contented." Despite their differences, William Jennings Bryan and Grover Cleveland are now comfortably lying in the same anti-imperialist cot. *Literary Digest*, July 9, 1898

In the initial moves toward rebuilding the party, Watterson propagandized for expansion and pressed his attacks on those in the party who refused to join him. Learning from the campaigns of 1896–97, when the popular will was arrayed against him, Watterson determined to capture the political and rhetorical initiative immediately, rather than be caught running after it. The *Courier-Journal* helped to focus the party's internal divisions, as it had done in the earlier period. Watterson now returned to his fullest voice. Nothing energized him like a battle for control of the party and the opportunity to apply bombast to a meaty set of issues. He filled multiple columns with detailed responses to his critics and again announced that the *Courier-Journal* "will in the end emerge from the [party] ordeal, still free, and glorious and great." He threatened disgrace, political destruction, and eternal damnation for those "greedy and lucky potwallopers" who refused to follow his lead and who "obstruct[ed] the march of the Universe." He attacked a Democratic anti-imperialist meeting in Boston's Faneuil Hall as unpatriotic, senselessly antiwar and anti-McKinley, and "certainly not desirable." Thus began a long series of engagements with this group on constitutional, economic, strategic, moral, racial, political, and historical grounds. Democratic papers as diverse as the *Minneapolis Times*, the *Salt Lake City Herald*, and the *Nashville American* in turn criticized Watterson for seeking an expansionist movement that was outside the party's interest and traditions.[25]

This intraparty dispute, which grew over time and was reported in papers across the country, centered as much upon whether Watterson was again flirting with party or sectional irregularity as it did upon the issue of expansionism. A typical exchange occurred between the *Augusta (GA) Chronicle* and the *Courier-Journal* over the true southern outlook on expansion. The *Chronicle* accused Watterson not only of deserting the Democratic Party by supporting expansionism but of "turn[ing] his back on his Confederate record of local self-government, just as he deserted the free coinage of silver for the gold standard." Watterson's response exemplified his new outlook. He announced the death of the "bucolic Republic of our Fathers" and argued that the future was always startling and unknown. It had "annihilated time and space." In this new world, the United States had to recognize and control its changed situation. "It means that Republicanism can not isolate itself, that it has become a part of the world's movement." In any case, he wrote, expansionism was not counter to southern traditions; it was their fulfillment. "The South was always a filibuster . . . its best hope lies in the direction of national expansion," he wrote.[26]

In general, Democratic papers accused Watterson of being a coward, a robber, and a traitor to the party, while he in turn chastised fellow Democrats for refusing to bypass narrow partisanship and support the self-evident benefits of Republican expansionism. The *Minneapolis Times*, among other papers, criticized Watterson for conspiring to send soldiers to "islands in far-off seas" so the "traitors at home may loot the country unmolested," and the *Nashville American* called for continued isolationism. Watterson countered, "The *Courier-Journal*, being a Democrat, would have the Democratic party take the larger, longer view. . . . It is simply amazing that a newspaper like the Nashville *American* . . . should counsel the policy of sticking the National head behind a rock, whilst the march of the universe goes on, and merely because a Republican Administration happens to be in power at Washington."[27] Watterson remained interested in material gain and long-term self-interest and was willing to overlook party labels or, if necessary, to counter Democratic traditions.

Perhaps the best single example of Watterson's transformed perspective was his nonresponse to the annexation of Hawaii, which he had of late vigorously opposed. It certainly was out of character for him to withhold comment on so important an issue. However, no longer considering this sort of expansion to be a party issue, he quietly abandoned most of his earlier positions. With all of the internal partisan bickering as a distraction, as well as the implications of a new "large policy," Watterson essentially abstained from commenting when Congress annexed Hawaii on July 7, 1898, by joint resolution. The debates over this action touched on the same economic and racial issues that had long dominated the Hawaiian annexation issue, but they lacked the severity of the earlier debate, and in any case, Watterson no longer deemed the issue worthy of attention.[28]

In general, southerners opposed annexation, but Watterson had discarded his previous opposition to acquiring the archipelago. He now believed that ownership of the islands was necessary to provide links with the Asian markets. He no longer feared that Hawaiian annexation would cause racial dissolution of the United States, which demonstrates how easily he trumped racial arguments with material ones. Other Watterson allies had not switched positions. Democratic representative John S. Rhea of Kentucky, for example, emphasized on the floor of the House the economic benefits of not annexing the islands because of the revenue value of existing reciprocity, and he mentioned the "bestiality and malignity that frequently lapses into crimes of lust and revenge" on the islands. Yet Watterson, within a few months of annexation, even scoffed at the *New York World* for discussing the supposed racial problems of foreign expansion, despite the fact that they had figured prominently in his own writings. Forget about the dangers of native populations abroad, he wrote gleefully, and instead "give us a classification of the population of New York."[29]

One critical aspect of Watterson's earlier antiexpansionist isolationism that he did not abandon, and that was also linked to racial ideas, was the promise of independence for Cuba. Midway through this short war, Watterson still assumed that it was a crusade waged for both American ideals and humanity. He tempered this view with what he considered a realistic assessment of the racial makeup of Cuba. On both grounds, he argued in July, the United States had to free the island after the war. He was not sanguine about the abilities of nonwhites to govern themselves in Cuba, especially given the "indolence" of the inhabitants. Although Watterson did not think that race made Cubans unsuitable for independence, he did believe that they were not destined to rule themselves successfully. "The Cubans labor under the double disability of climate and race," he wrote. This environmental disintegration threatened even whites who resided in the tropics. So, although the United States should not grab the islands as it had Hawaii, it did have an active role to play in guiding the island's independent future.[30]

Watterson likened Cuba's governance to the eternal southern problem of home rule. He thought both areas were dependent on rule by reasonable, stable, white individuals. Both also necessitated clear independence without a coercive and distant government demanding tribute or attempting to change what he considered the natural racial hierarchy. Watterson prescribed granting Cuba "a stable government," which really meant a white-dominated government, through the "friendly offices of the United States." The islands should not be turned over to the uneducated black population any more than the South should have been abandoned to freed slaves in the 1870s. "The Cuban negro has wholly failed to exhibit his superiority or even equality so far," he argued. Watterson thought that using external and unwelcome power to create unpopular minority regimes had been tried and found wanting after the Civil War. Later, he assured his readers that "the black man has no chance to make a Hayti out of the 'Pearl of the Antilles.'" "It is presumed," he told his audience, "that the United States will avoid the errors committed in the South in the days of reconstruction. To turn over the government of the island to the irresponsible elements of the population with liberty to prey upon the others would be to invite disaster and lead to the inevitable failure of our great humanitarian experiment."[31] He concluded that historical precedent, humanitarianism, and racial justice required the establishment of an independent Cuba under a suitably white regime, free from external, Republican meddling. In time, he thought, the island would realize that only incorporation into the United States could provide a stable future, just as the South had eventually found its place in the Union once white rule was reaffirmed. Presumably, a strong Democratic Party would be on hand to welcome Cuba into the fold and grant it the appropriate local autonomy.

Paradoxically, Watterson deemphasized race by ignoring the potential difficulties of eventually incorporating the nonwhite population into the country. Although he used charges of racial inferiority to support the establishment of a white Creole government in Cuba, he did so in the context of anticipating the eventual incorporation of the island into the United States. This was a dramatic shift from his earlier emphasis on race as a reason to maintain isolationism. At this juncture, with more than a trace of opportunism, he no longer envisioned the incorporation of racially diverse populations to be a problem. He similarly supported the idea of making Puerto Rico a state "as soon as it is desirable if not sooner," without referring to any racial complications. Watterson agreed that the language and cultural differences needed attention but also urged Americans to learn to pronounce Spanish names until a new, English-speaking generation came of age on the island. Although he thought "the people are at present unfit to govern themselves," he was unwilling to erect unnecessary barriers to union and remained generally unafraid to accept cross-cultural assimilation. This approach had a personal dimension as well. In 1901 Henry Watterson Jr., who had been a lieutenant in the army, married a Cuban woman named Blanca Esther Cassanova (the daughter of a Spanish general killed in action) without any protest from his father. Later, Watterson described U.S. annexation as entirely welcome and even romantic: "Porto Rico, for example, threw herself joyfully into the arms of the United States," he wrote.[32]

Watterson also refrained from applying racial limitations to the case of the Philippines. "The Filipino is as much entitled to life, liberty, and the pursuit of happiness as the Englishman or German," he wrote in his contradictory way, "but there are geographical as well as social and other reasons why he can not expect to assume a similar national position." Since the United States had the moral duty, political right, and self-interested motivation to take the islands, Watterson believed, it did not need to defend its expansionism with artificial racial justifications. Indeed, he consciously equated American control of the Philippines with the emancipation of the slaves. At other junctures, he wrote that Dewey "struck the shackles from the limbs of eight million slaves . . . eager for liberty." Watterson was ready "to continue our great work of emancipation" of the Philippines from Spain while rejecting both arbitration with Spain and total freedom for the archipelago.[33] He was not yet clear on how these goals could be reconciled.

Still, Watterson was convinced that the American public should decide the exact status of the islands. Although no promise had been made regarding Philippine independence, he predicted that the war would produce a new set of issues surpassing all others, including the tariff and the currency. "It would be interesting to know what these issues are," Watterson mused, thinking of their utility for political battle. He questioned McKinley's leadership and called for him to make up his mind about the Philippines. Meanwhile, Watterson girded himself and sought to rally the Democratic troops and to allay the "hopelessness of the mental confusion" of party leaders. "The fact is," he advised, "issues cannot be arbitrarily made in advance by one party. They have a way of shaping themselves, when the fight is actually on, in a manner that confounds all calculation." While waiting for this future battle, Watterson sought to consolidate support for expansion throughout the South.[34]

When hostilities ended on August 9, Watterson firmly supported a new policy of territorial expansionism in the Pacific, and he set about establishing the basic arguments that he would carry forward over the next two years.[35] These arguments jointly represented the basic worldview Watterson hoped would frame U.S. foreign policy throughout the twentieth century. He correctly predicted that the first party to support expansion, and the first to grab the "usufructs of the war" in the form of foreign market opportunity, would be the party of the twentieth century.

By the end of the summer of 1898, Watterson equated the expansion question with the party question. "The short-sighted persons who have got into the Democratic saddle do not know how to ride," Watterson wrote. Instead, the party leaders, including Bryan, had "disregard[ed] the plainest, simplest rules of political equestrianism." That is, they had followed misguided and misinformed ideas labeled "principles." Victory was there for the taking, and Watterson once more hoped to educate the Democracy toward this end. The first step was to convince the party to recognize that political reality and national destiny abroad were identical.[36]

"The whole bent of the national idea is Expansion," Watterson declared flatly; "the whole trend of the popular thought is expansion." There simply was no other program for the party to support. No party could "pull that flag down" and survive. Rather than "seize upon the spectre of Imperialism for an issue," Watterson called for "seizing upon Cuba, Porto Rico, the Philippines and everything else in sight and out of sight, and going the Republicans one better." In so doing, he laid out a careful and pragmatic program for party renewal. His call for expansion carried a large dollop of partisan self-interest. The Democrats had to exploit the mistakes of the Republicans, he wrote, and be "first to occupy fighting ground." Benefits would accrue to the more aggressive party as well as to the nation as a whole. Watterson saw no reason that the Republicans should be allowed to preside over this triumph.[37]

Democratic anti-imperialists, Watterson thought, should not assume party leadership unless they were willing to lead on to victory. It was necessary to "keep up with the procession" if the Democracy was to avoid falling victim like the failed parties that littered the past. Watterson held up the examples of 1860 and 1896 as times when the party had followed so-called principle to disaster and defeat, and he rejected, in addition, "the arguments of the timid of 1803, 1811, 1822, 1843, and later dates." Rather than follow these examples, Watterson counseled a return to Democratic traditions. He turned again to his favorite example: Jefferson and the Louisiana Purchase. Since "Jefferson was an ardent expansionist," Watterson found no legitimate grounds to oppose overseas expansion. "Did not Jackson fairly wallow in imperialism?" he asked. In an editorial titled "When This Old Hat Was New," Watterson laid out the case of historic Democratic expansionism, which he returned to many times over the next two years. He harkened back to "the good old days of pristine Democratic purity, when Jefferson buncoed Napoleon out of Louisiana and Monroe secured from Spain the reluctant cession of Florida, when Jackson laid the foundations for the annexation of Texas and Polk whisked California from the all-too-feeble grasp of the greasers, Democrats had plenty of elbow room. Uncle Sam was not only rich enough to give us all a farm, but [also] . . . there was never any serious want of an office for the faithful."[38]

Thus the Democratic Party could fulfill the policies of expansion it had pioneered and again offer up the spoils to the party faithful and the people at large. Instead of anti-imperialism, Watterson favored a Democratic battle cry of "the Legions of Jefferson and Jackson against the janizaries of McKinley, Alger, and Hanna!" Alongside the positive expansionist role models of Jefferson and Jackson, Watterson put Moses. He advised William Jennings Bryan to study up on these lessons and "overhaul his Pentateuch, along with the Book of Joshua."[39]

Watterson, like many others, also regularly argued that Americans since the time of Jefferson had not been unduly concerned with sentimental interpretations of the "doctrine of the consent of the governed." Watterson repeated this idea after August 1898, as the debate over the disposition of the Philippines intensified and the anti-imperialist movement raised this venerable American idea. He unblinkingly recounted how, at various times, slaves, women, minors, convicts, "lunatics and idiots," and even white southerners during Reconstruction were not allowed to vote. Even in 1898, some sections of the nation were not pleased with the ruling politicians. "The whole country is governed with consent of the governed," he wrote, "but small parts of it are governed whether they like it or not." There was, in short, no historical precedent blocking control of the Philippines. Theodore Roosevelt expressed the identical idea many times, arguing "the parallel between what Jefferson did with Louisiana and what is now being done in the Philippines is exact." Roosevelt hoped to utilize the Jeffersonian legacy to support imperialism and the Republicans while also preventing the Democrats from gaining additional political capital from these traditions. "The Bryanized Democracy has no right to claim one particle of heirship to the party founded by Jefferson and perpetuated by Jackson," he wrote. This was exactly the ideological hijacking Watterson sought to prevent.[40]

Although accurately describing the imperial legacies of the Democratic past, Watterson began to support governmental experimentation and growth that he would not have considered legitimate only months earlier. He professed to believe strongly in the strict interpretation of the Constitution, yet he recognized and accepted that colonialism in the Philippines required a new formulation of policy that was not explicitly supported in the document. This was flatly contradictory, but Watterson pretended otherwise. As he now claimed, "The Constitution is like the Bible in that all find in it warrant for what they want and ban for what they oppose." For Watterson, only "the bucolic dreamer, whose migrations are bounded by the apple-orchard on the one side and the willow-brook on the other, and whose life is a never-changing pastoral of happy fancies, would preserve forever the Republic conceived by Washington and Franklin." In other words, only the provincial and backward-looking rural elements (such as those drawn to the mirages of Populism and the mythical plantation Old South) would try to maintain an anachronistic or static system. Watterson explicitly told the South that its interests lay in a New Departure based upon a new outlook and a willingness to change.[41] Empires required new thinking, new ideas, and new regimes alongside the acquisition of new territory. The nation and its system had to adapt to globalization.

Watterson understood this administrative flexibility as one great source of national strength. He titled his critical editorial welcoming constitutional change "We Can Take Care of Ourselves." The radical implication of this idea was that the new America facing the twentieth century no longer needed the guidance of the founding fathers. "The American people will not be blindly and perpetually bound by limitations set by the century-dead upon conditions they could not foresee," he wrote. This was an especially bold statement from a man given to forms of ancestor worship in the cases of Jefferson, Jackson, and Tilden. Thus the same man who had constantly discussed the need for a strong Kentucky conservatism throughout 1897 to fight against radical change, and the same editor who stood for strict limits on federal power, now welcomed the "wisdom to amend it [the Constitution] and expand it to new conditions." The same Watterson who considered himself a spokesman for the eternal truth of the nation's founding ideals now declared, in a new spirit of independence, that "if the Constitution they left us is inadequate, we shall make it adequate."[42]

In dispensing with the ideological and traditional arguments against becoming a new imperial power, Watterson also very rapidly dispatched the "destiny" rhetoric he himself had employed in earlier editorials. It was economic realism that forced his reevaluation. He declared the real motivational force of history to be self-interest. "The arguments in favor of commercial expansion are numerous enough without assuming that

Providence is compelling us to take a particular course," he wrote. Earlier expansions, even in cases like the acquisitions of Louisiana, Florida, Texas, and California, came not from some happenstance but "in obedience to the demands of the commercial spirit that insisted on control of the Mississippi" and accompanying trade and markets. The greatest gains yet could be realized by annexing the Philippines and establishing a new free trade empire that facilitated the disposal of overproduced goods. "For years the *Courier-Journal* endeavored to show that what was wanting in the United States were wider markets." Now the country seemed to be paying attention. Certainly the proexpansion businessmen, Republican policymakers, and imperial propagandists were, and they urged everyone else not to miss this unprecedented opportunity. "By planting ourselves in Manila we will be in a position to take our share of the whole Pacific trade," Watterson declared.[43] The empire of free trade was nigh.

At this early date, Watterson believed that the New Departure that was signaled in the expansionist program would finally usher in the era of the Star-Eyed Goddess of tariff reform he had promised since the 1880s. It could be no other way. "The truth is," he wrote," the doctrine of territorial expansion is consistent only with the theories of the revenue tariff men. It is entirely at war with the system of trade restrictions." Global empire could be established only on open door terms. This idea, with its simple and attractive logic, was still not fully acceptable to the Republican imperialists, who had only recently begun to adopt reciprocity as a goal as well as an ideal. It would, finally, be the ground on which Watterson ended his heretofore strong support for the McKinley administration and the large policy. Watterson thought that the new territories would have to be granted an unrestricted relationship to the American market, but he would be sorely disappointed.[44]

In the fall of 1898, Watterson agitated for an open door with the Philippines and a fully open door at home. He was one of the first to do so, and perhaps the first to emphasize "a similar open door to the trade of the South." The links between the advance of the South and the expansion of overseas opportunity dominated his editorials. "The door to Southern trade stands open 365 days in the year and 366 days in leap years," he promised. Glowing editorials about the expansion of southern agriculture and manufacturing appeared regularly. New markets would bring prosperity, stability, and security. "The South 'Jes Laughs,'" crowed Watterson.[45]

Watterson trumpeted his commitment to Republican imperial expansion in his speech to the Patria Club of New York on December 9, 1898. The speech was reprinted in the *Courier-Journal*, in newspapers across the country, and in the *Saturday Evening Post* as half of a debate on the question, "Should the United States expand?" Watterson's speech supporting expansionism was juxtaposed with Andrew Carnegie's resounding "No!"[46]

Carnegie's article stressed the economic dangers of imperialism, including the impossibility of creating an open door with the Philippines, the need for high taxation and big government, the excessive costs of militarism, and the heightened danger of war. His article was methodical, rational, and pessimistic in tone, rather than moralistic or emotional. Carnegie did not achieve the rhetorical grandiosity that made Watterson such a prized speaker.[47] Watterson did not disappoint his readers on this count, although his speech was subdued compared to his grander, patriotic orations.

Like Carnegie, Watterson approached the expansion issue in fundamentally material terms, and his basic appeal was to economic self-interest. He began by quickly dispatching the very wide array of antiexpansion arguments. Watterson rejected imperialism's danger of leading to war with the European powers. He declared it impossible to allow Spain back into the Philippines or to abandon the islands either "as a temptation to the rapacity of other nations" or to "domestic anarchy." Using this phrasing, Watterson made American annexation seem like the reasonable middle path between two extremes. He also deftly handled the ideas of duty, destiny, and chance by declaring them all equally responsible for the Philippines' falling into the American lap. Militarism was "a danger we must risk," whereas the centralization of governmental power was merely a symptom of the modern era. Through no specific act, the federal government, and especially the president, had already developed powers "not contemplated [even] by the extremist theories of Hamilton and Adams." Watterson evinced no great concern about this revolutionary shift, despite that he had pushed strict construction of the Constitution and had long attacked Hamiltonian policies as illiberal, dangerous, and paternalistic.[48]

Watterson likewise quickly discarded any racial dangers of expansion. Instead, he argued, distantly ruling different races might even offer solutions "for the adjustment of hard problems nearer home." This was the precise reversal of his earlier arguments against Hawaiian annexation.

Watterson was never consistent in his racism, and this was especially true on the expansion issue. He never separated race and issues of racial justice from exact political calculations. Like other New South ideologues, he argued that "the race question and economic progress were inseparably bound together."[49] The race issue, whether at home or abroad, could not interfere with important political-economic issues. Simply put, too much was at stake. Yet it was impossible to separate the race question from the issue of overseas expansion. The decidedly material approach to his understanding of the significance of race in relation to politics and commerce did separate Watterson from some white southerners. Race typically defined political activity and identity, and many southerners enlisted racism as a fundamental argument against the desirability of a colonial policy. They simply did not want to increase the numbers of nonwhites in the United States. Some expansionist southerners, like John Tyler Morgan, were eager to export segregation. As C. Vann Woodward described it, "Events in the Philippines soon indicated that the Mississippi Plan had become the American Way." Watterson actually suggested that imperialism would eradicate, not intensify, the domestic racial question, although he did not explicitly outline a program of racial resettlement and colonization. "With National Expansion, why may we not find an outlet to this racial problem [at home]?" he asked, without offering any details.[50] He did not see any particular threat to the southern white supremacy that, not incidentally, also formed the basis of the Democratic Party.

It may seem curious that Watterson supported the Republican policy of imperialism as a means of answering Democratic southerners' racial fears, but he unabashedly (if vaguely) promised that "National Expansion is the one sure hope of the black belt of the South." Ironically, and for reasons that Watterson opposed, Edward E. Cooper, editor of the *Colored American*, supported imperialism as a means of generally increasing federal power and thereby weakening the relative position of southern white supremacy. Editor and publisher John Mitchell of the *Richmond Planet* disagreed; he feared that, in Cuba and the Philippines, "All the horrors of South Carolina, Mississippi, Louisiana and Texas will be repeated."[51]

Watterson did use some racial ideas to support colonial control of the Philippines. He believed that southern whites were especially suited for governing nonwhites. He argued that the best way to approach domestic race relations was with "the supervision and benevolent assistance of white men." Otherwise, he warned, the United States would turn into "Hayti or

San Domingo." Even more, he thought that all Americans were born imperialists because of their experience in subduing and ruling the Native Americans, and that the best example of the spread of white civilization was in the fight against savage freedom. Support for an independent Philippines was misplaced, he argued, as the United States had always ruled inferior groups by force and without consent. "We shall rule them as we rule the Indian Territory and Alaska," he wrote, evincing an attitude that was widely shared among imperialists. Watterson was astonished that "the savages far from home, with no grievance, get more encouragement than the savages at home who often have real grievances." Later, he admonished Republican anti-imperialist Senator George F. Hoar of Massachusetts by writing that, if his "ancestors had treated the Indians with the tender regard he would have Americans now show the Filipinos, we should have never had a New England."[52]

Watterson hurried through these various anti-imperialist arguments in his Patria Club address, leaving ample time for his fundamental argument for expansion, which was, predictably, the need for new and free international markets. These new commercial opportunities, he promised, would solve the problems of overproduction (which he called "the most serious danger that threatens us"), eliminate "the seeds of discontent" sowed by unoccupied or dissatisfied labor, and give the United States "an outlet for its superfluous energies." Echoing Brooks Adams, Watterson announced, "The world moves, and it is moving toward the Orient. . . . The sea-front of human activity may within the coming century be transferred from the Atlantic to the Pacific." Watterson told the country to follow this historical shift through the New Departure program he had developed. Following his own logic, he promised that "the new departure adopted by the Republic of 1900 will be no greater in its risks to liberty and law than was the departure adopted by the Republic in 1800." He welcomed this "total revolution" even as he stressed its congruence with American traditions. Expansion into the limitless markets of Asia was at once the novel solution to contemporary problems and the final realization of the American commercial potential of the last century.[53]

Watterson embraced this expansionist New Departure because he believed it would eliminate the Republican Party as a political force as easily as it would end overproduction and inaugurate the free trade era. Curiously, he supported McKinley's policies while fighting McKinleyism. He wrote to his friend John Hay, "As I am in agreement with what must inevitably be the foreign policy of the government, it is an added satisfaction to have the anticipation of cordially supporting you."[54] The cordial support never became public knowledge, however, and Watterson pressed what he perceived to be a political advantage.

Watterson's support for expansionism can be understood only in a broad political context. In expansion, he saw a means to reverse the party disarray that Populism had created, to end protectionism, to grant the South the final means of achieving strong independence within an even stronger Union, and to conclusively reveal the dangers of Republicanism at home and abroad. Imperialism and global market expansionism were indeed the paramount issues facing the nation, surpassing all others, including free silver. Here was an opportunity for the Democracy and the South to wave the Stars and Stripes as vigorously as the Republicans did and to realize the many subsequent gains. Watterson hoped to use expansionism as the base for his party's rebirth and for the achievement of his long-standing program of southern renewal. In this sense, Watterson began to fight the presidential campaign of 1900 more than a year early. He was himself so consumed with finding any route to electoral victory in 1900 that would avoid a repeat of the Democratic disaster of 1896 that, for a time, he even urged his fellow Democrats to forget their politics altogether and to support Admiral Dewey for president and Fitzhugh Lee for vice president on the platform "the Stars and Stripes, God bless them!" Dewey did put himself forward as a candidate on just such a platform—"the flag and the constitution"—but most commentators thought that it was either too vague or too silly to endorse. As it turned out, the admiral did not have a politician's skills and had never even voted.[55]

Watterson was only half joking when he proposed the ticket, but his point was clear. The Democrats would realize significant political advantages by avoiding all controversies that divided the nation and embracing the overtly patriotic and profitable program of expansion. "Don't let them write us down against the flag," he urged. "Don't let us seem to be opposed to the flag. The Declaration, yes. The Constitution, yes! But, ever and ever, and late and early, and right or wrong, the flag, the flag, the flag!"[56] Watterson was convinced that future Democratic victories would be assured, and the idiosyncrasies of the twentieth-century market met, if the entire party heeded his two-pronged message of national free trade expansionism and party unification. For the next two years, he proselytized for this vision.

7

We Done Expanded

> We are an Expansionist. But we would expand on Jeffersonian, not Caesaristic lines. We are an Expansionist. But we would have the Constitution follow the flag. We are an Expansionist. We rejoice in the knowledge that at last the scattered and discordant Confederacy, the uncertain and for a time dismembered Union, the belittled and despised Republic is a World Power, known, honored, respected of all men.
>
> —Henry Watterson, October 1, 1900

Henry Watterson desired an American empire, but only an empire of free trade. He lectured national audiences that territorial expansion into island colonies required the complementary extension of a free trade system.[1] Because he thought expansionism necessarily included the triumph of free trade and the opening of badly needed new markets, it also fulfilled his New Departure approach to southern political economy. He therefore admonished the South that only expansion could guarantee home rule, prosperity, stability, and racial peace. He directed the Democratic Party to support his expansionist program as the best means to unify and to win the presidential election of 1900. Because he saw so many advantages to imperialism, Watterson willingly accepted a large dose of Republicanism. Following the pattern of 1896, he challenged the orthodoxy of his party in favor of the program of his political enemies while claiming to speak for the true Democracy.

In the aftermath of the Spanish-American War, Watterson adopted a new foreign policy because he believed that the older, somewhat fitful policies of the nineteenth century needed to be folded into a coherent program of great power with equal parts colonialism and free trade imperialism. Watterson named his favored policy national expansion to distinguish it from the politically untenable (and Republican) labels of imperialism and colonialism. "Imperialism means simply the extension of our territory so as to make it equal to a great empire in area," he wrote disingenuously. "The word expansion conveys the idea better and is less calculated to mislead."[2] It was also less likely to offend American political sensibilities.

Watterson's hair-splitting distinctions between expansion and imperialism were frail, but he assessed differences based upon the relative importance of free trade and upon a shifting understanding of the meaning of "home rule." In his newest understanding, the South could achieve its final political and economic independence—its home rule—only through the blessings of expansionism and free trade. He therefore accepted both free trade imperialism and formal colonialism, so long as they promised acceptable political benefits to the South and to the broader cause of free trade. This paradox larded his arguments in favor of expansionism as the 1900 election slowly approached. Watterson decided that only the Democratic Party could resolve the paradoxes between these positions, because it adhered to a true understanding of strict constitutional limits, because it was southern, and because it was not Republican. As he fancifully put it, "Expansion upon the lines of Jefferson and expansion upon the lines of McKinley as far as we have gone is a gray horse of decidedly another color."[3]

The debate over imperialism congealed on December 10, 1898, when the Treaty of Paris ended hostilities between the United States and Spain. At this point, Watterson tried to identify his party with the Republican treaty, because he believed that its passing was the first necessary step toward world power. The debate in Congress, which lasted from January 4 until the treaty was passed on February 6, 1899, centered primarily on constitutional and racial issues rather than on the need for foreign markets. Both proponents and opponents of annexing the Philippines, in fact, agreed on the need for these commercial outlets. The treaty did not delineate the future status of the former Spanish colonies. An array of options existed, including freeing them, returning them to Spain, establishing an American protectorate over them, and selling them to another power, but the movement was toward outright annexation. Although Republicans pushed hard for the treaty's passage, McKinley was at first deliberately vague about his plans, as if wanting expansionist sentiment to be clearly expressed in the Senate before broaching the idea of colonial rule in the Philippines. He considered waiting to submit the treaty until after the newly elected, Republican-controlled Fifty-sixth Congress came into session. However, he extended American military rule to the Philippines on December 21, 1898.[4]

Watterson thought the expansion of trade was more quickly attainable through direct action of this sort. Unlike many Democrats, he welcomed McKinley's "benevolent assimilation" program for the islands and promised, "Our powers of assimilation are not yet exhausted." Other papers were not so sure. For example, the *Baltimore Sun* thought neither Indians nor blacks had ever been "satisfactorily assimilated" and did not welcome the challenge of assimilating Filipinos. The *Courier-Journal* pushed forward. It so clearly supported the imperial program that it ran Kipling's "The White Man's Burden" twice in a single day.[5]

Watterson traveled to Washington to witness the treaty battle firsthand and to nationalize his regional support for expansion by lobbying his various friends in Congress. He rejected all limitations on American expansion, such as those called for in a resolution by Senator Augustus O. Bacon of Georgia. This resolution broadly disclaimed "any disposition or intention to exercise permanent sovereignty, jurisdiction, or control over said islands" and called for eventual independence. Watterson alternatively pushed his hard-line desire for this very "permanent sovereignty in the Philippine Islands" that the Bacon resolution explicitly denied.[6]

Other critical support for the treaty came from unexpected quarters. William Jennings Bryan advanced the strange belief that his antiexpansionist cause would be best helped by the treaty's ratification. This was one of Bryan's great tactical blunders. To the bewilderment of other anti-imperialists, Bryan claimed that ratification "really clear[ed] the way for the recognition of a Philippine republic" and would subsequently save the United States from the evils of imperialism. He favored an "aggressive" fight in the public at large rather than a "defensive" fight against the treaty in the confines of the Senate. Bryan hoped that, once the war fever had passed, the public would soberly reject an imperialist policy and return to the currency issue.[7]

The Great Commoner's convoluted support for the treaty only heightened Watterson's disdain for him and for the anti-imperialists in general.

Watterson had strongly supported passing the treaty since early December, hoping that it would create the opportunity to use imperialism as a springboard in the coming presidential contest. He wanted to control the process, kill Bryan's campaign and political future, write the party's platform, and win the election for right-thinking Democrats. Several major southern newspapers, like the *Manufacturer's Record*, *Atlanta Constitution*, *Atlanta Journal*, *Charlotte Daily Observer*, *Memphis Commercial-Appeal*, and *Richmond Times*, joined in Watterson's support for the treaty for similar reasons. Watterson disregarded political restraints in supporting expansion, and he sought to similarly liberate his party. As he had done with the silver issue, once he established a clear platform from which to preach, Watterson returned to strident, uncompromising, and dialectical rhetoric. Just as he had offered his goldbug position as the logical choice between the extremes of Populist chaos and Republican paternalism, he now maneuvered between the two extremes of "aggression from abroad," in the form of the European imperial powers, and "anarchy at home," in the form of Philippine self-rule. Instead of these, Watterson offered the unifying "guiding hand of a superior race and a nation." It was, of course, a reformed, Wattersonian Democratic Party that could best guide this middle ground.[8]

This reformed party looked curiously like the party for which Watterson had propagandized throughout the previous three decades, and for good reason. He saw a seamless connection between the party of 1856 and that of 1900. It was during these years that failure had prevailed, and the true party had been twisting in the limbo of permanent opposition. From the Buchanan-Breckinridge ticket forward, Watterson argued, the true party had consistently supported "a platform of progressive Free Trade and National Expansion." When the party strayed from "organic questions," it was doomed to failure. Slavery, free silver, and anti-imperialism were all similarly dead questions. "There is no hope in threshing over the old straw of free silver and still less in declaring the war with Spain a failure," he argued. The Democracy should ignore Bryan and "return to the lines of Tilden, which was the line of Jackson, which was the line of Jefferson." Watterson understood the transcendent connections between these leaders to be the free market, expansion, and a conservative public order.[9]

This was the same program, newly retrofitted for foreign affairs, that Watterson had pushed since 1896. He knew it was essential for the Democrats to avoid the labels already being plastered upon them by the Republicans. Theodore Roosevelt had begun using the old Civil War–era comparisons to remind voters that the Democracy had a long history of national treachery. "In 1864 the name of liberty was invoked to secure the continuance of slavery," Roosevelt wrote. "In 1900 it is invoked to secure the abandonment of American honor and to throw the Philippines under the rule of a corrupt and tyrannous oligarchy."[10] Watterson deemed support for expansion the only protection from these slanders.

This outlook put the *Courier-Journal* in the vanguard of an anti-isolation movement that percolated out of the Midwest and Upper South. Writing from Washington to the Democratic Party as a whole, Watterson argued that theoretical debates over expansion such as were occurring during the treaty fight were utterly useless. Instead, the national discussion should focus on how best to exploit the spoils of war. The United States needed to learn how to wield its new standing, not quibble about the rise to imperial power. "With the 'open door' right ahead of us, with the country unified, with the bloody shirt in the old clo' basket, and the theory of Protection no longer needed or desired by anybody, old party issues pass away and the politics of the future turns upon the details of the expansion which is already here, not upon expansion itself," he wrote.[11]

The only relevant questions were how to set up and govern the new empire. Watterson's answers were immediate independence for Cuba and southern-style home rule for Puerto Rico. He favored colonial status for the Philippines, with a promise of autonomy within an American empire at an unspecified future date. Free trade would unite all of these areas and systems. Watterson advocated a long-term strategy of establishing free trade, as Britain had done, and then capturing the world's financial markets. "The Tariff story of England may be repeated in America," he mused. "William McKinley may become another Sir Robert Peel." He developed a series of slogans around which he hoped the public discourse would coalesce: "The Open Door is Free Trade. Expansion is the Outlet. The question of the future is commerce. Markets is the word."[12]

Democratic papers across the country attacked Watterson for weeks because of his conversion to the imperial program and his call for aggressive reformation of the party's political outlook. Watterson welcomed the challenge. For example, on February 7, 1899, while he defended himself against his critics in one column, the paper ran four other editorials on the expansion issue. Typically, Watterson called his critics reactionaries and equated all Democratic opposition to expansion with "that voice which forty years ago preached for divine origin of African slavery and the sovereign Kingship of Cotton, only to lure the South to its ruin." He appealed to the South with visions of greatness that awaited it overseas. He articulated a mantra on the wonders of the twentieth-century world market, with a strong new emphasis on the South dominating. "It is in expansion, in the canal, in the 'short-out' to the Pacific, that the South will find the speediest solution of the industrial problems with which they have to deal," he announced.[13] He had laid out his modernization program so often by this time that the phrasing and the image of the transition from the "idiosyncrasies of liberty" to the "idiosyncrasies of the market" were familiar to all his readers. The argument for economic self-interest dominated Watterson's editorials, but he also addressed the racial issues so important to his southern readers.

Watterson argued on the basis of tradition and made blunt use of the race issue he often muted when writing for northern audiences. The South had nothing to fear in the expansionist policy, Watterson reassured his readers, because it would not disrupt existing racial hierarchies. It offered "no greater perils to liberty than were embodied by the Indian problem and the Negro question." In these cases, order and white rule had been reasserted quickly. Watterson announced that the Republican mistakes of too quickly granting independence and rights to the freedman would not be repeated, especially not out of base political motivations. "The people of these regions are as ill-prepared for freedom as were the slaves of the South just after the war," he wrote. It was best to "wait and see" before making any final decision on their status, as "we are clearly responsible . . . for good or for evil."[14]

Watterson told southern white men that they had international responsibilities as well as rights. Most bitingly, he reminded antiexpansionist southerners, like Senator Donelson Caffery of Louisiana (who had been a staunch goldbug ally in the National Democratic movement of 1896), that they too shared in a long legacy of imperial rule in the form of white supremacy. The doctrine of consent of the governed was especially unimportant to the South, Watterson reminded his readers. Louisiana, Mississippi, and South Carolina had all given it "a fair trial . . . and they decided that it would not work." What was good for these areas in the form of voting restrictions and white rule would also be good for the Philippines. If blacks could not govern in the South, he asked his fellow

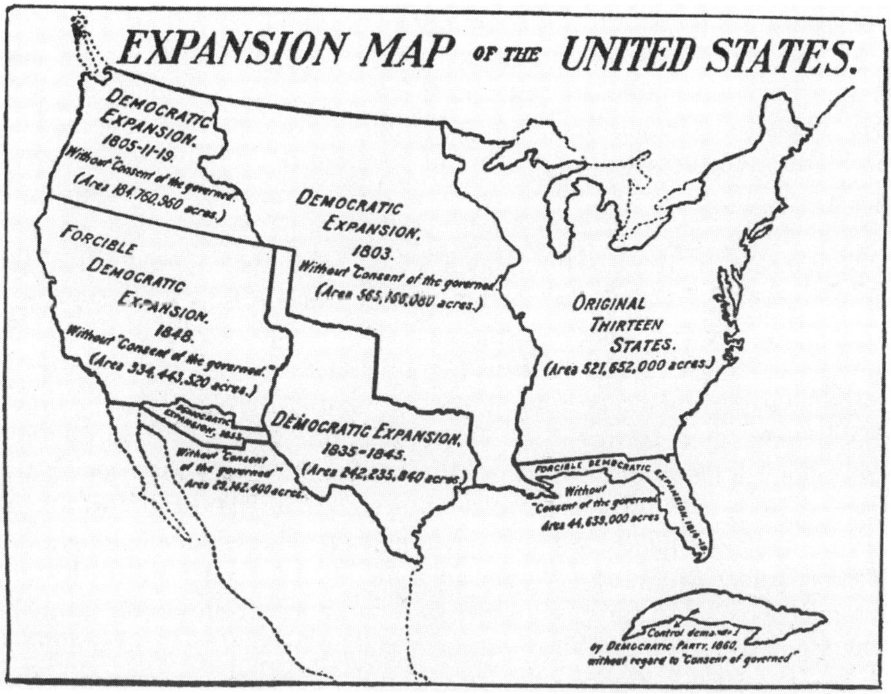

This "EXPANSION MAP OF THE UNITED STATES" appeared in 1900 Republican Party campaign materials as evidence of the many times the United States had expanded under the Democratic Party without reference to the "consent of the governed."

southerners, how could they govern in the Philippines? Republican pro-imperialist pamphlets, such as *Consent of the Governed: How it is Practised by Democrats Who Govern Against Republican Methods*, asked the same question, albeit more insinuatingly.[15]

Along with many others', Watterson's view of the Filipinos hardened significantly after the independence revolt began on February 4, 1899. Earlier, Watterson had broached the possibility of having to fight independence leader Emilio Aguinaldo at some future date, but he did not consider it a major concern. In any case, since the archipelago was taken "so cheaply" from the Spanish, "we can keep it easily." The only possible fighting against the "savages" might come as the United States built railroads throughout the islands, but Watterson did not mind that sort of conflict. "That is the old, established way of subjugating colonies by

English-speaking nations," the *Courier-Journal* told its readers. The Filipino revolt against American occupation strongly reaffirmed Watterson's support for annexation and a large American military presence in Asia. He now asserted that unconditional Filipino surrender had to come before attention turned toward issues of governance. With order restored, he wrote, the "work of emancipation of the Filipinos from savagery and chaos" could be properly accomplished.[16]

Ignoring the irony of the United States' fighting a colonial war, Watterson applied his universal Reconstruction analogy. His understanding of this analogy was especially strange given that anti-imperialists tended to employ the example of Reconstruction as a reason not to embark on a colonial experiment. For example, Senator James Berry of Arkansas drew negative parallels between imperialism and "the curse of carpetbag government," as he put it during the treaty debate. In Watterson's view, however, American control was critical and legitimate. The Filipino rebels were recapitulating the role of the wrongheaded Confederacy in fighting against a necessary union. Watterson argued that federal authority had to be reestablished in the Philippines as it had been in the South through the Civil War. The Filipino uprising was directly analogous to southern secession in 1861. Fighting the "insurgents" in the colony was as morally defensible and constitutionally justifiable as had been the fight against the Confederacy. Just as Congress had not declared war in 1861, Watterson wrote, it did not need to declare war in this instance. This was a war against internal rebels—not patriots, and certainly not a sovereign state—and it required no formal, congressional sanction. Indeed, Watterson thought opposition to expansion in 1898 was equivalent to supporting peace in 1861: a failure to understand that "the use of force is not necessarily dangerous to liberty."[17]

After this "internal rebellion" was subdued, Watterson thought, the islands could be ruled as a conquered province and the people uplifted without repeating the political and racial errors of Radical Republican Reconstruction. Watterson considered the South particularly well prepared for this task; it alone understood the necessity of limiting arbitrary governmental power while still providing for social stability. He told the Democrats and the nation to reject the legacies of Reconstruction through an enlightened colonial rule conforming to the southern spirit of stable governance and social (racial) order. The Democratic Party would not create carpetbag governments that "made the nigger as good as the white man, and in the Southern states a good deal better," and it would not follow the "coochy-coochy Ohio school of political thought." Instead, the Democracy would rule benevolently, firmly, and in line with national self-interest and tradition.[18]

Watterson went to great, often serpentine lengths to assure his southern audiences that he did not advocate an end to "personal liberty and home rule" even though he supported an aggressive overseas stance and the expansion of what many anti-imperialists were calling arbitrary power. Speaking at the Blue Grass Fair in Lexington, Watterson assured the crowd that expansion was consistent with constitutional limits on power, because the Constitution followed the flag: "Expansionist that I am, even jingo that I am, loving to hear the Eagle scream and to see Old Glory wave, fully conceiving the importance and portent of the advancing greatness of my country and rejoicing that it is at length a veritable world power—I yet stand to the belief that wherever the flag goes, the law must go; that there must be uniformity of freedom everywhere beneath that flag. . . . In other words, the Constitution is a clearly-defined chart of limited and enumerated powers, meant to . . . make the exercise of Arbitrary power impossible."[19]

The American system could expand, but its vital, internal constraints on arbitrary power must travel alongside. The constitutional system promised equal protection, liberty, and distributed sovereignty, even within an empire. Watterson was that rare imperialist who insisted on tightly reigned and defined national authority even in foreign territories held as colonies. His intransigence on the limits of authority in the political and economic realm, like his support for free trade, remained consistent throughout his life. He did not readily recognize the incoherency of attempting to reconcile limited government, liberty, and empire.

And yet, contradictorily, Watterson argued that the archipelago did not deserve the rights due to the individually sovereign states of the American system. This former Rebel and self-declared conservative defended the right of America to fight an undeclared war in defense of a questionably legitimate imperial land grab. He negated all comparisons of the Philippine revolt to the American Revolution, a standard anti-imperialist analogy. "The pretense that the people of the Philippine Islands are fighting for independence is distinctly false," Watterson countered in a persistent series of editorials. The Philippines were entirely subordinate to the United States, Watterson argued, and there was "absolutely no such thing as a Philippine government."[20]

Watterson searched for political leverage in the treaty fight, in his struggle for the control of the party's view, and in his attacks on the anti-imperialists. He was a political street fighter, and the Philippine revolt was a deeply useful weapon. By contrasting national self-interest with self-defeat, he saw great opportunities to attack his opponents. Watterson thought support for the new war effort was "good politics as well as good patriotism," and he urged his party to follow this advice. Only a coward could oppose this war or its logical end, he wrote, and there was no room for "manly difference" on this point.[21]

In attempting to convince the South of the benefits of expansion and to equate the fortunes of the policy with those of the region, Watterson portrayed the anti-imperialist movement as northeastern, weak, feminine, and aged. It represented a treasonous retrenchment of American power. He now had a specific enemy on which to focus his attacks, and he linked manliness, youthful vigor, and prosperity with the South, colonialism, and war. Expansion was "the voice of America," he announced, "not [of] a corner of New England." Indeed, Watterson fanned the flames of sectional dispute by reminding his readers and his enemies that it was New Englanders who had violated constitutional freedoms by suspending habeas corpus and locking up Confederates during the Civil War. The anti-imperialists, like "Granny" George F. Hoar, were "more compassionate toward the Filipinos than they were to the Anglo-Saxons of the South," Watterson warned.[22]

When the Philippine revolt began, Watterson started to refer regularly to anti-imperialists as either "Little Americans," grannies, or, in more common wordplay on their position, the "Aunties." It is unclear whether Watterson invented the moniker Aunties or simply was among the first to use it, which he did often. It fit quite well with his overall approach and reflected his use of gender concepts to strengthen his arguments. This language fused opposition to the war to a weak, irrelevant, and feminine older generation and allowed Watterson to ridicule his enemies and to counter their arguments. He linked the Aunties, who were out to destroy national manhood, with the forces out to destroy Democratic masculinity. The term was also a nice play on the idea that the anti-imperialists were "anti" all important issues facing the nation, unlike the optimistic New South. "The bugaboo of 'imperialism' will frighten no one," Watterson promised. "It may make a few he-grannies squirm and tickle a few ladylike mugwumps. But the brain and brawn of the nation are made of sterner stuff. The manhood of the time has its face set toward the future and keeps step to the music of progress."[23]

Of all the specific issues related to expansionism, the Philippine situation was especially likely to elicit this sort of gendered language from Watterson, reflecting his belief that colonialism arrested national emasculation. This effective rhetorical strategy sought to reinforce the vigor and patriotism of expansion. Watterson attacked the congressional agitation against the Treaty of Paris as the "gnawing of a file by the toothless gums of the Aunties [that] is in some quarters dignified with the name of statesmanship." Trying to frighten his fellow Democrats, Watterson warned that McKinley had "the young manhood of the country—yea, and excepting a few old grannies and aunties, its enlightenment—behind him." He dismissed the broader anti-imperialist movement as the "qualms of the weak, the quakes of the timorous, and the crotchets of the fogies." Finally, Watterson compared the spirit of activist and vibrant imperialist politicians like Theodore Roosevelt with that of the Civil War generation, who had also been willing to fight for national greatness, and implied that the new generation of antiwar weaklings were not up to the same standard. "Perhaps the turn of the government of the C.S.A. will yet come if our Aunties' unions hold out a little longer," he wrote.[24]

The Philippine revolt hardened Watterson's attitudes toward U.S. anti-imperialists, whom he considered to be traitors as well as fools of the highest order. They supported "national weakness, cowardice, selfishness and criminal chaos." Watterson joined numerous other newspapers in equating support for McKinley's Philippine policy with the need to destroy its detractors. Like other critics, Watterson strongly attacked the patriotism of anti-imperialist papers and politicians for ostensibly withholding support for troops in battle. He was especially sensitive to the Democratic vulnerability to the charge of copperheadism. "No party in this country has ever yet thrown itself across the highway of the country's progress [with soldiers in the field] . . . without marching to sure defeat," he warned. A month later he wrote the same, concluding, "No party ever can, or will, or ought."[25]

Watterson's support for the war effort in the Philippines was congruent with the majority of the nation's press, two-thirds of which endorsed the "aims and assumptions of the administration's policy." The major division among the papers derived from party affiliation and level of emotional response to the war, although sectional differences were important.

The *Courier-Journal* bemoaned that only in the South were the majority of newspapers antiexpansionist. It was bad policy and bad politics. It was decidedly atypical for a staunchly Democratic paper to support the McKinley administration so aggressively, although other papers did recognize specific commercial advantages in the Republican expansionist program. These included the *Jacksonville Times-Union*, *Atlanta Constitution*, *Baltimore Herald*, and *Memphis Commercial-Appeal*, as well as papers in Baton Rouge, Chattanooga, Galveston, Little Rock, Nashville, and New Orleans.[26]

To ensure that the Democratic Party did not follow Bryan again into the political wilderness, Watterson hoped to convince the South at large to support the expansionist program. The treaty battle and the growth of the anti-imperialist movement complicated this ongoing concern. The majority of southern senators were anti-imperialist, and southern public opinion was rather fluid because of racism, fear of a powerful state with a large military apparatus, potentially higher taxes, and partisanship.[27] Watterson's goal, therefore, was to articulate his interest in expansion in such a way that he convinced the southern public, the Democratic Party leaders, and other editors of the wisdom of the imperial program.

To convert his fellow southerners, Watterson linked the idea of regional economic self-interest to the broader national picture. "Selfish considerations may also be the highest reasons of state," he noted. He sought political allies who understood his vision for southern commercial supremacy, and he found one in his old punching bag, Senator John Tyler Morgan of Alabama. Morgan was the premier champion of the Nicaraguan canal and the end of "commercial thralldom" of the South. Increasingly, the *Courier-Journal* praised Morgan as one of the few southerners who understood absolutely what was at stake in the imperialism debate. Watterson declared Morgan to be a "thoroughbred," the "Apostle of that National Expansion which the prowess and valor of the Nation have brought us at last." Watterson even prominently supported Morgan's reelection and later rejoiced in his victory, so critical was the senator to the expansionist Democratic cause. The *Courier-Journal* also heaped praise upon Democratic senator Anselm J. McLaurin of South Carolina when he announced a proexpansion opinion. The fall 1899 elections seemed to indicate that anti-imperialism lacked political potency beyond Bryan's home state, Nebraska, a development that encouraged Watterson.[28]

Watterson found a receptive audience among New South businesses.

As happened nationwide, business elites in the New South formed an important consensus in support of expansion and commercial development. Southern cotton manufacturers in particular favored retaining the Philippines as the gateway to the legendary China market. These ideas appeared often in editorials like "The Southern Cotton Mill Boom," "The Boom in Cotton," and "Southern Prosperity Assured." Likewise, the *Memphis Commercial-Appeal* gloated over the "700,000,000 people who wear cotton" in Asia. Watterson asserted that southern mills had the competitive advantage against all foreign producers and, perhaps even more important, argued that "it is the Northern mill-owner who should be alarmed." In the South, he wrote, "the raw material . . . can be had at their doors, coal is cheap, labor is cheap, living is cheap." He bragged about fifty new southern cotton mills and the expansion of thirty-nine others and called again for mills to be built in Louisville, as he had periodically for the previous few years. "The construction of the Nicaragua Canal and the opening of the Cuban, Porto Rican and the Philippine markets to our manufacturers gives promise of indefinite trade growth," he promised.[29]

Achieving dominance in this tightly interconnected international commercial system was critical. "The world is shutting up like a telescope," Watterson wrote, "and through the smaller end one can see further than Jefferson saw through the larger." Watterson stressed "Our Great Export Trade" as the most important focus of a new imperial policy. Neither farmer nor manufacturer was independent of the world market. Watterson reveled in America's competitive edge, which he predictably related to his support for free trade. He pointed to "the solidarity of the commercial nations of the world in time of peace," which was becoming the single most important factor for a postprotection American economy. Accordingly, he recommended that national strength be measured in numbers of commercial craft rather than warships.[30] All that was needed to tap the riches of global trade was a reliable entry to the system. Watterson believed the Philippines and a canal offered exactly that opportunity.

Convincing the South of this insight required some careful argumentation, and the issue became hotly debated in southern Democratic papers in the middle of July 1899. Watterson, happily for himself and the *Courier-Journal*, dominated the discussion and set its extremes. The Philippine war had increased Watterson's need to rally southern support for what was now a war of conquest as well as of international markets and domestic political position. The United States had to "settle with Aguinaldo first and consider McKinley afterward." In a series of editorials expressly aimed at "the people of the Gulf States and the Southern States contiguous thereto," which was of course the entire former Confederacy, Watterson made his case. The most important of these editorials, presented in the multiple column format reserved only for big pronouncements, promised the South that imperialism would solve all of its concerns without imposing any difficulties. All of the ideas, and a good deal of the language, in this editorial were reused extensively in the following months. Watterson guaranteed that his New Departure of expansionism would utterly reform the economic and political subordination of the South in the U.S. system and erase all social instability. Indeed, he considered his imperial program to be so "far-reaching and overmastering" that "it will rehabilitate [the southern states] in their lost prestige and opulence, and may find them an avenue of escape from the conflict of races which overshadows their present life and menaces their future."[31]

Watterson never specifically described how expansion would solve the southern race problem, but he promised repeatedly that it could. He told the South that expansion was the only possible "outlet for our commerce and maybe for our niggers." Other expansionist southerners, particularly John Tyler Morgan, also supported using the new colonies as a safety valve for racial problems at home. Morgan had concerns about the racial makeup of the islands and was initially not interested in full, formal control of all of them for that reason. Later, he moved toward the outlandish idea of solving the domestic race problem by encouraging blacks to homestead in the Philippines.[32]

The biggest step in southern renewal was fully grasping the benefits of expansion into the Asian market, which Watterson considered "another New World." Once again, he relied on a string of historical analogies to prove that "the imperial idea" had always driven U.S. territorial expansion, adding the fresh examples of George Rogers Clark and "the Empire of Kaskaskia," as well as Pike, Fremont, and Lewis and Clark. Asia, Watterson asserted, was a "magic crucible whose elixir of life is to regenerate the South." In China and Japan, there were "myriads to be clothed and fed, to be educated in wants, . . . [and] elevated into Civilization and Markets," and the Philippines offered immediate access to this bottomless trough.[33] The idea of being "educated in wants" was a precise description

Senator John Tyler Morgan of Alabama, expansionist. Library of Congress, Prints and Photographs Division, LC-USZ62–51127

of the imperatives of an underconsuming capitalist system; the idea of being "elevated" to the markets was a fairly common understanding of American progress.

In addition to grabbing the Philippines, Watterson argued, building a Nicaraguan canal was crucial to southern domination of the Asian trade. From this point on, Watterson's support for expansion always included the canal caveat as a requirement for the South's prosperity. He dubbed the canal the fulcrum of an imperial policy, which would turn out to be an apt description. As globalization opened new markets, easy access would be essential, and the Isthmian canal would provide precisely this access. Watterson thought that building the canal was the only means for the South to achieve political independence as well as prosperity. He was not exaggerating the importance of the canal to economic or political success, because he knew that whatever party pushed the canal could command a newfound prosperity, public allegiance, and ballot success. Accordingly, he wrote to his friend John Hay, "These vast Territorial accessions will be but peg-legged affairs as far as the administration is concerned unless we [the South] get the canal."[34]

Although it was an important political prize, the canal would most of all be a boon to southern commerce. Those who discussed the canal at this time, with the conspicuous exception of John Tyler Morgan, tended to concentrate upon the benefits of linking the oceans for the coasts, rather than for the South. Watterson tried to recenter the debate around the South. He promised that the "the day is coming, . . . and when it does the South will become as thickly settled and wealthy as its natural advantages entitle it to be." Without this pathway between the oceans, he wrote, the Gulf of Mexico was, "if not a dead eddy, . . . an imperfect outlet . . . a pocket," and Mobile was stuck in a "watery cul-de-sac."[35]

Watterson argued that a canal offered the Gulf states a position from which to exploit the Asian market at will because, "with the Nicaraguan Canal, all of these regions are geographically ours." This emphasis was partly the result of the reopened discussion of exactly where to dig a canal, as Panama had fewer direct benefits for the South than did Nicaragua. Watterson envisioned the same benefits spreading throughout the Upper South and the whole Mississippi valley. Freight would turn south rather than continuing to go east, once the canal was built. Six railroads had their terminuses in New Orleans: the Southern Pacific, Queen and Crescent, Louisville and Nashville, Texas and Pacific, Yazoo and Mississippi Valley, and Illinois Central. The last was run by Watterson's old friend Stuyvesant Fish, who was interested in sending the "exportable surplus" of the Mississippi valley out through New Orleans. Watterson urged his readers to picture the future: "There is the mouth of the Mississippi drawing from the great [Old] Northwest exhaustless tribute to the Nicaragua outlet, sailing like an Argosy of golden fleece down the Father of Waters." Louisville, Memphis, Galveston, Mobile, and Pensacola would all prosper as the surplus goods of the United States flowed south, through the canal, and on to Asia. Watterson assured Dixie that "the policy of national Expansion, . . . as far as it relates to the Pacific, is but another name for the development of the South."[36]

Watterson was confident that the idiosyncrasies of the new Asian markets, laid open by a canal, would give the South back the "power and glory" that it had commanded in the nation before the Civil War. He argued that economic expansion into the markets of Asia would bring independence and solve all problems in the dependent regions of the United States, of which the South was the most suffering. The Pacific trade would free the South, in particular, from its orientation and its dependence on the Northeast and the "capitalists of England." Without a canal, Watterson warned, "there is no hope save that of fiscal and geographical dependency [on] . . . the ship-owners and money-changers of New York and its collateral branches, Philadelphia and Boston." Surely the South would not want to continue its subordination and dependence. The opportunity to demonstrate the region's competitiveness in Asia meant the beginning of a twentieth-century renewal: "All the states we have named [will] blossom like the traditional rose and regain their old-time splendor; independent in all things, tributary in nothing."[37]

These ideas, so forcefully presented, had a powerful impact on the debate over imperialism in the South, and Watterson spent the rest of the summer of 1899 responding to his critics and praising his supporters throughout the country. His presumption to speak from Kentucky for the Gulf states raised hackles in some newspapers, such as the *New Orleans Times-Democrat*. He referred to all such criticism, in general, as "the gyrations of some of Mr. Bryan's fool friends." Watterson sarcastically attacked his critics, as was his style, but he also supported his arguments with appeals to self-interest and the conflation of gender, imperialism, and race. He asked the highly critical *Tacoma (WA) News*, which had accused him of Republicanism, if it would "cast off her [the Philippines] now that she is within our embraces, her arms about her dear Uncle Samuel's neck and her kinky head resting lovingly upon his heaving but manly bosom? Perish the thought!" Watterson welcomed McKinley's increasingly forceful statements of imperial purpose in the Philippines and liberal benevolence toward Puerto Rico. It seemed clear that the policy would not (and should not) change, and therefore could not continue to be fruitfully disputed. McKinley said, "It is no longer a question of expansion with us; we have expanded. If there is any question at all it is a question of contraction; and who is going to contract?"[38]

Watterson picked up on this phrase and its implication, mostly seeking to convince his party of the futility of continuing to pretend that anti-imperialism had popular appeal. There was no longer an issue to be made of imperialism. "We done expanded," he often wrote, deliberately echoing McKinley, although adding a southern accent.[39] Since expansion was a reality, Watterson decided that the only new issue was how to apply the simple truths of home rule and free trade at home to the question of empire.

Despite Watterson's earnest hope that imperialism would not continue to divide the Democratic Party, it did. As the debate over it continued, and as the election of 1900 approached, Watterson concentrated on carving out an expansionist position that would somehow coalesce with his continued allegiance to the mainstream party. This became an increasingly difficult task when the party officially declared itself against colonization of the Philippines. Nevertheless, the benefits of expansion into the Pacific did have some new converts in the southern press. After a survey of southern press opinion on imperialism and trade expansionism, the *Macon (GA) Telegraph* concluded that the people should decide the Philippine issue in the election, but in so doing, they should recognize "our sympathies are strongly enlisted in behalf of every honorable means whereby trade expansion for the South and the whole country can be secured. And we think that this sentiment is now shared by a large majority of Southern people. The prospect of large gains for this section through the increased export of our manufacturers and otherwise is engaging the minds of all classes. The commercial and progressive South is fascinated with the vision of empire to come through an isthmian canal and Asiatic trade."[40]

Watterson likewise cajoled, teased, and ordered the Democratic Party to grab the political initiative by taking expansionism as its own and "developing it upon historic Democratic lines," rather than attempting to fight it. "Anti-expansion is anti-Democracy," Watterson wrote, twisting effectively the "Aunties'" idea that imperialism was antidemocratic. "Expansion does not mean imperialism unless Democrats surrender to the Republicans in advance and leave to them all the usufructs of War and Progress." At the very least, the party had to resist the forces of anti-imperialist "reaction" that were limiting its future room to maneuver. Political position mattered. David Healy characterizes this position as "the Hearst-Watterson blend of political opportunism and economic aspiration." He argues that, "without Bryan, the Democratic stand on foreign policy would have differed considerably from that to which he led it," especially because of the influence of people like Watterson and John Tyler Morgan. Watterson characteristically insisted he was preaching a middle course and not an extremist position: "It is because the *Courier-Journal* is an Expansionist and not an Imperialist, a Democrat and not a Republican, that we counsel greater moderation and caution," he wrote.[41]

Accordingly, Watterson thought control and utilization of the empire should be the primary focus of Democratic political action, as that was the first step to control of national politics. Watterson condemned his party and the South for failing to grasp the fundamental fact that it was not possible to separate foreign affairs from domestic affairs. The Republicans relied on the fact that Democratic "schoolboy orators" like Bryan were incapable of understanding the interrelatedness of the modern world. They subsequently misled their often "simple and primitive" constituents. "They would put a horse's head on the body of a man and make it sing like a bird," Watterson wrote to illustrate the confusion.[42]

Watterson thought the isolationist, anti-imperialist approach was "grotesque, incongruous, out of date and out of line; playing directly into the hands of the Republicans." The Republicans agreed, and they welcomed his support. The editor had, after all, helped rally conservative Democratic support for McKinley in 1896. Marcus Hanna, for instance, read Watterson's major editorial "Expansion and Imperialism" from early August and sent him "a word of congratulations upon the clear and forcible manner in which you have put it before the southern people." Hanna concluded, "I hope they will profit by it."[43] Watterson knew he was potentially playing into Republican hands when he earned such praise, and he refused to aid the Republicans in 1900 as he had four years earlier. A party bolt would have been counterproductive, since it would court the commercial disasters that came after 1896 and would leave the Democrats on the wrong side of the issue. The Republicans would be left shaping the American empire. Watterson instead attempted to burnish his party credentials by insisting on his own party regularity despite the obvious contradictions of this position.

Watterson insisted, at great length, that expansion was not a Republican issue and that he was not a closeted Republican. "The Editor of the Courier-Journal is too dyed-in-the-wool of his Democracy to become a Republican," he wrote cheerfully in his favored third-person voice. "He may remain what he seems to be, a Democrat in bad standing." He derided "the party of Mammon, the party of Unrighteousness, the party of Reconstruction with the Money Devil in the person of Mark Hanna at its head." Watterson understood the danger that, through expansion, the Republicans could destroy the South's chance to revive. If Bryan were successful in determining the Democratic outlook, Watterson warned, McKinley would be reelected "while the poor, deluded banjo players [of the South] suck their thumbs and swear at the returns."[44]

To avoid that fate, and to render Bryan irrelevant, Watterson suggested a new party focus on the centrality of foreign affairs in producing future prosperity. He contrasted his own, self-consciously sophisticated and synthetic understanding with that of the anti-imperialists, North and South. "What do our hayseed statesmen know about the treaty of Tientsin or the open door, or the Siberian Railway, or the schemes of Bruin, or the Concert of Powers, or the dismemberment of the Mongolian Empire, and the relation of these things to our own future?" he asked. Surely these hayseeds saw no connections, which was "the characteristic answer of fools." In contrast, Watterson believed that his sophisticated understanding of the South's commercial interest gave him a clear view of the future, and he saw that the future of the United States was tightly linked with events in Asia. "We already have two thousand miles of Occidental frontage," he wrote, and the United States could not escape the "world-movement to the Pacific" even if it wanted to.[45] It was time for the Democracy to modernize its politics for this new reality and to capitalize on its massive potential.

In fact, with the country seemingly in support of expansion, and with the reality of imperial control accomplished, Watterson thought the time was at hand to achieve "Democratic government on Jeffersonian lines at home and abroad!" A successful foreign policy could produce political and commercial success at home. By ignoring this truth, the party courted doom. With the right policy, however, the Democratic Party could win with any candidate. Only the party of empire could carry the day. Watterson asked, "But how many votes do these gentlemen think they can poll in 1900 on a back-action reversing-the-engine, out-of-coal and out-of-date campaign, with only the warmed over victuals to sustain them against McKinley flying the flag?" Four years earlier, the party had met disaster because of shoddy leadership, social chaos, and economic disruption: "Depression everywhere, the Open Door nowhere." Now, things had changed, and the party had another chance.[46]

Rather than focusing on individual political posturing, Watterson hoped to refocus the party on the basic advantages of the policy itself. To this end, and in immense contradiction with his stated positions, Watterson slowly and painfully decided to support William Jennings Bryan as the party's candidate. The editor made this decision almost entirely out of political expediency, which he certainly knew well. Watterson did not wish to further divide his weakened party. Since he could not block this nomination, he sought to contain its ultimate effects on the party's stance. The editor tried hard to make a Bryan candidacy seem like less than a total disaster to his overall vision for the future. The futile effort of the National Democrats in 1896, and the ongoing disastrous attempts to reshape the party throughout 1897–99, made it clear that acting only on the periphery of the party was ineffective. Even as he urged the party to admit "we done expanded" and move to exploit the new policy, Watterson accepted that Bryan was inevitably going to win the party's nomination. Watterson thus sought to consolidate the party center around his new emphasis on assertive foreign policy.

Watterson first signaled this change early in 1900 in an editorial titled "Expansion and Protection," in which he laid out what he considered the most important difference between the parties: free trade. He implied that it was the overall ideology of a party that mattered, not the views of an individual politician. Since the Democracy was the only party of free trade expansionism, it was necessary to support it and whomever it chose to run in the fight against McKinleyism. Watterson promised that a Democratic victory would usher in a new era as the American system was spread throughout the world: "National Expansion goes hand in hand, if not with free trade, at least with freer trade than we had heretofore had. The tendency of expansion is toward free trade. . . . Every new bit of territory that becomes a part of the United States extends the area of the free trade that has always prevailed among the States and Territories of the Union."[47]

Because the realization of free trade was imminent, Watterson admitted quietly that he would toe the party line and support Bryan as the candidate. On the occasion of "St. Jackson's Day," his favorite time to rally the party faithful, Watterson downplayed his support for Bryan by emphasizing that the real focus should be strictly on party victory. Only a Democratic president could oversee the development of global free trade rather than a closed imperial system. If the party grabbed the appropriate issues, which Watterson had delineated at great length, then the "Jeffersonian gospel of Constitutional freedom [would] prevail over the military gospel of Caesar and Caesarism." Under these circumstances, the party could win despite Bryan. All Watterson asked in return was for Bryan to assure the country, and especially the South, that, "as to National development, there will be no retrograde movement" away from free trade.[48]

This bargain on continued party support for free trade became the basis of Watterson's support for Bryan and of his willingness to act wholly within the confines of the official party. Watterson was also interested in maintaining his future legitimacy in the party. Other Democratic leaders followed the same difficult path. In the words of one historian, "Desperate for a standard bearer, the inescapable fact that it had to be Bryan, whom they viewed as a demagogue and a radical, drove the non-Bryanites to the brink of a new desperation." For example, William Randolph Hearst, despite his early belief in retaining the Philippines, started the *American* in Chicago to support Bryan in the Midwest. The antisilver and anti-Bryan *Charleston News and Courier*, *Atlanta Journal*, and *Memphis Commercial-Appeal* all endorsed Bryan in the spirit of party unity. The latter pushed for a new emphasis on trust-busting and tariff revision to replace anti-imperialism as the issues with national appeal. "The negro question will keep most of the Southern States for the Democracy" in any case, it argued.[49]

Watterson did not wish for his party to lose on the basis of a personnel disagreement, especially when so much was at stake for the South. Expansion promised "redemption from the stagnation and poverty" that had afflicted the South since its escape from Radical Republican rule. Watterson was terrified that these gains would be lost. In dozens of editorials, he implied that national expansion might actually offer revenge for decades of political and regional subordination by liberating the Democratic Party. The Republicans had historically taken good policies to radical extremes: "It has been sometimes a fanatic and sometimes an opportunist." Since that party could not resist making "expansion a new era of Reconstruction," Democrats only had to be patient and the Republicans would reveal their true nature, as they had after the Civil War. "It is already beginning to be apparent that the Republicans, if given enough rope in arranging the government of our new territory, will hang themselves," Watterson wrote in February 1900. The Democrats had to use these blunders against them.[50]

The southern party was facing a crisis it had not known since the Civil War because of the generational switch and the vigor of the imperialism issue. Watterson was desperate for this new issue to arrive so that the Democrats would have something on which to build a proactive

In this undated cartoon, Watterson is much chagrined to find himself appointed press agent for William Jennings Bryan. Against all of his wishes, Watterson found himself forced to support Bryan in successive presidential campaigns in the interests of the Democratic Party. Library of Congress, Manuscripts Division, Henry Watterson Papers

platform. He had concerns that the "Young South," in the form of the post–Civil War generation, was "already hanging upon the ragged edge of Republicanism" and might fall over it if not given an attractive alternative. These youth, insufficiently schooled in a Democracy unterrified and undefiled, were being "dazzled" by the promises, glory, and success of the imperial policies of McKinley, Hanna, and Roosevelt. Watterson warned they would be bored or repelled by a revival of "dead issues." Watterson thought Bryan had degraded the party's appeal by steering it away from "organic" issues and muscular appeals to national power toward senseless moralizing and weakness. The Solid South was crumbling. The Democrats had to choose, Watterson wrote: "It is the Young South, solid as ever, or Granny Hoar and Aguinaldo."[51]

When Bryan visited Frankfort, Kentucky, in the middle of January 1900, the *Courier-Journal* greeted him with three editorials that reiterated the idiosyncrasy of the market ideas developed over the previous two years. What is most striking in these and subsequent editorials is the emphasis they placed on the "traditions and instincts" of the Republican Party, particularly its "Imperialism of the Reconstruction brand."[52] Watterson attempted to dominate the southern debate and now reverted to the ultimate reasoning for supporting his former bitter enemy. How could any self-respecting southerner support Republicanism and carpetbaggery if the alternative was merely acquiescing to Auntie Bryan as a candidate?

In delicately embracing the Boy Orator of the Platte, Watterson exposed himself to criticism from other southern papers. He refused to be baited about the switch to supporting Bryan and refused to change his own position. "The *Courier-Journal* is wearing no sack-cloth to speak of," he told his critics at the *Charlotte (NC) Observer*. "We see no hope for the South except in Expansion, and we welcome Expansion." Rather, Watterson argued, it was the silverite and anti-imperialist papers that ought to be ashamed of their positions. He no longer admitted fearing Bryan's taking office and destroying the public credit and order. "As for silver! Tralala! By the time Mr. Bryan gets warm in his seat in the White House we shall have other and bigger fish to fry." Later, Watterson promised possible voters that, "at his worst, Mr. Bryan would be powerless to do any serious or lasting harm," whereas the tentacles of the Republicans would be impossible to eradicate in the future.[53]

This argument directly contradicted Watterson's stance in 1896, when he told southerners that the nation could survive another four years of McKinley and protectionism but would be utterly destroyed by free silver. Now, he argued that protectionism had returned as the greatest threat to the Republic. Watterson was unconcerned that even a Bryanite Democracy would reverse the course of globalization that he so eagerly anticipated. It certainly helped that Bryan, like most of the anti-imperialists, never disputed the desirability and necessity of increasing American access to foreign markets, just the means. In a letter on June 7, 1900, Bryan assured Watterson that the two actually agreed on general principles, writing, "I note what you say on the subject of imperialism. I believe that we should draw the line between Expansion and imperialism. Expansion is the taking in of territory which can be created into States; the enlargement of a republic without a change in its character. Imperialism is the conversion of a republic into an empire, wherein part of the people govern themselves and also govern the colonies."[54] More concerned with ends than means, Watterson found Bryan's economic expansionism palatable indeed.

The bigger fish Watterson wished to fry was the establishment and maintenance of a free trade system in the new empire. This was his vision for the future, as well as the means of stopping Republican bedazzlement of the "Young South." He thus again turned to the tariff issue to magnify the political issues at stake and to separate the parties and their approaches to governance. Although this time he was concerned with imperial tariffs and the management of empire rather than internal revenue and economic development, he viewed the issues as tightly interconnected. As usual, he asserted that economic questions determined the true ideological and partisan disputes.

Watterson pointed to the Republican establishment of Puerto Rican and Philippine tariffs as "The Issue" on which to base the campaign of 1900. The creation of tariffs in the new empire animated debate across the country, and Watterson eagerly joined. Since expansion was a fait accompli, the Democracy should dispute the mechanics of Republican colonial administration and exploit their "contradictions and absurdities." Watterson also knew that the colonial tariff itself was going to last for only two years, so it was essential to exploit it while the issue was fresh. He raised the specter of the Republicans' importing their tariff shenanigans into internal territories, like Alaska, New Mexico, Arizona, and Oklahoma, and beginning to practice overt imperialism domestically. Most of all, Watterson attacked the Republicans for their inability to understand that it was free trade that had made the Union strong, and free trade that would make the colonial empire strong.[55]

The Puerto Rican tariff question grew out of the search for coherent economic policy in the wake of Spain's defeat. As early as May 19, 1898,

McKinley had set up trade with the Philippines based upon the United States' collecting the former Spanish tariffs, although military and colonial government supplies entered duty free. Some type of selectively applied tariff continued to be placed on the colony from that point. One historian called this system "the reconciliation of imperialism and protection." The maintenance of the Philippine tariff system was based upon the Foraker Act of 1900, which established dutiable rates for Puerto Rico. The tariffs later achieved legitimacy through the Supreme Court in a series of decisions called the insular cases.[56]

The tariff issue was Watterson's ideal issue: it was simultaneously clarifying and polarizing. Since an empire of protection was exactly the sort of system he feared would be projected abroad by the McKinley administration, he concentrated his attacks on the relations between the tariff and the idea of Republican neo-Reconstructionism. For Watterson, the tariff clearly signaled that the new American empire would be improperly governed under the congenitally paternalistic Republicans. An imperial tariff destroyed trade and freedom because it violated the essential tenets of Watterson's preferred system—home rule and free trade. The expansion of sovereignty required the expansion of liberty and opportunity.

The Puerto Rican tariff was especially useful in clarifying the distinction Watterson made between his version of free trade expansionism and McKinley's imperialism. The question of managing the new empire was the key. "It is not imperialism to acquire new territory," he commonly put it, "but imperialism may appear in the manner of governing it." The Republicans simply could not allow the area of freedom to grow; it ran counter to their instincts. The colonial tariffs were more of the same policy they had pursued since the Civil War. Historian Goran Rystad argues that "the [real] issue was not Puerto Rico, but the Philippines, Cuba, and in general the foundations of American expansion." The tariff did in fact reveal the decidedly self-interested manner in which the United States initially structured its relationship with both its new empire and, in turn, the international political economy. The debate over it (and the earlier Dingley tariff) highlighted the complexities of moving toward a system of reciprocity and free trade as the underpinnings of American expansionism. Oddly, the colonial tariff is not an issue that has inspired historians of foreign affairs, despite its importance to the conception of the American imperial system. It is usually discussed only fleetingly. The racial and constitutional aspects of the imperialism debate are often considered to be more attractive or valuable topics, although they are in fact inseparable from the tariff, sovereignty, and jurisdictional questions.[57]

That the tariff issue would gain prominence in the imperialism debate was not simply the delusion of a man who had dedicated most of his political energies over the years to the Star-Eyed Goddess of tariff reform. The *Courier-Journal* did often give more room to the tariff than other papers gave to editorials overall, but the tariff controversy gained significant traction in the national political debate. Most major papers and politicians of Watterson's day quickly recognized the significance of the issue, and it dominated the nation's editorial pages throughout the spring of 1900. Bryan was occupying lonely ground when he insisted that imperialism was "still the most important question," comparable to a heart attack, whereas "the tariff question can be compared to the stomach ache, which is uncomfortable but not vital." He was inconsistent, to say the least. Paolo Coletta wrote, "Bryan may have erred in championing too many issues. On one day he was an anti-imperialist, the next a silverite, on the third a trust-buster, the fourth a friend of labor, the fifth an Anglophobe working for the German and Irish vote, the sixth an advocate of the income tax. . . . The wonder is that he did so well with such a heavy load."[58]

The precise nature of trade relations within the new empire was of great importance to the national economy and to the structure of future American foreign affairs, and it focused the minds of both politicians and journalists. Differing positions on the issue tended to reflect broader understandings of economic development's proper course, of political rights, and of political expediency. Globalization necessitated open markets and liberalized trade networks, but domestic politics had other constraints. Businesses that faced competition from colonial producers were not eager to confront the challenge. Yet American exporters wished to have unencumbered access to the new colonial markets, free of foreign competition. Southern congressmen and senators were often apprehensive of making Puerto Ricans citizens. Free trade relations between the island and the United States, they feared, would start a trend toward miscegenation or racial chaos. Historian Ronald Fernandez put it well: "Puerto Rico was stranded in a sea of ambiguity, racism, good intentions, whimsy, audacity, contradiction, indifference, and political compromise."[59]

In keeping with his new emphasis on open markets (as signaled in the move toward reciprocity), McKinley had originally sought the long-term establishment of free trade relations with Puerto Rico. This delighted

Watterson. The head of McKinley's Insular Commission, Henry K. Carroll, initiated the debate by arguing that the island deserved free trade with the United States but that "the statehood issue is really not an issue." In his annual address of 1899, the president declared, "Our plain duty is to abolish all customs tariffs between the United States and Puerto Rico and give her products free access to our markets." Despite this seemingly clear intent, McKinley was hampered by internal wrangling in his party and fear over setting an unwelcome precedent for the Philippines. Senate Republicans briefly warmed to an unbalanced system in which American goods would be admitted to Puerto Rico without restriction but trade from the island would face duties. As economist R. F. Hoxie noted shortly thereafter, "Its significance was of course perfectly apparent. It was a plan for colonial exploit pure and simple." Senator Joseph B. Foraker, who headed the Senate committee on the new territorial dependencies, eventually accepted a lower, two-year compromise tariff based on 15 percent of the high Dingley rates. The money raised would be used for administration of the new possession. Protectionism was saved for a time.[60]

The Foraker compromise tariff did not please everyone, and both Republican and Democratic papers called for a new policy. A wide array of midwestern and southern papers were strongly united in their opposition to the tariff, with exceptions in sugar-growing areas like Louisiana. There remained among protectionists a great deal of fear that a new colonial system would damage the domestic market if not carefully managed. In general, only hard-line protectionist papers, like the *St. Louis Globe-Democrat* and Whitelaw Reid's *New York Tribune*, were satisfied with the tariff. Reid, Watterson's old friend from the 1870s and the negotiator of the Treaty of Paris, understood that the imperatives of globalization were changing the dynamics of domestic economic policy. He fought to keep the Constitution and political and economic rights from spreading to the islands. Reid suggested that, since one could not complain about the "barbarous Chinese Wall" of a tariff and then want to enclose the islands in it, imperial free trade might well destroy protectionism itself. He feared that treating the territories like states would cause "the whole tariff system [to be] thus plucked up by the roots."[61] This was, of course, Watterson's hope.

Empire and the opportunities of globalization seemed to have deepened the faint stirrings of trade liberalization occurring among some protectionists. McKinley and prominent friends of reciprocity, including the *Chicago Inter-Ocean*, *Chicago Evening Post*, *Cincinnati Commercial*, *Baltimore American*, *Boston Journal*, and *Indianapolis Journal*, opposed the Foraker tariff in large numbers. They argued that the United States could not manage the territories on an exclusionary basis. Although these papers were not threatening to leave their party, they were realigning their policies. The *Inter-Ocean* called the tariff "an outrage," and the *Chicago Times-Herald*, usually a Watterson foe, seemed to echo his best lines when it argued, "The tariff line marks the boundary where republicanism becomes imperialism."[62]

A large portion of the dispute over colonial tariffs centered on whether Puerto Rico was to be granted territorial or colonial status, which in turn raised a broader series of constitutional, racial, and economic questions. Territorial status traditionally led to statehood, and opponents of direct congressional rule of Puerto Rico argued that the island could be constitutionally held only as a state. Congress debated whether this land was, in the words of Foraker, "a possession or dependency, a district, a territory, or otherwise . . . restricted or restrained by the provisions and limitations of the Constitution."[63] In this context, the tariff debate became representative of the larger dispute over establishing and governing the empire, and for what ends.

One major issue of this process was whether keeping and ruling Puerto Rico was even allowed under national law. The political questions, mirroring the broader imperial debate, centered on general government acquisition of territory and the subsequent status of annexed lands. The Foraker Act of May 1900 finally established clear American legal control of Puerto Rican life and politics and brought the island into regulated trade union with the United States. Watterson thought the country needed a single "uniform and equitable rule for dealing with its new possessions." He gloated when the *Chicago Tribune* crossed party lines to oppose the Foraker Act and was pleased about the wider turmoil within the Republican Party. Yet Watterson detected a conspiracy to destroy political liberties as well as commerce in the Foraker compromise. He did not approve of its construction or its intent, and he did not believe it protected either the nation's or the colony's interests. Most of all, however, he thought the question moved beyond that of mere protection of industry (of which Puerto Rico had none to speak of) or commercial sectors, like agriculture, and into the realm of political rights.[64]

All sides in the public debate over the Foraker Act rallied around the

Constitution. Benjamin Harrison and other anti-imperialists argued that the Puerto Rican tariff violated the essential principles of the Constitution and set a double standard. They insisted that the Constitution be strictly interpreted and uniformly applied. Traditional McKinley supporters, such as the *Outlook*, argued that "Puerto Rico is not under the Constitution" but that the only sensible policy was "absolute free trade; in other words, the immediate practical admission of Puerto Rico into the commercial union of the States, but not . . . into the political union." The *Nation* called a tariff erected against Puerto Rico a "Middle-Age monstrosity" and claimed that the unwillingness of the United States to apply the open door to the island indicated that it had only reenslaved it. "In this respect, liberation from Spanish commercial oppression means for the islanders a falling back into worse oppression." Sounding like Watterson, the Democratic *Washington Times* declared the colonial tariff to be in defiance of "the basic law of the Union" and, therefore, a political gold mine. "The Democracy has been looking for a paramount issue upon which to rally all its scattered and divided forces," it wrote. "Here is one, and a better could not be conceived: 'Honesty, humanity, and the Constitution!'"[65]

Watterson used the same constitutional arguments that the anti-imperialists used, but in support of welcoming Puerto Rico into both the commercial and the political union. He thought that the Constitution had to follow the flag, right along with home rule, free trade, and sound money. He was unafraid of expanding political connections so long as economic freedoms accompanied them. The two were inseparable. "Why not give our own people the benefit of the 'open door,'" he asked archly, "subject only to the revenue needs of the Government?" The Puerto Rican tariff, with its implication of separateness and inequality, violated the Constitution because it held the island in unrepresented limbo and economic exploitation. Later, in the insular decisions, Justice John Marshall Harlan described this limbo as "disembodied shade." Watterson and others saw this as the essence of Republicanism. An anonymous author, "An Ex-Democrat," wrote in a 1901 recap of the presidential election in the *Forum*, "It would at least furnish the ironically inclined historian with a pungent parable should the party of Franklin Pierce and James Buchanan free the Filipino from the party of Abraham Lincoln and Ulysses S. Grant."[66]

Watterson did not recognize the right of the United States to tax the free inhabitants of Puerto Rico any more than he recognized its right to tax Kentuckians, and he welcomed the islanders to full and immediate civil parity with Americans. He accepted this idea more sweepingly than most did. Since Puerto Ricans indeed deserved to be citizens, they had as much right to commercial freedom within the Union as did southerners. In Watterson's understanding, this was a fundamental right and benefit of home rule. Ignoring the dominant southern fear that imperialism created new, dangerous race questions, he fully welcomed Puerto Rico into confederation with the United States. This position followed his established opinions that overseas expansion would only ease domestic racial problems and that the Puerto Ricans had escaped the racial degradation of southern blacks. The Republicans had blurred the issue, but Watterson would not accept that lack of clarity. "The people of Porto Rico are either citizens of the United States or foreigners," he wrote. If the Republican Party wanted to reap the benefits of controlling Puerto Rico, it would have to take the necessary step of incorporating the island as a self-governing entity into a decentralized but solid federal union. Otherwise, it could not make laws to govern the island. "If they are foreigners," he asked, "what right have we to tax them?" Let them be citizens, and he was sure they would wisely choose free trade.[67]

The insular tariff question was essentially parallel in Watterson's mind to the Reconstruction question. Both turned on the issues of the nature of federal sovereignty, home rule within the Union, the party question, and commercial and political freedom. The GOP simply could not resist returning to its exploitative roots when it became drunk with power. "With sublime effrontery the Republican organs, fell into the familiar line of carpetbaggery, scallawaggery and skullduggery just like cavalry horses trained never to forget, although out of practice." Watterson compared the political situation in Kentucky under Republican rule to the destruction of free government and home rule in Puerto Rico under McKinley: "The State of Kentucky is a republic, and it is menaced by imperialism just as the United States are menaced." In an editorial titled "A Tale of Two Eras," he described "the spirit that underlay Caesarism, Grantism, [and] Imperialism." He further argued that the Republicans wanted nothing more than "carpetbag colonies to be governed by force and robbed at will . . . Cuba another Louisiana; Porto Rico another South Carolina." He argued that the South faced the same choice in 1900 that it had in 1876: to prevent further corruption, arbitrary power, and economic stagnation, it needed a Democratic victory.[68]

As he had since the Civil War, Watterson understood the tariff issue to be as much about political power and ideology as about economic policy. He recalled his promise to the South that expansion would not entail the growth of arbitrary power, and he recognized the danger. The colonial tariff question, he wrote when it came before the Supreme Court, "invokes the very nature of our Government." The question was whether Congress could rule where the Constitution did not extend. Watterson asserted that the delegated powers at the heart of the federal system forbade it. "There was no notion of creating a Government with any innate power," he argued. Once a war ended, the country had to either formally acquire foreign territory it held by conquest or leave it. Watterson believed that this was the Jeffersonian legacy. Colonial protectionism could be destructive of the domestic system if Congress ruled possessions with absolute power. If the Constitution were ignored in empire, "the door is open to arbitrary power everywhere."[69]

Watterson welcomed overseas territorial expansion and its "boodle" in the form of new foreign market opportunities, and he was initially quite willing to bend or expand the Constitution to achieve these ends. He compromised on the expansion of federal sovereignty when it was necessary to achieve specific, clear, and defensible foreign policy ends but erected limits on the creation of arbitrary powers when they violated the internal rules he had developed over the years. He expected his readers to follow his convoluted lead because he articulated their greater concerns and defended southern interests. He was not entirely successful in this regard. In many ways, Watterson embraced Republican policies without convincing many southerners of their value or fully grasping their long-term implications himself.

Watterson had welcomed the Republican Open Door policy (the first notes of which were sent on September 6, 1899, and the second on July 3, 1900) as a step in the right direction and proof that McKinley indeed understood the need for open markets and liberalized trade. These diplomatic notes were sent to the European great powers in an attempt to maintain open access to markets within a territorially secure China. They represented the clear commitment of the United States to market expansionism and globalization. This move strengthened Watterson's feeling that the Puerto Rican tariff was "opportunism run mad." Now that the United States was not just a reunited nation but a world power urging free trade, he argued, it needed to modernize its commercial policies along his favored lines. "Protection is the expedient of small and inaccessible communities," he wrote; "it is not for a great and growing country." One reason for his growing, if stubborn, admiration for the McKinley administration after the Spanish-American War was its apparent understanding of the connections between territorial expansion, great power, and commercial dominance. The Puerto Rican tariff nullified all previous achievements. Surely, Watterson pleaded, "that great protectionist leader . . . recognized the fact that this [expansion] meant an extension of the area of free trade."[70]

Watterson had long supported free international markets and efforts to keep them free through most-favored nation systems like the Open Door, so it followed that he welcomed this series of diplomatic notes written by his old friend John Hay. Watterson encouraged Hay in letters. Since he opposed allowing the Republicans to gain political capital from issues he had long supported, in the *Courier-Journal* Watterson claimed convincingly that the Open Door was a "distinctly Democratic doctrine," along with "commercial expansion" and "Reciprocal Trade." He understood that this policy, and its effect on U.S. economic supremacy, would greatly expand the area of free trade, and he moved to claim at least some of the credit for himself and, most important, for his party. He told his readers, "The Free Trade question is working round to an Open Door, which will in many ways change our commercial outlook."[71]

Many others were arguing similar positions, and Watterson drew from them to bolster his arguments. For instance, he fully accepted Cleveland's former secretary of state Richard Olney's argument that both isolationism and protectionism had to end because of their incompatibility with modern great power. Olney thought that this was especially true in the case of the new dependencies. "If we claim the 'open door' of the Powers dominating China, how are we to deny it to them in our own dependencies and especially in the Philippines?" he asked. The *Courier-Journal* applauded this article. It did not accept that reciprocity treaties, such as the one with Hawaii, were the best way to slowly open trade, and it refused entirely to tolerate "new measures [that] are devised to restrict it."[72]

Although the Democratic platform mirrored Watterson's general approach to open doors and his opposition to the Puerto Rican tariff, the document most prominently reinforced exactly the anti-imperialism that Watterson warned against as a political issue and tactic. The platform echoed Bryan's ideas on making imperialism the "paramount issue" of the campaign and declared "that no nation can long endure half republic and half empire." It also reaffirmed the currency planks of the Chicago platform of 1896 that Watterson had so vehemently opposed. However, the trade issues were not insignificant. Criticizing the Dingley tariff at home, the platform prominently attacked the Puerto Rican tariff "as a bold and open violation of the nation's organic law and a flagrant breach of the national good faith" that, as the "first act of [the McKinley] imperialistic programme," signaled a move away from "republican institutions." Democrats also endorsed foreign trade expansion and supported "the immediate construction, ownership and control of the Nicaragua Canal." Commentators were surprised that the Republican platform did not mention the Puerto Rican tariff. Henry Litchfield West called it "curious" and presumed that "the omission carries with it the confession that the action of Congress was either indefensible or discreditable."[73]

Watterson continued to support the Democratic ticket despite its prominent anti-imperialism. He announced that party platforms were meaningless, "glittering generalities or muddled evasions," and that this one was particularly so. Given his past roles in writing platforms, especially his two-year struggle for the free trade "mandate" of the 1892 platform, this was a surprising statement. He justified it lightly: "There was a time when the Editor of the *Courier-Journal* gave a good deal of respect for party platforms, and wasted some precious moments that might have been better given over to his natural rest, upon their construction." The *Courier-Journal* reprinted the platform together with Bryan's anti-imperialist speech from the convention and thereafter avoided discussing the divisive issues in detail. Watterson refused to be driven from his party. He had nowhere to go and so announced that it was "not the business of a newspaper to call conventions and to set up tickets which nobody will vote for." This contrasted markedly with what he had argued four years earlier, when he urged a principled dissent from the Democracy's mainstream radicalism despite the certainty of defeat.[74]

Watterson elaborately justified changing his mind with grand statements of the *Courier-Journal*'s fortitude and independence. Most of all, he urged the party to overlook its massive divisions in order to win. "If the *Courier-Journal* can stand it," he intoned, "surely any Democrat can." Bryan quietly and privately thanked Watterson. "Am glad to see the C.J. coming around so gallantly," the candidate wrote.[75] Although Watterson usually resorted to alarmist cries about the impending destruction of the

Constitution, nation, and party, it seems clear that the prospect of another Republican administration did not terrify Watterson. He accepted his own declaration that "we done expanded." Aside from the horrible missteps over the Puerto Rican tariff—which might have been expected from the protectionist McKinley, of all people—Watterson did not worry that the essentials of his New Departure were in danger. The Foraker Act had a two-year limit, after all. Although Watterson still detected dangerous threats to freedom and the southern way of life, it was unnecessary to revisit the apocalyptic defiance of 1896. Accordingly, he essentially opted out of the campaign until the late fall, choosing instead to vacation and to avoid strong support for Bryan. This reticence was unprecedented, particularly in a presidential year.

When Watterson returned to writing about the campaign in October, the *Courier-Journal* became, briefly and strangely, indistinguishable

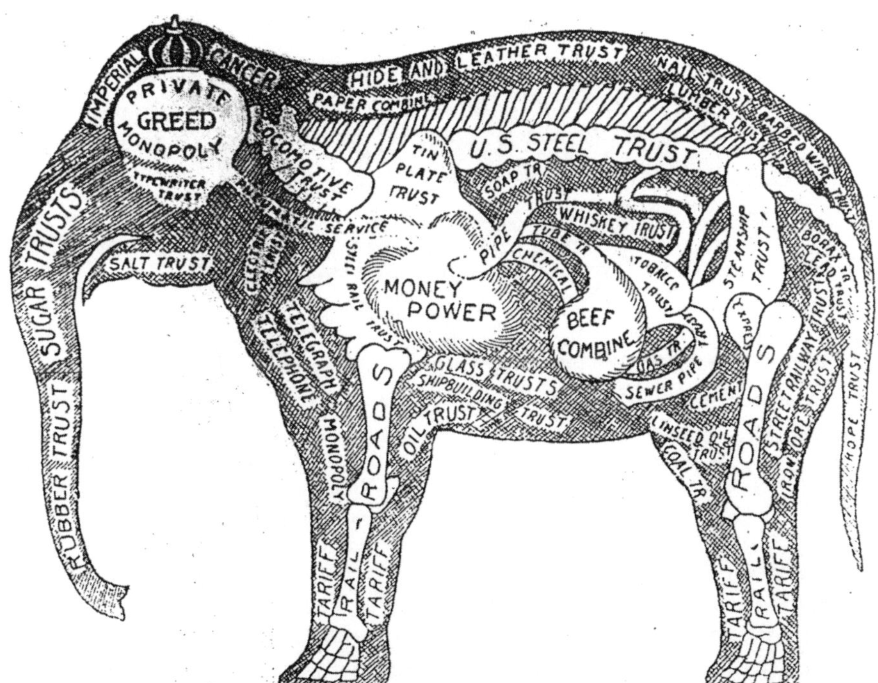

Louisville Courier-Journal cartoon detailing what makes the Republican elephant tick, such as greed, trusts, and the "IMPERIAL CANCER." *Louisville Courier-Journal*, September 15, 1902

"The Burden of Imperialism and the Man Who Bears It." The working man burdened by the "TRUST HOG," an imperial army and navy, and a massive war tax. *Louisville Courier-Journal*, October 1, 1900

from any other Democratic, anti-imperialist paper. On the occasion of an Indiana meeting of the Democrats, two entire sections of the paper were given over to anti-imperialism. In addition to reprinting numerous political speeches and the party platform, the paper ran a cartoon of "Napoleon McKinley, who would be Emperor," and another of the American working man bent double carrying the "TRUST HOG," covered with dollar signs and wearing the crown of imperialism, as well as the weight of the "IMPERIAL NAVY," the "IMPERIAL ARMY," and a billion-dollar war tax.[76]

The sentiment in these cartoons signaled the Democratic Party's new tactics. Bryan highlighted the new approach when he argued, "The issue presented in the campaign of 1900 is the issue between plutocracy and democracy." The trust issue was not new to Watterson, as he had long linked it with the protective tariff. To downplay the party's anti-imperialism, he had tried to emphasize the class issue when the campaign began in earnest. He contrasted the "hewers of wood and the drawers of water" with the "growing circle of indolence and culture, avarice and proscription." Watterson proved quite capable of aligning himself with the sort of social upheaval he had tried to silence earlier, if only because it deemphasized his attractions to the McKinley policies. Throughout, Watterson argued that he was a proud social conservative and a supporter of economic stability and legitimate business interests. "The *Courier-Journal* is a Conservative, not a radical," he wrote in one of his commonplace moments of self-definition. "It will not be bamboozled by the cheap Johns of commerce." It helped Watterson that these Johns, in the form of trusts, were usually northern and supportive of the Republican Party. Watterson contrasted the "Democratic masses" with "the regular troops of the governing classes . . . the armored legionnaires of prerogative and power; stall-fed oxen of the steel-clad trusts; sleek race horses out of the Aegean stables of political corruption, each mounted by a trained jockey from the school of Platt, Quay and Hanna; an omnium gatherum of gamblers with a limitless treasury of boodle to draw upon."[77]

This language recalled the capital-labor divisions he had dwelled upon a few years earlier, when he promised to fuse the interests of capital and labor in a reformed Democratic Party. The editorial was also a well-written attempt to dodge what Bryan was helplessly trying to make the major issue of the campaign. Watterson preferred to return to the ground on which he had so often battled. He stressed the tariff issue and attacked the Republicans as "the party of Cant, Rant and Corruption." In so doing, he even defended Bryan from Republican charges that he would destroy the business interests of the country, charges that often echoed his own writings of 1896. Theodore Roosevelt, for example, wrote an article in which he accused Bryan of wanting to install "a government of a disorderly mob, by the demagogue, for the shiftless and disorderly and the criminal and the semicriminal." Watterson instead slammed "the dizzy old cocotte! the freckled old jaybird! The Painted Harlot of Protection! Fob! Take her away!"[78]

These tactics, though amusing and illustrative of the editor's particular preoccupations, had little effect on the outcome of the election. McKinley rode to overwhelming victory, even in the Great Commoner's home state of Nebraska, on the strength of the national economy and foreign policy. Watterson had been correct that his party could not win if it concentrated on anti-imperialism rather than focusing on the benefits of the imperial project itself. Historian Thomas A. Bailey concludes that the election of 1900 was a mandate on almost none of its major issues, and certainly not on foreign policy or imperialism. "The American people were interested primarily in hogs, corn, and wheat; and only secondarily in the Filipinos," he wrote. Bryan attributed his loss to "money, war and better times." He managed to win Kentucky, but by such a narrow margin that the once solid Kentucky Democracy seemed near death. McKinley even carried Jefferson County, which included Louisville.[79]

Watterson was not surprised, and therefore not particularly disappointed, by the results of the election. He approved, after all, of most of the Republicans' policies. He did not even write about the loss until a few days had passed, which was also highly unusual for him. Papers from all over the South and elsewhere sent telegrams asking for his analysis of the election and the path the party should take to reform itself. The *New Orleans Picayune* telegraphed, "What must [the] Democratic party do to be saved"? The *Atlanta Evening News* asked Watterson to express what he thought of "reorganizing [the] Democratic party on old lines." The *New York Herald* asked how to restore the party to "its old prestige."[80]

Watterson remained deeply disappointed that the Puerto Rican argument had not inflamed the public and that the Republicans would continue to do violence to the Constitution through tariff policy. Historian Goran Rystad has argued that the tariff question in general was, along with race, totally unimportant to the 1900 election because emotional "party loyalty" had replaced "ideological commitment." He believes that partisan division had become an end in itself, a static system, and that the parties had become mere "clans" of self-identity.[81] In these terms, Watterson can be viewed as among the last of the ideologues. Although he intellectually crossed party lines, he refused to accept a convergence of the two groups. He continued to believe that the different moral and ideological approaches to the tariff question—and thus to the true nature of American expansionism—divided the parties clearly and permanently.

Bryan, as architect of the anti-imperialism issue, received all of Watterson's blame for the loss. The editor wrote that Bryan lost support every time he opened his mouth. But rather than returning to flog the dead horse of Bryan's campaign, Watterson looked forward to the next battle and to reshaping the party. He considered the election of 1900 to be similar to that of 1872, when the public had not been wise enough to reject Grant. The "Jeffersonian ideal" had died that year, wrote Watterson, as the country plunged back into the nightmare of Reconstruction. But the ideal returned with Tilden four years later, when the public rose to end the tyranny of Reconstruction. Watterson anticipated that "the issue of imperialism, that is, of the administration of the [new] territory," would likewise grow in the public mind. Although the Republicans had evaded responsibility in 1900, they would be forced to face a public reckoning. "Even as Tilden overthrew the Boa Constrictor of Reconstruction, will some future Tilden overthrow the monster of maladministration in the outlying provinces, making Republicanism hideous abroad, odious at home," and slowing clarifying the threats to the Constitution.[82]

From this point on, Watterson continuously fought for control of the Democratic Party so that its politics could be remade along truly free trade lines. He spent virtually all of 1901–2 demanding and offering plans for the reorganization of the party. Like clockwork, with each new electoral defeat he worked to remake the party in the only image he ever trusted—that of the Star-Eyed Goddess of tariff reform. The continual failures of the *Courier-Journal* to control Democratic fortunes did not corrode Watterson's resolve. The failures were mitigated by the facts that, at heart, he supported much of the Republican imperial foreign policy, and that neither he nor his paper ever relinquished its iconoclasm. The 1896 party implosion had almost destroyed the *Courier-Journal*, and Watterson had responded by following strict, official party regularity, despite his very clear dissatisfaction. Now, in the wake of a fiasco he had predicted in 1898, Watterson meant to reestablish his position in the party. "The *Courier-Journal* is a Democrat," he wrote in another of his self-definitions. "It is once again a Leader of Democrats. It resumes its old place at the head of the column."[83]

Watterson unabashedly set out again to remake the party and rescue it from Bryanism, anti-imperialism, and any other ism that deviated from

THE HAVANA POST

GEORGE M. BRADT, Publisher

EVERY DAY IN THE YEAR

Entered at the Havana, Cuba, Post-office as Second-Class Matter.

ZULUETA 28.

Telephone, A-2662; P. O. Box, 989
Cable Address, "Post"

MEMBER OF
THE ASSOCIATED PRESS

SUBSCRIPTION RATES

Subscriptions Payable in Advance
By Mail or City Delivery by Carrier

1 Month...$1.00 6 Months..$4.00
3 Months..$2.50 12 Months..$7.50

Above subscription rate applies to all countries in the Postal Union; all other countries, $10.00 a year

SUNDAY EDITION

One Year..............Two Dollars

OUR BEAUTIFUL FLAG

The Star Spangled Banner! Was ever flag so beautiful, did ever flag so fill the souls of men?—

Henry Watterson

Undated *Havana Post* clipping of a patriotic Watterson quote, demonstrating the wide distribution of his words. Library of Congress, Manuscripts Division, Henry Watterson Papers

his middle path to free trade globalization. "Perhaps it is that we have drunk too much and too deep of the waters of the Mississippi and the Ohio," Watterson wrote to the party faithful, but he remained confident that his blend of southern nationalism through home rule, flexible constitutionalism, and free trade expansionism would lead his region and party to prosperity and immortality. Watterson was convinced that events always vindicated his positions. The cause of free trade would prevail, he told the Manhattan Club in February 1901, and "it will surely conduct us out of the long, dark night of dissension and into the dawning light of the days of a Democracy, reunited, unterrified, and undefiled!"[84]

Conclusion

The Compromises of Empire

When I say Back to the Constitution, I address myself equally to Republicans and Democrats.

—Henry Watterson

In a 1901 *New York Tribune* cartoon, "Miss Democracy of 1904" is seen unpacking a trunk of clothing sent to her by Henry Watterson with a note offering her a new "1904 outfit . . . [because] the old ones you have are 'shopworn.'" Her new wardrobe prominently includes a hat of "EXPANSION" and "PROGRESS."[1] Watterson, of course, equated the two, and he never stopped trying to dress the Democratic Party according to his vision. He designated himself the prophet of expansion and progress and pressed hard for his party and the South to follow his lead. From the Civil War on, he remained uncompromising on establishing free trade in ever-expanding international markets, on limiting government power, and on advancing southern prosperity and independence through globalization. In the 1890s, following the crisis of the depression years, Henry Watterson willingly transformed his own ideological positions and challenged his party's traditions in a new attempt to achieve these long-standing goals. The transformation of the American economy, global markets, and geopolitical realities required new policies and new energy to pursue them, counseled Watterson. The opportunities offered by these expanding markets required compromise with empire.

The market was the centerpiece of Watterson's outlook, and free trade was the solvent for all of his contradictions. He felt vindicated in his un-

"WANTS TO MAKE A 'NEW WOMAN' OF MISS DEMOCRACY. Miss Democracy—Oh, Henry, how could you!" Watterson's plan to dress the Democratic Party in new garments, since its old outfits were "shopworn." *New York Daily Tribune*, May 31, 1901

wavering defense of it and impatiently waited for policymakers in both parties to adopt his free trade prescription. As he stated repeatedly, a system based on the holy trinity of home rule, sound money, and free trade would solve every problem facing the United States.

Watterson's obsession with the free trade and southern questions, in conjunction with his willingness to reverse many of his earlier positions in pursuit of an expansionist solution, distinguished him from other New South editors who did not leap onto the imperial bandwagon in the 1890s. His strong support for achieving southern prosperity and independence through a combination of overseas territorial empire and free market expansion was decidedly uncommon in the Democratic South, elevating him into the rarefied company of committed expansionists such as Senator John Tyler Morgan of Alabama and editor Joseph Bryan of Virginia.

Yet Watterson also must be viewed in the broader context of the New South ideologues, a uniquely energetic and driven group of journalists, politicians, businessmen, and boosters who eagerly sought economic solutions to the South's condition. These men consistently emphasized the southern aspect of national problems, pursued increased investment in southern industrialization and infrastructure, agitated for political autonomy, and sought a stable and conservative social order. Settling on economic development and opportunities in new markets as the means to achieve their goals, these politicians and journalists connected defined regional interests with an increasingly internationalist perspective and an interest in actively opening foreign markets to American goods. The concerns of the most outward-looking southerners soon converged on support for an empire of free trade. In adopting empire as their policy, these expansionists helped articulate the policy of globalization that would come to dominate twentieth-century American foreign relations.[2]

Watterson stood on the vanguard of this broadening bipartisan engagement with globalization. As he had argued at length, the global market system did indeed become the "idiosyncrasy of the twentieth century," or at least the dominant ideological paradigm of American policymakers. The United States' relationship to the world was radically transformed, and both Republicans and Democrats moved to exploit the new benefits of the international market system. Neither party had disputed the need to penetrate foreign markets in the 1890s, only the means of doing so. Watterson's arguments in favor of expansion and an empire of free trade correctly anticipated the appeal of the perceived benefits of globalization, including unprecedented national prosperity, an end to sectionalism, the exportation of the social question, and political success for free trade's champions. Empire seemed to offer great promise.

One clear sign of the accelerating uniformity of support for globalization and an empire of free trade at the dawn of the twentieth century was signaled in McKinley's firm embrace of reciprocity in trade relations in 1901. In his final speech to the Pan-American Exposition in Buffalo, New York, on September 5, 1901, delivered just before his assassination, McKinley succinctly described international interconnectedness and the need for liberalized trade relations that produced the rapid trajectory of globalization. This was the moment, wrote Alfred Eckes Jr., in which "McKinley emerged as an internationalist." The president declared that an emerging world system had changed everything. Prices were now being set by global markets. International communications, the flow of information, and new transportation systems had become so rapid that distance was no longer a limiting factor in commercial relations. "Isolation is no longer possible or desirable," McKinley announced. "The age of exclusiveness is past. The expansion of our trade and commerce is the pressing problem."[3] The United States needed a new set of policies to grapple with the changed circumstances and to ensure the nation's dominance within them.

Most important, McKinley seized upon the idiosyncrasy of the market and the necessity of liberalized trade. In particular, he saw that opportunities in global political economy had created a dominant national need to buy and sell in unencumbered and expanding foreign markets. "We must not repose in fancied security that we can forever sell everything and buy little or nothing . . . what we produce beyond our domestic consumption must have a vent abroad. The excess must be relieved through a foreign outlet," McKinley announced in words that must have been strikingly familiar to *Courier-Journal* readers. The president called for a merchant marine, an Isthmian canal, a Pacific cable, and, most centrally, increased reciprocal trade agreements to open up and sustain new markets. Each of these goals was a central feature of the emerging era of globalization, and each formed a vital role in America's emerging hegemony.[4]

McKinley's internationalist turn basically recapitulated lines of argument Watterson had been pushing since even before the 1890 McKinley tariff had reinvigorated protectionism. Despite its source, Watterson cautiously welcomed this shift. McKinley's program did not meet Watterson's strict criteria for truly free trade; reciprocity was only a step, a very small step, toward the free trade he deemed necessary to ensure southern rejuvenation and to bolster national prosperity. "Reciprocity, be it borne in mind, is merely Free Trade by Treaty, Free Trade in broken doses, Free Trade homeopathically taken," Watterson wrote. He demanded more, and he thought the Democracy should too.[5]

Although Watterson's defense of the virtues of free trade expansion anticipated the logic behind the later, bipartisan embrace of globalization, he did not account for its often contradictory results at home. Market-oriented expansionism brought changes of a political, social, and diplomatic nature that he was unable to accept. In particular, empire required and encouraged the growth of the state, which he feared. Watterson balked at accepting the new administrative structures of world power alongside its material benefits. In the twentieth century, he proved incapable of moving beyond his fundamental free trade formula—or his own fitful construction of constitutional limitations—toward a broader conception of America's evolving hegemony. Free trade and unhampered globalization did not immediately appear after the War of 1898, nor did they magically liberate the South from its relative thralldom within the Union. Solidifying the new order would require the development of an activist state, decades of entanglement, and two world wars. Watterson did not anticipate this result. Furthermore, he could neither tolerate nor fully comprehend the expansion of federal authority that accompanied the effort to project the free trade he had so stridently pursued. His compromise with empire had strict limitations and consequences he did not envision in the debates of 1899–1900.

Accordingly, Watterson was unable to articulate a coherent program in response to the enormous expansion of the federal government after 1900. He had blithely and vaguely assured Democrats and southerners that expansionism guaranteed strict limits on federal growth and intervention, even in colonial possessions, but he rapidly discovered that he was mistaken. In his last twenty years, as he reacted poorly to this unanticipated consequence of empire, Watterson became a caricature of his earlier activist days, a victim of his own rhetorical excesses, and, to his chagrin, an anachronism in the new imperial system that he originally welcomed.

This new system that distressed him was characterized by an enormous expansion and concentration of power, coordination, and control within both the federal government and the business world during the administrations of Roosevelt, Taft, and Wilson. This was a time of dramatic and far-reaching change, a transformative moment. During the Progressive Era, as one historian describes it, a new "organizational sector" emerged "between the market and political ones" that had defined the nineteenth-century system. In this new "corporatist order," unelected, elite professionals and their organizations increasingly controlled policy-making decisions. The doctrine of laissez-faire in political economy and the emphasis on the free market in which Watterson had invested such promise were inexorably replaced by more functional and interventionist forms of governance and control. Nongovernmental institutions and impersonal, international market forces created imperatives and shaped national responses that blunted the impact of individuals. These nongovernmental organizations became the hallmark of the globalization era. They further eroded regional and national authority and autonomy, which was precisely what Watterson feared. In this environment, mid-

“SEEIN’ THINGS.” Undated cartoon depicting Watterson’s fear of Theodore Roosevelt’s Caesarism haunting even his dreams. Library of Congress, Manuscripts Division, Henry Watterson Papers

level opinion leaders and personalities like Watterson became increasingly marginalized and irrelevant. Instead of forming a vital connection between the public and political leaders, as they had in the nineteenth century, this group found itself isolated from those in power.[6]

Watterson’s editorials reflected this alienated distress, fairly shrieking against the wind. He adopted the ranting tone and capitalization of the politically impotent: “We are told, and most of us believe, that those are best governed who are least governed. Yet we have one big congress in the nation’s capital and forty-eight little congresses in the several state capitals

CONSTANTLY IN SESSION TO MAKE AND UNMAKE LAWS to vex the people and confuse the courts. Seeing the Evils of too much legislation we call for more . . . We are CREATING A SYSTEM OF CENTRALIZED BUREAUCRACY and . . . we have A STANDING ARMY OF OFFICIALS."[7]

Like government, journalism became more professionalized and bureaucratized. The increasing power of advertisers and the influence of broad commercial concerns on newspaper form and content greatly constrained the latitude of idiosyncratic editors like Watterson. Business principles dominated newspaper management, and news began to be marketed as a commodity.[8] The rise of this new professionalism and commercialism brought an end to the partisan journalism Watterson had mastered, and it placed a greater emphasis on profit motives, in which he had little interest.

The discourse of the new century shifted from Watterson's grasp. He had commanded a transitional moment when the interpretation of political interests fell to middle-stratum editors like him, but that moment rapidly passed after 1900. Congealed in the public mind as "the last of the personal journalists," Watterson became unmoored even as he gained celebrity status. He was left promoting, in the words of Bryant Crittenden Biggerstaff of the *St. Joseph (MO) Gazette*, "the gospel of a return to the primitive ethics of what was a glorious day."[9] Watterson was unwilling and unable to assimilate the imperial system he had helped to create, unable to understand the new corporatist order, and unable to fully accept the immense political, commercial, and ideological challenges of modernity.

In retrospect, it is clear that, during the imperialism debates at the end of the nineteenth century, Watterson was both at the apogee of his abilities and influence in southern political culture and at the end of his campaign for southern home rule and prosperity. Capitalizing on his vitality at that moment, he saw significant aspects of his New Departure foreign policy adopted. The compromise with empire he championed accomplished many of its intended results, although not fully in the manner he expected and in good measure because he attached himself to Republican policies.

Empire and globalization did, in some essential respects, solve the home rule, sound money, and free trade questions. These results were not all immediately obvious in 1900, but Watterson felt vindicated in articulating his trinity over the years following the Spanish-American War. He had aggressively supported expansionism because he predicted its positive effects on national and southern prosperity and social order, and he turned out to be at least partially correct. The war ushered in the final decline of the sectional question, just as Watterson and many other New South propagandists had hoped and predicted. The "bloody shirt" ceased to exist in the twentieth century. The war and its expansionist aftermath ended the persistent sovereignty and development questions of Reconstruction as much as they offered an expansionist solution to the social and overproduction crisis wrought by the panic of 1893. The South, no longer subordinate and insecure, freely pursued its own particular home rule in the forms of widespread capitalist development, white supremacy, state sovereignty, and continued single-party dominance. The nation remained economically healthy and globally unchallenged for years. The political utility of empire would be grasped by the swift and the clever of the future. However, Watterson's attempt to shape the party in the image of his New Departure did not create the immediate Democratic dominance he envisioned.

The national Democracy proved to be remarkably difficult to overhaul and redirect, but Watterson's personal influence in party circles continued to grow in the early twentieth century. He remained one of the party's most influential and respected spokesmen for tariff revision, carrying the battles of his earlier years into the new era. In the first decade of the new century, he was seriously mentioned as a candidate for Kentucky senator and governor, as well as for president. Each time, he declined to run, standing firm on his declaration that he preferred the freedom of journalism to the slavery of political office. "I am now, as ever and always, a free-nigger and not a slave-nigger," Marse Henry told the *New York Times* on July 14, 1912, deliberately sounding like the old Kentucky Colonel the public knew. "My master is my conscience, and, [I owe] nothing to any political organism, having not a dollar of money, nor a letter of credit for a lifetime of service to the Democratic party."[10] Watterson's disconnection from politics is evident in his desire not to be ensnared in it.

Watterson bragged of political independence and continued to issue bold pronouncements, but in truth, he was slowly forfeiting responsibility for the direction of the party. The deep political divisions wrought during the tumultuous 1890s had lasting negative effects on both national party organization and unity. The national Democratic Party was defeated and seemingly directionless for years, which Watterson had foreseen as the

"THE KENTUCKY SENATORSHIP." Watterson is considered as a dark horse candidate for the Kentucky senatorship in 1908. Note the "LOST CAUSE" jug hanging on the wall behind him. *Washington Evening Star,* January 16, 1908

penalty of its opposition to expansion in 1900. By 1908, when again he supported William Jennings Bryan as the presidential candidate, it was clear that the editor had blurred and even abandoned the battle lines of uncompromised, capital-*t* Truth in favor of simple party regularity and reluctant resignation.

The party faced years of political exile from the White House, until the election of Woodrow Wilson, whom Watterson condemned as a self-righteous "school-teacher" and opposed fitfully and rather unsuccessfully. Indeed, the editor tried to derail Wilson's 1912 presidential bid, an attempt that Arthur S. Link attributed largely to Watterson's age, irrationality, and "ante-bellum sense of honor and friendship" with *North American Review* and *Harper's* publisher George Harvey. Watterson told the *New York Times* that Wilson was "an able man, with an intellect highly trained, tyrannous by nature and despotic by the vocation and habit of a lifetime." But the editor eventually reached an accommodation in the interests of the Democratic Party. In 1916 the *Milwaukee Free Press* ran a cartoon of a sobbing Marse Henry being fed a "bitter pill" in the shape of Wilson, held by the hand of "PARTY REGULARITY." By the time a Democrat got to the White House, Watterson had moved beyond party strictures and settled comfortably into his status as a living legend of the old school rather than a party warrior of the new. "These are not party times. The old parties are in abeyance," he wearily wrote to a good friend. "Just two old empty bottles with two old dirty labels."[11] Watterson came to prefer commiserating with his surviving cronies in the Manhattan Club to grappling intellectually with the issues of the day.

Increasingly, Watterson became an unpredictable curmudgeon. He unrelentingly attacked the "despotic experimentation" and adventurism of "that would-be Autocrat of America . . . Kaiser Roosevelt," despite the fundamental agreement the two shared on the ends of American foreign policy. Watterson never accepted Republican management of the American empire, even when it pursued goals he personally supported. He based his political stances less on the direct statements of self-interest he produced in the 1880s and 1890s and more on his overriding obsession with the dangers of expanding government power and his personal antipathy to each successive president. He was at least consistent throughout his life in seeming to hate Democratic presidents more than Republican ones. "Things have come to a hell of a pass/When a man can't whip his own jackass," he famously quipped, by way of explanation.[12]

Until his death in 1921, Watterson counseled a retreat to strict construction of the Constitution and dedicated the bulk of his energy to preventing the expansion of what he viewed as arbitrary governmental power. "Back to the Constitution" became the mantra of his columns in those years, replacing his earlier insistent chant of "Home Rule, Sound Money, and Free Trade." He spent his last twenty years in reaction to fed-

"A Bitter Pill for Marse Henry." Watterson accepts Wilson as a candidate in the interest of party regularity, but he does not have to like it. *Milwaukee Free Press*, September 24, 1916

eral growth, drawing connections with critiques of power and employing his old rhetoric. "Rooseveltism is like Bryanism in 1896—like it in many ways," Watterson wrote in 1904. "Bryan would have Mexicanized our currency. Roosevelt's election will Mexicanize the State." Watterson dismissed "the fad called 'progressivism'" as a plot to destroy individual and state liberties. He attacked Wilsonian internationalism as a plot to destroy the nation's independence through entanglements abroad and warned that Wilson himself would "Mexicanize the government and Diazify the Presidency."[13]

Since he considered the southern question to be satisfactorily solved, Watterson no longer felt a need to compromise with empire and overseas adventurism, or with expanded national power and internationalism. This was a marked shift from the 1890s, when he considered foreign affairs the culmination of his New Departure. With the conclusion of his post–Civil War development and independence program and the promise of continued overseas trade along open door principles, Watterson turned his attention inward and no longer considered foreign policy a vital extension of domestic politics.

With this shift, Watterson's positions on foreign affairs became highly erratic, even when compared to his earlier frequent and contradictory realignments. His declarations often seemed designed more to stimulate wide news coverage than to advance the national dialogue. For example, Watterson refused, largely out of wounded pride and partisanship instead of legitimate national interest, to transfer his long-standing support for a Nicaraguan canal to what he memorably called the "abortion across Panama" that Roosevelt secured. At varying times, Watterson called for annexation of Cuba and all of Mexico, but he opposed adventurism in Nicaragua. He supported selling the Philippines to Japan and "send[ing] the memory of the Monroe Doctrine to grass and its ghost to the boneyard." He favored Canadian reciprocity and international arbitration in 1911, strongly advocated war against Germany in 1914, but then utterly opposed the League of Nations in 1919.[14]

Watterson's unpredictability developed in part from his growing disengagement from political issues and his new emphasis on travel and leisure. He stopped his theretofore popular public speaking tours after the death of his son in 1908, wrote less in the *Courier-Journal*, and enjoyed the semiretirement he had postponed in 1895. Increasingly, he turned to convivial leisure activities and to the cultivation of his wide connections, friendships, and historical image. His letters from this time reflect at length on the pleasures of card playing and drinking. Watterson acted as a bit of a scoundrel, even inserting his own handwritten "damn" into typed letters, since, as he wrote a friend, "my stenographer is a religious blonde who don't say 'damn.'"[15] Although his flamboyant personality had always had a prominent role in his political outlook and writings, between 1900 and 1921 he indulged himself significantly more than he had in his first thirty years as an editor. His opinions were still news in themselves, and his editorials continued to be reprinted all over the country, but they were famous for their flash rather than for their substance.

Writing less frequently, Watterson no longer limited himself to exacting discussions of politics and foreign affairs. He instead regularly announced outrageous positions and basked in the predictable public attention and national press they brought. To be sure, these statements made Watterson's editorials a continued delight to read. They also increased his national stature when papers across the nation responded to "the latest sensation started by Mr. Watterson," as *Public Opinion* characterized one such instance. For example, Watterson's 1903 attack on the Monroe Doctrine yielded three hundred replies from national newspapers, all but two of which were negative. But such excesses also made it more likely that he would contradict himself or sound like an irascible crank (or a drunk) instead of a powerful, relevant editor. In 1909 the *Albany (NY) Journal* described one of Watterson's attacks on Roosevelt as a "harangue [bearing] evidence of his well known skill as a phrase-maker, and of his utter inability to get down to sound, sane, argument."[16] Watterson's "profuseness of vituperation" also endangered the *Courier-Journal*'s profitability in instances in which he overstepped the bounds of public acceptance. This occurred toward the end of his career, when he printed vicious, nativist, anti-German editorials during World War I in heavily German Louisville. Watterson refused to moderate his stance despite the appeals of his publisher Bruce Haldeman, who suffered the negative commercial effects of these writings.

Watterson had always simplified his political positions into catchy phrases to further their mass appeal and acceptance, but these slogans were meant to represent broader political positions. In the twentieth century, he moved toward mere phrasemaking in place of political analysis as part of a reactionary response to the evolving new system. He feared becoming irrelevant, and in response, he lashed out at modernity and its changes. This, in turn, made him even more irrelevant. He spent his last years fitfully fighting the modern dangers he saw in women's suffrage, the rise of corporate journalism, Prohibition, and "the dry rot of wealth wasting itself in self-indulgence." His 1919 autobiography is in spots rambling and almost incoherent, as it devolves from discussions of nineteenth-century events into ranting attacks on his new fixations. Watterson considered internationalism, Prohibition, and women's suffrage to be similarly "revolutionary" movements "driv[ing] deep into the vitals of the home and the state." They were designed to "break down equally the limitations

"Hol' On, There, Marse Henry!" Watterson produced a national uproar when he suggested taking all of Mexico and marching all the way to Panama. His battle cry was "On to Panama!" as seen here on the flag. This editorial splash, which was reprinted across the country, was a good example of his continuing to make news with outrageous positions. *Baltimore Sun*, April 24, 1914 of sex and the barriers of the organic law and [to] set up at Washington a centralized oligarchy foreign to the letter and the spirit of the original compact." Watterson cursed the twin dangers of the twentieth century. "To Hell with Feminism!" he wrote in letters to friends. "To Hell with Prohibition!"[17]

Despite his growing irregularity, Watterson's name retained such power and public renown throughout his life that he was eagerly sought after to chair a wide array of organizations interested in political reform, humanitarian aid, and social reaction. He anchored various national fights against Prohibition, women's suffrage, and the League of Nations. He was a contributing editor of the decidedly reactionary *Woman Patriot*, which described itself as "a National Newspaper For Home and National Defense Against Woman Suffrage, Feminism, and Socialism." In this paper, he indulged his expanding obsession with the profound dangers of gender equity. In the first issue, he excoriated "the Feminist goal of blatant infidelity, rejecting the Religion of Christ and Him Crucified and repudiating the man-made Bible of Moses and the Prophets." Watterson was also tapped to be the president of the major Republican anti–League of Nations organization, the League for the Preservation of American Independence. He unerringly chose the losing side of these signature antimodern battles.[18]

Watterson's intellectual decline and alienation were reflected at the end of his professional career in a similar disengagement from his own newspaper. Watterson's traditional mooring was loosened with the death of his old partner and friend Walter Newman Haldeman in 1901. Majority ownership of the Courier-Journal Company passed to Haldeman's children, with Watterson retaining his percentage and editorship. Bruce Haldeman, the youngest son, took managerial control of the *Courier-Journal* and the *Louisville Times*. In this capacity, he increasingly clashed with the volatile Watterson over the erratic content of his editorials, his profligate spending, and the general direction of the paper in a newly competitive business environment. When Watterson and his friend (*Times* editor and elder son) William B. Haldeman wrested control away from the young Bruce in 1917, they soon found themselves unable to run the papers effectively as businesses, even with the aid of subordinates like Arthur Krock, Tom Wallace, and Young E. Allison. Subsequently, in August 1918, both properties were sold to Robert W. Bingham.[19]

The Bingham era in the history of the *Courier-Journal* marked the end

"THE SAME OLD WATTERSON." Watterson holds his ground against autocracy during World War I, while Samuel Tilden looks down on his old friend Marse Henry in this undated *Sacramento Bee* cartoon. Library of Congress, Manuscripts Division, Henry Watterson Papers of Henry Watterson's reign as "dictator of Kentucky," although he briefly continued at his old post as an ill-defined "editor emeritus." Watterson accepted that title to lend the new owner a patina of legitimacy, since, in his own words, "my writing possessed a certain commercial value." In 1919 the *Courier-Journal* was undistinguished without Marse Henry. Bingham, a loyal Wilsonian Democrat on a rapid ascent to national political influence, and Watterson, a self-proclaimed Jeffersonian Democrat well on his way to irrelevance, thereafter clashed bitterly on the three big issues that dominated Watterson's thinking in his later days: Prohibition, women's suffrage, and the Treaty of Versailles.[20]

When the First World War began, Watterson pushed aggressively for preparedness and intervention and described the war as an "irrepressible conflict between Absolutism and Democracy, between the claim Diabolic of Kings and Kaisers and the Right Divine of the People." He ended his famous, Pulitzer Prize–winning diatribe against the Central powers, "To Hell with the Hapsburgs and Hohenzollern!" Watterson liked this phrase so much that, with typical excess, he ran it in the *Courier-Journal* throughout the war.[21] He argued that the United States had a responsibility to save Europe and the world from militarism and autocracy by going to war, but he then pitilessly eviscerated Wilson's plan for the League of Nations as a dangerous entanglement. Watterson called it "a Utopian scheme" that "subordinates our national sovereignty" and "antagonizes our wisest counsels and oldest traditions." He warned that it would "diminish not increase our moral power as a nation."[22] These were rather common isolationist sentiments at the time, and they offered clear evidence of Watterson's inward turn.

It was the debate over the League of Nations that drove the final division between the old editor and the new publisher, just as it marked the great failure of early-twentieth-century internationalism. "Shinny on your side of the ocean and we shinny on our side," Watterson told the Europeans a number of times, embracing the isolationism he had rejected so thoroughly at the turn of the century. Although he reached new heights of rhetorical excess and wrote voluminously on this issue, Watterson had nothing new or critical to add to the national debate about America's global position, aside from rejecting the "universal hari-kari in Europe." In contrast to their influence in the nineteenth century, his arguments no longer dominated or directed national discussion.[23]

Meanwhile, Bingham strongly supported the League in his new pa-

Henry Watterson on Miami Beach in 1919. Library of Congress, Manuscripts Division, Henry Watterson Papers

per. The *Courier-Journal* continued, for a time, to print both of their perspectives on the League—even placing the editorials side by side. The obvious paradox and inherent eccentricity of promoting the two men's opposing positions eventually became an irreconcilable difference. On March 22, 1919, Watterson wrote to Bingham that he had "no interest in the policies to be pursued by the *Courier-Journal*, nor do I desire to write for that or any other publication."[24]

In this quiet way, the end of the Watterson era arrived. Marse Henry Watterson finally retired from the daily political battles that had defined his incredible life. He spent his remaining year and a half of life relaxing in his favorite haunts in New York and Florida, recalling his struggles in the great events of his youth and withdrawing from an increasingly strange new world.

Notes

Abbreviations

AKP	Alexander Konta Papers, Filson Historical Society, Louisville, KY
CJ	*Louisville Courier-Journal*
CR	*Congressional Record*
ERP	Elihu Root Papers, Manuscripts Division, Library of Congress
GCP	Grover Cleveland Papers, Manuscripts Division, Library of Congress
HFP	Haldeman Family Papers, Filson Historical Society, Louisville, KY
HWP-FHS	Henry Watterson Papers, Filson Historical Society, Louisville, KY
HWP-LC	Henry Watterson Papers, Manuscripts Division, Library of Congress
HWP-UL	Henry Watterson Papers, University of Louisville Archives (microfilm edition), Louisville, KY
JHP	John Hay Papers, Manuscripts Division, Library of Congress
JQ	*Journalism Quarterly*
JTMP	John Tyler Morgan Papers, Manuscripts Division, Library of Congress
LD	*Literary Digest*
MMMP	Manton Malone Marble Papers, Manuscripts Division, Library of Congress
MVHR	*Mississippi Valley Historical Review*
NAR	*North American Review*
NYT	*New York Times*
NYTB	*New York Tribune*
PHR	*Pacific Historical Review*
RWBP	Robert Worth Bingham Papers, Manuscripts Division, Library of Congress
WCWP	William C. Whitney Papers, Manuscripts Division, Library of Congress
WMP	William McKinley Papers, Manuscripts Division, Library of Congress
WQGP	Walter Q. Gresham Papers, Manuscripts Division, Library of Congress
YEAP	Young E. Allison Papers, Filson Historical Society, Louisville, KY

Introduction: A New Empire for the New South

1. *Lexington Leader*, n.d., series 6, reel 6, p. 99, HWP-UL; *NYTB*, 13 July 1896. The influence of the *CJ* is described in respectful terms in the *New Orleans Item, Fort Worth Record, Montgomery Advertiser*, and *Quincy (IL) Daily Herald*, series 6, reel 5, pp. 733–1407, 1414, and reel 6, p. 98, HWP-UL. As Arthur Krock wrote, "To mention the *Courier-Journal*—everyone knows it as Henry Watterson's paper." Arthur Krock, "A Newspaper Career with a Purpose," *Advertiser's Magazine*, May 1910, 25–26. Also see Thomas D. Clark, "The Country Newspaper: A Factor in Southern Opinion, 1865–1930," *Journal of Southern History* 14 (February 1948): 4–5, 8.

2. O. O. Stealey, "Claims of the Candidates: Henry Watterson," *NAR* 187 (1908): 841; *Houston Post*, January 1920, vol. 2, AKP; *Fourth Estate*, 11 December 1909, 3, 12–13; *NYTB*, 21 June 1899, 2, 8. Watterson's prominence is well supported in the memoir literature of journalists and politicians of the time and in the letters to him from a vast array of both prominent and unknown individuals, all discussing his arguments and importance. For just a few examples, see the autobiography of the former editor of the *Sun* (Edward P. Mitchell, *Memoirs of an Editor: Fifty Years of American Journalism* [New York: Scribner's Sons, 1924], 134) and R. H. P. Day to Watterson, 10 June 1914 ("Who that reads newspapers printed in the United States is not familiar with the name of Henry Watterson?"), and Joseph Cannon to Watterson, 24 March 1910 and 24 September 1910, boxes 2 and 1, HWP-LC. Watterson's files of clippings, spread over three manuscript collections (HWP-FS, HWP-LC, and HWP-UL), are quite a haphazard and incomplete collection. Nevertheless, it is staggering how widely Watterson's editorials were reprinted. These files show clearly that his opinions were widely sought across the country by papers large and small. These collections have clippings from, among other papers, the *Chicago Times, Inter-Ocean, Journal, Record, Examiner*, and *Tribune*; *Indianapolis News and Sentinel*; *Philadelphia Inquirer* and *Public Ledger*; *St. Louis Christian Evangelist* and *Chronicle*; *Tacoma Morning Union*; *Baltimore Sun, American*, and *News*; *New York Tribune, Times, Commercial Advertiser, Sun, Herald*, and *World*; *Cincinnati Tribune* and *Times-Star*; *Kansas City Star* and *Tribune*; *Cleveland Plain-Dealer*; *Knoxville Journal, Sentinel*, and *Tribune*; *Washington Post* and *Star*; *Dayton Journal*; *Hartford Courant*; *Hazard (KY) Herald*; *Pueblo (CO) Chieftain*; *Portland (ME) Argus*; *Nashville Tennessean*; *Birmingham Daily News*; *Boston Herald* and *Transcript*; *Youngstown (OH) Vindicator*; *Troy (NY) Daily Times*; *Columbus (OH) Dispatch*; *Des Moines Capital*; *Buffalo Commercial* and *Times*; *Miami Herald*; *Fort Worth Record*; *Florida Times-Union*; *New Orleans Picayune*; *Colorado Springs Gazette*; *Ashland (KY) Daily Independent*; *Russellville (AR) Twice-a-Week Record*; *South Bend (IN) News-Times*; *Houston Post*; *Tampa Times*; *Rochester Democrat-Chronicle* and *Post Express*; *Lebanon (KY) Enterprise*; *Pittsburgh Gazette-Times*; *Omaha Bee*; *Springfield (MO) Republican*; *Minneapolis Journal*; *Seattle Times*; *Wichita*

Eagle; *London Daily Telegraph*; *Brooklyn Eagle* and *Standard-Union*; *Jackson (KY) Times*; *San Francisco Chronicle*; *Galveston Daily-News*; *Syracuse Herald*; *Huntington (WV) Advertiser*; *Gallatin Examiner-Tennessean*; *Hattiesburg (MS) News*; *Knickerbocker Press (Albany, NY)*; *Spokane Review*; *Milwaukee Sentinel*; *Davenport (IA) Democrat*, *Times*, and *Leader*; *Asheville (NC) Citizen*; *Meridian (MS) Evening Star*; *London (KY) Mountain Echo*; *Ocala (FL) Banner and Demands*; *Richmond Virginian*; *Columbia (SC) Record and State*; *Morning Oregonian*; and *Evansville (IN) Courier*.

3. Cassius Marcellus Clay, *The Life of Cassius Marcellus Clay: Memoirs, Writings, and Speeches*, vol. 1 (Cincinnati, OH: Brennan, 1886), 1:507; *Tammany Times*, 2 December 1893; *Oakland (CA) Tribune*, 20 June 1914; *Fulton (KY) Fultonian*, 3 March 1893; Tom Wallace, "Henry Watterson: A Man of Salient Characteristics," *Southern Newspaper Publishers Association Bulletin Special*, 1 April 1950, 3–11; Henry Watterson, *The Editorials of Henry Watterson*, ed. Arthur Krock (New York: Doran, 1923); Arthur Krock, *Myself When Young: Growing Up in the 1890s* (Boston: Little, Brown, 1973), 101–14, 162; Arthur Krock, *Louisville Times*, 23 December 1912; *Omaha World Herald*, 6 December 1903; *Washington Star*, n.d., box 17, misc. clippings, HWP-LC (the same language can be found in *Tampa Tribune*, 17 June 1906); Oswald Garrison Villard, *Some Newspapers and Newspapermen* (New York: Knopf, 1923), 260–67. Also see *Tacoma Ledger*, 17 July 1913; *Havana Post*, 28 February 1915; *Portland (ME) Express*, 1 March 1915; *Indianapolis Journal*, n.d., *Houston Chronicle*, n.d., and *Cleveland Plain-Dealer*, n.d.—all series 6, reel 5, pp. 1400–13, HWP-UL; Walter Emerson, "Marse Henry Watterson—An Appreciation by One of His Boys," *Cincinnati Commercial Tribune*, 27 April 1919; Isaac Frederick Marcosson, *"Marse Henry": A Biography of Henry Watterson* (New York: Dodd, Mead, 1951), 4; and Isaac Frederick Marcosson, *Before I Forget: A Pilgrimage to the Past* (New York: Dodd, Mead, 1959), 67.

4. *Harper's Weekly*, 3 February 1877, 188. This image greatly rankled Watterson, and it remained a sore spot for decades. He wrote to his friend Whitelaw Reid forty years later, "I think toward the close of his life Nast was a little ashamed of his brutality." Watterson to Reid, 6 May 1911, box 11, HWP-LC.

5. Thomas D. Clark, "Kentuckians Read Watterson First and the *Courier-Journal* Second," unidentified newspaper clipping, n.d., Watterson clippings file, box 27, folder 236, HFP; *Boston Transcript*, 8 March 1919.

6. Joseph Frazier Wall, *Henry Watterson: Reconstructed Rebel* (New York: Oxford University Press, 1956), 215–17; Henry Watterson, *"Marse Henry": An Autobiography*, 2 vols. (New York: George H. Doran, 1919), 1:17; *Washington Post*, 5 January 1907.

7. Lena Crain Logan, "Henry Watterson, Border Nationalist, 1840–1877" (PhD diss., Indiana University, 1942); Joseph Niel Plummer, "The Political Leadership of Henry Watterson" (PhD diss., University of Wisconsin–Madison, 1940); George Christopher Wharton, "Henry Watterson—A Study of Selected

Speeches on Reconciliation in the Post-Bellum Period" (PhD diss., Louisiana State University, 1974); Carl R. Osthaus, *Partisans of the Southern Press: Editorial Spokesmen of the Nineteenth Century* (Lexington: University Press of Kentucky, 1994), 150.

8. Osthaus, *Partisans of the Southern Press*, 164; Gaines M. Foster, *Ghosts of the Confederacy: Defeat, The Lost Cause, and the Emergence of the New South, 1865 to 1913* (New York: Oxford University Press, 1987), 80. An important exception to the simple view of Watterson is Paul M. Gaston, *The New South Creed: A Study in Southern Mythmaking* (New York: Knopf, 1970).

9. The literature on the personal journalists is very large; see the bibliography for relevant works. Also see Henry Watterson, "George Denison Prentice" (speech, 22 February 1870), in Henry Watterson, *The Compromises of Life; and Other Lectures and Addresses, Including Some Observations on Certain Downward Tendencies of Modern Society* (New York: Fox, Duffield, 1903), 3–23; and Gerald J. Baldasty, "The Nineteenth-Century Origins of Modern American Journalism," *Proceedings of the American Antiquarian Society* 100, no. 2 (1990): 407–19.

10. Mark Wahlgren Summers, *The Press Gang: Newspapers and Politics, 1865–1878* (Chapel Hill: University of North Carolina Press, 1994), 47, 98, 208; James L. Baughman, "'The World is Ruled By Those Who Holler the Loudest': The Third-Person Effect in American Journalism History," *Journalism History* 16, nos. 1–2 (Spring–Summer 1989): 12–19; Ferald J. Bryan, *Henry Grady or Tom Watson? The Rhetorical Struggle for the New South, 1880–1890* (Macon, GA: Mercer University Press, 1994).

11. Henry Watterson, "The Ideal in Public Life" (speech, Emerson Centenary, Waldorf-Astoria, 25 May 1903), in Watterson, *Compromises of Life*, 373.

12. Tennant S. McWilliams, *The New South Faces the World: Foreign Affairs and the Southern Sense of Self, 1877–1950* (Baton Rouge: Louisiana State University Press, 1988), 47–48.

13. CJ, 19 July 1899.

14. CJ, 21 December 1898, 17 April 1900.

15. CJ, 20, 21 December 1897.

16. CJ, 2 November 1897.

17. James M. Lindgren, "The Apostasy of a Southern Anti-Imperialist: Joseph Bryan, the Spanish-American War, and Business Expansion," *Southern Studies* 2, no. 2 (Summer 1991): 151–78.

18. A clear discussion of the processes that constituted globalization and some of their results at the turn of the nineteenth century can be found in Alfred E. Eckes Jr. and Thomas W. Zeiler, *Globalization and the American Century* (Cambridge: Cambridge University Press, 2003), 1–37. Louis A. Perez Jr. explores the evolving meaning and understanding of the Spanish-American War in *The War of 1898: The United States and Cuba in History and Historiography* (Chapel Hill: University of North Carolina Press, 1998). A succinct and unified analysis of American foreign policy interests at this time is Thomas Schoonover,

Uncle Sam's War of 1898 and the Origins of Globalization (Lexington: University Press of Kentucky, 2003), although still unsurpassed are Thomas J. McCormick, *China Market: America's Quest for Informal Empire, 1893–1901* (Chicago: Quadrangle Books, 1967); and Walter LaFeber, *The New Empire: An Interpretation of American Expansion, 1865–1898* (Ithaca, NY: Cornell University Press, 1963).

19. New attention is being focused on the impact of empire and globalization on the South, for example, Peter Coclanis, "Globalization before Globalization: The South and the World to 1950," in *Globalization and the American South*, ed. James C. Cobb and William Stueck (Athens: University of Georgia Press, 2005), 19–35.

20. Joseph A. Fry, *John Tyler Morgan and the Search for Southern Autonomy* (Knoxville: University of Tennessee Press, 1992), 72, 259–61, 104. Also see Fry's excellent survey, *Dixie Looks Abroad: The South and U.S. Foreign Relations, 1789–1973* (Baton Rouge: Louisiana State University Press, 2002), 106–38.

1. Toward the Star-Eyed Goddess

1. Watterson, "*Marse Henry*," 1:15–16.

2. Ibid., 20, 25–27, 53; Wall, *Henry Watterson*, 4, 8.

3. Wall, *Henry Watterson*, 10, 16–17.

4. Watterson, "*Marse Henry*," 1:33–38. Watterson enumerated the presidents he knew in *CJ*, 19 March 1911, in a good example of his cultivation of his own image.

5. *CJ*, 27 July 1879, 8 January 1897.

6. Young E. Allison, "Henry Watterson," *Illustrated American*, 5 July 1890, 67, series 6, reel 5, p. 1369, HWP-UL; Morton M. Casseday, "Henry Watterson," *Mid-Continent Magazine*, May 1895, 7; Wall, *Henry Watterson*, 22–23; *The Biographical Encyclopedia of Kentucky of the Dead and Living Men of the Nineteenth Century* (Cincinnati, OH: Armstrong, 1878); Watterson, "*Marse Henry*," 1:17–18; Hay quoted in unidentified newspaper clipping, n.d., misc. clippings, box 18, HWP-LC. No issues of *New Era* from this period have survived, although the paper continued to be published after the Civil War.

7. Watterson, "*Marse Henry*," 1:55. In his autobiography, Watterson spelled her name "Casneau," although historians spell it "Cazneau." She changed her name so often, or used pseudonyms, that this confusion is not a surprise. See the very enlightening Linda S. Hudson, *Mistress of Manifest Destiny: A Biography of Jane McManus Storm Cazneau, 1807–1878* (Austin: Texas State Historical Association, 2001); the description of Mann is on p. 163. Robert May, "Marse Henry and His Lady Insurrecto: A Case Study of Fictional Reminiscences for the High School History Classroom," *International Journal of Social Education* 6, no. 3 (1991–92): 41–67.

8. Hudson, *Mistress of Manifest Destiny*, chap. 3, offers the case on Cazneau as the author of "manifest destiny"; chap. 7 details her later politics. Robert May,

"'Plenipotentiary in Petticoats': Jane M. Cazneau and American Foreign Policy in the Mid-Nineteenth Century," in *Women and American Foreign Policy: Lobbyists, Critics, and Insiders*, ed. Edward P. Crapol (New York: Greenwood Press, 1987), 19–44; Watterson, "*Marse Henry*," 1:56–57.

9. Watterson, "*Marse Henry*," 1:56–57; Cazneau to Watterson, 14 October 1868, box 3, HWP-LC; *CJ*, 25 September 1895.

10. Watterson, "*Marse Henry*," 1:78.

11. Henry Watterson, "Abraham Lincoln," *Cosmopolitan Magazine*, March 1909, 363; *CJ*, 18 August 1897; Merrill D. Peterson, *Lincoln in American Memory* (Oxford: Oxford University Press, 1994), 49–50, 85, 138, 178–79, 191, 251; *CJ*, 8, 10, 20 May 1895, 27 October 1895; *Public Opinion*, 9 September 1897, 296–97; Henry Watterson, "The Hampton Roads Conference" (speech, Confederate Veteran Camp of the City of New York annual banquet, 26 January 1903); Watterson, *Compromises of Life*, 363–69; Henry Watterson, *"Abraham Lincoln": An Oration Delivered before the Lincoln Union, Chicago Auditorium, February 12, 1895* (Louisville, KY: Courier-Journal Job Printing, 1899). Watterson's popular "Abraham Lincoln" address was delivered all over the country for years. Watterson went abroad for a year to write a Lincoln biography, but the article cited and some speeches are all that seem to have resulted. The book was never completed, despite Watterson's allusions to a book contract and forthcoming release when he returned stateside at the end of 1896. *NYT*, 29 November 1896.

12. Watterson, "*Marse Henry*," 1:59, 81–82; Wall, *Henry Watterson*, 32–33.

13. Watterson, "*Marse Henry*," 1:82; Logan, "Henry Watterson, Border Nationalist," 42; *CJ*, 26 October 1870; Henry Watterson, "The Humor and Tragedy of the Greeley Campaign," *Century Magazine*, November 1912, 27.

14. Henry Watterson, "The Reunited Union," *NAR* 140 (1885): 24; *CJ*, 12 December 1898; Henry Watterson, "An Abortive Hero," *NAR* 193 (1911): 38. Also see Henry Watterson, "The Southern Confederacy," *Chautauquan*, May 1892, 147–52, which is something of a repudiation of the rebellion.

15. *NYTB*, 16 January 1901; Henry Watterson, "Let Us Have Peace" (speech, Society of the Army of Tennessee annual banquet, Chicago, 9 October 1891), in Watterson, *Compromises of Life*, 297; *CJ*, 1 July 1902.

16. Henry Watterson, "The Compromises of Life," in *Compromises of Life*, 47. He also told this story in "*Marse Henry*," 1:28.

17. Watterson, "*Marse Henry*," 1:85.

18. J. Cutler Andrews, *The South Reports the Civil War* (Princeton, NJ: Princeton University Press, 1970), 40–41, 345–46; *Chattanooga Rebel*, 26 August 1863, 5 September 1863.

19. *Chattanooga Rebel*, 13 January 1863; James W. Livingood, "The Chattanooga *Rebel*," *East Tennessee Historical Society's Publications* 39 (1967): 51; Wall, *Henry Watterson*, 40–44; Watterson to Rebecca Ewing, 5 January 1865, box 14, HWP-LC. Wall has a good overall discussion of Watterson's war years, chap. 3.

20. Watterson, "Southern Confederacy," 152; Watterson, "*Marse Henry,*" 1:241.

21. Wall, *Henry Watterson,* 51–57; Logan, "Henry Watterson, Border Nationalist," 71g. Wall sees a unity in Watterson's actions at the time (and at most times) that does not allow for a more honest, critical perspective of his actions at the end of the war, although Wall does provide a useful narrative of Watterson's interaction with President Andrew Johnson during those years.

22. Donald W. Curl, *Murat Halstead and the* Cincinnati Commercial (Boca Raton: University Press of Florida, 1980), 49–50; Watterson quoted in Marcosson, "*Marse Henry,*" 243.

23. E. Merton Coulter, *William G. Brownlow, Fighting Parson of the Southern Highlands* (Knoxville: University of Tennessee Press, 1971), 285; Wall, *Henry Watterson,* 58–64, Watterson quoted on p. 60; Eric Foner, *Reconstruction: America's Unfinished Revolution, 1863–1877* (New York: Harper & Row, 1988), 189–90; Martin Abbott, ed., "A Southerner Views the South, 1865: Letters of Harvey M. Watterson," *Virginia Magazine of History and Biography* 68 (October 1960): 478–89.

24. Wall, *Henry Watterson,* 42, 54–55; Watterson family letters throughout HWP-FHS and HWP-UL; *Havana Post,* 31 December 1915, box 18, WP-LC.

25. Bett Carolyn Congleton, "George D. Prentice: Nineteenth Century Southern Editor," *Register of the Kentucky Historical Society* 65 (1967): 94–119.

26. C. Vann Woodward, *Origins of the New South, 1877–1913* (Baton Rouge: Louisiana State University Press, 1951), 6; E. Merton Coulter, *The Civil War and Readjustment in Kentucky* (Chapel Hill: University of North Carolina Press, 1926); William E. Ellis, *Robert Worth Bingham and the Southern Mystique: From the Old South to the New South and Beyond* (Kent, OH: Kent State University Press, 1997), 17; Wall, *Henry Watterson,* 76; Thomas L. Connelly, "Neo-Confederatism or Power Vacuum: Post-War Kentucky Politics Reappraised," *Register of the Kentucky Historical Society* 64 (1966): 258–59. Other views of Kentucky as a microcosm of the tensions facing the postwar South are Ross A. Webb, "Kentucky: Pariah among the Elect," in *Radicalism, Racism, and Party Realignment: The Border States during Reconstruction,* ed. Richard O. Curry (Baltimore: Johns Hopkins University Press, 1969), 1065–145; and Ross A. Webb, *Kentucky in the Reconstruction Era* (Lexington: University Press of Kentucky, 1979).

27. Peter R. Knights, "'Competition' in the U.S. Daily Newspaper Industry, 1865–68," *JQ* 45 (1968): 473–80; Henry Watterson, "The History of a Great Newspaper," *CJ,* 8 November 1918; Ardnt M. Stickles, *Simon Bolivar Buckner: Borderland Knight* (Chapel Hill: University of North Carolina Press, 1940), 299–300; J. H. Battle, W. H. Perrin, and G. C. Kniffen, *Kentucky: A History of the State* (Louisville, KY: Battery, 1885), 495–98. The merger agreements and financial papers are in boxes 21–23, HFP, and in the Walter N. Haldeman file, box 5, HWP-LC. On Haldeman, who has, unfortunately, been almost totally ignored by historians, see Dennis Charles Cusick, "Gentleman of the Press: The

Life and Times of Walter Newman Haldeman" (master's thesis, University of Louisville, 1987).

28. Watterson, "History of a Great Newspaper"; *Louisville Commercial* quoted in Cusick, "Gentleman of the Press," 170.

29. Watterson, "History of a Great Newspaper"; George P. Rowells, *American Newspaper Directory* (New York: Printer's Ink, 1869–94); Edwin Alden and Brothers, *American Newspaper Catalogue* (Cincinnati, OH: Alden, 1868–94); Osthaus, *Partisans of the Southern Press*, 195; Alfred McClung Lee, *The Daily Newspaper in America: The Evolution of a Social Instrument* (New York: Macmillan, 1937), 122; *CJ*, 27 February 1898.

30. Henry Watterson, "The Personal Equation in Journalism," *Atlantic Monthly*, July 1910, 41; Wall, *Henry Watterson*, 174–75; *NYTB*, 3 January 1902.

31. Wallace, "Henry Watterson," 3–11; "Watterson's Editorial Writers Once Outnumbered Reporters," *Editor and Publisher*, 30 December 1939, 5. N.b., in the current work, if there is any chance that Watterson did not write an editorial, it is attributed in the text to the *CJ*.

32. Henry Watterson, "English and American Journalism," *Munsey's Magazine*, January 1906, 425; *CJ*, 12 August 1893; Henry Watterson, "The American Newspaper," in Watterson, *Compromises of Life*, 258.

33. Watterson to John Hay, 26 October 1898, WP-LC.

34. *CJ*, 14 October 1879; Woodward, *Origins of the New South*, 6.

35. *CJ*, 25 May 1870; Henry Watterson, "The South in Light and Shade," in Watterson, *Compromises of Life*, 101.

36. *CJ*, 9 November 1868, 5 December 1870, 6, 14 April 1871, 24 June 1871; Hambleton Tapp and James C. Klotter, *Kentucky: Decades of Discord, 1865–1900* (Frankfort: Kentucky Historical Society, 1977), 471n1.

37. Watterson, "History of a Great Newspaper"; Foner, *Reconstruction*, 416–17, 421; Watterson, "History of a Great Newspaper."

38. *CJ*, 6 April 1871, 3 July 1872; Watterson, "*Marse Henry*," 1:177; *Frankfort Weekly Commonwealth*, 22 July 1870. Also see William Elsey Connelley and E. Merton Coulter, *History of Kentucky* (Chicago: American Historical Society, 1922), 2:918; E. Merton Coulter, *The South during Reconstruction, 1865–1877* (Baton Rouge: Louisiana State University Press, 1947), 344–45; and Horace Samuel Merrill, *Bourbon Democracy of the Middle West, 1865–1896* (Baton Rouge: Louisiana State University Press, 1953), 65–67. For the relationship between northern and southern Democrats on the confluence of these political and economic issues, see Terry L. Seip, *The South Returns to Congress: Men, Economic Measures, and Intersectional Relationships, 1868–1879* (Baton Rouge: Louisiana State University Press, 1983), 291–92.

39. Henry Watterson, "The South and Its Colored Citizens," *Cosmopolitan Magazine*, May 1890, 116; *CJ*, 8 April 1895, 7 January 1902; Watterson, "South in Light and Shade," 100; *CJ*, 17, 29 June 1870, 24 October 1870.

40. Watterson, "South and Its Colored Citizens," 116; Henry Watterson

(speech, Carnegie Hall, 11 January 1908), quoted in Alonzo W. Draine to Watterson, 27 January 1908, box 1, folder 3, HWP-FHS.

41. George C. Wright, *Life behind a Veil: Blacks in Louisville, Kentucky, 1865–1930* (Baton Rouge: Louisiana State University Press, 1985), 24–27; Watterson, "South and Its Colored Citizens," 113–16; Henry Watterson, "The Negro in America," *Chautauquan*, April 1892, 20–24; Henry Watterson, *Harper's Weekly*, 11 October 1890, 787; *CJ*, 27 September 1899, 26 August 1900; Henry Watterson, "Massachusetts and Kentucky, with a Word or Two about Reciprocity and Expansion" (speech, Merchants Association of Boston Banquet, 10 December 1901), box 11, folder 170, speeches, 1899–1904, HWP-FHS; Watterson to Konta, 7 November 1919, vol. 2, AKP. Robert K. Thorp, "Marse Henry and the Negro: A New Perspective," *JQ 46* (1969): 467–74, covers the limitations of Watterson's racial liberalism during the Reconstruction years. Wall (*Henry Watterson*), in contrast, almost never cites Watterson using the word "nigger," although it was commonplace in his editorials and speeches. This sort of language would have soured Wall's portrait of the editor as a liberal original, and even as a progressive. Also see Allen J. Share, *Cities in the Commonwealth: Two Centuries of Urban Life in Kentucky* (Lexington: University Press of Kentucky, 1982), 94–96.

42. Watterson, *Editorials*, 313; Victor B. Howard, "The Kentucky Press and the Black Suffrage Controversy, 1865–1872," *Filson Club History Quarterly* 47, no. 3 (1973): 215–37; Victor B. Howard, "The Kentucky Press and the Negro Testimony Controversy, 1866–1872," *Register of the Kentucky Historical Society* 71 (1973): 25–50; *CJ*, 7 August 1895, 17 February 1897. The New Southerners' understanding of the race question is well covered in Gaston, *New South Creed*, 119–50, 207–14.

43. *CJ*, 15 October 1868, 27 October 1870; Watterson quoted in Share, *Cities in the Commonwealth*, 74.

44. Connelley and Coulter, *History of Kentucky*, 2:926. For a few examples of Watterson's consistency over the years, see *CJ*, 23 June 1871, 6 August 1881, 5 October 1882, 15 January 1895, 25 December 1895, 13 July 1898, 1, 29 August 1898, and 13 May 1900. The critical railroad dispute and the *CJ*'s role in it are well described in Leonard P. Curry, *Rail Routes South: Louisville's Fight for the Southern Market, 1865–1872* (Lexington: University of Kentucky Press, 1969).

45. *DeBow's Review*, January–June 1868, 442, quoted in Connelley and Coulter, *History of Kentucky*, 2:925.

46. *CJ*, 27 October 1870, 16 November 1876; Watterson, "*Marse Henry*," 2:127; Watterson quoted in Share, *Cities in the Commonwealth*, 69; *CJ*, 4 August 1879; Henry Watterson, "The Man in Gray," in Watterson, *Compromises of Life*, 353; Henry Watterson, "The Nation's Dead," in Watterson, *Compromises of Life*, 281.

47. *CJ*, 9 May 1893, 9–14 September 1895; Wharton, "Henry Watterson," 155; Henry Watterson, "The Blue and the Gray," in *Memorable Addresses by American Patriots*, ed. John Clark Ridpath (Chicago: Elliot-Madison, 1919); *CJ*, 9 July 1895.

48. Wharton, "Henry Watterson," 234; *CJ*, 10 May 1893.

49. Richard Franklin Bensel, *Sectionalism and American Political Development, 1880–1980* (Madison: University of Wisconsin Press, 1984), 4, 21–29, 50–51; *CJ*, 17 May 1872.

50. *CJ*, 3 July 1872.

51. Wall, *Henry Watterson*, 101.

52. Wall, *Henry Watterson*, 106–8; Tapp and Klotter, *Kentucky*, 119–21; Lena C. Logan, "Henry Watterson and the Liberal Convention of 1872," *Indiana Magazine of History*, December 1944, 319–40. The details of the nomination fight and Watterson's role in the campaign are covered from Watterson's memory in Watterson, "Humor and Tragedy"; the quote is on p. 43.

53. Earle D. Ross, "Horace Greeley and the South, 1865–1872," *South Atlantic Quarterly* 16 (1917): 324–38; Joseph P. Kenkel, *Progressives and Protection: The Search for a Tariff Policy, 1866–1936* (Lanham, MD: University Press of America, 1983), 19.

54. The daily circulation increased from a low of 10,500 in 1873 (a depression year) to 12,633 three years later, and the weekly circulation increased from 17,500 to 28,300 in the same time frame. George P. Rowells, *American Newspaper Directory* (New York: Printer's Ink, 1873–75).

55. Henry Watterson, *History of the Manhattan Club: A Narrative of the Activities of Half a Century* (New York: Manhattan Club, 1915), 147.

56. Watterson, "*Marse Henry*," 1:69–70, 2:21–22; *CR*, 44th Cong., 1st sess., 12 August 1876, vol. 4, pt. 6, p. 5557; *CR*, 44th Cong., 2nd sess., 13 December 1876, vol. 5, pt. 1, p. 177; *CR*, 44th Cong., 2nd sess., 11 January 1877, vol. 5, pt. 1, p. 577; *House of Representatives Journal*, 44th Cong., 2nd sess., 14 December 1876, p. 75; Watterson, "*Marse Henry*," 2:115; Bowles to Watterson, quoted in George S. Merriam, *The Life and Times of Samuel Bowles* (New York: Century, 1885), 2:418–19. In 1883, Watterson was nominated for senator from Kentucky by state senator J. R. W. Smith. *Journal of the Regular Session of the Senate of the Commonwealth of Kentucky*, 30 January 1883, 236. In 1896, in a very tense political atmosphere in the state, Watterson was again nominated for senator. Tapp and Klotter, *Kentucky*, 357–58; *NYTB*, 14, 15 August 1902. Also see "The Watterson Boom," n.d., series 6, reel 6, p. 487, HWP-UL.

57. Henry Watterson, "The Hayes-Tilden Contest for the Presidency: Inside History of a Great Political Crisis," *Century Magazine*, May 1913, 3–20. Wall's largest contribution is undoubtedly his discussion of the Tilden campaign and the compromise. Wall, *Henry Watterson*, 123–71. Also see Keith Ian Polakoff, *The Politics of Inertia: The Election of 1876 and the End of Reconstruction* (Baton Rouge: Louisiana State University Press, 1973); C. Vann Woodward, *Reunion and Reaction: The Compromise of 1877 and the End of Reconstruction* (Boston: Little, Brown, 1951); and Alexander Clarence Flick, *Samuel Jones Tilden: A Study in Political Sagacity* (Westport, CT: Greenwood Press, 1939), 300–402.

58. *Official Proceedings of the National Democratic Convention, Held in St.*

Louis, MO, June 27th, 28th and 29th, 1876 (St. Louis: Woodward, Tiernan & Hale, 1876), 21; S. Walter Poulshock, *The Two Parties and the Tariff in the 1880s* (Syracuse, NY: Syracuse University Press, 1965), 15; Watterson, "Hayes-Tilden Contest," 4–7; *CJ*, 25 May 1876, 8 November 1898.

59. Woodward, *Reunion and Reaction*, 110–11, 121; *CJ*, 8 January 1877; Wall, *Henry Watterson*, 149–52; W. A. Swanberg, *Pulitzer* (New York: Scribner, 1967), 37.

60. Watterson to Manton Marble, 5 April 1878, vol. 50, MMMP; *CR*, 44th Cong., 2nd sess., 26 January 1877, vol. 5, pt. 2, pp. 1005–8.

61. Henry Watterson, "The Solid South," *NAR* 128 (1879): 49.

62. *Proceedings of the Convention of the American Bankers Association held at Louisville, Kentucky, October 10th and 11th, 1883* (New York: Bankers Publishing Association, 1883), 73–74.

63. *CJ*, 25 October 1870; Festus B. Summers, *William L. Wilson and Tariff Reform: A Biography* (1953; repr., Westport, CT: Greenwood Press, 1974), 136; Poulshock, *Two Parties and the Tariff*, 44; *Birmingham Age* quoted in *CJ*, 28 April 1883; Henry Watterson, "The Political Outlook," *Forum*, January 1898, 569–70; Watterson, "Southern Confederacy," 147; Watterson, *"Marse Henry,"* 2:249. On Watterson and tariff reform, also see Wall, *Henry Watterson*, 195–96. *CJ*, 14 April 1883, has a wide array of press comment on Watterson's obsession with the tariff, much of it critical, in such papers as the *Nashville American*, *Philadelphia Times*, *Kansas City Journal*, *New York Commercial Advertiser*, *St. Louis Globe-Democrat*, *Chicago Tribune*, and *Memphis Avalanche*. Also see the antitariff breakdown in box 2, folder 35, HWP-FHS; and Clarence Lee Miller, *The States of the Old Northwest and the Tariff, 1865–1888* (Emporia, KS: Emporia Gazette Press, 1929), 137, 182. On southerners and the tariff, see Patrick J. Heardon, *Independence and Empire: The New South's Cotton Mill Campaign, 1865–1901* (DeKalb: Northern Illinois University Press, 1982), 6; Judith Goldstein, *Ideas, Interests, and American Trade Policy* (Ithaca, NY: Cornell University Press, 1993), 79; and Seip, *South Returns to Congress*, 162–69.

64. *CJ*, 19 January 1893; Carlisle quoted in H. W. Furber, ed., *Which? Protection, Free Trade, or Revenue Reform* (Hartford, CT: Park, 1884), 441; John H. Allen, *The Tariff and Its Evils, or Protection Which Does Not Protect* (New York: Putnam's Sons, 1888), 33; *CJ*, 6 August 1881.

65. Miller, *States of the Old Northwest*, 181–82; Adams quoted in Seip, *South Returns to Congress*, 163; Sarah McCanless Howell, "The Editorials of Arthur S. Coylar, Nashville Prophet of the New South," *Tennessee Historical Quarterly* 27, no. 3 (1968): 262–67.

66. Tom E.Terrill, *The Tariff, Politics, and American Foreign Policy, 1874–1901* (Westport, CT: Greenwood Press, 1973), 9, 24–25, 32, 213; Cynthia A. Hody, *The Politics of Trade: American Political Development and Foreign Economic Policy* (Hanover, NH: University Press of New England, 1996), 43–44; Bensel, *Sectionalism*, 62 and passim; Peter Trubowitz, *Defining the National In-*

terest: Conflict and Change in American Foreign Policy (Chicago: University of Chicago Press, 1998), chap. 2.

67. Terrill, *Tariff, Politics, and American Foreign Policy*, 184.

68. James Tice Moore, "Redeemers Reconsidered: Change and Continuity in the Democratic South, 1870–1900," *Journal of Southern History* 44 (August 1978): 376; Democratic platform quoted in Edward Stanwood, *American Tariff Controversies in the Nineteenth Century*, 2 vols. (Boston: Houghton Mifflin, 1903), 2:199.

69. *CJ*, 4 September 1879; *Elizabeth (NJ) Evening Times*, n.d., series 6, reel 6, p. 835, HWP-UL.

70. F. W. Taussig, *The Tariff History of the United States* (New York: Putnam's Sons, 1892), 249; Ida M. Tarbell, *The Tariff in Our Times* (New York: Macmillan, 1911), 109–32; *CJ*, 21 July 1879, 14 November 1879, 11 April 1883.

71. *CJ*, 11 April 1883 (the same sentiments are expressed at length in *CJ*, 14, 21, 28 April 1883).

72. *CJ*, 14, 16 September 1887.

73. Allan Nevins, *Grover Cleveland: A Study in Courage* (New York: Dodd, Mead, 1932), 367–82; Godkin to Watterson, 16 November 1888, series 1, reel 1, pp. 44–46, HWP-UL; James D. Richardson, ed., *A Compilation of the Messages and Papers of the Presidents* (New York: Bureau of National Literature, 1897), 11:5169–75; Terrill, *Tariff, Politics, and American Foreign Policy*, 96–97, 120–21; Nevins, *Grover Cleveland*, 383–442; John Edgar McDaniel Jr., "The Presidential Election of 1888" (PhD diss., University of Texas at Austin, 1970).

74. Henry Watterson, "The Tariff ['For Revenue Only']," *Harper's Monthly*, January 1888, 272–85.

75. John G. Carlisle, "The National Revenues," in *The National Democratic Party: Its History, Principles, Achievements and Aims*, ed. William L. Wilson (Baltimore: Harvey, 1888), 308.

76. *Official Proceedings of the National Democratic Convention, Held in St. Louis, MO, June 5th, 6th, and 7th, 1888* (St. Louis: Woodward, Tiernan & Hale, 1888), 98; John R. Lambert, *Arthur Poe Gorman* (Baton Rouge: Louisiana State University Press, 1953), 140–42; George T. McJimsey, *Genteel Partisan: Manton Marble, 1834–1917* (Ames: Iowa State University Press, 1971), 249. McDaniel called Watterson's plank "radical" ("The Presidential Election of 1888," 91–93); Nevins, supportive of Cleveland's tariff revision idea, did not stress the tension at the convention (*Grover Cleveland*, 400–401).

77. Watterson to *New York Sun*, draft, 1888, box 10, HWP-LC.

78. *Louisville Times*, 7 November 1884; Watterson to Cleveland, 18 June 1885, series 2, reel 14, and Watterson to Cleveland, 6 November 1885, series 2, reel 23, GCP; *CJ*, 17 October 1887.

79. Watterson to Cleveland, 9 March 1890, 13 April 1890, 21 November 1890, series 2, reel 68, GCP.

80. *CJ*, 13, 25 September 1890, 21 May 1894, 20 September 1895; David A.

Lake, "The State and American Trade Strategy in the Pre-Hegemonic Era," *International Organization* 42, no. 1 (Winter 1988): 40. On the details of the McKinley tariff, see Terrill, *Tariff, Politics, and American Foreign Policy*, 159–83.

81. *NYTB* quoted in Terrill, *Tariff, Politics, and American Foreign Policy*, 171; Watterson to Cleveland, 21 November 1890.

82. Michael Perman, *Struggle for Mastery: Disfranchisement in the South, 1888–1908* (Chapel Hill: University of North Carolina Press, 2001), 38–47; Stanley P. Hirshson, *Farewell to the Bloody Shirt: Northern Republicans and the Southern Negro, 1877–1893* (Chicago: Quadrangle Books, 1962), 145; Richard E. Welch Jr., "The Federal Elections Bill of 1890: Postscripts and Prelude," *Journal of American History* 52, no. 3 (December 1965): 511–26.

83. Watterson, "Southern Confederacy," 151; Watterson, "South and Its Colored Citizens," 113–16.

84. *New York Mail and Express*, 6 April 1895. Clippings from newspapers' coverage of Watterson's speeches are in box 18 and misc. printed matter, box 21, HWP-LC. The Watterson Club constitution and minutes are in the Filson Historical Society Library, Louisville, KY.

85. *New York Herald*, 22 January 1892 (the idea of Watterson's candidacy is also discussed on 14, 16, 19, 25, 28 January 1892 and 18, 23 February 1892); *CJ*, 23 February 1892; Henry Watterson (speech, Kentucky state Democratic convention, Louisville, 1892), box 17, HWP-LC, also in Watterson, *Editorials*, 71. Also see George Harman Knoles, *The Presidential Campaign and Election of 1892* (Palo Alto, CA: Stanford University Press, 1942), 31; and Nevins, *Grover Cleveland*, 485. On Watterson's opposition to Cleveland, see Knoles, *Presidential Campaign and Election of 1892*, 23–28.

86. *Official Proceedings of the National Democratic Convention, Held in Chicago, Ill., June 21st, 22nd and 23rd, 1892* (Chicago: Cameron, Amberg, 1892), 82–92, 95–101; William L. Wilson, "The Tariff Plank at Chicago," *NAR* 155 (1892): 280–86; Summers, *William L. Wilson*, 141; Stanwood, *American Tariff Controversies*, 315; Watterson, *"Marse Henry,"* 2:134–39. The platform fight is discussed in Knoles, *Presidential Campaign and Election of 1892*, 80–86.

87. Cleveland quoted in Horace Samuel Merrill, *Bourbon Leader: Grover Cleveland and the Democratic Party* (Boston: Little, Brown, 1957), 164.

88. Cleveland-Watterson correspondence described in Watterson, *"Marse Henry,"* 2:132–43; Nevins, *Grover Cleveland*, 492.

89. Watterson to Whitney, 12 November 1892, box 1, folder 1, HWP-FHS.

90. *CJ*, 25 January 1893, 2 January 1893 (similar sentiment in *CJ*, 9 August 1893, 4 March 1893, and 7 March 1893).

91. *CJ*, 14 April 1893, 3 April 1893, 23 May 1893, 2 August 1892.

92. *Public Opinion*, 18 January 1894, 381–82; Tarbell, *Tariff in Our Times*, 209–36; Stanwood, *American Tariff Controversies*, 319–59; Terrill, *Tariff, Politics, and American Foreign Policy*, 185–97; Hody, *Politics of Trade*, 48; Lambert, *Arthur Poe Gorman*, 200–238; LaFeber, *New Empire*, 159–72; *CJ*, 9 May 1894.

93. Merrill, *Bourbon Leader*, 188; Watterson, *"Marse Henry,"* 2:159; *NYT*, 12 August 1895; *CJ*, 3 October 1895; Charles W. Stein, *The Third Term Tradition: Its Rise and Collapse in American Politics* (New York: Columbia University Press, 1943), 122; *Cincinnati Tribune*, 12 November 1894; Marcosson, *"Marse Henry,"* 137.

94. U.S. Department of State, *Papers Relating to the Foreign Relations of the United States, 1895* (Washington, DC: U.S. Government Printing Office, 1896), pt. 1, 554–55; *CJ*, 5, 9, 18–31 December 1895; *NYTB*, 13 July 1896.

95. *CJ*, 9 March 1895, 8 January 1895.

2. Sound Money, Home Rule, and Free Trade

1. *CJ*, 29 January 1895, 8 July 1895.

2. Lindgren, "Apostasy of a Southern Anti-Imperialist," 151–78.

3. *CJ*, 9 October 1896.

4. Wall, *Henry Watterson*, 221–22; *CJ*, 2 December 1895.

5. *American Newspaper Annual* (Philadelphia: Ayer & Son, 1891–95); *CJ*, 16 May 1895. Violence statistics discussed in *CJ*, 18 August 1895, and in Edward Wiltz, "The 1895 Election: A Watershed in Kentucky Politics," *Filson Club History Quarterly* 37, no. 2 (1963): 118.

6. *CJ*, 9 October 1896; *NYT*, 29 November 1896.

7. *CJ*, 9, 20 May 1895.

8. *CJ*, 2 July 1895; Charles S. Campbell, *The Transformation of American Foreign Relations, 1865–1900* (New York: Harper & Row, 1976), 143; Edward Atkinson, "Jingoes and Silverites," *NAR* 161 (1895): 554–60; *CJ*, 10 May 1895.

9. McCormick, *China Market*, 31–32; Campbell, *Transformation*, 141–42; *CJ*, 16 July 1895.

10. Wall, *Henry Watterson*, 224; *CJ*, 23 September 1895, 17 May 1895.

11. *NYT*, "Watterson on Politics," 29 November 1896.

12. *CJ*, 10 February 1895, 10, 17 May 1895, 3 October 1895, 22 August 1896, 2 August 1897.

13. LaFeber, *New Empire*, 154–59.

14. J. C. Hemphill, "Free Coinage and the Loss of Southern Statesmanship," *Forum*, March–August 1892, 297.

15. *CJ*, 22 May 1895, 2 August 1897.

16. Rydell, *All the World's a Fair*, 74, 89–93; *CJ*, 9 November 1895; Walter G. Cooper, *The Cotton States and International Exposition and South, Illustrated; Including the Official History of the Exposition* (Atlanta, GA: Illustrator, 1896); Edward Atkinson, "The Atlanta Exposition," *NAR* 161 (1895): 385–93.

17. Gretchen Ritter, *Goldbugs and Greenbacks: The Antimonopoly Tradition and the Politics of Finance in America* (New York: Cambridge University Press, 1997), 28–61; Merrill, *Bourbon Leader*, 112–17; Paul W. Glad, *McKinley, Bryan, and the People* (Philadelphia: Lippincott, 1964), 94. Hollingsworth de-

scribes these divisions in detail. J. Rogers Hollingsworth, *The Whirligig of Politics: The Democracy of Cleveland and Bryan* (Chicago: University of Chicago Press, 1963), 39–47, 69–83.

18. *CJ*, 15 May 1895, 7 November 1895, 22 July 1897. Wall supplies only three vague sentences on the crucial state party battles discussed here. Wall, *Henry Watterson*, 225. Also see Franklin T. Lambert, "Free Silver and the Kentucky Democracy, 1891–1895," *Filson Club History Quarterly* 53, no. 2 (1979): 146, 171.

19. Tapp and Klotter, *Kentucky*, 404–9.

20. Thomas J. Brown, "The Roots of Bluegrass Insurgency: An Analysis of the Populist Movement in Kentucky," *Register of the Kentucky Historical Society* 78 (1980): 219–42; Gaye Keller Bland, "Populism in Kentucky, 1887–1896" (PhD diss., University of Kentucky, 1979); Bruce Palmer, *Man over Money: The Southern Populist Critique of American Capitalism* (Chapel Hill: University of North Carolina Press, 1980).

21. *CJ*, 15 May 1891, quoted in Lambert, "Free Silver," 149; *CJ*, 27 June 1895.

22. Lambert, "Free Silver," 159–60; *CJ*, 25 May 1895.

23. *CJ*, 9, 11, 22 May 1895. For statewide press response to Buckner's declarations on sound money, see *CJ*, 9 May 1895.

24. Charles E. Barker (of Pembroke, KY) to Watterson, n.d., box 1, HWP-LC; Wiltz, "1895 Election," 127–28; George Lee Willis, *Kentucky Democracy: A History of the Party and Its Representative Members—Past and Present* (Louisville, KY: Democratic Historical Society, 1935), 1:354; *CJ*, 17 May 1895.

25. *CJ*, 26 July 1895; Lambert, "Free Silver," 165–61; *CJ*, 12 March 1896, 11 December 1895; Lowell H. Harrison and James C. Klotter, *A New History of Kentucky* (Lexington: University Press of Kentucky, 1997), 268. Also see Wiltz, "1895 Election," 134; Webb, "Kentucky: Pariah among the Elect," 145; and Tapp and Klotter, *Kentucky*, 348–55.

26. *CJ*, 3 October 1895; Willis, *Kentucky Democracy*, 1:356; Wiltz, "1895 Election," 117.

27. Watterson, *Editorials*, 80; James A. Barnes, *John G. Carlisle: Financial Statesman* (New York: Dodd, Mead, 1931), 437–43; Clark quoted in Barnes, *John G. Carlisle*, 431; Stanley Jones, *The Presidential Election of 1896* (Madison: University of Wisconsin Press, 1964), 55–57. Also see James A. Barnes, "The Gold Standard Democrats and the Party Conflict," *MVHR* 17 (1930–31): 422–50.

28. *CJ*, 21 May 1895; Lambert, "Free Silver," 156–59; *CJ*, 18, 11 May 1895; Tapp and Klotter, *Kentucky*, 348.

29. *CJ*, 7 May 1895, 25 June 1895, 24 May 1876, 8, 12 October 1895. For the same argument applied, conversely, to the gold standard, see *Chicago Dispatch*, quoted in *LD*, 19 September 1896, 649.

30. *CJ*, 12 October 1895; *Raleigh News and Observer*, 23 April 1895, quoted in Joseph L. Morrison, *Josephus Daniels Says . . . : An Editor's Political Odyssey*

from Bryan to Wilson and F.D.R., 1894–1914 (Chapel Hill: University of North Carolina Press, 1962), 93; Jones, *Presidential Election of 1896*, 266.

31. *CJ*, 2, 9 July 1895, 8 October 1895, 26 July 1895, 23 September 1895, 13 May 1895; Wall, *Henry Watterson*, 225, 230.

32. *CJ*, 2 December 1895.

33. Ibid.

34. Ibid.; *CJ*, 9 October 1896. For discussions of the problems of gold Democrats, especially southerners, see Hollingsworth, *Whirligig of Politics*, 39–47, 69–83; Jones, *Presidential Election of 1896*, 264–75; and Barnes, "Gold Standard Democrats," 422–50.

35. *NYTB*, 13 July 1896; Hearst to Watterson, 4 December 1896, box 5, HWP-LC; *CJ*, 22 August 1896. Watterson had always claimed he was impartial as an editor in any case.

36. John M. Palmer, *Personal Recollections of John M. Palmer: The Story of an Earnest Life* (Cincinnati, OH: Clarke, 1901), 591; Haldeman to Watterson, 22 August 1896, box 5, HWP-LC; *Newspaper Maker*, 10 September 1896, 4; Baldasty, "Nineteenth-Century Origins," 410; Woodward, *Origins of the New South*, 286–87; Hollingsworth, *Whirligig of Politics*, 69–70; Harold A. Williams, *The Baltimore Sun, 1837–1987* (Baltimore: Johns Hopkins University Press, 1987), 94–95; Jones, *Presidential Election of 1896*, 265–69.

37. William Jennings Bryan, *The First Battle: A Story of the Campaign of 1896* (Chicago: Conkey, 1896), 445–48.

38. *CJ*, 14 July 1896; *NYTB*, 14 July 1896; *NYT*, 16 July 1896; Watterson to Whitney, 27 July 1896, WCWP; *NYTB*, 16 August 1896. The *CJ* crowed the phrase "No compromise with dishonor" for the duration of the campaign. Wall cites a rough draft of a letter to an unidentified person that makes a point similar to that in the letter to Whitney. Wall, *Henry Watterson*, 226–27.

39. *CJ*, 22 August 1896.

40. *CJ*, 9 October 1896; William B. Haldeman to Watterson, 8 October 1896, box 5, HWP-LC; *CJ*, 22 August 1896, 7 April 1897.

41. *CJ*, 7 April 1897.

42. *CJ*, 21 August 1896; Haldeman to Watterson, 22 August 1896.

43. Haldeman to Watterson, 8 October 1896. Wall has a solid narrative of Watterson's refusal to run. Wall, *Henry Watterson*, 226–29. Also see Barnes, *John G. Carlisle*, 434–40.

44. Haldeman to Watterson, 22 August 1896.

45. *NYT*, 16 July 1896; *New York Herald* interview quoted in Wall, *Henry Watterson*, 228; *New York Herald*, Paris edition, 29 August 1896, 5 September 1896, series 6, reel 6, p. 442, HWP-UL.

46. Watterson, "*Marse Henry*," 1:268, 18–19.

47. Watterson to Ewing Watterson, 8 September 1896, box 1, folder 1, HWP-FHS.

48. *NYT*, 2 September 1896. Jones wrote that Watterson's "candidacy was hampered by a misunderstanding regarding his availability," but this is a misread-

ing of Watterson's unwillingness to run, as described above. Jones, *Presidential Election of 1896*, 270.

49. Nevins, *Grover Cleveland*, 707; *CJ*, 21 August 1896; *LD*, 12 September 1896, 610–11.

50. Horace Samuel Merrill, *William Freeman Vilas: Doctrinaire Democrat* (Madison: State Historical Society of Wisconsin, 1954), 235–41; Hollingsworth, *Whirligig of Politics*, 80–83; Paolo E. Coletta, *William Jennings Bryan*, vol. 1, *Political Evangelist, 1860–1908* (Lincoln: University of Nebraska Press, 1964), 170–71; *Campaign Textbook of the National Democratic Party, 1896* (Chicago, 1896), 6–7; Palmer, *Personal Recollections*, 595; Bryan, *First Battle*, 386–89; George Thomas Palmer, A *Conscientious Turncoat: The Story of John M. Palmer, 1817–1900* (New Haven, CT: Yale University Press, 1941), 277–78. On the National Democrats, in addition to the sources cited above, see Elbridge Gerry Dunnell, "The Rise of the 'National Democracy': The Movement for Sound Money and the Indianapolis Convention," *Review of Reviews* 14, no. 4 (October 1896): 434–45.

51. *Campaign Textbook*, 12–24; Stickles, *Simon Bolivar Buckner*, 407–13; *CJ*, 9 October 1896; *NYT*, 5 September 1896.

52. Watterson, "Political Outlook," 568–73; *CJ*, 7 April 1897; Jones, *Presidential Election of 1896*, 349. See Jones, 340–50, for a detailed discussion of the vote nationwide.

53. Walter Dean Burnham, *Critical Elections and the Mainsprings of American Politics* (New York: Norton, 1970), 71–90; Walter Dean Burnham, "The System of 1896: An Analysis," in *The Evolution of American Electoral Systems*, by Paul Kleppner, Walter Dean Burnham, Ronald P. Formisano, Samuel P. Hays, Richard Jensen, and William G. Shade (Westport, CT: Greenwood Press, 1981), 158–65.

54. Barnes, "Gold Standard Democrats," 445. For a statistical breakdown of the 1896 election results by county, see Jasper B. Shannon and Ruth McQuown, *Presidential Politics in Kentucky, 1824–1948: A Compilation of Election Statistics and an Analysis of Political Behavior* (Lexington: University of Kentucky Press, 1950), 68–73.

55. Haldeman to Watterson, 8 October 1896.

56. There were 26 dailies and 234 weeklies in the state in 1895, alongside many other smaller ones. *American Newspaper Directory* (New York: Rowell, 1894), 280; *American Newspaper Directory* (New York: Rowell, 1895), 292; *American Newspaper Directory* (New York: Rowell, 1896), 337. Financial statements are in Haldeman Family Papers; also see Cusick, "Gentleman of the Press," 174–75; Wall, *Henry Watterson*, 232; and Plummer, "Political Leadership of Henry Watterson," 46.

57. Hendrick to Watterson, 24 August 1907, box 6, HWP-LC; Haldeman to Watterson, 8 October 1896; Watterson to H. T. MacDonald, 5 October 1906, box 8, HWP-LC.

58. *CJ*, 9 October 1896, reprinted in Watterson, *Editorials*, 86.
59. *NYT*, 29 November 1896; *CJ*, 12 June 1900.
60. *CJ*, 15 March 1897.

3. Democracy Unterrified and Undefiled

1. *CJ*, 8 April 1897, 15 January 1897.
2. *CJ*, 15 July 1897, 27 May 1897, 18 March 1897.
3. "Now, the *Courier-Journal*, having had its head chopped off long ago, has nothing to fear or to lose, and it can afford . . . to say what it please to say." *CJ*, 27 September 1899.
4. Watterson, "Political Outlook," 573; *CJ*, 16 April 1897.
5. *CJ*, 15 March 1897; Wall, *Henry Watterson*, 233; Thomas D. Clark, *A History of Kentucky* (New York: Prentice-Hall, 1937), 606; *CJ*, 8 September 1897.
6. *CJ*, 30 January 1897, 18, 27 March 1897.
7. Watterson, " Reciprocity and Expansion," in Watterson, *Compromises of Life*, 418–19; *CJ*, 15 March 1897, 16, 22 November 1895, 15 December 1895. For a description of what newspapers looked like at the end of the nineteenth century, see Frank Luther Mott, *American Journalism: A History, 1690–1960*, 3rd ed. (New York: Macmillan, 1962), 577–92.
8. *CJ*, 21 May 1897.
9. *CJ*, 24 September 1899.
10. *CJ*, 22 September 1897, 15 January 1897, 8 April 1897, 15 March 1897.
11. Wall, *Henry Watterson*, esp. 243–46.
12. *CJ*, 28 June 1899.
13. *CJ*, 14, 15 January 1897, 18 March 1897, 15 July 1897, 14, 22 September 1897, 4 July 1897, 19 October 1897, 26 February 1897.
14. *Stanford Interior-Journal* quoted in *CJ*, 26 March 1897; *CJ*, 27 March 1897; Watterson, "Political Outlook," 576.
15. *CJ*, 27 April 1897. Also see *CJ*, 22 September 1897. On Herbert's southern boosterism, see Hugh B. Hammett, *Hilary Abner Herbert: A Southerner Returns to the Union* (Philadelphia: American Philosophical Society, 1976), and Tennant McWilliams, "The Lure of Empire: Southern Interest in the Caribbean, 1877–1900," *Mississippi Quarterly* 29 (Winter 1975–76): 52–53.
16. *CJ*, 4 June 1897, 14, 22 September 1897.
17. *CJ*, 28 August 1897, 22 September 1897. Watterson's gendered language was in keeping with that of his day. Gail Bederman, *Manliness and Civilization: A Cultural History of Gender and Race in the United States, 1880–1917* (Chicago: University of Chicago Press, 1996), 27.
18. *CJ*, 9 January 1897.
19. Ibid.
20. Ibid.

21. Ibid.
22. Ibid.
23. Ibid.
24. Ibid.; *CJ*, 9 July 1897.
25. *CJ*, 9 July 1897.
26. *CJ*, 18 March 1897; Tapp and Klotter, *Kentucky*, 365.
27. *CJ*, 15 July 1897, 1.
28. Ibid.
29. Ibid., 2.
30. Ibid.
31. Ibid.
32. Ibid., 3.
33. Ibid.
34. *CJ*, 26, 28, 29 October 1897, 22 September 1897.
35. *CJ*, 27 May 1897, 3 August 1897.
36. *CJ*, 3 August 1897.
37. Tapp and Klotter, *Kentucky*, 366.
38. Nicholas C. Burckel, "Progressive Governors in the Border States: Reform Governors of Missouri, Kentucky, West Virginia, and Maryland, 1900–1918" (PhD diss., University of Wisconsin–Madison, 1971), 171. Important editorials are *CJ*, "The *Courier-Journal* and Its Enemies," 2 March 1898, and others throughout that month, as well as *CJ*, 14 July 1899, 2, 12, 14 September 1899, and February 1900. For a discussion of general political violence and lawlessness and a solid account of the Goebel campaign, see Tapp and Klotter, *Kentucky*, 377–454. The secondary literature on the election and assassination is relatively small, but there are some important works. The best overview and synthesis are James C. Klotter, *William Goebel: The Politics of Wrath* (Lexington: University Press of Kentucky, 1977); Burckel, "Progressive Governors," 170–206; and Nicholas C. Burckel, "William Goebel and the Campaign for Railroad Regulation in Kentucky, 1888–1900," *Filson Club History Quarterly* 48, no. 1 (1974): 43–60. Also useful are Thomas D. Clark, "The People, William Goebel, and the Kentucky Railroads," *Journal of Southern History* 5 (February 1939): 34–48, and R. E. Hughes, F. W. Schaefer, and E. L. Williams, *That Kentucky Campaign, or The Law, the Ballot and the People in the Goebel-Taylor Contest* (Cincinnati, OH: Clarke, 1900).
39. Wall, *Henry Watterson*, 236–39; *CJ*, 2 March 1899, 1 July 1899, 26 October 1899.
40. *CJ*, 30 January 1897, 8 April 1897.
41. *Inaugural Addresses of the Presidents of the United States from George Washington 1789 to George Bush 1989* (Washington, DC: U.S. Government Printing Office, 1989), 196–97; F. W. Taussig, "The United States Tariff Act of 1897," *Economic Journal* 7, no. 28 (December 1897): 592–98.
42. *CJ*, 18 March 1897; *Inaugural Addresses*, 197.

43. McCormick, *China Market*, 51; Paul Wolman, *Most Favored Nation: The Republican Revisionists and U.S. Tariff Policy, 1897–1912* (Chapel Hill: University of North Carolina Press, 1992), 1–26.

44. *CJ*, 6 March 1897.

45. *CJ*, 7 April 1897, 3, 13 August 1897.

46. Henry Watterson, "Massachusetts and Kentucky" (speech, Merchants Association of Boston Banquet, 10 December 1901), box 11, folder 170, speeches, 1899–1904, HWP-FHS; McCormick, *China Market*, 21–52; Watterson, "Political Outlook," 577–78.

47. Watterson to McClure, 24 January 1897, microfilm edition, series 1, reel 1, WMP; Margaret Leech, *In the Days of McKinley* (New York: Harper, 1959), 22.

48. Watterson to Ridgely, [October 1896], reel 10, vol. 16, JHP; Herman Kohlsaat to John Hay, 18 October 1896, reel 10, vol. 16, JHP; Watterson to Hay, 16 March 1899, reel 11, vol. 17, JHP; Watterson to McClure, 24 January 1897; Watterson to Hay, n.d., box 6, folder 49, HWP-FHS; Watterson to Allison, 11 July 1898, box 1, folder 1, HWP-FHS. (The comparison of his editorials to shotgun blasts is an apt one.) Watterson later told Hay, "The memory of the old days is yet radiant with me." Watterson to John Hay, 26 October 1898, reel 10, vol. 16, JHP. On Kohlsaat and the election of 1896, see Leech, *In the Days of McKinley*, 73, 108–10.

49. *CJ*, 18 March 1897; Coletta, *William Jennings Bryan*, 1:215; *CJ*, 8 July 1897, 14 January 1897. On the connections between silver and the tariff as political and campaign issues, see Stanwood, *American Tariff Controversies*, 2:360–78, 389–90.

50. Donald Bruce Johnson and Kirk H. Porter, eds., *National Party Platforms, 1840–1972*, 5th ed. (Urbana: University of Illinois Press, 1973), 107–8; *Inaugural Addresses*, 172; Leech, *In the Days of McKinley*, 140; Kenkel, *Progressives and Protection*, 3; H. Wayne Morgan, *William McKinley and His America* (Syracuse, NY: Syracuse University Press, 1963), 277.

51. McCormick, *China Market*, 51; Leech, *In the Days of McKinley*, 142.

52. *CJ*, 30 January 1897.

53. *Inaugural Addresses*, 174; *CJ*, 30 January 1897.

54. *CJ*, 18, 25 March 1897, 6 April 1897.

55. *CJ*, 3, 6 August 1897.

56. *CJ*, 3 August 1897.

4. The Idiosyncrasy of the Market

1. *CJ*, 27 May 1897.

2. Henry Watterson, "Money and Morals," in Watterson, *Compromises of Life*, 105; Watterson, "*Marse Henry*," 2:198–203.

3. *CJ*, 26 September 1897, 10 October 1897, 9 January 1898, 8 February 1898.

4. *CJ*, 13 May 1898.

5. *CJ*, 19 July 1899, 16 January 1900; Watterson, "Massachusetts and Kentucky" (speech, Merchants Association of Boston Banquet, 10 December 1901), box 11, folder 170, speeches, 1899–1904, HWP-FHS.

6. *CJ*, 28 August 1897; Watterson, "Massachusetts and Kentucky."

7. *CJ*, 13 February 1897, 13 December 1897.

8. *CJ*, 17 July 1897, 11 November 1897; W. F. Axton, *Tobacco and Kentucky* (Lexington: University Press of Kentucky, 1975), 82–86; McCormick, *China Market*, 36; Wolman, *Most Favored Nation*, chap. 2; Kenkel, *Progressives and Protection*, 42, 143; Martin J. Sklar, "The N.A.M. and Foreign Markets on the Eve of the Spanish-American War," *Science and Society* 23 (1959): 133–62; Charles S. Campbell, *Special Business Interests and the Open Door Policy* (New Haven, CT: Yale University Press, 1951), 1–18; *CJ*, 2, 19, 25, 29 January 1898, 2, 28 February 1898.

9. *CJ*, 4 February 1897, 18 September 1898, 25 January 1898.

10. Richard Franklin Bensel, *Yankee Leviathan: The Origins of Central State Authority in America, 1859–1877* (Cambridge: Cambridge University Press, 1990); Stephen Skowronek, *Building a New American State: The Expansion of National Administrative Capacities, 1877–1920* (Cambridge: Cambridge University Press, 1982); Martin J. Sklar, *The Corporate Reconstruction of American Capitalism, 1890–1916: The Markets, the Law, and Politics* (Cambridge: Cambridge University Press, 1988); *CJ*, 2 February 1898.

11. *CJ*, 2 February 1898. Also see *CJ*, 18 November 1895, 19 March 1897, and 18 May 1897.

12. *CJ*, 25 May 1897, 3 March 1897.

13. *CJ*, 15 November 1897, 16 February 1898.

14. *CJ*, 28 January 1897.

15. See William Langer, *The Diplomacy of Imperialism, 1890–1902*, 2nd ed. (New York: Knopf, 1951), 195–210.

16. *CJ*, 2 December 1895.

17. Langer, *Diplomacy of Imperialism*, 385–412, 445–80; *CJ*, 5, 8, 13 January 1898, 14 February 1898, 12 March 1898, 7 May 1895; Robert McClellan, *The Heathen Chinee: A Study of American Attitudes toward China, 1890–1905* (Columbus: Ohio State University Press, 1971), 163–202; *CJ*, 10 January 1898, 16 April 1898, 26 December 1897.

18. *CJ*, 26 December 1897.

19. Ibid. McClellan covers these attitudes well. McClellan, *Heathen Chinee*, 3–129.

20. *CJ*, 15 June 1895.

21. Ibid.; *CJ*, 11 August 1895, 17 September 1895.

22. *CJ*, 18 August 1895. Also see *CJ*, 24 August 1895.

23. Bradford Perkins, *The Great Rapprochement: England and the United States, 1895–1914* (New York: Atheneum, 1968), 27–30; Nelson M. Blake, "The Olney-Pauncefote Treaty of 1897," *American Historical Review* 50 (1945): 228–

43; Edward P. Crapol, *America for Americans: Economic Nationalism and Anglophobia in the Late Nineteenth Century* (Westport, CT: Greenwood Press, 1973), 225; *CJ*, 22 February 1897.

24. *CJ*, 25 January 1897, 3, 10 February 1897, 5 April 1897.

25. Fry, *John Tyler Morgan*, 96, 107–9; *CJ*, 25 January 1897, 20 March 1897.

26. *CJ*, 28 June 1897, 6 July 1897; Henry Watterson, "European Society Contrasted with Ours," *Cosmopolitan Magazine*, November 1905, 3–12; *CJ*, 23 June 1897; Fry, *John Tyler Morgan*, 106–7 and passim; *CJ*, 15 November 1897, 17 May 1898.

27. *CJ*, 16 February 1898, 1 July 1897, 21 February 1898.

28. *CJ*, 24 March 1898.

29. *CJ*, 15 May 1898; Fry, *John Tyler Morgan*, 72–74, 125. A strong case in support of the idea of the South's subordination within the "core-periphery allocation of functions within the nation," as well as the relationship with specific political developments, is Bensel, *Sectionalism*, 3–103; also see Crapol, *America for Americans*, 91–141, 193–94, and passim; Woodward, *Origins of the New South*, 291–320; Gavin Wright, *Old South, New South: Revolutions in the Southern Economy since the Civil War* (New York: Basic Books, 1986); and Roger V. Clements, "The Farmers' Attitude toward British Investment in American Industry," *Journal of Economic History* 15, no. 2 (March 1955): 151–59.

30. *CJ*, 1 January 1898.

31. *CJ*, 15 February 1898.

32. *CJ*, 8 February 1898; Perman, *Struggle for Mastery*, 1–172.

33. *CJ*, 8 February 1898.

34. Ibid.; *CJ*, 15 February 1898.

35. *CJ*, 21 February 1897, 25 October 1897, 6, 31 July 1897. On the relationships between the private sector and government promotion of economic activity, see David Healy, *Drive to Hegemony: The United States in the Caribbean, 1898–1917* (Madison: University of Wisconsin Press, 1988), 14–23.

36. *CJ*, 1 March 1897.

37. *CJ*, 4 December 1897.

38. *CJ*, 13 March 1897; *American Newspaper Annual* (Philadelphia: Ayer & Son, 1898), 1045; Harrison and Klotter, *New History of Kentucky*, 302–3; *CJ*, 2 July 1901, 12 May 1898, 13 July 1898, 1, 10 February 1898. The best work on the connections between this New South movement and market expansionism is Heardon, *Independence and Empire*.

39. Watterson, "Abortive Hero," 43.

5. The *New* New Departure

1. *CJ*, 18 October 1895. The details of the Cuban revolution will not be presented here. The discussion draws from Jose Hernandez, *Cuba and the Unit-*

ed States: Intervention and Militarism, 1868–1933 (Austin: University of Texas Press, 1993); Jules Robert Benjamin, *The United States and the Origins of the Cuban Revolution: An Empire of Liberty in an Age of National Liberation* (Princeton, NJ: Princeton University Press, 1989); David Healy, *The United States in Cuba, 1898–1902: Generals, Politicians, and the Search for Policy* (Madison: University of Wisconsin Press, 1963); LaFeber, *New Empire*; and Morgan, *William McKinley*, 328. On the bases of John Tyler Morgan's support for annexation of Cuba, see Fry, *John Tyler Morgan*, 154–58. On southerners and the Cuban issue, see Marshall E. Schott, "The South and American Foreign Policy, 1894–1904: Regional Concerns during the Age of Imperialism" (PhD diss., Louisiana State University, 1995), 75–85.

2. *CJ*, 7 May 1895, 23 June 1895, 22 March 1895.

3. *CJ*, 26 March 1895, 9 May 1895.

4. *LD*, 13 July 1895, 303; *CJ*, 17 October 1895. On other editors' perceptions of the power of the yellow press and their critiques of sensationalism, see James L. Baughman, "'The Louder It Shrieks, the Less Attention Is Paid to It': The Third-Person Effect and the Critics of Sensational Journalism, 1895–1898" (paper delivered at the Association for Education in Journalism and Mass Communication annual convention, 8 August 1992); Joseph E. Wisan, *The Cuban Crisis as Reflected in the New York Press, 1895–1898* (New York: Columbia University Press, 1934), 70–73; William M. Armstrong, *E. L. Godkin and American Foreign Policy, 1865–1900* (New York: Bookman Associates, 1957); Mark Welter, "The 1895–98 Cuban Crisis in Minnesota Newspapers: Testing the 'Yellow Journalism' Theory," *JQ* 47 (1970): 719–24; and Stanley Lemons, "The Cuban Crisis of 1895–1898: Newspapers and Nativism," *Missouri Historical Review* 60 (1965): 63–74.

5. *CJ*, 13 April 1895; Morgan, *William McKinley*, 329–32; George W. Auxier, "The Propaganda Activities of the Cuban Junta in Precipitating the Spanish-American War, 1895–1898," *Hispanic American Historical Review* 19 (1939): 286–305; *CJ*, 23 February 1898; Hearst to Watterson, 28 February 1896, box 6, HWP-LC. Also good for comparing news coverage in the South are Roger P. Leemhuis, "South Carolina Newspapers and American Foreign Policy in the 1890s," *Proceedings of the South Carolina Historical Association* 50 (1980): 133–47, and George H. Gibson, "Attitudes in North Carolina Regarding the Independence of Cuba, 1868–1898," *North Carolina Historical Review* 43, no. 1 (1966): 43–65, esp. 54–65.

6. *CJ*, 3 May 1895, 9, 29 June 1895, 11, 21 July 1895, 1 September 1895.

7. *CJ*, 29 September 1895; *LD*, 18 January 1896, 335–36; Hernandez, *Cuba and the United States*, 24; Wisan, *Cuban Crisis*, 99–141.

8. *CJ*, 8 January 1897.

9. *CJ*, 7, 17, 29 October 1895.

10. *CJ*, 21 May 1897.

11. Morgan, *William McKinley*, 332–33; *CJ*, 28 November 1895.

12. *CJ*, 6 January 1897, 26 February 1897, 25 October 1897.

13. *CJ*, 26 February 1897, 25 October 1897.

14. *CJ*, 20, 27 January 1897. The changing interpretations of McKinley's Cuban policy are very well covered in Joseph A. Fry, "William McKinley and the Coming of the Spanish-American War: A Study of the Besmirching and Redemption of an Historical Image," *Diplomatic History* 3, no. 1 (Winter 1979): 77–97.

15. *CJ*, 27 May 1897; Fry, *John Tyler Morgan*, 159–60.

16. *CJ*, 28 May 1897, 31 December 1898.

17. *CJ*, 13 June 1897, 6 November 1897; Hannis Taylor, "A Review of the Cuban Question in Its Economic, Political, and Diplomatic Aspects," *NAR* 165 (1897): 610.

18. *CJ*, 27 May 1897, 15 December 1897, 11 June 1897, 7 August 1897, 24 September 1897, 3 October 1897.

19. *CJ*, 6 October 1897.

20. Ibid.

21. This idea remained the same whenever Watterson discussed it; for example, *CJ*, 20 June 1893, 26 February 1897, 24 February 1898, 29 January 1899.

22. *CJ*, 23 December 1897.

23. *CJ*, 10, 11, 19, 23 March 1893, 15, 18 April 1893, 29 May 1893, 3 June 1893, 9 August 1893, 18 December 1893, 31 January 1894, 6, 8 February 1894, 2 April 1894. Also see Watterson to Walter Q. Gresham, 12 November 1893, vol. 41, WQGP. For a comparison of how other writers' ideas changed, see Linda Heffernan, "From Independent Nation to Client State: The Metamorphosis of the Kingdom of Hawai'i in the Pages of the *North American Review* in the Nineteenth Century," *Hawaiian Journal of History* 22 (1988): 209–27. The southern fight is described in Tennant S. McWilliams, "James H. Blount, the South, and Hawaiian Annexation," *PHR* 57 (1988): 25–46. Also see George F. Pearce, "Assessing Public Opinion: Editorial Comment and the Annexation of Hawaii—A Case Study," *PHR* 43 (1974): 324–41, and Thomas J. Osborne, "Trade or War? America's Annexation of Hawaii Reconsidered," *PHR* 50 (1981): 285–307.

24. Thomas J. Osborne, *"Empire Can Wait": American Opposition to Hawaiian Annexation, 1893–1898* (Kent, OH: Kent State University Press, 1981), 85–86; LaFeber, *New Empire*, 362–33; Fry, *John Tyler Morgan*, 165–68; Richardson, *Compilation of the Messages and Papers*, 13:6241; *CJ*, 18 June 1897.

25. *CJ*, 18, 16 June 1897.

26. *CJ*, 31 March 1897, 21 October 1897, 20, 23 November 1897, 17 February 1898, 2 July 1897.

27. *CJ*, 18 February 1898, 15 September 1897, 13 May 1897; the arguments against a big navy are found in *CJ*, 21 October 1897, 1, 16, 21 December 1897, and 4, 20 January 1898, among other times; *CJ*, 29 June 1897, 28, 30 July 1897, 16 October 1897, 23 December 1897, 18 February 1898.

28. *CJ*, "The Hawaiian Conspiracy," 5 August 1897; *CJ*, 29 November 1897, 3 November 1897, 4 August 1897.

29. *CJ*, 24 December 1897, 18 May 1899 (response to *Salt Lake Tribune*).

30. Fry, *John Tyler Morgan*, 168; *CJ*, 26 January 1898.

31. *CJ*, 21 October 1898, 14, 15 January 1898.

32. *CJ*, 24 November 1897; Johnson and Porter, *National Party Platforms*, 108.

33. *CJ*, 20 March 1897. The same sentiment was expressed in *CJ*, 28 July 1897, 29 April 1897, and 7 February 1898.

34. *CJ*, 18 June 1897.

35. *CJ*, 17, 21, 24 June 1897, 20 November 1897, 23 December 1898, 5 February 1898, and many others. These ideas are also discussed in Rubin Francis Weston, *Racism in U.S. Imperialism: The Influence of Racial Assumptions on American Foreign Policy, 1893–1946* (Columbia: University of South Carolina Press, 1972), 57–68; *CJ*, 17, 30 December 1897, 1 July 1897.

36. *CJ*, 9 February 1898; Fry, *John Tyler Morgan*, 166–67; Weston, *Racism in U.S. Imperialism*, 14; Christopher Lasch, "The Anti-Imperialists, the Philippines, and the Inequality of Man," *Journal of Southern History* 24 (February–November 1958): 319–31; *CJ*, 3 September 1897, 17, 18 November 1897, 21 October 1897.

37. *CJ*, 23 December 1897.

38. Ibid.; Osborne, *"Empire Can Wait,"* 86–108; *CJ*, 18 March 1898.

39. John Offner, *An Unwanted War: The Diplomacy of the United States and Spain over Cuba, 1895–1898* (Chapel Hill: University of North Carolina Press, 1992); Lewis L. Gould, *The Spanish-American War and President McKinley* (Lawrence: University Press of Kansas, 1982); Morgan, *William McKinley*, 351–78; Gerald F. Linderman, *The Mirror of War: American Society and the Spanish-American War* (Ann Arbor: University of Michigan Press, 1974).

40. *CJ*, 11 April 1898.

41. Morgan, *William McKinley*, 355–57; LaFeber, *New Empire*, 347; George W. Auxier, "Middle-Western Newspapers and the Spanish-American War, 1895–1898," *MVHR* 26 (1940): 531–32; Schott, "South and American Foreign Policy," 123–24; *CJ*, 11 February 1898.

42. *CJ*, 26 March 1898, 1 May 1898; also see *CJ*, 9 May 1898; William Inglis, "A Democratic Presidential Possibility: 'Marse Henry' Watterson of Kentucky," *Harper's Weekly*, 8 August 1907, 1230; Mark Welter, "Minnesota Newspapers and the Cuban Crisis, 1895–1898: Minnesota as a Test Case for the 'Yellow Journalism' Theory" (PhD diss., University of Minnesota, 1970), chap. 1; Welter, "1895–1898 Cuban Crisis in Minnesota Newspapers," 719–24; Marcus M. Wilkerson, *Public Opinion and the Spanish-American War: A Study in War Propaganda* (1932; repr., New York: Russell & Russell, 1967), 17–20; Benedict Karl Zobrist, "How Victor Lawson's Newspapers Covered the Cuban War of 1898," *JQ* 38 (1961): 323–31; Auxier, "Middle-Western Newspapers," 528–29, 532–33.

43. McWilliams, *New South Faces the World*, 47–48; Lindgren, "Apostasy of a Southern Anti-Imperialist," 158.

44. Morgan, *William McKinley*, 360–68; LaFeber, *New Empire*, 348–51; Wilkerson, *Public Opinion and the Spanish-American War*, 101; *CJ*, 31 October 1895.

45. *CJ*, 16–19 February 1898.

46. *CJ*, 19, 22, 25, 26 February 1898, 8, 15 March 1898.

47. *CJ*, 10 March 1898.

48. Bensel, *Sectionalism*, 62–63; *CJ*, 11, 15 March 1898.

49. *CJ*, 12, 13, 15, 18, 23 March 1898.

50. *CJ*, 25 March 1898.

51. *CJ*, 2 March 1898.

52. *CJ*, 3 April 1898.

53. *CJ*, 18 March 1898.

54. *CJ*, 19, 25 March 1898, 19 April 1898.

55. *CJ*, 26, 29 March 1898. The significance of Proctor's speech is described in Gould, *Spanish-American War*, 40, and Morgan, *William McKinley*, 365–66.

56. *CJ*, 26 March 1898, 2 April 1898.

57. *CJ*, 28 March 1898.

58. Ibid.

59. Ibid.

60. Ibid.

61. Morgan, *William McKinley*, 371–77; *CJ*, 3 April 1898.

62. *CJ*, 1–10 April 1898.

63. Morgan, *William McKinley*, 377–78; Richardson, *Compilation of the Messages and Papers*, 6281–92.

64. *CJ*, 12, 13 April 1898.

65. *CJ*, 10, 11 April 1898.

66. *CJ*, 11 April 1898.

67. Ibid.

68. *CJ*, 17, 20 April 1898.

69. *CJ*, 18 April 1898.

70. *CJ*, 14–18, 21, 22, 24 April 1898; *CR*, 55th Cong., 2nd sess., 13 April 1898, vol. 31, pt. 4, pp. 3731–33, 3776; Schott, "South and American Foreign Policy," 149–50.

71. *CJ*, 6 April 1898.

72. *CJ*, 9 March 1898, 14, 17, 20, 22 April 1898, 1 May 1898.

73. Henry Watterson, "Farewell to the Kentucky Troops," in Watterson, *Compromises of Life*, 432; *CJ*, 30 April 1898.

74. Watterson, "Farewell to the Kentucky Troops," 428–37.

75. *CJ*, 20 April 1898.

76. *Raleigh News and Observer*, 3 May 1898; Foster, *Ghosts of the Confederacy*, 145–49.

77. Woodward, *Origins of the New South*, 369; Edward L. Ayers, *The Promise of the New South: Life after Reconstruction* (New York: Oxford University Press,

1992), 328–33; Henry Watterson, "The Reunited Sections," in Watterson, *Compromises of Life*, 329; Watterson, "*Marse Henry*," 2:123–25; *CJ*, 30 August 1898.

78. Henry Watterson, *History of the Spanish-American War: Embracing a Complete Review of Our Relations with Spain* (Louisville, KY: Courier-Journal Job Printing, 1898), vii–viii. Another example is *CJ*, 7 September 1898. Watterson's *History of the Spanish-American War* was ghostwritten by Watterson's close friend and *CJ* city editor Young E. Allison, and the original manuscript, in Allison's handwriting, can be found in box 28, YEAP. Watterson's familiar style is clearly evident in the preface, and the rest of the book pales in comparison. The book did not sell well, perhaps because the writing was so pedestrian, or because it was a straightforward narrative without any Watterson-style digressions. Nevertheless, Watterson was proud of it. Watterson to Hay, 26 October 1898, reel 10, vol. 16, JHP. It was not until Wall's 1956 book that Allison's descendants revealed the real author of the book. Wall, *Henry Watterson*, 347n5.

79. Schott, "South and American Foreign Policy," 139–43; Heardon, *Independence and Empire*, xv.

80. *CJ*, 25 April 1898; Watterson's speech quoted in *NYTB*, 31 May 1899.

6. War Has Its Compensations

1. *CJ*, 22 August 1898.

2. Wolman, *Most Favored Nation*, 10–11.

3. *CJ*, 4 April 1898, 3 June 1898, 1 May 1898.

4. *CJ*, 21 June 1898, 29 April 1898.

5. *CJ*, 16 June 1898, 1–3 May 1898; *Raleigh News and Observer*, 2 May 1898.

6. *CJ*, 3 May 1898.

7. *CJ*, 9 June 1898, 6 May 1898.

8. *CJ*, 5, 6 May 1898.

9. *CJ*, 9, 17, 18 May 1898.

10. *CJ*, 13, 22, 30 May 1898.

11. *Raleigh News and Observer*, 3 May 1898; *LD*, 14 May 1898, 571–73; *LD*, 11 June 1898, 696–97.

12. Fry, *John Tyler Morgan*, 171–75; John T. Morgan, "What Shall We Do with the Conquered Islands?" *NAR* 166 (1898): 641–49.

13. *CJ*, 2, 10 August 1898.

14. *CJ*, 2 June 1898.

15. *CJ*, 17 August 1898, 6 June 1898.

16. *CJ*, 7 June 1898.

17. Ibid.; *CJ*, 28 June 1898, 8, 25 August 1898.

18. *CJ*, 9–19 July 1898, 2–8, 20 August 1898, and many others.

19. *CJ*, 29, 14 July 1898.

20. *CJ*, 21 July 1898. Watterson also began to ridicule the antiexpansionists' own use of historical examples. *CJ*, 5 November 1898.

21. *CJ*, 12, 29 August 1898, 1, 7 February 1899.

22. *CJ*, 16, 24 June 1898, 4 August 1898.

23. *LD*, 9 July 1898, 32.

24. *CJ*, 12 July 1898.

25. *Minneapolis Times*, *Salt Lake City Herald*, and *Nashville American* cited in *CJ*, 25 August 1898, 13 July 1898, and 19 June 1898; E. Berkeley Tompkins, *Anti-Imperialism in the United States: The Great Debate, 1890–1920* (Philadelphia: University of Pennsylvania Press, 1970), 120–39; Robert L. Beisner, *Twelve against Empire: The Anti-Imperialists, 1898–1900* (New York: McGraw-Hill, 1968); Fred H. Harrington, "The Anti-Imperialist Movement in the United States, 1898–1900," *MVHR* 22 (1935): 211–30; Richard E. Welch Jr., "Motives and Policy Objectives of Anti-Imperialists, 1898," *Mid-America* 51, no. 2 (1969): 119–29; Jim Zwick, "The Anti-Imperialist Movement, 1898–1921," in *Whose America? The War of 1898 and the Battles to Define the Nation*, ed. Virginia M. Bouvier (Westport, CT: Praeger, 2001), 171–77.

26. *Augusta (GA) Chronicle* quoted and responded to in *CJ*, 25 August 1898. Gaines M. Foster wrote that, in general, "the Confederate past . . . did little to cause Southerners to question imperialism." Foster, *Ghosts of the Confederacy*, 150.

27. *Minneapolis Times* and *Nashville American* quoted and responded to in *NYTB*, 4 July 1898, and *CJ*, 14 July 1898. The *NYTB* defended the logic of Watterson's case, supported expansionism and McKinley, and asked, "What is the matter with the 'Times,' anyhow?" *NYTB*, 4 July 1898.

28. *CR*, 55th Cong., 2nd sess., 15 June 1898, vol. 31, pt. 6, p. 5974.

29. Bensel, *Sectionalism*, 97; Fry, *John Tyler Morgan*, 170; Schott, "South and American Foreign Policy," 60–67; Osborne, "*Empire Can Wait*," 109–34, 160n26; Thomas A. Bailey, "The United States and Hawaii during the Spanish-American War," *American Historical Review* 36 (1931): 552–60; *CJ*, 16 December 1898. For southerners' attitudes toward annexation, see John Tyler Morgan, "The Duty of Annexing Hawaii," *Forum*, March 1898, 11–16, and Philip S. Foner and Richard C. Winchester, eds., *The Anti-Imperialist Reader: A Documentary History of Anti-Imperialism in the United States*, vol. 1, *From the Mexican War to the Election of 1900* (New York: Holmes & Meier, 1984), 69–108. For the discussion of the economics of annexation, see *CR*, 55th Cong., 2nd sess., 23 June 1898, vol. 31, pt.6, pp. 6269–70, 6355. For the discussion of the racial makeup of the islands, see Senate Report no. 681, 55th Cong., 2nd sess., 16 March 1898, vol. 3, nos. 621–906, p. 43.

30. *CJ*, 21 July 1898.

31. Ibid.; *CJ*, 10 December 1898.

32. *CJ*, 10 July 1898, 1, 9 August 1898, 27 September 1898, 1 November 1898, 19 October 1900; *NYTB*, 16 August 1901.

33. *CJ*, 20 August 1898, 19 July 1898.

34. *CJ*, 19 July 1898, 8, 10, 12 August 1898.

35. *CJ*, "Peace," 13 August 1898.

36. *CJ*, 26 August 1898, 3 October 1898.

37. *CJ*, 22 October 1898.

38. *CJ*, 1 February 1899, 24 October 1899, 27 August 1898.

39. *CJ*, 3 October 1898, 11 December 1898, 1 February 1899, 9 January 1899.

40. *CJ*, 15 October 1898, 15, 16 December 1898, 13 January 1899; Theodore Roosevelt, "Acceptance Letter," in *The Works of Theodore Roosevelt*, nat. ed. (New York: Scribner's Sons, 1926), 14:365–66, 393–94; Theodore Roosevelt, "The Louisiana Purchase," in Roosevelt, *Works*, 11:315–20; Theodore Roosevelt, "The Strenuous Life," in Roosevelt, *Works*, 13:329–30. For a brief discussion of the uses of Jefferson in this debate, see Merrill D. Peterson, *The Jefferson Image in the American Mind* (New York: Oxford University Press, 1962), 266–70.

41. *CJ*, 30 November 1898, 12 July 1898.

42. *CJ*, 30 November 1898.

43. *CJ*, 7 October 1898, 18 November 1898, 1, 30 August 1898, 3 September 1898.

44. *CJ*, 1, 5, 14, 21 October 1898.

45. *CJ*, 25 August 1898, 24, 25 November 1898.

46. *CJ*, 13 December 1898; *New York Herald*, 10 December 1898; *Saturday Evening Post*, 28 January 1899, 476–91.

47. *New York Herald*, 10 December 1898.

48. *Saturday Evening Post*, 28 January 1899, 491.

49. Ibid.; Gaston, *New South Creed*, 125–26. See Watterson, "South and Its Colored Citizens," 113–16, and "Negro in America," 20–24.

50. Lasch, "Anti-Imperialists," 319–31; Weston, *Racism in U.S. Imperialism*, 4–56; Foster, *Ghosts of the Confederacy*, 150–52; Frank Furedi, *The Silent War: Imperialism and the Changing Perception of Race* (New Brunswick, NJ: Rutgers University Press, 1998); Edwina C. Smith, "Southerners on Empire: Southern Senators and Imperialism, 1898–1899," *Mississippi Quarterly* 31 (Winter 1977–78): 97–99; McWilliams, *New South Faces the World*, 66; Woodward, *Origins of the New South*, 324–25; *CJ*, 10 December 1898. On race and the anti-imperialism movement generally, see Richard E. Welch Jr., *Response to Imperialism: The United States and the Philippine American War, 1899–1902* (Chapel Hill: University of North Carolina Press, 1979), 101–16.

51. *CJ*, 2 November 1899; Willard B. Gatewood Jr., "Black Editor on American Imperialism: Edward E. Cooper of the *Colored American*, 1898–1901," *Mid-America* 57, no. 1 (1975): 3–19; John Mitchell quoted in Willard B. Gatewood Jr., "A Negro Editor on Imperialism: John Mitchell, 1898–1901," *JQ* 49 (1972): 48. Also see George P. Marks III, "Opposition of Negro Newspapers to American Philippine Policy, 1899–1900," *Midwest Journal* 4, no. 1 (Winter 1951–52):

1–25, and George P. Marks III, ed., *The Black Press Views American Imperialism, 1898–1900* (New York: Arno Press, 1971). On Mitchell, also see Ann Field Alexander, *Race Man: The Rise and Fall of the "Fighting Editor," John Mitchell Jr.* (Charlottesville: University of Virginia Press, 2002).

52. *CJ*, 2 April 1899, 17 August 1899, 12 January 1899, 14 December 1898, 16 March 1899; Walter L. Williams, "United States Indian Policy and the Debate over Philippine Annexation: Implications for the Origins of American Imperialism," *Journal of American History* 66, no. 4 (March 1980): 810–30; *CJ*, 2 March 1901. Also useful is Hazel M. McFerson, *The Racial Dimension of American Overseas Colonial Policy* (Westport, CT: Greenwood Press, 1997), 23–50.

53. *CJ*, 18 September 1899; *Saturday Evening Post*, 28 January 1899, 491.

54. Watterson to John Hay, 26 October 1898, reel 10, vol. 16, JHP.

55. *NYTB*, 2 January 1899; *LD*, 14 April 1900, 443–45; Louis W. Koenig, *Bryan: A Political Biography of William Jennings Bryan* (New York: Putnam's Sons, 1971), 315–16; *CJ*, 30 September 1899, 20 April 1900; Hearst to Watterson, n.d., box 6, HWP-LC.

56. *CJ*, 5 March 1901.

7. We Done Expanded

1. *CJ*, 1 January 1899, 18 March 1899.

2. *CJ*, 21 November 1898.

3. *CJ*, 10 September 1900. Wall's discussion of Watterson on imperialism is essentially one sentence, in which he notes that "Watterson performed all sorts of sophistical gymnastics in semantics to show that there was a difference between expansionism and imperialism" but does not go further to explain why the editor made these distinctions, which is the critical point discussed here. Wall, *Henry Watterson*, 245. Watterson's acceptance of both free trade imperialism and formal colonialism can be contrasted with the consistent anti-imperialism of Benjamin Tillman, for example, in Tillman, "Bryan or McKinley: Causes of Southern Opposition to Imperialism," *NAR* 171 (1900): 439–46.

4. John A. S. Grenville and George Berkeley Young, *Politics, Strategy, and American Diplomacy: Studies in Foreign Policy, 1873–1917* (New Haven, CT: Yale University Press, 1966), 287; Paolo E. Coletta, "Bryan, McKinley, and the Treaty of Paris," *PHR* 26 (1957): 136; Paolo E. Coletta, "McKinley, the Peace Negotiations, and the Acquisition of the Philippines," *PHR* 30 (1961): 341–50; Gould, *Spanish-American War*, 151–60; Robert L. Beisner, *From the Old Diplomacy to the New, 1865–1900*, 2nd ed. (Arlington Heights, IL: Harlan Davidson, 1986), 107–24, 140–50; Welch, *Response to Imperialism*, chap. 1.

5. *CJ*, 20–25 January 1899; Williams, *The Baltimore Sun, 1837–1987*, 96; *CJ*, 5 February 1899.

6. *CR*, 55th Cong., 3rd sess., 6 February 1899, vol. 32, pt. 2, p. 1489; Lala Carr Steelman, "Senator Augustus O. Bacon: Champion of Philippine Indepen-

dence," in *Essays in Southern Biography* (Greenville, NC: Department of History, East Carolina College, 1965), 93.

7. William Jennings Bryan, *Bryan on Imperialism* (New York: Arno Press, 1970), 16–17, 37–38; William Jennings Bryan, *The Second Battle, or The New Declaration of Independence, 1776–1900* (Chicago: Conkey, 1900), 126; *NYT*, 7 September 1900; H. W. Brands, *Bound to Empire: The United States and the Philippines* (Oxford: Oxford University Press, 1992), 24–35; Tompkins, *Anti-Imperialism in the United States*, 183–95; Ephraim K. Smith, "'A Question from Which We Could not Escape': William McKinley and the Decision to Acquire the Philippine Islands," *Diplomatic History* 9, no. 4 (Fall 1985): 363–75; Coletta, "Bryan, McKinley," 145; Merle Eugene Curti, *Bryan and World Peace* (New York: Octagon, 1969), 129.

8. *CJ*, 1 December 1898, 11, 12 January 1899; McWilliams, *New South Faces the World*, 66n47; *CJ*, 23–28 January 1899, 16, 17 February 1899, 1, 29 January 1899.

9. *CJ*, 1, 29, 31 January 1899.

10. Roosevelt, *Works*, 14:351.

11. *CJ*, 20, 31 January 1899, 8, 9 February 1899.

12. William G. Carleton, "Isolationism and the Middle West," *MVHR* 33 (1946): 378; *CJ*, 20, 31 January 1899, 8, 9 February 1899.

13. *CJ*, 31 January 1899.

14. *CJ*, 9 February 1899.

15. Ibid.; *CJ*, 11 March 1899; "*Collected Campaign Documents—1900 Campaign*," Special Collections, Wisconsin Historical Society, Madison. Also see Heardon, *Independence and Empire*, 46.

16. Brian McAllister Linn, *The Philippine War, 1899–1902* (Lawrence: University Press of Kansas, 2000), 3–181; Stuart Creighton Miller, "*Benevolent Assimilation*": *The American Conquest of the Philippines, 1899–1903* (New Haven, CT: Yale University Press, 1982), 31–128; *CJ*, 27 January 1899, 18 February 1899, 29 April 1899.

17. *CR*, 55th Cong., 3rd sess., 31 January 1899, vol. 32, pt. 2, p. 1298; Schott, "South and American Foreign Policy," 197, 206; *CJ*, 1, 21 May 1899, 1 June 1899. Watterson based some of his arguments on a pamphlet by Colonel Charles H. Clark titled *Imperialism in 1861 and 1898*. *CJ*, 5 January 1899.

18. *CJ*, 27 May 1899.

19. *Lexington Herald* [1899?], misc. clippings, box 19, HWP-LC.

20. *Anti-Imperialist*, 4 July 1899; *CJ*, 7 January 1899.

21. *CJ*, 18, 24 February 1899, 1 March 1899, 5 May 1899.

22. *CJ*, 24 August 1899, 3 July 1899.

23. *CJ*, 7 March 1899, 2, 3 August 1899. Welch cites the use of "aunties" in the *Indianapolis Journal* of 19 October 1899, which was long after Watterson began using the term. Welch, *Response to Imperialism*, 52. Also see the important discussion in Kristen L. Hoganson, *Fighting for American Manhood: How*

Gender Politics Provoked the Spanish-American and Philippine-American Wars (New Haven, CT: Yale University Press, 2000), 156–79. Hoganson notes the use of gender stereotypes in Watterson's ghostwritten *History of the Spanish-American War,* but she does not examine his extensive editorial writings in the same vein. Also see Judith Papachristou, "American Women and Foreign Policy, 1898–1905: Exploring Gender in Diplomatic History," *Diplomatic History* 14, no. 4 (Fall 1990): 493–509.

24. *CJ*, 29 November 1899, 3 March 1900, 5 May 1899.

25. *CJ*, 15 August 1899; *LD*, 13 May 1899, 541–42; *Public Opinion*, 11 May 1899, 583–84; Welch, *Response to Imperialism*, 51–54; *CJ*, 2 August 1899, 18 September 1899.

26. Richard E. Welch Jr., "'The Philippine Insurrection' and the American Press," *Historian* 36 (1973): 36–37, 46–49; Foster, *Ghosts of the Confederacy*, 151; Hollingsworth, *Whirligig of Politics*, 141n54; *Memphis Commercial-Appeal*, 20 July 1898, 3 May 1899; *Atlanta Constitution*, 22 May 1899; Schott, "South and American Foreign Policy," 212; Thomas Harrison Baker, *The Memphis Commercial-Appeal: The History of a Southern Newspaper* (Baton Rouge: Louisiana State University Press, 1971), 198–201; *LD*, 4 February 1899, 121–23; *LD*, 8 April 1899, 387–89; *CJ*, 17 December 1898.

27. Smith, "Southerners on Empire," 90; McWilliams, *New South Faces the World*, 66; Tillman, "Bryan or McKinley," 439–46; Schott, "South and American Foreign Policy," 301.

28. *CJ*, 21 August 1899, 6 September 1899, 28 October 1899, 22 November 1899, 16, 17 April 1900; O. Lawrence Burnette Jr., "John Tyler Morgan and Expansionist Sentiment in the New South," *Alabama Review* 18, no. 3 (July 1965): 170; *CJ*, 11 November 1899. On Morgan's political challenges in Alabama, see Fry, *John Tyler Morgan*, 110–53. Morgan's newspaper clipping files contain a large number of laudatory editorials from Watterson. Microfilm reels 7, 8, JTMP.

29. Heardon, *Independence and Empire*, 135–37; Baker, *The* Memphis Commercial-Appeal, 200; *CJ*, 25 January 1900, 4, 6 February 1900, 1 May 1900; *Memphis Commercial-Appeal*, December 1899; *CJ*, 14 June 1899.

30. *CJ*, 12 July 1899, 20 April 1899, 2 February 1899, 2 March 1899, 3, 9, 11 May 1899, 29 June 1899, 21 July 1899, 12 September 1899.

31. *CJ*, 12 July 1899.

32. Watterson made virtually identical claims about expansion and the southern race problem in *CJ*, 12, 26 July 1899, 26 August 1899, 23 September 1899, and 24 October 1899. Joseph O. Baylen and John Hammond Moore, "Senator John Tyler Morgan and Negro Colonization in the Philippines, 1901–1902," *Phylon* 29 (Spring 1968): 65–75; Fry, *John Tyler Morgan*, 183–87; John Tyler Morgan, "The Territorial Expansion of the United States," *Independent* 50 (July 1898): 10–12.

33. *CJ*, 19, 12 July 1899.

34. Watterson to Hay, 8 March 1901, reel 14, vol. 21, JHP.

35. Fry, *John Tyler Morgan*, chap. 6; *CJ*, 7 April 1899, 5 September 1899.

36. *CJ*, 25 October 1899, 19 July 1899, 10 May 1900.

37. *CJ*, 12 July 1899; Warner Miller, "The Nicaragua Canal," *Forum*, November 1898, 331–42.

38. *CJ*, 15–20 July -1899, 25 July 1899, 25 August 1899, 9 September 1899; E. Berkeley Tompkins, "Scylla and Charybdis: The Anti-Imperialist Dilemma in the Election of 1900," *PHR* 36 (1967): 149; Koenig, *Bryan*, 294–95; *CJ*, 15, 29 August 1899; William McKinley, second annual address, Richardson, *Compilation of the Messages and Papers*, 13:6391–99. McKinley stated several times that, once the archipelago was pacified, government could be established and the Philippines developed. "The hour of victory will be the hour of clemency and reconstruction," he said. Morgan, *William McKinley*, 436.

39. *CJ*, 31 March 1900.

40. *NYTB*, 21 June 1899; *Macon (GA) Telegraph*, 7 January 1900.

41. *CJ*, 9 January 1899; David Healy, *U.S. Expansionism: The Imperialist Urge in the 1890s* (Madison: University of Wisconsin Press, 1970), 223–25; *CJ*, 4 August 1899.

42. *CJ*, 3 August 1899.

43. Hanna to Watterson, 2 August 1899, box 6, HWP-LC.

44. *CJ*, 3 August 1899.

45. Ibid.

46. *CJ*, 7 March 1899, 18 September 1899.

47. *CJ*, 3 January 1900.

48. *CJ*, 8 January 1900.

49. Baker, *The* Memphis Commercial-Appeal, 201–2; Healy, *U.S. Expansionism*, 226; Harold Baron, "Anti-Imperialism and the Democrats," *Science and Society* 21 (1957): 234; Tompkins, "Scylla and Charybdis," 144; William Jennings Bryan, "The Issue in the Presidential Campaign," *NAR* 170 (1900): 753–71; *Memphis Commercial-Appeal*, 15 January 1900.

50. *CJ*, 7 February 1900.

51. *CJ*, 15 January 1900.

52. *CJ*, 16 January 1900.

53. Ibid.

54. *CJ*, 30 March 1900, 21 September 1900; Bryan, *Bryan on Imperialism*, 37–43; Bryan, *Second Battle*, 191–92; Bryan to Watterson, 7 June 1900, box 2, HWP-LC.

55. *CJ*, 7 February 1900.

56. Pedro E. Abelarde, *American Tariff Policy towards the Philippines, 1898–1946* (Morningside Heights, NY: King's Crown Press, 1947), 5–6 and, for a description of Spanish tariff policies, 6–15, 20–22, 32–38; F. W. Taussig, *Some Aspects of the Tariff Question* (Cambridge, MA: Harvard University Press, 1929), 70–72; Frank H. Golay, "The Search for Revenues," in *Reappraising an*

Empire: New Perspectives on Philippine-American History, ed. Peter W. Stanley (Cambridge, MA: Harvard University Press, 1984), 32–37. The connections between the Philippine and Puerto Rican tariff systems, particularly relating to the sugar interests, are discussed in Luzviminda Bartolome Francisco and Jonathan Shepard Fast, *Conspiracy for Empire: Big Business, Corruption, and the Politics of Imperialism in America, 1876–1907* (Quezon City, Philippines: Foundation for Nationalist Studies, 1985), 211–18, and David M. Pletcher, *The Diplomacy of Trade and Investment: American Economic Expansion in the Hemisphere, 1865–1900* (Columbia: University of Missouri Press, 1998), 357–60.

57. *CJ*, 5 March 1900, 19 October 1900; Wolman, *Most Favored Nation*, 15. Especially useful (and rare) is Goran Rystad's *Ambiguous Imperialism: American Foreign Policy and Domestic Politics at the Turn of the Century* (Lund, Sweden: Esselte Studium, 1975), an extended study of the Puerto Rican question in domestic politics and the election of 1900, particularly in Indiana. The only major flaw of this work is that it relies on generalized summaries of the positions of various papers and politicians without discussing the actual arguments presented in each. The quote is on p. 85. Also see Edward J. Berbusse, *The United States in Puerto Rico, 1898–1900* (Chapel Hill: University of North Carolina Press, 1966), and Julius W. Pratt, *America's Colonial Experiment: How the United States Gained, Governed, and in Part Gave Away a Colonial Empire* (New York: Prentice-Hall, 1950), 167–68. Specialized studies of the issues involved and their legal and political effects are also helpful, such as James Edward Kerr, *The Insular Cases: The Role of the Judiciary in American Expansionism* (Port Washington, NY: Kennikat Press, 1982), especially the historical background discussed in pp. 3–39, and Juan R. Torruella, *The Supreme Court and Puerto Rico: The Doctrine of Separate and Unequal* (Rio Piedras: University of Puerto Rico, 1985), 7–39. Puerto Rico has been relatively absent from studies of United States foreign relations, as Francisco A. Scarano argues in "Intervention or Possession? Puerto Rico, the War of 1898, and the American Colonial Periphery," in Bouvier, *Whose America*, 161–69.

58. *CJ*, 24 October 1898, 8 December 1898; Bryan quoted in Genevieve Forbes Herrick and John Origen Herrick, *The Life of William Jennings Bryan* (Chicago: Buxton, 1925), 195; Coletta, *William Jennings Bryan*, 1:283.

59. Ronald Fernandez, *The Disenchanted Island: Puerto Rico and the United States in the Twentieth Century*, 2nd ed. (Westport, CT: Praeger, 1996), 2. Race is discussed in the context of the Puerto Rican tariff debate in Justin Libby, "'Our Plain Duty': Senator Joseph B. Foraker and the First Civil Government in Puerto Rico," *Mid-America* 69, no. 1 (January 1987): 54–55, and in Weston, *Racism in U.S. Imperialism*, 192.

60. Henry K. Carroll, "How Shall Puerto Rico Be Governed?" *Forum*, November 1899, 257–59; McKinley quoted in Richardson, *Compilation of the Messages and Papers*, 13:6402–3; R. F. Hoxie, "The American Colonial Policy and the Tariff," *Journal of Political Economy* 11, no. 2 (March 1903): 204–5; Rystad, *Ambiguous Imperialism*, 73–80. Another Republican view of Puerto Rico is H.

G. Curtis, "The Status of Puerto Rico," *Forum*, December 1899, 403–11. The academic debate on the constitutional issues is covered in Rystad, *Ambiguous Imperialism*, 61–67. The contemporary debate on these issues is outlined in Charles Kendall Adams, "Colonies and Other Dependencies," *Forum*, March 1899, 33–46. A good, short description of the major issues disputed in the negotiations and debate in the Senate is in Libby, "'Our Plain Duty,'" 39–56. For the party-line, protectionist, and procolonial status, see George L. Bolen, "Hawaii and Porto Rico as Colonies," *Gunton's Magazine*, January 1900, 26–32.

61. *CJ*, 4 January 1900; Whitelaw Reid, *Problems of Expansion as Considered in Papers and Addresses* (New York: Century, 1900), 188, 245–51, 278; Harry W. Baehr Jr., *The New York Tribune since the Civil War* (New York: Octagon Books, 1972), 260–61. A good regional breakdown of newspapers' positions on the tariff is in *LD*, 7 April 1900, 413–14. Rystad summarizes the positions of an array of papers. Rystad, *Ambiguous Imperialism*, 80–85.

62. *LD*, 24 March 1900, 355; *LD*, 7 April 1900, 413–14; *LD*, 14 April 1900, 445–46; *LD*, 21 April 1900, 475.

63. Joseph B. Foraker, "The United States and Puerto Rico," *NAR* 170 (1900): 467–68.

64. Fernandez, *Disenchanted Island*, 11–14; Raymond Carr, *Puerto Rico: A Colonial Experiment* (New York: New York University Press, 1984), 35–36; Wolman, *Most Favored Nation*, 15; Stephen Pfeil, "The Status of Porto Ricans in Our Polity," *Forum*, February 1901, 716–21; *CJ*, 8 May 1900.

65. Beisner, *Twelve against Empire*, 216; *Anti-Imperialist*, 15 September 1899, 43–44; *Outlook*, 24 February 1900, 438; *Outlook*, 10 March 1900, 569–70; *Nation*, 24 November 1898, 383–84; *LD*, 10 March 1900, 295.

66. *CJ*, 25 November 1899, 1 May 1900; Harlan quoted in Carr, *Puerto Rico*, 39; An Ex-Democrat, "The Rehabilitation of the Democratic Party," *Forum*, February 1901, 651.

67. *CJ*, 17 February 1900, 29, 30 March 1900. On the nature of racial ideas in U.S.–Puerto Rican relations, see McFerson, *Racial Dimension*, 117–38; on southern racial ideas in particular, see chap. 3.

68. *CJ*, 2, 4, 6, 10, 31 October 1900.

69. *CJ*, 19 November 1900, 19, 20 December 1900, 4 January 1901. Two interesting contemporary views are Sidney Webster, *Two Treaties of Paris and the Supreme Court* (New York: Harper Brothers, 1901), a discussion of the legalities in the insular cases, and Alpheus H. Snow, *A Historical Statement in Attempted Interpretation of the Provisions of the Constitution Relating to the Power of the American Union over Annexed Regions not Represented in the Congress* (N.p., 1908; Wisconsin Historical Society Library, Madison), a comparison with earlier expansions.

70. McCormick, *China Market*, 117–120; Schoonover, *Uncle Sam's War*, 83–87; *CJ*, 16 February 1900.

71. Watterson to Hay, 26 December 1900, reel 13, vol. 20, JHP; *CJ*, 13 January 1899, 3 January 1900, 17, 28 March 1900, 5 April 1900, 2 May 1900, 15, 20,

28 June 1900, 16, 17 July 1900, 26 August 1900, 26 November 1900, 4 December 1900, 9 January 1901.

72. Richard Olney, "Growth of Our Foreign Policy," *Atlantic Monthly*, March 1900, 295; *CJ*, 2 March 1900, 3 March 1900.

73. William J. Stone, "The Campaign of 1900 from a Democratic Point of View," *Forum*, September 1900, 99–108; Johnson and Porter, *National Party Platforms*, 112; Henry Litchfield West, "The Republican and Democratic Platforms Compared," *Forum*, September 1900, 86–98.

74. *CJ*, 14 April 1900, 5 May 1900, 12 June 1900.

75. *CJ*, 7 July 1900; Bryan to Watterson, [1900?], box 2, HWP-LC.

76. *CJ*, 1 October 1900.

77. Bryan, "Issue in the Presidential Campaign," 753–71; *CJ*, 3 July 1900, 25 October 1900, 6 July 1900.

78. *CJ*, 2 October 1900; Coletta, *William Jennings Bryan*, 1:282–83; Theodore Roosevelt, "Menace of the Demagogue," in *Works*, 14:262; *CJ*, 23 September 1900. For Whitelaw Reid's campaign against Bryan, see Baehr, *The* New York Tribune *since the Civil War*, 264.

79. Walter LaFeber, "Election of 1900," in *History of American Presidential Elections, 1789–1968*, ed. Arthur M. Schlesinger Jr. (New York: Chelsea House, 1971), 3:1877–1917; Thomas A. Bailey, "Was the Presidential Election of 1900 a Mandate on Imperialism?" *MVHR* 24 (1937): 43–52; William Jennings Bryan, "The Election of 1900," *NAR* 170 (1900): 790. Also see Hollingsworth, *Whirligig of Politics*, 186; Morgan, *William McKinley*, 499–508; and Shannon and McQuown, *Presidential Politics in Kentucky*, 74–77.

80. *New Orleans Picayune* to Henry Watterson, telegram, 8 November 1900, box 10; *Atlanta Evening News* to Henry Watterson, telegram, 7 November 1900, box 1; *New York Herald* to Henry Watterson, telegram, 7 November 1900, box 10. Also see *Atlanta Journal* to Henry Watterson, telegram, 7 November 1900, box 1, and other telegrams from around the country, boxes 6, 14. All telegrams are in HWP-LC.

81. Rystad, *Ambiguous Imperialism*, 306. He follows the argument of Albert Shaw, "The American Presidential Election," *Contemporary Review* 78 (1900): 609.

82. *CJ*, 8, 13 November 1900. As time passed, Tilden began to shine the brightest in Watterson's political constellation, and a few months later, Watterson called Andrew Jackson "the Tilden of his day!" *CJ*, 8 January 1901.

83. *CJ*, 8 January 1901.

84. Henry Watterson, Manhattan Club Banquet speech letter, February 1901, misc. clippings, box 17, HWP-LC.

Conclusion: The Compromises of Empire

1. *NYTB*, 31 May 1901.

2. The best overview of the southern approach to foreign affairs is Fry, *Dixie Looks Abroad*.

3. Alfred E. Eckes Jr., *Opening America's Market: U.S. Foreign Trade Policy since 1776* (Chapel Hill: University of North Carolina Press, 1995), 77; "President McKinley's Last Public Utterance to the People, Buffalo, N.Y., September 5th, 1901," in Richardson, *Compilation of the Messages and Papers*, 14:6619.

4. "President McKinley's Last Public Utterance," 6621; Eckes and Zeiler, *Globalization and the American Century*, 17.

5. *CJ*, 17 September 1901, 9 October 1901, 18 May 1901, 10 June 1901. Also see Watterson, "Reciprocity and Expansion," 412–27.

6. The corporatist model is best defined in Ellis W. Hawley, "The Discovery and Study of a Corporate Liberalism," *Business History Review* 52, no. 3 (Autumn 1978): 309–20. The quote is on p. 310. The model's utility is best explained in Thomas J. McCormick, "Drift or Mastery? A Corporatist Synthesis for American Diplomatic History," *Reviews in American History* 10 (December 1982): 318–30. A stimulating discussion of the response of "second tier" non-elites to their marginalization under corporatist structures and governance is in Beth McKillen, "The Corporatist Model, World War I, and the Public Debate over the League of Nations," *Diplomatic History* 15, no. 2 (Spring 1991): 171–97.

7. Henry Watterson, "Reform by Reason, Not by Emotion," *Galveston Tribune*, 7 August 1913.

8. For a discussion of these changes in journalism, driven by the changing influence of the market, see Gerald J. Baldasty, *The Commercialization of News in the Nineteenth Century* (Madison: University of Wisconsin Press, 1992), chaps. 4–6. Richard L. Kaplan discusses the changing conception of the role of the press in *Politics and the American Press: The Rise of Objectivity, 1865–1920* (Cambridge: Cambridge University Press, 2002).

9. Biggerstaff to Watterson, n.d., box 1, HWP-LC; *Brooklyn Eagle*, "Remarks of Henry Watterson, Banquet of the New York Press Club, given in his honor, May 28, 1910," box 1, folder 4, HWP-FHS. For Watterson's attacks on the new commercialism of journalism, see *New York Herald*, 6 December 1909, and clippings in series 6, reel 5, pp. 310–38, HWP-UL. For Watterson's critique of the rise of "counting-room journalism," see Watterson, "Personal Equation in Journalism," 40–47.

10. Claude E. Barfield, "'Our Share of the Booty': The Democratic Party Cannonism, and the Payne-Aldrich Tariff," *Journal of American History* 57, no. 2 (September 1970): 318; *NYT*, 14 July 1912. For examples of Watterson's potential run for political office, see *Louisville Evening Post*, 15, 22 October 1901; "The Watterson Boom," box 19, HWP-LC; and Inglis, "Democratic Presidential Possibility," 1230–31, 1248.

11. Arthur S. Link, *Wilson: The Road to the White House* (Princeton, NJ: Princeton University Press, 1947), 365–78; *NYT*, 14 July 1912; *Milwaukee Free Press*, 24 September 1916; Watterson to Konta, 22 January 1921, vol. 2, AKP.

12. *CJ*, 7 January 1902; Watterson quoted, from *NYT*, 23 December 1921, in Wall, *Henry Watterson*, 317.

13. *CJ*, 15 May 1909; *Davenport Democrat*, [1904], series 6, reel 6, p. 453, HWP-UL; *NYT*, 14 July 1912; Henry Watterson, *Editor and Publisher*, 3 March 1918.

14. *CJ*, 21 June 1902, 30 December 1902; Watterson to Elihu Root, 30 November 1906, and Watterson to Root, 31 March 1907, ERP; *New York World*, [1911], box 19, HWP-LC; *Omaha Bee*, 2 August 1913; Henry Watterson, "Arbitration Treaties" (speech, Carnegie Hall, 12 December 1911), series 5, reel 5, pp. 354–57, HWP-UL; William Borah to Watterson, 8 August 1913, box 1, HWP-LC; Ronald R. Alexander, "Henry Watterson and World War I," *Journal of the West Virginia Historical Association* 1, no. 1 (Spring 1977): 15–25.

15. For example, Watterson to Konta, 28 May 1917, vol. 1, AKP; Watterson to Konta, 5 April 1920, vol. 2, AKP.

16. *Public Opinion*, 8 January 1903, 38–39; *Albany (NY) Journal*, 7 September 1909.

17. *New York Herald*, 20 January 1918. Watterson employed the "to hell" line very often and for a variety of purposes. Two examples are Watterson to Konta, 17 December 1920, and 1 September 1921, vol. 2, AKP.

18. *Woman Patriot*, 27 April 1918, box 11, folder 166, HWP-FHS; *New York Herald*, 20 January 1918.

19. Relevant letters and legal documents are in boxes 8, 20–21, 27, HFP. Also see *CJ*, June–July 1917, and *Editor and Publisher*, 30 June 1917, 1.

20. Watterson to Bingham, April 1919, box 5, folder 33, HWP-FHS; Ellis, *Robert Worth Bingham*, 65–66. Watterson's changing relationship with Bingham is revealed in their letters, box 26, RWBP.

21. Henry Watterson, "Uncle Sam for Umpire" (lecture, 10 November 1917), box 11, folder 175, HWP-FHS; *CJ*, 3 September 1914.

22. Watterson to unknown recipient, telegram, 2 May 1919, box 5, folder 33, HWP-FHS.

23. Watterson, *Marse Henry*, 2:279; Henry Watterson, "The Bolsheviki Are On the Way," unidentified newspaper clipping, 1919, box 11, folder 161, HWP-FHS.

24. Watterson to Bingham, 22 March 1919, box 26, RWBP.

Bibliography

Manuscript Collections

Manuscripts Division, Library of Congress

Albert Beveridge Papers
Robert Worth Bingham Papers
William E. Borah Papers
Grover Cleveland Papers
Josephus Daniels Papers
Walter Q. Gresham Papers
John Hay Papers
Manton Malone Marble Papers
William McKinley Papers
John Tyler Morgan Papers
Elihu Root Papers
Henry Watterson Papers
William C. Whitney Papers

Filson Historical Society, Louisville, KY

Young E. Allison Papers, 1853–1932
Belknap Family Papers, 1856–1904
Haldeman Family Papers, 1843–1985
Alexander Konta Papers, 1915–22
Mayors of Louisville Papers, 1870–1909
Thorn Family Papers
Henry Watterson Papers

Department of Rare Books and Special Collections, Princeton University, Princeton, NJ

Ford Family Papers
Archives of Henry Holt & Co., Correspondence
Laurence Hutton Correspondence

Arthur Krock Papers
Don C. Seitz Papers
Julian Street Papers, series 2

University of Louisville Archives and Records Center, Louisville, KY

Henry Watterson Papers, 1857–1983, 1882–1921, microfilm edition

Primary Sources

Adams, Brooks. *The Law of Civilization and Decay.* New York: Macmillan, 1896.

———. *America's Economic Supremacy.* New York: Macmillan, 1900.

———. "Reciprocity or the Alternative." *Atlantic Monthly,* August 1901, 145–55.

———. *The New Empire.* New York: Macmillan, 1902.

Allen, John H. *The Tariff and Its Evils, or Protection Which Does Not Protect.* New York: Putnam's Sons, 1888.

Atkinson, Edward. "Jingoes and Silverites." *North American Review* 161 (1895): 554–60.

Audran, Ernest. A *Retrospect on Events Which Made Possible the Late Baltimore Convention and a Complement to the Same.* Baltimore: Murphy, 1890.

Blake, Tiffany. "The Editorial: Past, Present and Future." *Colliers,* September 23, 1911, 18, 35–37.

Bryan, Charles G. "Scrapbook on Henry Watterson." Filson Historical Society Library, Louisville, KY.

Bryan, William Jennings. *The First Battle: A Story of the Campaign of 1896.* Chicago: Conkey, 1896.

———. "The Election of 1900." *North American Review* 170 (1900): 788–800.

———. "The Issue in the Presidential Campaign." *North American Review* 170 (1900): 753–71.

———. *The Second Battle, or The New Declaration of Independence, 1776–1900.* Chicago: Conkey, 1900.

———. *The Real Bryan.* Compiled by Richard L. Metcalfe. Des Moines, IA: Personal Help, 1908.

Bryan, William Jennings, and Mary Baird Bryan. *The Memoirs of William Jennings Bryan.* Philadelphia: Winston, 1925.

Burgess, John W. "The Decisions of the Supreme Court in the Insular Cases." *Political Science Quarterly* 16 (1901): 486–504.

Campaign Textbook of the National Democratic Party, 1896. Chicago, 1896.

Casseday, Morton M. "Henry Watterson." *Mid-Continent Magazine,* May 1895, 3–22.

Clark, Champ. *My Quarter Century of American Politics*. New York: Harper & Brothers, 1920.

Clay, Cassius M., Jr. *The Speeches, Addresses and Writings of Cassius M. Clay, Jr.* New York: Winthrop Press, 1914.

Clay, Cassius Marcellus. *The Life of Cassius Marcellus Clay: Memoirs, Writings, and Speeches*. Vol. 1. Cincinnati, OH: Brennan, 1886.

Cleveland, Grover. *Letters of Grover Cleveland, 1850–1908*. Edited by Allan Nevins. Boston: Houghton Mifflin, 1933.

Collection of Campaign Documents—1900 Presidential Campaign. N.p., n.d. Wisconsin Historical Society Library, Madison.

Dunnell, Elbridge Gerry. "The Rise of the 'National Democracy': The Movement for Sound Money and the Indianapolis Convention." *Review of Reviews* 14, no. 4 (October 1896): 434–45.

Edwards, Elisha Jay. "Henry Watterson." *Munsey's Magazine*, January 1906, 437–40.

Ellis, Edward S., ed. *The Great Leaders and National Issues of 1896*. Philadelphia: Winston, 1896.

Ellwanger, Ella Hutchinson. "Henry Watterson: World-Famous Editor of the *Louisville Courier-Journal*." *Register of the Kentucky Historical Society* 9 (1911): 43–49.

Ex-Democrat, An. "The Rehabilitation of the Democratic Party." *Forum*, February 1901, 641–52.

Furber, H. W., ed. *Which? Protection, Free Trade, or Revenue Reform*. Hartford, CT: Park, 1884.

Gibson, Edgar J. "Reciprocity and Foreign Trade." *Forum*, December 1901, 466–80.

Grady, Henry W. *The Complete Orations and Speeches of Henry W. Grady*. Edited by Edwin Du Bois Shurter. Austin, TX: South-west, 1910.

Hemphill, J. C. "Free Coinage and the Loss of Southern Statesmanship." *Forum*, March–August 1892, 295–99.

Henry, R. H. *Editors I Have Known since the Civil War*. Jackson, MS: Jackson Clarion-Ledger, 1922.

History of the Ohio Falls Cities and Their Counties with Illustrations and Biographical Sketches. Cleveland, OH: Williams, 1882.

Hoxie, R. F. "The American Colonial Policy and the Tariff." *Journal of Political Economy* 11, no. 2 (March 1903): 198–219.

Inglis, William. "A Democratic Presidential Possibility: 'Marse Henry' Watterson of Kentucky." *Harper's Weekly*, 8 August 1907, 1230–31, 1248.

Johnson, Donald Bruce, and Kirk H. Porter, eds. *National Party Platforms, 1840–1972*. 5th ed. Urbana: University of Illinois Press, 1973.

Krock, Arthur. "A Newspaper Career with a Purpose." *Advertiser's Magazine*, May 1910, 25–26.

———. *Memoirs: Sixty Years on the Firing Line*. New York: Funk & Wagnalls, 1968.

———. *Myself When Young: Growing Up in the 1890s*. Boston: Little, Brown, 1973.

Lauck, W. Jett. "The Political Significance of Reciprocity." *Journal of Political Economy* 12, no. 4 (September 1904): 495–524.

Leon, T. C. de *Inauguration of President Watterson: Gormanius or, The Battle of Reps-Demos; The Temple of Trusts, Honesty and Venality and Other Travesties*. New York: American Writers' Trust, 1902.

McCulloch, Hugh. *Men and Measures of Half a Century*. New York: Scribner's Sons, 1889.

McKinley, William. *The Tariff in the Days of Henry Clay and Since: An Exhaustive Review of Our Tariff Legislation from 1812 to 1896*. New York: Clay, 1896.

Merriam, George S. *The Life and Times of Samuel Bowles*. 2 vols. New York: Century, 1885.

Mitchell, Edward P. *Memoirs of an Editor: Fifty Years of American Journalism*. New York: Scribner's Sons, 1924.

Morgan, John T. "What Shall We Do with the Conquered Islands?" *North American Review* 166 (1898): 641–49.

Official Proceedings of the National Democratic Convention, Held in St. Louis, MO, June 27th, 28th and 29th, 1876. St. Louis: Woodward, Tiernan & Hale, 1876.

Official Proceedings of the National Democratic Convention, Held in Chicago, Ill., July 8th, 9th, 10th and 11th, 1884. New York: Taylor's Democratic Printing House, 1884.

Official Proceedings of the National Democratic Convention, Held in St. Louis, MO, June 5th, 6th, and 7th, 1888. St. Louis: Woodward, Tiernan & Hale, 1888.

Official Proceedings of the National Democratic Convention, Held in Chicago, Ill., June 21st, 22nd and 23rd, 1892. Chicago: Cameron, Amberg, 1892.

Olney, Richard. "Growth of Our Foreign Policy." *Atlantic Monthly*, March 1900, 290–301.

Palmer, John M. *Personal Recollections of John M. Palmer: The Story of an Earnest Life*. Cincinnati, OH: Clarke, 1901.

The Perry Memorial and Centennial Celebration under the Auspices of the National Government and the States of Ohio, Pennsylvania, Michigan, Illinois, Wisconsin, New York, Rhode Island, Kentucky, Minnesota, and Indiana. Cleveland, OH: Inter-state Board of the Perry's Victory Centennial Commissioners, 1913.

Prentice, George Denison. *Prenticeana, or Wit and Humor in Paragraphs*. New York: Derby and Jackson, 1860.

Proceedings of the Convention of the American Bankers Association held at Louisville, Kentucky, October 10 & 11th, 1883. New York: Bankers Publishing Association, 1883.

Reid, Whitelaw. *Problems of Expansion as Considered in Papers and Addresses.* New York: Century, 1900.

Richardson, James D., ed. *A Compilation of the Messages and Papers of the Presidents.* New York: Bureau of National Literature, 1897.

Roosevelt, Theodore. *The Works of Theodore Roosevelt.* National ed. 20 vols. New York: Scribner's Sons, 1926.

Smith, Ballard. "Henry Watterson." *Harper's Weekly,* 20 August 1887, 600.

Snow, Alpheus H. *A Historical Statement in Attempted Interpretation of the Provisions of the Constitution Relating to the Power of the American Union over Annexed Regions not Represented in the Congress.* N.p., 1908. Wisconsin Historical Society Library, Madison.

Stealey, O. O. *Twenty Years in the Press Gallery.* New York: Publishers Printing, 1906.

———. "Claims of the Candidates: Henry Watterson." *North American Review* 187 (1908): 841–44.

———. *130 Pen Pictures of Live Men.* Washington DC: Publishers Printing, 1910.

Taussig, F. W. "The McKinley Tariff Act." *Economic Journal* 1, no. 2 (June 1891): 326–50.

———."Reciprocity." *Quarterly Journal of Economics* 7, no. 1 (October 1892): 26–39.

———. "The United States Tariff Act of 1897." *Economic Journal* 7, no. 28 (December 1897): 592–98.

Tilden, Samuel J. *Letters and Literary Memorials of Samuel J. Tilden.* Edited by John Bigelow. 2 vols. New York: Harper, 1908.

Tillman, Benjamin. "Bryan or McKinley: Causes of Southern Opposition to Imperialism." *North American Review* 171 (1900): 439–46.

Villard, Oswald Garrison. *Some Newspapers and Newspapermen.* New York: Knopf, 1923.

Watterson, Henry. "The Solid South." *North American Review* 128 (1879): 47–58.

———. "The Reunited Union." *North American Review* 140 (1885): 22–29.

———. "The Tariff ['For Revenue Only']." *Harper's Monthly,* January 1888, 272–85.

———. "The South and Its Colored Citizens." *Cosmopolitan Magazine,* May 1890, 113–16.

———. "The Negro in America." *Chautauquan,* April 1892, 20–24.

———. "The Southern Confederacy." *Chautauquan,* May 1892, 147–52.

———. *History of the Spanish-American War: Embracing a Complete Review of Our Relations with Spain.* Louisville, KY: Courier-Journal Job Printing, 1898.

———. "The Political Outlook." *Forum,* January 1898, 568–78.

———. *"Abraham Lincoln": An Oration Delivered before the Lincoln Union,*

Chicago Auditorium, February 12, 1895. Louisville, KY: Courier-Journal Job Printing, 1899.

———. *The Compromises of Life; and Other Lectures and Addresses, Including Some Observations on Certain Downward Tendencies of Modern Society*. New York: Fox, Duffield, 1903.

———. "Expansion." In *The Best American Orations of Today*, edited by Harriet Blackstone, 160–62. New York: Noble and Noble, 1903.

———. "European Society Contrasted with Ours." *Cosmopolitan Magazine*, November 1905, 3–12.

———. "English and American Journalism." *Munsey's Magazine*, January 1906, 424–26.

———. "Strange Prophecy About Roosevelt: A Midwinter Fantasy." *Cosmopolitan Magazine*, January 1908, 302–8.

———. "Abraham Lincoln." *Cosmopolitan Magazine*, March 1909, 363–75.

———. "The Wisdom of Watterson." *Harper's Weekly*, 27 March 1909, 25, 31.

———. "The Personal Equation in Journalism." *Atlantic Monthly*, July 1910, 40–47.

———. "An Abortive Hero." *North American Review* 193 (1911): 35–46.

———. "The Great Unwritten Law." *Harper's Weekly*, 20 April 1912, 7.

———. "The Humor and Tragedy of the Greeley Campaign." *Century Magazine*, November 1912, 27–43.

———. "The Hayes-Tilden Contest for the Presidency: Inside History of a Great Political Crisis." *Century Magazine*, May 1913, 3–20.

———. *History of the Manhattan Club: A Narrative of the Activities of Half a Century*. New York: Manhattan Club, 1915.

———. "The Blue and the Gray." In *Memorable Addresses by American Patriots*, edited by John Clark Ridpath. Chicago: Elliot-Madison, 1919.

———. "Looking Backward: Men, Women, and Events During Eight Decades of American History." Pts. 1–6. *Saturday Evening Post*, 1 March 1919, 3–4, 130, 133; 8 March 1919, 18–19, 65; 15 March 1919, 18–19, 60; 22 March 1919, 18–19, 45; 29 March 1919, 14–15; 5 April 1919, 23–24, 26, 77–78.

———. *"Marse Henry": An Autobiography*. 2 vols. New York: Doran, 1919.

———. *The Editorials of Henry Watterson*. Edited by Arthur Krock. New York: Doran, 1923.

Watterson Club Revised Constitution. Louisville, KY: Courier-Journal Job Printing, 1892.

"What Shall We Do With It?" (Meaning the Surplus): Taxation and Revenue Discussed. New York: Harper & Brothers, 1888.

Wilson, William L. *The National Democratic Party: Its History, Principles, Achievements and Aims*. Baltimore: Harvey, 1888.

———. "The Tariff Plank at Chicago." *North American Review* 155 (1892): 280–86.

———. "The Republican Policy of Reciprocity." *Forum*, October 1892, 255–64.

Wilson, Woodrow. *Division and Reunion, 1829–1889.* New York: Longmans, Green, 1893.

Secondary Sources

Books

Abelarde, Pedro E. *American Tariff Policy towards the Philippines, 1898–1946.* Morningside Heights, NY: King's Crown Press, 1947.

Adler, Selig. *The Isolationist Impulse: Its Twentieth-Century Reaction.* New York: Collier Books, 1961.

Alexander, Ann Field. *Race Man: The Rise and Fall of the "Fighting Editor," John Mitchell Jr.* Charlottesville: University of Virginia Press, 2002.

Altschuler, Glenn C., and Stuart M. Blumin. *Rude Republic: Americans and Their Politics in the Nineteenth Century.* Princeton, NJ: Princeton University Press, 2000.

Andrews, J. Cutler. *The South Reports the Civil War.* Princeton, NJ: Princeton University Press, 1970.

Armstrong, William M. *E. L. Godkin and American Foreign Policy, 1865–1900.* New York: Bookman Associates, 1957.

Axton, W. F. *Tobacco and Kentucky.* Lexington: University Press of Kentucky, 1975.

Ayers, Edward L. *The Promise of the New South: Life after Reconstruction.* New York: Oxford University Press, 1992.

Baker, Jean H. *Affairs of Party: The Political Culture of Northern Democrats in the Mid- Nineteenth Century.* 1983. Reprint, New York: Fordham University Press, 1998.

Baker, Thomas Harrison. *The* Memphis Commercial-Appeal: *The History of a Southern Newspaper.* Baton Rouge: Louisiana State University Press, 1971.

Baldasty, Gerald J. *The Commercialization of News in the Nineteenth Century.* Madison: University of Wisconsin Press, 1992.

Barnes, James A. *John G. Carlisle: Financial Statesman.* New York: Dodd, Mead, 1931.

Bass, Herbert J. *"I Am a Democrat": The Political Career of David Bennett Hill.* Syracuse, NY: Syracuse University Press, 1961.

Battle, J. H., W. H. Perrin, and G. C. Kniffen. *Kentucky: A History of the State.* Louisville, KY: Battery, 1885.

Beard, Charles A. *The American Party Battle.* New York: Macmillan, 1929.

———. *The Idea of National Interest: An Analytical Study in American Foreign Policy.* New York: Macmillan, 1934.

Becker, William H. *The Dynamics of Business-Government Relations: Industry and Exports, 1893–1921.* Chicago: University of Chicago Press, 1982.

Bederman, Gail. *Manliness and Civilization: A Cultural History of Gender and*

Race in the United States, 1880–1917. Chicago: University of Chicago Press, 1996.

Beisner, Robert L. *Twelve against Empire: The Anti-Imperialists, 1898–1900*. New York: McGraw-Hill, 1968.

———. *From the Old Diplomacy to the New, 1865–1900*. 2nd ed. Arlington Heights, IL: Harlan Davidson, 1986.

Benjamin, Jules Robert. *The United States and Cuba: Hegemony and Dependent Development, 1880–1934*. Pittsburgh, PA: University of Pittsburgh Press, 1977.

———. *The United States and the Origins of the Cuban Revolution: An Empire of Liberty in an Age of National Liberation*. Princeton, NJ: Princeton University Press, 1989.

Bensel, Richard Franklin. *Sectionalism and American Political Development, 1880–1980*. Madison: University of Wisconsin Press, 1984.

———. *Yankee Leviathan: The Origins of Central State Authority in America, 1859–1877*. Cambridge: Cambridge University Press, 1990.

Blight, David W. *Race and Reunion: The Civil War in American Memory*. Cambridge, MA: Belknap Press of Harvard University Press, 2001.

Bouvier, Virginia M., ed. *Whose America? The War of 1898 and the Battles to Define the Nation*. Westport, CT: Praeger, 2001.

Bowers, Claude. *Beveridge and the Progressive Era*. Boston: Houghton Mifflin, 1932.

Braeman, John. *Albert J. Beveridge: American Nationalist*. Chicago: University of Chicago Press, 1971.

Brands, H. W. *Bound to Empire: The United States and the Philippines*. Oxford: Oxford University Press, 1992.

Brown, Charles H. *The Correspondents' War: Journalists in the Spanish-American War*. New York: Scribner's Sons, 1967.

Bryan, Ferald J. *Henry Grady or Tom Watson? The Rhetorical Struggle for the New South, 1880–1890*. Macon, GA: Mercer University Press, 1994.

Buck, Paul H. *The Road to Reunion, 1865–1900*. Boston: Little, Brown, 1937.

Burnham, Walter Dean. *Critical Elections and the Mainsprings of American Politics*. New York: Norton, 1970.

Calhoun, Charles W. *Gilded Age Cato: The Life of Walter Q. Gresham*. Lexington: University Press of Kentucky, 1988.

Campbell, A. E., ed. *Expansion and Imperialism*. New York: Harper & Row, 1970.

Campbell, Charles S. *Special Business Interests and the Open Door Policy*. New Haven, CT: Yale University Press, 1951.

———. *From Revolution to Rapprochement: The United States and Great Britain, 1783–1900*. New York: Wiley & Sons, 1974.

———. *The Transformation of American Foreign Relations, 1865–1900*. New York: Harper & Row, 1976.

Carr, Raymond. *Puerto Rico: A Colonial Experiment.* New York: New York University Press, 1984.

Carter, Hodding. *Their Words Were Bullets: The Southern Press in War, Reconstruction, and Peace.* Athens: University of Georgia Press, 1969.

Chiles, Paul Nelson. *The Puerto Rican Press Reaction to the United States, 1888–1898.* New York: Arno Press, 1975.

Clark, E. Culpepper. *Francis Warrington Dawson and the Politics of Restoration: South Carolina, 1874–1889.* Tuscaloosa: University of Alabama Press, 1980.

Clayton, Charles C. *Little Mack: Joseph B. McCullagh of the* St. Louis Globe-Democrat. Carbondale: Southern Illinois University Press, 1969.

Clements, Kendrick A. *William Jennings Bryan: Missionary Isolationist.* Knoxville: University of Tennessee Press, 1982.

Clift, G. Glenn. *Governors of Kentucky, 1792–1942.* Cynthiana, KY: Hobson Press, 1942.

Clymer, Kenton J. *John Hay: The Gentleman as Diplomat.* Ann Arbor: University of Michigan Press, 1975.

Cobb, James C., and William Stueck, eds. *Globalization and the American South.* Athens: University Press of Georgia, 2005.

Cohen, William. *At Freedom's Edge: Black Mobility and the Southern Quest for Racial Control, 1861–1915.* Baton Rouge: Louisiana State University Press, 1991.

Coletta, Paolo E. *William Jennings Bryan.* Vol. 1, *Political Evangelist, 1860–1908.* Lincoln: University of Nebraska Press, 1964.

Collins, Lewis. *History of Kentucky.* Covington, KY: Collins, 1874.

Connelley, William Elsey, and E. Merton Coulter. *History of Kentucky*, edited by Charles Kerr. Vol. 2. Chicago: American Historical Society, 1922.

Cooper, John Milton, Jr. *Walter Hines Page: The Southerner as American, 1855–1918.* Chapel Hill: University of North Carolina Press, 1977.

Cooper, William J., Jr., and Thomas E. Terrill. *The American South: A History.* New York: Knopf, 1990.

Coulter, E. Merton. *The Civil War and Readjustment in Kentucky.* Chapel Hill: University of North Carolina Press, 1926.

———. *The South during Reconstruction, 1865–1877.* Baton Rouge: Louisiana State University Press, 1947.

Crapol, Edward P. *America for Americans: Economic Nationalism and Anglophobia in the Late Nineteenth Century.* Westport, CT: Greenwood Press, 1973.

———, ed. *Women and American Foreign Policy: Lobbyists, Critics, and Insiders.* New York: Greenwood Press, 1987.

———. *James G. Blaine: Architect of Empire.* Wilmington, DE: Scholarly Resources, 2000.

Curl, Donald W. *Murat Halstead and the* Cincinnati Commercial. Boca Raton: University Press of Florida, 1980.

Curry, Leonard P. *Rail Routes South: Louisville's Fight for the Southern Market, 1865–1872*. Lexington: University of Kentucky Press, 1969.

Curry, Richard O., ed. *Radicalism, Racism, and Party Realignment: The Border States during Reconstruction*. Baltimore: Johns Hopkins University Press, 1969.

Curti, Merle Eugene. *Bryan and World Peace*. New York: Octagon, 1969.

Dabney, Virginius. *Liberalism in the South*. 1932. Reprint, New York: AMS Press, 1970.

Dearing, Mary R. *Veterans in Politics: The Story of the* G.A.R. Baton Rouge: Louisiana State University Press, 1952.

Degler, Carl N. *The Other South: Southern Dissenters in the Nineteenth Century*. New York: Harper & Row, 1974.

———. *Place over Time: The Continuity of Southern Distinctiveness*. Baton Rouge: Louisiana State University Press, 1977.

Dicken-Garcia, Hazel. *Journalistic Standards in Nineteenth-Century America*. Madison: University of Wisconsin Press, 1989.

Dickerson, Donna Lee. *The Course of Tolerance: Freedom of the Press in Nineteenth-Century America*. Westport, CT: Greenwood Press, 1990.

Doyle, Don H. *New Men, New Cities, New South: Atlanta, Nashville, Charleston, Mobile, 1860–1910*. Chapel Hill: University of North Carolina Press, 1990.

Drinnon, Richard. *Facing West: The Metaphysics of Indian-Hating and Empire Building*. New York: New America Library, 1980.

Duncan, Bingham. *Whitelaw Reid: Journalist, Politician, Diplomat*. Athens: University of Georgia Press, 1975.

Ealy, Lawrence. *Yanqui Politics and the Isthmian Canal*. University Park: Pennsylvania State University Press, 1971.

Eckes, Alfred E., Jr. *Opening America's Market: U.S. Foreign Trade Policy since 1776*. Chapel Hill: University of North Carolina Press, 1995.

Eckes, Alfred E., Jr., and Thomas W. Zeiler. *Globalization and the American Century*. Cambridge: Cambridge University Press, 2003.

Ellis, William E. *Robert Worth Bingham and the Southern Mystique: From the Old South to the New South and Beyond*. Kent, OH: Kent State University Press, 1997.

Evans, Herndon J. *The Newspaper Press in Kentucky*. Lexington: University Press of Kentucky, 1976.

Faulkner, Harold V. *Politics, Reform and Expansion, 1890–1900*. New York: Harper & Row, 1963.

Fenton, John H. *Politics in the Border States: A Study of the Pattern of Political Organization and Political Change, Common to the Border States: Maryland, West Virginia, Kentucky, and Missouri*. New Orleans, LA: Hauser Press, 1957.

Fernandez, Ronald. *The Disenchanted Island: Puerto Rico and the United States in the Twentieth Century*. 2nd ed. Westport, CT: Praeger, 1996.

Flick, Alexander Clarence. *Samuel Jones Tilden: A Study in Political Sagacity.* Westport, CT: Greenwood Press, 1939.

Foner, Eric. *Reconstruction: America's Unfinished Revolution, 1863–1877.* New York: Harper & Row, 1988.

Foner, Philip S., and Richard C. Winchester, eds. *The Anti-Imperialist Reader: A Documentary History of Anti-Imperialism in the United States.* Vol. 1, *From the Mexican War to the Election of 1900.* New York: Holmes & Meier, 1984.

Ford, Edwin, and Edwin Emery, eds. *Highlights in the History of the American Press.* Minneapolis: University of Minnesota Press, 1954.

Foster, Gaines M. *Ghosts of the Confederacy: Defeat, The Lost Cause, and the Emergence of the New South, 1865 to 1913.* New York: Oxford University Press, 1987.

Francisco, Luzviminda Bartolome, and Jonathan Shepard Fast. *Conspiracy for Empire: Big Business, Corruption, and the Politics of Imperialism in America, 1876–1907.* Quezon City, Philippines: Foundation for Nationalist Studies, 1985.

Frederickson, George M. *The Black Image in the White Mind: The Debate on Afro-American Character and Destiny, 1817–1914.* New York: Harper & Row, 1971.

Fry, Joseph A. *John Tyler Morgan and the Search for Southern Autonomy.* Knoxville: University of Tennessee Press, 1992.

———. *Dixie Looks Abroad: The South and U.S. Foreign Relations, 1789–1973.* Baton Rouge: Louisiana State University Press, 2002.

Furedi, Frank. *The Silent War: Imperialism and the Changing Perception of Race.* New Brunswick, NJ: Rutgers University Press, 1998.

Gaston, Paul M. *The New South Creed: A Study in Southern Mythmaking.* New York: Knopf, 1970.

Gillette, William. *Retreat from Reconstruction, 1869–1879.* Baton Rouge: Louisiana State University Press, 1979.

Glad, Paul W. *The Trumpet Soundeth: William Jennings Bryan and His Democracy, 1896–1912.* Lincoln: University of Nebraska Press, 1960.

———. *McKinley, Bryan, and the People.* Philadelphia: Lippincott, 1964.

Goldstein, Judith. *Ideas, Interests, and American Trade Policy.* Ithaca, NY: Cornell University Press, 1993.

Goodwyn, Lawrence. *Democratic Promise: The Populist Movement in America.* New York: Oxford University Press, 1976.

Gould, Lewis L. *The Spanish-American War and President McKinley.* Lawrence: University Press of Kansas, 1982.

Grantham, Dewey W., Jr. *Hoke Smith and the Politics of the New South.* Baton Rouge: Louisiana State University Press, 1958.

———, ed. *The South and the Sectional Image: The Sectional Theme since Reconstruction.* New York: Harper & Row, 1967.

Grenville, John A. S., and George Berkeley Young. *Politics, Strategy, and American Diplomacy: Studies in Foreign Policy, 1873–1917*. New Haven, CT: Yale University Press, 1966.

Hammett, Hugh B. *Hilary Abner Herbert: A Southerner Returns to the Union*. Philadelphia: American Philosophical Society, 1976.

Harris, Brayton. *Blue and Gray in Black and White: Newspapers in the Civil War*. Washington DC: Brassey's, 1999.

Hart, Roger L. *Redeemers, Bourbons, and Populists: Tennessee, 1870–1896*. Baton Rouge: Louisiana State University Press, 1975.

Hartz, Louis. *The Liberal Tradition in America*. New York: Harcourt, Brace & World, 1955.

Healy, David. *The United States in Cuba, 1898–1902: Generals, Politicians, and the Search for Policy*. Madison: University of Wisconsin Press, 1963.

———. *U.S. Expansionism: The Imperialist Urge in the 1890s*. Madison: University of Wisconsin Press, 1970.

———. *Drive to Hegemony: The United States in the Caribbean, 1898–1917*. Madison: University of Wisconsin Press, 1988.

Heardon, Patrick J. *Independence and Empire: The New South's Cotton Mill Campaign, 1865–1901*. DeKalb: Northern Illinois University Press, 1982.

Hendrick, Burton J. *The Life and Letters of Walter H. Page*. 3 vols. Garden City, NY: Doubleday, Page, 1925.

Hernandez, Jose. *Cuba and the United States: Intervention and Militarism, 1868–1933*. Austin: University of Texas Press, 1993.

Herr, Kincaid. *The Louisville and Nashville Railroad, 1850–1963*. Louisville, KY: Public Relations Department, Louisville and Nashville, 1964.

Hibben, Charles A. *The Peerless Leader: William Jennings Bryan*. New York: Farrar and Reinhart, 1929.

Hilderbrand, Robert C. *Power and the People: Executive Management of Public Opinion in Foreign Affairs, 1897–1921*. Chapel Hill: University of North Carolina Press, 1981.

Hirshson, Stanley P. *Farewell to the Bloody Shirt: Northern Republicans and the Southern Negro, 1877–1893*. Chicago: Quadrangle Books, 1962.

Hody, Cynthia A. *The Politics of Trade: American Political Development and Foreign Economic Policy*. Hanover, NH: University Press of New England, 1996.

Hofstadter, Richard. *The Paranoid Style in American Politics and Other Essays*. Chicago: University of Chicago Press, 1979.

Hogan, Michael J. *The Panama Canal in American Politics: Domestic Advocacy and the Evolution of Policy*. Carbondale: Southern Illinois University Press, 1986.

Hoganson, Kristen L. *Fighting for American Manhood: How Gender Politics Provoked the Spanish-American and Philippine-American Wars*. New Haven, CT: Yale University Press, 2000.

Hollingsworth, J. Rogers. *The Whirligig of Politics: The Democracy of Cleveland and Bryan*. Chicago: University of Chicago Press, 1963.

Howard, Victor B. *Black Liberation in Kentucky: Emancipation and Freedom, 1862–1884*. Lexington: University Press of Kentucky, 1983.

Hudson, Linda S. *Mistress of Manifest Destiny: A Biography of Jane McManus Storm Cazneau, 1807–1878*. Austin: Texas State Historical Association, 2001.

Hunt, Michael H. *The Making of a Special Relationship: The United States and China to 1914*. New York: Columbia University Press, 1983.

Huntzicker, William. *The Popular Press, 1833–1865*. Westport, CT: Greenwood Press, 1999.

Hyman, Michael R. *The Anti-Redeemers: Hill Country Political Dissenters in the Lower South from Redemption to Populism*. Baton Rouge: Louisiana State University Press, 1990.

Johannsen, Robert W., Sam W. Haynes, and Christopher Morris. *Manifest Destiny and Empire: American Antebellum Expansionism*. College Station: Texas A&M University Press, 1997.

Johnson, Gerald W., Frank R. Kent, H. L. Mencken, and Hamilton Owens. *The Sunpapers of Baltimore, 1837–1937*. New York: Knopf, 1937.

Jones, Stanley. *The Presidential Election of 1896*. Madison: University of Wisconsin Press, 1964.

Juergens, George. *News from the White House: The Presidential-Press Relationship in the Progressive Era*. Chicago: University of Chicago Press, 1981.

Kaplan, Amy. *The Anarchy of Empire in the Making of U.S. Culture*. Cambridge, MA: Harvard University Press, 2005.

Kaplan, Richard L. *Politics and the American Press: The Rise of Objectivity, 1865–1920*. Cambridge: Cambridge University Press, 2002.

Kenkel, Joseph P. *Progressives and Protection: The Search for a Tariff Policy, 1866–1936*. Lanham, MD: University Press of America, 1983.

Kerr, James Edward. *The Insular Cases: The Role of the Judiciary in American Expansionism*. Port Washington, NY: Kennikat Press, 1982.

Kielbowicz, Richard B. *News in the Mail: The Press, Post Office, and Public Information, 1700–1860s*. New York: Greenwood Press, 1989.

Klein, Maury. *History of the Louisville and Nashville Railroad*. New York: Macmillan, 1972.

Klotter, James C. *William Goebel: The Politics of Wrath*. Lexington: University Press of Kentucky, 1977.

———. *Kentucky: Portrait in Paradox, 1900–1950*. Frankfort: Kentucky Historical Society, 1996.

Knoles, George Harman. *The Presidential Campaign and Election of 1892*. Palo Alto, CA: Stanford University Press, 1942.

Koch, Tom. *The News as Myth: Fact and Context in Journalism*. New York: Greenwood Press, 1990.

Koenig, Louis W. *Bryan: A Political Biography of William Jennings Bryan*. New York: Putnam's Sons, 1971.

Kousser, J. Morgan. *The Shaping of Southern Politics: Suffrage Restriction and the Establishment of the One-Party South, 1880–1910*. New Haven, CT: Yale University Press, 1975.

LaFeber, Walter. *The New Empire: An Interpretation of American Expansion, 1865–1898*. Ithaca, NY: Cornell University Press, 1963.

Lambert, John R. *Arthur Poe Gorman*. Baton Rouge: Louisiana State University Press, 1953.

Langer, William. *The Diplomacy of Imperialism, 1890–1902*. 2nd ed. New York: Knopf, 1951.

Lee, Alfred McClung. *The Daily Newspaper in America: The Evolution of a Social Instrument*. New York: Macmillan, 1937.

Lee, James Melvin. *History of American Journalism*. Boston: Houghton Mifflin, 1917.

Leech, Margaret. *In the Days of McKinley*. New York: Harper, 1959.

Leonard, Thomas C. *The Power of the Press: The Birth of American Political Reporting*. New York: Oxford University Press, 1986.

Link, Arthur S. *Wilson: The Road to the White House*. Princeton, NJ: Princeton University Press, 1947.

Link, William A. *The Paradox of Southern Progressivism, 1880–1930*. Chapel Hill: University of North Carolina Press, 1992.

Linn, Brian McAllister. *The Philippine War, 1899–1902*. Lawrence: University Press of Kansas, 2000.

Marcosson, Isaac F. *"Marse Henry": A Biography of Henry Watterson*. New York: Dodd, Mead, 1951.

Marks, George P., III, ed. *The Black Press Views American Imperialism, 1898–1900*. New York: Arno Press, 1971.

Marszalek, John F., and Wilson D. Miscamble, eds. *American Political History: Essays on the State of the Discipline*. Notre Dame, IN: University of Notre Dame Press, 1997.

May, Ernest R. *American Imperialism: A Speculative Essay*. New York: Atheneum, 1968.

———. *Imperial Democracy: The Emergence of America as a Great Power*. New York: Harper & Row, 1973.

McClellan, Robert. *The Heathen Chinee: A Study of American Attitudes toward China, 1890–1905*. Columbus: Ohio State University Press, 1971.

McCormick, Thomas J. *China Market: America's Quest for Informal Empire, 1893–1901*. Chicago: Quadrangle Books, 1967.

McFarland, Gerald. *Mugwumps, Morals, and Politics*. Amherst: University of Massachusetts Press, 1975.

McFerson, Hazel M. *The Racial Dimension of American Overseas Colonial Policy*. Westport, CT: Greenwood Press, 1997.

McGerr, Michael E. *The Decline of Popular Politics: The American North, 1865–1928*. New York: Oxford University Press, 1986.
McJimsey, George T. *Genteel Partisan: Manton Marble, 1834–1917*. Ames: Iowa State University Press, 1971.
McWilliams, Tennant S. *Hannis Taylor: The New Southerner as an American*. Tuscaloosa: University of Alabama Press, 1978.
———. *The New South Faces the World: Foreign Affairs and the Southern Sense of Self, 1877–1950*. Baton Rouge: Louisiana State University Press, 1988.
Merrill, Horace Samuel. *Bourbon Democracy of the Middle West, 1865–1896*. Baton Rouge: Louisiana State University Press, 1953.
———. *William Freeman Vilas: Doctrinaire Democrat*. Madison: State Historical Society of Wisconsin, 1954.
———. *Bourbon Leader: Grover Cleveland and the Democratic Party*. Boston: Little, Brown, 1957.
Miller, Clarence Lee. *The States of the Old Northwest and the Tariff, 1865–1888*. Emporia, KS: Emporia Gazette Press, 1929.
Miller, Stuart Creighton. *"Benevolent Assimilation": The American Conquest of the Philippines, 1899–1903*. New Haven, CT: Yale University Press, 1982.
Morgan, H. Wayne. *William McKinley and His America*. Syracuse, NY: Syracuse University Press, 1963.
———, ed. *The Gilded Age*. Syracuse, NY: Syracuse University Press, 1970.
———. *Unity and Culture: The United States, 1877–1900*. London: Allen Lane, 1971.
Morrison, Joseph L. *Josephus Daniels Says . . . : An Editor's Political Odyssey from Bryan to Wilson and F.D.R., 1894–1914*. Chapel Hill: University of North Carolina Press, 1962.
———. *Josephus Daniels: The Small-d Democrat*. Chapel Hill: University of North Carolina Press, 1966.
Mott, Frank Luther. *American Journalism: A History, 1690–1960*. 3rd ed. New York: Macmillan, 1962.
Mott, George Fox. *Survey of Journalism*. New York: Barnes and Noble, 1937.
Musicant, Ivan. *Empire by Default: The Spanish-American War and the Dawn of the American Century*. New York: Holt, 1998.
Muzzey, David Saville. *James G. Blaine: A Political Idol of Other Days*. New York: Dodd, Mead, 1934.
Nerone, John. *Violence against the Press: Policing the Public Sphere in U.S. History*. New York: Oxford University Press, 1994.
Nevins, Allan. *Grover Cleveland: A Study in Courage*. New York: Dodd, Mead, 1932.
———. *Abram S. Hewitt, with Some Account of Peter Cooper*. New York: Harper & Brothers, 1935.
Nixon, Raymond B. *Henry Grady: Spokesman of the New South*. New York: Russell & Russell, 1969.

Nord, David Paul. *Newspapers and New Politics: Midwestern Municipal Reform, 1890–1900*. Ann Arbor, MI: UMI Research Press, 1981.
Offner, John. *An Unwanted War: The Diplomacy of the United States and Spain over Cuba, 1895–1898*. Chapel Hill: University of North Carolina Press, 1992.
O'Rourke, Kevin H., and Jeffrey G. Williamson. *Globalization and History: The Evolution of a Nineteenth-Century Atlantic Economy*. Cambridge, MA: MIT Press, 1999.
Osborne, Thomas J. *"Empire Can Wait": American Opposition to Hawaiian Annexation, 1893–1898*. Kent, OH: Kent State University Press, 1981.
Osthaus, Carl R. *Partisans of the Southern Press: Editorial Spokesmen of the Nineteenth Century*. Lexington: University Press of Kentucky, 1994.
Painter, Nell Irvin. *Standing at Armageddon: The United States, 1877–1914*. New York: Norton, 1989.
Palmer, Bruce. *Man over Money: The Southern Populist Critique of American Capitalism*. Chapel Hill: University of North Carolina Press, 1980.
Palmer, George Thomas. *A Conscientious Turncoat: The Story of John M. Palmer, 1817–1900*. New Haven, CT: Yale University Press, 1941.
Perez, Louis A., Jr. *The War of 1898: The United States and Cuba in History and Historiography*. Chapel Hill: University of North Carolina Press, 1998.
Perkins, Bradford. *The Great Rapprochement: England and the United States, 1895–1914*. New York: Atheneum, 1968.
Perman, Michael. *Reunion without Compromise: The South and Reconstruction, 1865–1868*. New York: Cambridge University Press, 1973.
———. *The Road to Redemption: Southern Politics, 1869–1879*. Chapel Hill: University of North Carolina Press, 1984.
———. *Struggle for Mastery: Disfranchisement in the South, 1888–1908*. Chapel Hill: University of North Carolina Press, 2001.
Persky, Joseph J. *The Burden of Dependency: Colonial Themes in Southern Economic Thought*. Baltimore: Johns Hopkins University Press, 1992.
Peterson, Merrill D. *The Jefferson Image in the American Mind*. New York: Oxford University Press, 1962.
———. *Lincoln in American Memory*. Oxford: Oxford University Press, 1994.
Peterson, Norma L. *Freedom and Franchise: The Political Career of B. Gratz Brown*. Columbia: University of Missouri Press, 1965.
Pletcher, David M. *The Awkward Years: American Foreign Relations under Garfield and Arthur*. Columbia: University of Missouri Press, 1962.
———. *The Diplomacy of Trade and Investment: American Economic Expansion in the Hemisphere, 1865–1900*. Columbia: University of Missouri Press, 1998.
———. *The Diplomacy of Involvement: American Economic Expansion across the Pacific, 1784–1900*. Columbia: University of Missouri Press, 2001.
Polakoff, Keith Ian. *The Politics of Inertia: The Election of 1876 and the End of Reconstruction*. Baton Rouge: Louisiana State University Press, 1973.

Pollard, James E. *The Presidents and the Press*. New York: Macmillan, 1947.
Pomeroy, William J. *American Neo-Colonialism: Its Emergence in the Philippines and Asia*. New York: International Publishers, 1970.
Poulshock, S. Walter. *The Two Parties and the Tariff in the 1880s*. Syracuse, NY: Syracuse University Press, 1965.
Pratt, Julius W. *America's Colonial Experiment: How the United States Gained, Governed, and in Part Gave Away a Colonial Empire*. New York: Prentice-Hall, 1950.
———. *Expansionists of 1898: The Acquisition of Hawaii and the Spanish Islands*. Chicago: Quadrangle Books, 1964.
Pressly, Thomas J. *Americans Interpret Their Civil War*. New York: Free Press, 1962.
Rabinowitz, Howard N. *Race Relations in the Urban South, 1865–1890*. New York: Oxford University Press, 1978.
Richardson, Heather Cox. *The Greatest Nation of the Earth: Republican Economic Policies during the Civil War*. Cambridge, MA: Harvard University Press, 1997.
———. *The Death of Reconstruction: Race, Labor, and Politics in the Post–Civil War North, 1865–1901*. Cambridge, MA: Harvard University Press, 2001.
Ritter, Gretchen. *Goldbugs and Greenbacks: The Antimonopoly Tradition and the Politics of Finance in America*. New York: Cambridge University Press, 1997.
Rosewater, Victor. *History of Cooperative News-Gathering in the United States*. New York: Appleton, 1930.
Rutland, Robert A. *The Newsmongers: Journalism in the Life of the Nation, 1690–1972*. New York: Dial Press, 1973.
Rydell, Robert W. *All the World's a Fair: Visions of Empire at American International Expositions, 1876–1916*. Chicago: University of Chicago Press, 1984.
Rystad, Goren. *Ambiguous Imperialism: American Foreign Policy and Domestic Politics at the Turn of the Century*. Lund, Sweden: Esselte Studium, 1975.
Sachsman, David B., S. Kittrell Rushing, and Debra Reddin van Tuyll, eds. *The Civil War and the Press*. New Brunswick, NJ: Transaction, 2000.
Salmon, Lucy Maynard. *The Newspaper and the Historian*. New York: Oxford University Press, 1923.
Santis, Vincent P. de *Republicans Face the Southern Question: The New Departure Years, 1877–1897*. Baltimore: Johns Hopkins University Press, 1959.
Schirmer, Daniel B. *Republic or Empire: American Resistance to the Philippine War*. Cambridge, MA: Schenkman, 1972.
Schoonover, Thomas. *Uncle Sam's War of 1898 and the Origins of Globalization*. Lexington: University Press of Kentucky, 2003.
Schroth, Raymond A. *The* Eagle *and Brooklyn: A Community Newspaper, 1841–1955*. Westport, CT: Greenwood Press, 1974.
Seip, Terry L. *The South Returns to Congress: Men, Economic Measures, and*

Intersectional Relationships, 1868–1879. Baton Rouge: Louisiana State University Press, 1983.

Sellers, Charles Grier, Jr., ed. *The Southerner as American*. Chapel Hill: University of North Carolina Press, 1960.

Shannon, Jasper B., and Ruth McQuown. *Presidential Politics in Kentucky, 1824–1948: A Compilation of Election Statistics and an Analysis of Political Behavior*. Lexington: University of Kentucky Press, 1950.

Share, Allen J. *Cities in the Commonwealth: Two Centuries of Urban Life in Kentucky*. Lexington: University Press of Kentucky, 1982.

Silbey, Joel H. *A Respectable Minority: The Democratic Party in the Civil War Era, 1860–1868*. New York: Norton, 1977.

———. *The American Political Nation, 1838–1893*. Palo Alto, CA: Stanford University Press, 1991.

Sklar, Martin J. *The Corporate Reconstruction of American Capitalism, 1890–1916: The Markets, the Law, and Politics*. Cambridge: Cambridge University Press, 1988.

Skowronek, Stephen. *Building a New American State: The Expansion of National Administrative Capacities, 1877–1920*. Cambridge: Cambridge University Press, 1982.

Socolofsky, Homer E., and Allan B. Spetter. *The Presidency of Benjamin Harrison*. Lawrence: University Press of Kansas, 1987.

Sproat, John G. *"The Best Men": Liberal Reformers in the Gilded Age*. 1968. Reprint, Chicago: University of Chicago Press, 1982.

Spurr, David. *The Rhetoric of Empire: Colonial Discourse in Journalism, Travel Writing, and Imperial Administration*. Durham, NC: Duke University Press, 1993.

Stanley, Peter W., ed. *Reappraising an Empire: New Perspectives on Philippine-American History*. Cambridge, MA: Harvard University Press, 1984.

Stanwood, Edward. *American Tariff Controversies in the Nineteenth Century*. 2 vols. Boston: Houghton Mifflin, 1903.

Steele, Janet E. *The Sun Shines for All: Journalism and Ideology in the Life of Charles A. Dana*. Syracuse, NY: Syracuse University Press, 1993.

Stein, Charles W. *The Third-Term Tradition: Its Rise and Collapse in American Politics*. New York: Columbia University Press, 1943.

Stickles, Ardnt M. *Simon Bolivar Buckner: Borderland Knight*. Chapel Hill: University of North Carolina Press, 1940.

Suggs, Henry Leavis, ed. *The Black Press in the South, 1865–1979*. Westport, CT: Greenwood Press, 1983.

Summers, Festus B. *William L. Wilson and Tariff Reform: A Biography*. 1953. Reprint, Westport, CT: Greenwood Press, 1974.

Summers, Mark Wahlgren. *The Era of Good Stealings*. New York: Oxford University Press, 1993.

———. *The Press Gang: Newspapers and Politics, 1865–1878*. Chapel Hill: University of North Carolina Press, 1994.

———. *Rum, Romanism, and Rebellion: The Making of a President, 1884*. Chapel Hill: University of North Carolina Press, 2000.

———. *Party Games: Getting, Keeping, and Using Power in Gilded Age Politics*. Chapel Hill: University of North Carolina Press, 2004.

Tapp, Hambleton, and James C. Klotter. *Kentucky: Decades of Discord, 1865–1900*. Frankfort: Kentucky Historical Society, 1977.

Taussig, F. W. *The Tariff History of the United States*. New York: Putnam's Sons, 1892.

———. *Free Trade, the Tariff, and Reciprocity*. New York: Macmillan, 1920.

———. *Some Aspects of the Tariff Question*. Cambridge, MA: Harvard University Press, 1929.

Tebbel, John, and Sarah Miles Watts. *The Press and the Presidency: From George Washington to Ronald Reagan*. New York: Oxford University Press, 1985.

Terrell, Russell Franklin. *A Study of the Early Journalistic Writings of Henry W. Grady*. New York: Beckman, 1974.

Terrill, Tom E. *The Tariff, Politics, and American Foreign Policy, 1874–1901*. Westport, CT: Greenwood Press, 1973.

Thompson, John Herd, and Stephen J. Randall. *Canada and the United States: Ambivalent Allies*. Athens: University of Georgia Press, 1994.

Tindall, George Brown. *The Persistent Tradition in New South Politics*. Baton Rouge: Louisiana State University Press, 1975.

Tompkins, E. Berkeley. *Anti-Imperialism in the United States: The Great Debate, 1890–1920*. Philadelphia: University of Pennsylvania Press, 1970.

Torruella, Juan R. *The Supreme Court and Puerto Rico: The Doctrine of Separate and Unequal*. Rio Piedras: University of Puerto Rico, 1985.

Trubowitz, Peter. *Defining the National Interest: Conflict and Change in American Foreign Policy*. Chicago: University of Chicago Press, 1998.

Vandiver, Frank E., ed. *The Idea of the South*. Chicago: University of Chicago Press, 1964.

Varg, Paul. *Missionaries, Chinese, and Diplomats: The American Protestant Missionary Movement in China, 1890–1952*. Princeton, NJ: Princeton University Press, 1958.

Verdier, Daniel. *Democracy and International Trade: Britain, France, and the United States, 1860–1990*. Princeton, NJ: Princeton University Press, 1994.

Villard, Oswald Garrison. *The Disappearing Daily: Chapters in American Newspaper Evolution*. New York: Knopf, 1944.

Waldstreicher, David. *In the Midst of Perpetual Fetes: The Making of American Nationalism, 1776–1820*. Chapel Hill: University of North Carolina Press, 1997.

Wall, Joseph Frazier. *Henry Watterson: Reconstructed Rebel*. New York: Oxford University Press, 1956.

Weaver, Richard M. *The Southern Tradition at Bay: A History of Postbellum Thought*. New Rochelle, NY: Arlington House, 1968.

Webb, Ross A. *Benjamin Helm Bristow: Border State Politician.* Lexington: University Press of Kentucky, 1969.

Webster, Sidney. *Two Treaties of Paris and the Supreme Court.* New York: Harper & Brother, 1901.

Welch, Richard E., Jr. *George Frisbie Hoar and the Half-Breed Republicans.* Cambridge, MA: Harvard University Press, 1971.

———. *Response to Imperialism: The United States and the Philippine American War, 1899–1902.* Chapel Hill: University of North Carolina Press, 1979.

———. *The Presidencies of Grover Cleveland.* Lawrence: University Press of Kansas, 1988.

Welter, Rush. *The Mind of America, 1820–1860.* New York: Columbia University Press, 1975.

Weston, Rubin Francis. *Racism in U.S. Imperialism: The Influence of Racial Assumptions on American Foreign Policy, 1893–1946.* Columbia: University of South Carolina Press, 1972.

Wiebe, Robert H. *The Search for Order, 1877–1920.* New York: Hill and Wang, 1967.

Wilkerson, Marcus M. *Public Opinion and the Spanish-American War: A Study in War Propaganda.* 1932. Reprint, New York: Russell & Russell, 1967.

Williams, Harold A. *The* Baltimore Sun, *1837–1987.* Baltimore: Johns Hopkins University Press, 1987.

Williams, R. Hal. *Years of Decision: American Politics in the 1890s.* New York: Wiley & Sons, 1978.

Williams, William Appleman. *The Roots of the Modern American Empire: A Study of the Growth and Shaping of Social Consciousness in a Marketplace Society.* New York: Vintage, 1969.

———. *Tragedy of American Diplomacy.* 2nd ed. New York: Dell, 1972.

———. *The Contours of American History.* New York: Norton, 1988.

Williamson, Joel. *A Rage for Order: Black-White Relations in the American South since Emancipation.* New York: Oxford University Press, 1986.

Willis, George Lee. *Kentucky Democracy: A History of the Party and Its Representative Members—Past and Present.* 3 vols. Louisville, KY: Democratic Historical Society, 1935.

Wilson, Charles Reagan. *Baptized in Blood: The Religion of the Lost Cause, 1865–1920.* Athens: University of Georgia Press, 1980.

Wisan, Joseph E. *The Cuban Crisis as Reflected in the New York Press, 1895–1898.* New York: Columbia University Press, 1934.

Wolman, Paul. *Most Favored Nation: The Republican Revisionists and U.S. Tariff Policy, 1897–1912.* Chapel Hill: University of North Carolina Press, 1992.

Woodward, C. Vann. *Tom Watson: Agrarian Rebel.* New York: Macmillan, 1938.

———. *Origins of the New South, 1877–1913.* Baton Rouge: Louisiana State University Press, 1951.

———. *Reunion and Reaction: The Compromise of 1877 and the End of Reconstruction.* Boston: Little, Brown, 1951.

———, ed. *The Comparative Approach to American History*. New York: Basic Books, 1968.

———. *The Strange Career of Jim Crow*. 3rd ed. New York: Oxford University Press, 1974.

Wright, George C. *Life behind a Veil: Blacks in Louisville, Kentucky, 1865–1930*. Baton Rouge: Louisiana State University Press, 1985.

———. *Racial Violence in Kentucky, 1865–1940: Lynchings, Mob Rule, and "Legal Lynchings."* Baton Rouge: Louisiana State University Press, 1996.

Young, Marilyn Blatt. *The Rhetoric of Empire: American China Policy, 1895–1901*. Cambridge, MA: Harvard University Press, 1968.

Articles

Abbott, Martin, ed. "A Southerner Views the South, 1865: Letters of Harvey M. Watterson." *Virginia Magazine of History and Biography* 68 (October 1960): 478–89.

Alexander, Ronald R. "Henry Watterson and World War I." *Journal of the West Virginia Historical Association* 1, no. 1 (Spring 1977): 15–25.

Anderson, Stuart. "'Pacific Destiny' and American Policy in Samoa, 1872–1899." *Hawaiian Journal of History* 12 (1978): 45–60.

Auxier, George W. "The Propaganda Activities of the Cuban Junta in Precipitating the Spanish-American War, 1895–1898." *Hispanic American Historical Review* 19 (1939): 286–305.

———. "Middle-Western Newspapers and the Spanish-American War, 1895–1898." *Mississippi Valley Historical Review* 26 (1940): 523–34.

Bailey, Thomas A. "The United States and Hawaii during the Spanish-American War." *American Historical Review* 36 (1931): 552–60.

———. "Was the Presidential Election of 1900 a Mandate on Imperialism?" *Mississippi Valley Historical Review* 24 (1937): 43–52.

Baldasty, Gerald J. "The Nineteenth-Century Origins of Modern American Journalism." *Proceedings of the American Antiquarian Society* 100, no. 2 (1990): 407–19.

Barfield, Claude E. "'Our Share of the Booty': The Democratic Party Cannonism, and the Payne-Aldrich Tariff." *Journal of American History* 57, no. 2 (September 1970): 308–23.

Barnes, James A. "The Gold Standard Democrats and the Party Conflict." *Mississippi Valley Historical Review* 17 (1930–31): 422–50.

Baron, Harold. "Anti-Imperialism and the Democrats." *Science and Society* 21 (1957): 222–39.

Baughman, James L. "'The World is Ruled By Those Who Holler the Loudest': The Third-Person Effect in American Journalism History," *Journalism History* 16, nos. 1–2 (Spring–Summer 1989): 12–19.

Beard, William E. "Henry Watterson—Last of the Oracles." *Tennessee Historical Magazine*, July 1931, 234–52.

Billington, Ray Allen. "The Origins of Middle Western Isolationism." *Political Science Quarterly* 60 (1945): 44–64.

Bishop, Robert L., and Stephen Friedman. "Campaign Coverage—1876 Style by the *Chicago Tribune*." *Journalism Quarterly* 45 (1968): 481–86.

Blake, Nelson M. "The Olney-Pauncefote Treaty of 1897." *American Historical Review* 50 (1945): 228–43.

Brown, Thomas J. "The Roots of Bluegrass Insurgency: An Analysis of the Populist Movement in Kentucky." *Register of the Kentucky Historical Society* 78 (1980): 219–42.

Burnette, O. Lawrence, Jr. "John Tyler Morgan and Expansionist Sentiment in the New South." *Alabama Review* 18, no. 3 (July 1965): 163–82.

Calhoun, Charles W. "Morality and Spite: Walter Q. Gresham and U.S. Relations with Hawaii." *Pacific Historical Review* 52 (1983): 292–311.

Carleton, William G. "Isolationism and the Middle West." *Mississippi Valley Historical Review* 33 (1946): 377–90.

Castle, Alfred L. "Tentative Empire: Walter Q. Gresham, U.S. Foreign Policy, and Hawai'i, 1893–1895." *Hawaiian Journal of History* 29 (1995): 83–96.

Clark, Thomas D. "The Country Newspaper: A Factor in Southern Opinion, 1865–1930." *Journal of Southern History* 14 (February 1948): 3–33.

Clements, Roger V. "The Farmers' Attitude toward British Investment in American Industry." *Journal of Economic History* 15, no. 2 (March 1955): 151–59.

Cobb, James C. "Beyond Planters and Industrialists: A New Perspective on the New South." *Journal of Southern History* 54 (February 1988): 45–68.

Coletta, Paolo E. "Bryan, McKinley, and the Treaty of Paris." *Pacific Historical Review* 26 (1957): 131–46.

———. "McKinley, the Peace Negotiations, and the Acquisition of the Philippines." *Pacific Historical Review* 30 (1961): 341–50.

Congleton, Bett Carolyn. "The *Louisville Journal*: Its Origin and Early Years." *Register of the Kentucky Historical Society* 62 (1964): 87–103.

———. "George D. Prentice: Nineteenth Century Southern Editor." *Register of the Kentucky Historical Society* 65 (1967): 94–119.

Connelly, Thomas L. "Neo-Confederatism or Power Vacuum: Post-War Kentucky Politics Reappraised." *Register of the Kentucky Historical Society* 64 (1966): 257–69.

Crapol, Edward P. "Coming to Terms with Empire: The Historiography of Late-Nineteenth Century American Foreign Relations." *Diplomatic History* 16, no. 4 (Fall 1992): 573–97.

Cumming, Carman. "The *Toronto Daily Mail*, Edward Farrer, and the Question of Canadian-American Union." *Journal of Canadian Studies* 24, no. 1 (1989): 121–39.

DeConde, Alexander. "The South and Isolationism." *Journal of Southern History* 24 (August 1958): 332–46.

Degler, Carl N. "Thesis, Antithesis, Synthesis: The South, The North, and the Nation." *Journal of Southern History* 53 (February 1987): 3–18.

Eiteman, Wilford J. "The Rise and Decline of Orthodox Tariff Propaganda." *Quarterly Journal of Economics* 45, no. 1 (November 1930): 22–39.

Ensor, Allison R. "The House United: Mark Twain and Henry Watterson Celebrate Lincoln's Birthday 1901." *South Atlantic Quarterly* 74 (1975): 259–68.

Faulkner, Ronnie W. "North Carolina Democrats and Silver Fusion Politics, 1892–1896." *North Carolina Historical Review* 59, no. 3 (1982): 230–51.

Fry, Joseph A. "William McKinley and the Coming of the Spanish-American War: A Study of the Besmirching and Redemption of an Historical Image." *Diplomatic History* 3, no. 1 (Winter 1979): 77–97.

———. "John Tyler Morgan's Southern Expansionism." *Diplomatic History* 9, no. 4 (Fall 1985): 329–46.

Gatewood, Willard B., Jr. "A Negro Editor on Imperialism: John Mitchell, 1898–1901." *Journalism Quarterly* 49 (1972): 43–50, 60.

———. "Black Editor on American Imperialism: Edward E. Cooper of the *Colored American*, 1898–1901." *Mid-America* 57, no. 1 (1975): 3–19.

Gaughan, Anthony. "Woodrow Wilson and the Legacy of the Civil War." *Civil War History* 43, no. 3 (1997): 225–42.

Gibson, George H. "Attitudes in North Carolina Regarding the Independence of Cuba, 1868–1898." *North Carolina Historical Review* 43, no. 1 (1966): 43–65.

Harrington, Fred H. "The Anti-Imperialist Movement in the United States, 1898–1900." *Mississippi Valley Historical Review* 22 (1935): 211–30.

Harris, Paul W. "Cultural Imperialism and American Protestant Missionaries: Collaboration and Dependency in Midnineteenth Century China." *Pacific Historical Review* 60 (1991): 309–38.

Havard, William C. "The Journalist as Interpreter of the South." *Virginia Quarterly Review* 59, no. 1 (Winter 1983): 1–21.

Hawke, G. R. "The United States Tariff and Industrial Protection in the Late Nineteenth Century." *Economic History Review* 28, no. 1 (1975): 84–99.

Hawley, Ellis W. "The Discovery and Study of a Corporate Liberalism." *Business History Review* 52, no. 3 (Autumn 1978): 309–20.

Heffernan, Linda. "From Independent Nation to Client State: The Metamorphosis of the Kingdom of Hawai'i in the Pages of the *North American Review* in the Nineteenth Century." *Hawaiian Journal of History* 22 (1988): 209–27.

Henretta, James A. "The 'Market' in the Early Republic." *Journal of the Early Republic* 18, no. 2 (Summer 1998): 289–304.

Hoffman, Charles. "The Depression of the Nineties." *Journal of Economic History* 16, no. 2 (June 1956): 137–64.

Holbo, Paul S. "Presidential Leadership in Foreign Affairs: William McKinley and the Turpie-Foraker Amendment." *American Historical Review* 72 (1967): 1321–55.

Hollander, J. H. "The Cincinnati Southern Railway: A Study in Municipal Activity." *Johns Hopkins University Studies in Historical and Political Science* 12, nos. 1–2 (January–February 1894): 7–96.

Howell, Sarah McCanless. "The Editorials of Arthur S. Coylar, Nashville Prophet of the New South." *Tennessee Historical Quarterly* 27, no. 3 (1968): 262–76.

Ireland, Robert M. "The Politics of the Elective Judiciary during the Period of Kentucky's Third Constitution." *Register of the Kentucky Historical Society* 93 (1995): 387–421.

Irwin, Douglas A. "Changes in U.S. Tariffs: The Role of Import Prices and Commercial Policies." *American Economic Review* 88, no. 4 (September 1998): 1015–26.

Kelley, Robert. "The Thought and Character of Samuel J. Tilden: The Democrat as Inheritor." *Historian* 26 (1964): 176–205.

Kielbowicz, Richard B., and Linda Lawson. "Protecting the Small-Town Press: Community, Social Policy and Postal Privileges, 1845–1970." *Canadian Review of American Studies* 19 (Spring 1988): 23–45.

Knights, Peter R. "'Competition' in the U.S. Daily Newspaper Industry, 1865–68." *Journalism Quarterly* 45 (1968): 473–80.

Kuehl, Warren F. "Midwestern Newspapers and Isolationist Sentiment." *Diplomatic History* 3, no. 3 (Summer 1979): 283–306.

LaFeber, Walter. "The Constitution and United States Foreign Policy." *Journal of American History* 74, no. 3 (December 1987): 695–717.

Lake, David A. "The State and American Trade Strategy in the Pre-Hegemonic Era." *International Organization* 42, no. 1 (Winter 1988): 33–58.

Lambert, Franklin T. "Free Silver and the Kentucky Democracy, 1891–1895." *Filson Club History Quarterly* 53, no. 2 (1979): 145–76.

Lasch, Christopher. "The Anti-Imperialists, the Philippines, and the Inequality of Man." *Journal of Southern History* 24 (February–November 1958): 319–31.

Lebergott, Stanley. "The Returns of U.S. Imperialism, 1890–1929." *Journal of Economic History* 40, no. 2 (June 1980): 229–52.

Leemhuis, Roger P. "South Carolina Newspapers and American Foreign Policy in the 1890s." *Proceedings of the South Carolina Historical Association* 50 (1980): 133–47.

Lemons, Stanley. "The Cuban Crisis of 1895–1898: Newspapers and Nativism." *Missouri Historical Review* 60 (1965): 63–74.

Leuctenburg, William E. "Progressivism and Imperialism: The Progressive Movement and American Foreign Policy, 1898–1952." *Mississippi Valley Historical Review* 39 (1952): 483–504.

Lindgren, James M. "The Apostasy of a Southern Anti-Imperialist: Joseph Bryan, the Spanish-American War, and Business Expansion." *Southern Studies* 2, no. 2 (Summer 1991): 151–78.

Livingood, James W. "The Chattanooga *Rebel*." *East Tennessee Historical Society's Publications* 39 (1967): 42–55.

Logan, Lena C. "Henry Watterson and the Liberal Convention of 1872." *Indiana Magazine of History*, December 1944, 319–40.

Marks, George P., III. "Opposition of Negro Newspapers to American Philippine Policy, 1899–1900." *Midwest Journal* 4, no. 1 (Winter 1951–52): 1–25.

May, Robert E. "Marse Henry and His Lady Insurrecto: A Case Study of Fictional Reminiscences for the High School History Classroom." *International Journal of Social Education* 6, no. 3 (1991–92): 41–67.

McCormick, Thomas J. "Drift or Mastery? A Corporatist Synthesis for American Diplomatic History." *Reviews in American History* 10 (December 1982): 318–30.

McKillen, Beth. "The Corporatist Model, World War I, and the Public Debate Over the League of Nations." *Diplomatic History* 15, no. 2 (Spring 1991): 171–97.

McWilliams, Tennant S. "The Lure of Empire: Southern Interest in the Caribbean, 1877–1900." *Mississippi Quarterly* 29 (Winter 1975–76): 43–63.

———. "James H. Blount, the South, and Hawaiian Annexation." *Pacific Historical Review* 57 (1988): 25–46.

Moore, James Tice. "Redeemers Reconsidered: Change and Continuity in the Democratic South, 1870–1900." *Journal of Southern History* 44 (August 1978): 357–78.

Nichols, Jeanette P. "Silver Diplomacy." *Political Science Quarterly* 48 (1933): 565–88.

Osborne, Thomas J. "Trade or War? America's Annexation of Hawaii Reconsidered." *Pacific Historical Review* 50 (1981): 285–307.

Papachristou, Judith. "American Women and Foreign Policy, 1898–1905: Exploring Gender in Diplomatic History." *Diplomatic History* 14, no. 4 (Fall 1990): 493–509.

Pearce, George F. "Assessing Public Opinion: Editorial Comment and the Annexation of Hawaii—A Case Study." *Pacific Historical Review* 43 (1974): 324–41.

Pletcher, David M. "Rhetoric and Results: A Pragmatic View of American Economic Expansionism, 1865–98." *Diplomatic History* 5, no. 2 (Spring 1981): 93–105.

Plummer, Leonard Niel. "Henry Watterson's Editorial Style: An Interpretive Analysis." *Journalism Quarterly* 23 (1946): 58–65.

Rable, George C. "Bourbonism, Reconstruction, and the Persistence of Southern Distinctiveness." *Civil War History* 39, no. 2 (1983): 135–53.

Rollins, John W. "The Anti-Imperialists and Twentieth Century American Foreign Policy." *Studies on the Left* 3 (November 1962): 9–24.

Ross, Earle D. "Horace Greeley and the South, 1865–1872." *South Atlantic Quarterly* 16 (1917): 324–38.

Ruiz, George W. "The Ideological Convergence of Theodore Roosevelt and Woodrow Wilson." *Presidential Studies Quarterly* 19, no. 1 (1989): 159–77.

Schlup, Leonard. "Conservative Counterattack: Adlai E. Stevenson and the Compromise of 1892 with Democrats in Tennessee and the South." *Tennessee Historical Quarterly* 53, no. 2 (1994): 114–29.

———. "Bourbon Democrat: Thomas C. Catchings and the Repudiation of Silver Monometallism." *Journal of Mississippi History* 57, no. 3 (1995): 207–23.

———. "Kentucky's Native Son: Adlai Stevenson and the Politics of Persuasion." *Filson Club History Quarterly* 69, no. 3 (1995): 227–54.

Sklar, Martin J. "The N.A.M. and Foreign Markets on the Eve of the Spanish-American War." *Science and Society* 23 (1959): 133–62.

Smith, Edwina C. "Southerners on Empire: Southern Senators and Imperialism, 1898–1899." *Mississippi Quarterly* 31, no. 1 (Winter 1977–78): 89–107.

Smith, Ephraim K. "'A Question from Which We Could not Escape': William McKinley and the Decision to Acquire the Philippine Islands." *Diplomatic History* 9, no. 4 (Fall 1985): 363–75.

Smythe, Ted Curtis. "Pulitzer's World and the Venezuela Boundary Dispute." *Journalism Quarterly* 46 (1969): 807–11.

Steelman, Lala Carr. "Senator Augustus O. Bacon, Champion of Philippine Independence." In *Essays in Southern Biography*, 91–113. Vol. 2 of *East Carolina College Publications in History*. Greenville, NC: Department of History, East Carolina College, 1965.

Thorp, Robert K. "Marse Henry and the Negro: A New Perspective." *Journalism Quarterly* 46 (1969): 467–74.

Tompkins, E. Berkeley. "Scylla and Charybdis: The Anti-Imperialist Dilemma in the Election of 1900." *Pacific Historical Review* 36 (1967): 143–61.

Vaughan, Christopher A. "The 'Discovery' of the Philippines by the U.S. Press, 1898–1902." *Historian* 57 (1995): 303–14.

Vevier, Charles. "American Continentalism: An Idea of Expansion, 1845–1910." *American Historical Review* 65 (1960): 323–35.

Wall, Joseph F. "Marse Henry: Reconstructed Once Again." *Filson Club History Quarterly* 61, no. 2 (1987): 247–55.

Wallace, Tom. "Henry Watterson: A Man of Salient Characteristics." *Southern Newspaper Publishers Association Bulletin Special*, April 1, 1950, 3–11.

Webb, Samuel L. "A Jacksonian Democrat in Postbellum Alabama: The Ideology and Influence of Journalist Robert McKee, 1869–1896." *Journal of Southern History* 52 (1996): 239–274.

Welch, Richard E., Jr. "The Federal Elections Bill of 1890: Postscripts and Prelude." *Journal of American History* 52, no. 3 (December 1965): 511–26.

———. "Motives and Policy Objectives of Anti-Imperialists, 1898." *Mid-America* 51, no. 2 (1969): 119–29.

———. "'The Philippine Insurrection' and the American Press." *Historian* 36 (1973): 34–51.

Welter, Mark. "The 1895–98 Cuban Crisis in Minnesota Newspapers: Testing the 'Yellow Journalism' Theory." *Journalism Quarterly* 47 (1970): 719–24.

Wilkerson, Marcus M. "The Press and the Spanish-American War." *Journalism Quarterly* 9 (1932): 129–48.

Williams, Walter L. "United States Indian Policy and the Debate over Philippine Annexation: Implications for the Origins of American Imperialism." *Journal of American History* 66, no. 4 (March 1980): 810–30.

Williams, William Appleman. "Brooks Adams and American Expansion." *New England Quarterly* 25, no. 2 (June 1952): 217–32.

Wiltz, Edward. "The 1895 Election: A Watershed in Kentucky Politics." *Filson Club History Quarterly* 37, no. 2 (1963): 117–36.

Wisan, Joseph E. "The Cuban Crisis as Reflected in the New York Press, 1895–1898." *Columbia University Studies in History, Economics, and Public Law* 403 (1934): 455–60.

Wood, Richard E. "The South and Reunion, 1898." *Historian* 31 (1969): 415–30.

Zimmerman, James A. "Who Were the Anti-Imperialists and Expansionists of 1893 and 1899? A Chicago Perspective." *Pacific Historical Review* 46 (1977): 589–601.

Zobrist, Benedict Karl. "How Victor Lawson's Newspapers Covered the Cuban War of 1898." *Journalism Quarterly* 38 (1961): 323–31.

Unpublished Theses and Dissertations

Alexander, Ronald R. "From Isolation to Intervention: The Louisville *Courier-Journal* and the Period of American Neutrality, 1914–1917." Master's thesis, University of Kentucky, 1967.

Cope, Neil B. "A History of the *Memphis Commercial-Appeal*." PhD diss., University of Missouri, 1969.

Cusick, Dennis Charles. "Gentleman of the Press: The Life and Times of Walter Newman Haldeman." Master's thesis, University of Louisville, 1987.

Edwards, Rebecca B. "Gender in American Politics, 1880–1900." PhD diss., University of Virginia, 1995.

Logan, Lena Crain. "Henry Watterson, Border Nationalist, 1840–1877." PhD diss., Indiana University, 1942.

McDaniel, John Edgar, Jr. "The Presidential Election of 1888." PhD diss., University of Texas at Austin, 1970.

Ogle, Arthur Harrison, Jr. "Nationalism and American Foreign Policy: A Series of Case Studies on the Influence of an Idea." PhD diss., University of Virginia, 1971.

Phillips, George Howard. "An Analysis of 835 Articles in the Leading American Periodicals for the Period 1890–1914 to Determine What Was Said about American Daily Newspapers." PhD diss., University of Iowa, 1962.

Plummer, Joseph Niel. “The Political Leadership of Henry Watterson.” PhD diss., University of Wisconsin–Madison, 1940.

Rabourn, June. “The *Louisville Courier-Journal* and International Problems, 1918–1922.” Master’s thesis, University of Kentucky, 1956.

Schott, Marshall E. “The South and American Foreign Policy, 1894–1904: Regional Concerns during the Age of Imperialism.” PhD diss., Louisiana State University, 1995.

Wharton, George Christopher. “Henry Watterson—A Study of Selected Speeches on Reconciliation in the Post-Bellum Period.” PhD diss., Louisiana State University, 1974.

Index